AF575667

Also by Jerome R. Corsi, Ph.D.

Coup d'État: Exposing Deep State Treason and the Plan to Re-Elect President Trump

Silent No More: How I Became a Political Prisoner of Mueller's "Witch Hunt"

Dr. Corsi Investigates: Why The Democratic Party Has Gone Communist

Goodnight Obama: A Parody

The Truth about Energy, Global Warming, and Climate Change: Exposing Climate Lies in an Age of Disinformation

How the Coming Global Crash Will Create a Historic Gold Rush

THE TRUTH

ABOUT NEO-MARXISM, CULTURAL MAOISM, and ANARCHY

EXPOSING WOKE INSANITY in an AGE OF DISINFORMATION

JEROME R. CORSI, Ph.D.

A POST HILL PRESS BOOK
ISBN: 978-1-63758-521-4
ISBN (eBook): 978-1-63758-522-1

The Truth about Neo-Marxism, Cultural Maoism, and Anarchy:
Exposing Woke Insanity in an Age of Disinformation

Cover design by Mark Karis

Post Hill Press
New York • Nashville
posthillpress.com

Published in the United States of America
1 2 3 4 5 6 7 8 9 10

Dedicated to Two Warriors for Truth and Freedom
Stephen Coughlin

and

In Memory of the Late, Great Richard Higgins
Coauthors of the 2019 Book
Re-Remembering the Mis-Remembered Left:
The Left's Strategy and Tactics to Transform America

and

Cofounders of UnconstrainedAnalytics.org

Also Dedicated to a Trusted, Long-Term Friend
Jim Garrow

A Wise Counselor Who Encouraged
Me to Write This Book

Thank You

TABLE OF CONTENTS

INTRODUCTION

The Twenty-First Century "Woke" Social Justice Popular Delusion

We find that whole communities suddenly fix their minds upon one object, and go mad in its pursuit; that millions of people become simultaneously impressed with one delusion and run after it, till their attention is caught by some new folly more captivating than the first.

—**Charles Mackay**, *Extraordinary Popular Delusions and the Madness of Crowds*, 1852[1]

Marx recognized that Hegel's dialectic does not advance cultures under its sway but rather ***nihilizes them.*** *Marx envisioned a critical philosophy* ***to tear down Western culture*** *and a proletariat of middle-class nihilists to do so. From Marx to Alinsky,* ***a dark, destructive nihilist strain that runs through the Left as characterized by numerous homages to Satan****, et al.*

—**Stephen Coughlin and Richard Higgins**, *Re-Remembering the Mis-Remembered Left: The Left's Strategy and Tactics to Transform America*, 2019.[2]

A DARK, EVIL IDEOLOGY HAS descended over America.

Universities across the country have indoctrinated a generation of young adults with the idea that America is a racist nation founded by slaveholders who perpetuate social injustice. This dangerous neo-Marxist generation, the first ever to rise in this land, is rapidly gaining power, pervading the federal bureaucracy, politicizing our institutions of justice, dominating our military, setting out to control the Supreme Court, and willing to steal the presidency if necessary. Trained in the techniques of critical theory, these young revolutionaries are in the process of imposing a totalitarian standard of their truths on all who dare oppose them.

Admiring the techniques of Mao Tse-tung's Cultural Revolution, this rising generation of revolutionaries is determined to impose their totalitarian standard of political correctness on public communications in this country. Versed in Mao's Long March tactics, these young revolutionaries have extended their control over the nation's corporations. Determined to negate all that is good about America, this new generation of radicals has already captured public education down to the kindergarten level, aiming to extend their reach into all subsequent generations. Applying lessons from Antonio Gramsci's "march through the institutions,"[3] these young adults have captured control over crucial social networking websites as well as the mainstream broadcast and print media. Pushing to achieve their utopian dreams, this new generation of cultural Maoist devotees aim to destroy the Judeo-Christian tradition our Founding Fathers correctly believed was required to perpetuate the liberties they bestowed upon us.

I am writing this second volume of my Great Awakening Trilogy in the hope and prayer that by exposing the demonic political philosophy that gave birth to this "woke" generation, we may yet save the world from plunging into the apocalyptic abyss. We should understand that World War III has already begun with Russia invading Ukraine, much as Hitler invaded Poland in 1939. With the Joe Biden administration giving the green light to Iran to develop nuclear weapons, we are on the verge of a historic attempt to wipe Israel from the map. With the development of hypersonic nuclear weapons by Russia, China, and now the United States, the logic of mutually assured destruction that has prevented a nuclear holocaust is shifting. Despite the midnight darkness of the current hour, I have persisted in completing this second volume. I remain with the certainty that, in the end, God always wins. Yet I fear how horrible "in the end" may be for us to experience unless we act now to proclaim truth to cast a needed beam of light into this dark and evil night of this disinformation age.

In the first volume, *The Truth about Energy, Global Warming, and Climate Change: Exposing Climate Lies in an Age of Disinformation*,[4] published in August 2022, I explained the false philosophical premises and the twisted science this revolutionary "woke" movement has used to make humans fear that industrial progress has polluted even the air we breathe.

The "save the planet" hysteria is a repeat and perhaps the final chapter in the popular delusions and the madness of crowds that have always plagued human existence. This second volume explains the anarchy the social justice theories have already caused to become pervasive in America, presaging the Maximilien Robespierre Reign of Terror, which the neo-Marxists/cultural Maoists are planning to unleash in America to force the country into submission.

Standing in the wings, waiting to be the new evil masters, are the godless globalists. Convinced that their technological advances have placed them on the throne of God, these globalists, once in power, will quickly eliminate the neo-Marxist/cultural Maoists who have destroyed America to pave the road for their New World Order. As in the prelude to World War II, the socialist Nazis are ready to send to the concentration death camps the woke rabble-rousers who brought them to power.

Fronted by the World Economic Forum, these New World Order globalist mobsters and their multinational corporate accomplices are preparing to be the ultimate masters of the world. In a wave of transgender transhumanism, the globalist demons believe they have the technology to create the final Nietzschean *Übermensch* to rule over an enslaved, vastly diminished, worldwide population of subservient mortals willing to obey just to receive their daily bread. At the end of their Reign of Terror, the woke generation may finally realize they have birthed their demise—a realization they will not experience until they are herded off to the gulag or walk up the steps with their hands bound behind their backs to face the guillotine.

This second volume in the Great Awakening Trilogy explains how the woke ideology was crafted, beginning with Immanuel Kant and Georg Wilhelm Friedrich Hegel, continuing through Antonio Gramsci, the Frankfurt School, and concluding with postmodern thinkers like Jean Baudrillard. Unless we understand how the woke social justice phenomenology and political philosophy evolved away from biblical principles of natural law and natural rights, we will never be able to turn back this evil. Thus, the first volume on energy, global warming, and climate change demonstrates that the "woke" ideology depends upon scientific lies that are credible only in this age of disinformation. This second volume on neo-Marxism, cultural Maoism, and anarchy explains "why" these woke totalitarians lie. This second volume demonstrates that political philosophers starting with Kant and Hegel, progressing through Marx and Mao, to the Frankfurt School and Herbert Marcuse, as refined by postmodernist theory, have created a subjective, schizophrenic phenomenology that forces the woke generation to live in a value-relative world that is foreign and hostile to a natural law worldview.

Thus, Volume 1 of the Great Awakening Trilogy, *The Truth about Energy, Global Warming, and Climate Change: Exposing Climate Lies in an Age of Disinformation*, demonstrated that climate-change/global-warming hysteria is nothing but a political ideology. That book documented the proven lies the neo-Marxist radical Left has told to demonize carbon dioxide, a molecule we exhale. Volume 1 further documented that the climate-change/global-warming ideology is not legitimate environmentalism. Depopulationists like Harrison Brown and Paul Ehrlich co-opted the environmental movement at the end of World War II. In Volume 1, I explained how neo-Marxists in recent years have further co-opted the depopulation movement to focus on our use of hydrocarbon fuels, claiming that our use of hydrocarbon fuels constitutes an existential threat to human survival. The neo-Marxists chose to demonize carbon dioxide because hydrocarbon fuels emit carbon dioxide. Without hydrocarbon fuels, capitalism and the modern industrial state cannot support the billions of lives globally that have thrived in this global interglacial warming period we are experiencing on Earth.

Volume 2 explains the development in phenomenology and political philosophy that has led to today's woke social justice ideology. Properly understood, woke social justice philosophy is an advanced form of the Hegelian dialectic aimed at negating capitalism, destroying the United States as a global superpower, and instituting a bureaucratically controlled totalitarian state intolerant of any dissent. While Volume 1 necessarily included discussion of mathematical and scientific concepts, Volume 2 necessarily includes an extensive discussion of phenomenology and political philosophy. What should be clear to readers of Volume 2 is that the neo-Marxists, cultural Maoists, and anarchists live in a fundamentally different view of reality. Moreover, they operate with a set of values that redefines truth to be subjective.

The radical Left today intends to negate America by deconstructing the Enlightenment understanding of how we perceive reality and value life. The reconstructed "woke" phenomenology and ethics involve a worldview dictated by a vaguely articulated utopia that the radical Left believes involves a reengineered human being. With Volume 2, we are forced to consider reality as a language construct, as articulated by philosophers like Ludwig Wittgenstein and postmodernists like Jean Baudrillard. Unfortunately, Volume 2, like Volume 1, is complex. But understanding, and hopefully defeating, critical theory and social justice ideology leaves us no other choice.

Volume 1 demonstrated that climate change and global warming true believers do not necessarily believe their arguments are true (in an Enlightenment sense), but they believe they are necessary (in a utopian sense). Volume 2 demonstrates that the worldview (in German, the *Weltanschauung*) in which the woke live is schizophrenic, necessarily self-constructed, and intolerant of discussion, debate, or disagreement. While the journey is complex, those who persist to read both books entirely will understand that the neo-Marxists, cultural Maoists, and anarchists we are experiencing today live in a bizarre, twisted metaverse that attempts to create a synthetic reality in which they expect future generations will live. In this woke metaverse all truth is fiction, all values are relative, and all reality is an illusion.

This Volume 2 explains the ideology the neo-Marxists have constructed to self-justify their lying. Volume 3 will explain where the neo-Marxists are headed if they are permitted to succeed. Volume 3 will show that the future these maniacs plan will be one of marvelous machines designed to allow an unnamed global elite to be in total control of our every thought, emotion, and action. Our cell phones and iPads create a marvelously seductive metaverse in which we live. But what happens when behind the scenes the anonymous masters pull the cord and unplug the electricity? Thus, Volume 3 will cover themes of transhumanism, transgenderism, artificial intelligence, mass surveillance, and totalitarian control. Volume 3 will expose the New World Order globalists and their twisted view that a small, elite minority together with the willing assistance of multinational corporations can create a utopia with their machines. Volume 3 explains the ultimate goal toward which these mad Malthusian utopians are aiming.

The "heaven on earth" these globalist oligarchs seek to create will be "hell on earth" for the rest of us. The question we face as a civilized society is whether we turn over the asylum to the management of these neo-Marxist, cultural Maoist, anarchistic lunatics. The reality of human existence here is that we did not create this world or set the rules. The dialectic certainty proclaimed at the heart of this woke madness is that Hegel, Marx, and Mao would die long before their godless utopia on earth had been realized. Life here has remained the same since *Homo sapiens* first walked upon this planet. God rules here, and living the moral code God established is possibly the only eternal or utopian experience we humans can ever expect to encounter.

But trying to explain this to the intolerant woke generation is pointless. How do you explain true reality to those who think there is no truth and there is no reality? The woke have already been seduced and brainwashed to live in a metaverse constructed to give them the illusion that their personal metaverse is all that exists. The evil masters who created this nightmare are nihilists who believe our experience is illusionary and will not have happened once all is gone. The devils behind these evil masters know better. The genius demons acknowledge God exists because they exist not to deny God but to hate Him. The woke reality is evil because its metaverse is demon-devised. The woke believe social justice critical theory will liberate us, without understanding the evil monsters who created this ideology did so to enslave us.

The reader should approach the three volumes of the Great Awakening Trilogy much as one would listen to a symphony. The themes introduced in each book will resonate and be developed in all three books, much like musical themes weave through a classical opus. Volume 3 will cover themes of transhumanism, transgenderism, artificial intelligence, and perpetual life extension as we explore the dystopian nature of the neo-Marxist utopia that the globalist New World Order plans as our future. In summary, Volume 1 explained that the neo-Marxists lie.

I pray America will awaken, to reject being woke. America must return to God if we are to have any hope of preventing these Satanic maniacs from actualizing the totalitarian future their ideology dictates. Yet, all is not lost. Ultimately, the God of Genesis who willed "Let there be light" may stop the malicious Four Horsemen of the book of Revelation from riding the world to destruction. God can and will pull the plug on this world when and if God so chooses. As Eve came sorrowfully to realize, biting the fruit containing the knowledge of good and evil was partaking not of divine wisdom but the serpent's great lie rooted in hatred of God.

I am writing this book in the hope that it is not too late to beg God's forgiveness. We should have protested in the 1940s when the Supreme Court began taking God out of the schools. But in the spirit of 2 Chronicles 7:14, we are assured victory if we get on our knees and beg God for forgiveness for our sins. As I have said repeatedly, in the end God always wins! In writing this book, the only fear I have is to contemplate just what "in the end" might mean if we fail to turn from these wicked ways. What is at stake is the end of a God-inspired morality and the loss of the freedoms bequeathed to us by our Founding Fathers.

CHAPTER 1

Neo-Marxist Political Warfare

National policy has come under the influence of constructed narratives that mainstream and conservative leaders neither understand nor control.

—**Stephen Coughlin and Richard Higgins**, *Re-Remembering the Mis-Remembered Left*, 2019[5]

The ordinary acceptation of words in their relation to things was changed as men thought fit.

—**Thucydides**, *History of the Peloponnesian War*, Book III, Chapter LXXXII, 4[6]

The abuse of political power is fundamentally connected with the sophistic abuse of the word, indeed, finds in it the fertile soil in which to hide and grow and get ready, so much so that the latent potential of the totalitarian poison can be ascertained, as it were, by observing the symptom of public abuse of language. The degradation, too, of man through man, alarmingly evident in the acts of physical violence committed by all tyrannies, has its beginning, certainly much less alarmingly, at that almost imperceptible moment when the word loses its dignity.

—**Josef Pieper**, *Abuse of Language—Abuse of Power*, 1974[7]

Communists long ago realized that it's difficult to achieve the social disintegration needed to ready a country for communist revolution by promoting class division alone. Class is amorphous; it can change within a generation. In a free society, an ambitious individual can rise from beggar to billionaire in a lifetime. Class is an unreliable wedge for revolutionaries, especially in Western free-market societies. Ethnic, religious, and especially racial differences are more stable.

The divisions are deeper; the differences, more obvious; and their histories, more imbued with bitterness and hatred. Few people care that their grandparents were poor, but many might care that they were slaves or dispossessed of their ancestral lands by a rival racial or ethnic group. Such resentments can last for generations. Therefore, modern Marxists-Leninists have consistently, even scientifically, exploited ethnic and racial divisions to achieve revolutionary ends.

—**Trevor Loudon**, "Communists and Race," 2019[8]

IN THIS SECOND DECADE OF the twenty-first century, America has never been at greater risk of losing the individual freedoms defined by a broad embrace of classical liberalism that has prevailed in this country since the Continental Congress adopted the Declaration of Independence on July 4, 1776. The radical Left elite running our nation's elite educational institution has now indoctrinated two generations of Americans—first the millennials and now the Gen Z "Zoomers." These are the first two generations to reach adulthood and enter power in this country trained to "hate America." At the core of this hate-America sentiment is the accusation the United States is and has always been a racist country.

Those desiring to use race to divide America trace the accusation of racism back to our Founding Fathers and the Constitutional Convention in Philadelphia in 1787. Unable to convince the southern states to renounce slavery, our Founding Fathers chose to create the union that in 1787 they could create. However, a close reading of the words written makes clear the language of the Constitution does not mention the institution of slavery or the designation of race specifically. Nor does the Constitution repudiate the Declaration of Independence.[9] Still, a radical Left remains determined to declare the Constitutional Convention's failure to abolish the institution of slavery as the "fatal flaw" in the founding of this nation that branded America once and for all as a racist state.

On November 19, 1863, President Abraham Lincoln delivered the Gettysburg Address. Speaking on that great battlefield of the Civil War, Lincoln said 272 words that "remade America," as Garry Wills, an emeritus professor of history at Northwestern University and a prolific author, wrote in his 1992 book *Lincoln at Gettysburg*.[10] Like the Constitution, Wills noted that Lincoln's Gettysburg Address does not mention slavery. Wills wrote:

> The Gettysburg Address does not mention Gettysburg. Nor slavery. Nor—more surprising—the Union. (Certainly not the South.) The other major message of 1863, the Emancipation Proclamation, is not mentioned, much less defended or vindicated. The "great task" mentioned in the Address is not emancipation but the preservation of self-government. We assume, today, that self-government includes self-rule by blacks as well as whites; but at the time of his appearance at Gettysburg Lincoln was not advocating, even eventually, the suffrage for African Americans. The Gettysburg Address, for all its artistry and eloquence, does not directly address the prickliest issues of its historic moment.[11]

Yet, as Wills noted, Lincoln's Gettysburg Address was transcendental in its impact. Wills made that point as follows:

> The Gettysburg Address has become an authoritative expression of the American spirit—as authoritative as the Declaration itself, and perhaps even more influential, since it determines how we read the Declaration. For most people now, the Declaration means what Lincoln told us it means, as a way of correcting the Constitution itself without overthrowing it. It is this correction of the spirit, this intellectual revolution, that makes attempts to go back beyond Lincoln to some earlier version so feckless. The proponents of states' rights may have arguments, but they have lost their force, in courts as well as in the popular mind. By accepting the Gettysburg Address, its concept of a single people dedicated to a proposition, we have been changed. Because of it, we live in a different America.[12]

Wills's point is that with the Gettysburg Address, Lincoln wrote the proposition that "all men are created equal" into our founding principles. By declaring that five words, "all men are created equal," were the proposition to which this nation was dedicated, Lincoln subtly advanced the Declaration of Independence take precedence over the Constitution in defining what, since that day on the Gettysburg battlefield, Americans understand to be the true meaning of "conceived in liberty." The principle that Lincoln declared to the nation on November 19, 1863, was direct. Regardless of race or the tragedy of slavery, all human beings are created by God to have equal human rights. Despite the many differences we all have at birth, including race, we all exist equally in the eyes of God. Lincoln established, by implication, the principle that equal status as human beings applied equally to all as what Thomas Jefferson meant in 1776 when penning the relevant sentence into the Declaration of Independence. That God created all human beings equal in rights, Lincoln declared, was the founding principle upon which our Founding Fathers brought forth this "new nation" upon the face of the earth.

With the Gettysburg Address, Lincoln clarified the uniqueness in the founding of America. Throughout history, no other nation had ever articulated its founding principle as equal rights for all, regardless of our differences, including race. Wills's book *Lincoln at Gettysburg* received the 1993 Pulitzer Prize for General Nonfiction. Today, Wills may well have experienced difficulty getting his analysis into print, let alone winning a Pulitzer Prize.

Today, the millennials and the Gen Z "Zoomers" are coming of age. At the same time, the "Greatest Generation" that fought to defeat Benito Mussolini's fascism in Italy, Adolf Hitler's fascism in Germany, and the imperial ambitions of near-feudal, emperor-ruled Japan are rapidly passing from the face of the earth. Indoctrinated by educational institutions and a popular culture dominated by the radical Left, the millennials and Gen Z "Zoomers" are the first generations of Americans to reach adulthood harboring a neo-Marxist brand of cultural Maoism-shaped hate-America values. Today, these "hate-America" youthful leaders are taking over the institutions of this nation with a frightful ignorance of all things, including American history. Their inability to understand or appreciate Western civilization's traditions or understand American exceptionalism creates an intellectual vacuum sadly filled by an ideological fervor to dismantle our constitutional freedoms and destroy capitalism once and for all. Today, the neo-Marxist, cultural Maoist radical Left considers rights equal only for the woke.

The Political Warfare Battlefield

Stephen Coughlin and Richard Higgins are two former intelligence officers who understand we are in an ideological war with the neo-Marxist Left. Experienced in military counterinsurgency tactics, Coughlin and Higgins apply a political warfare analysis "to reframe the political environment in order to provide timely anticipatory situation awareness in support of decision-making" in a last-ditch attempt to preserve this country as a beacon of freedom for ourselves and all peoples of the world. Let's expand the quotation from Coughlin and Higgins's remarkable 2019 book *Re-Remembering the Mis-Remembered Left*. The full excerpt reads as follows:

> National policy has come under the influence of constructed narratives that mainstream and conservative leaders neither understand nor control. Lacking situational awareness to recognize the operational nature of information campaigns directed against national policy, **responses tend to be tactically limited and predictably reactive** along scripted action-reaction cycles built into the operational sequencing of information campaigns controlled by the Left. These powerful but misunderstood narratives drive policy. At their core, these narratives are not American. Rather, they are dialectically driven Neo-Marxist memes that infuse mass line efforts operating at the cultural level intent on powering down into the political space. This furthers the Left's political warfare effort to impose conformance resulting in the non-enforcement of laws by those tasked with their oversight and enforcement. As these narratives transition into prevailing cultural memes, non-enforcement becomes institutionalized and enforced by an opposition that increasingly comes under the control of those narratives.[13]

One of the key strategies in the neo-Marxist campaign to destroy the United States is to rewrite American history. The neo-Marxist goal is to change the cultural understanding of our founding principles. Traditionally, American history has been taught from the perspective that our Founding Fathers created a form of limited government, a republic, not a democracy. Principles such as separation of powers—i.e., the division of ruling authority between coequal executive, legislative, and judicial branches of government—aimed to prevent the emergence of a dictatorship. Finally, as the Declaration of Independence articulated, preserving God-bestowed individual rights and liberties was the central purpose of the new government the Constitutional Convention created in 1787. The neo-Marxist rewrite portrays our Founding Fathers not as defenders of freedom but as racists who devised a system of white privilege that institutionalized slavery. Neo-Marxists condemn the United States beyond redemption based on the argument that our Founding Fathers were determined to create a system of government that bestowed God-endowed individual rights only to white men owning property.

President Lincoln's 1862 message to Congress expressed the urgency the Civil War had created to remedy the fundamental flaw in the nation's creation that the Constitutional Convention had failed to fix. In that message, Lincoln said: "In giving freedom to the slave, we assure freedom to the free—honorable alike in what we give, and what we preserve. We shall nobly save, or meanly lose, the last best hope of earth."[14] Lincoln fought the Civil War not to free the slaves but to preserve the Union, renouncing the legitimacy of the states' rights argument used by the Southern states to justify succession. But by January 1, 1863, the date he issued the Emancipation Proclamation, Lincoln knew that freeing the slaves had become an unavoidable issue that the Civil War had to resolve if the nation, as articulated by the Declaration of Independence, was to survive. On January 31, 1865, the U.S. Congress passed the Thirteenth Amendment when the House of Representatives, in a second vote, narrowly passed the measure that abolished slavery approximately two months before General Robert E. Lee surrendered to General Ulysses S. Grant at Appomattox Court House on April 9, 1865. Watching Steven Spielberg's 2012 movie *Lincoln*, virtually nothing is said to clarify that Lincoln was a Republican and the opposition to the Thirteenth Amendment came mainly from Southern Democrats.

Yet, in its stubborn insistence, the neo-Marxist Left ignores Lincoln's determination to extend the Declaration of Independence's statement of equal rights to all Americans, including the slaves. The historian Howard Zinn, an admitted anarchist and socialist who preferred to call himself a democratic socialist,[15] made this point abundantly clear in his 1980 college textbook *A People's History of the United States*.[16] "There is not a country in the world in which racism has been more important, for so long a time, as the United States," Zinn wrote in chapter 2, "Drawing the Color Line."[17] Zinn argued that even Thomas Jefferson, in the drafting of the Declaration of Independence, was a racist. Zinn explained as follows:

> Thomas Jefferson had written a paragraph of the Declaration accusing the King of transporting slaves from Africa to the colonies and "suppressing every legislative attempt to prohibit or to restrain this execrable commerce." This seemed to express moral indignation against slavery and the slave trade (Jefferson's personal distaste for slavery must be put alongside the fact that he owned hundreds of slaves to the day he died). Behind it was the growing fear among Virginians and some other southerners about the growing number of black slaves in the colonies (20 percent of the total population) and the threat of slave revolts as the number of slaves increased. Jefferson's paragraph was removed by the Continental Congress, because slaveholders themselves disagreed about the desirability of ending the slave trade. So even that gesture toward

> the black slave was omitted in the great manifesto of freedom of the American Revolution.[18]

Zinn begged the reader to understand that his intent is not to put "impossible moral burdens on that time [i.e., 1776]" but "to try to understand the way in which the Declaration functioned to mobilize certain groups of Americans, ignoring others."[19] In the language of today's critical race theory, Zinn's point is that Thomas Jefferson's declaration that "all men are created equal" was, in reality, a statement affirming "white male privilege."[20] Not willing to excuse Jefferson from a charge of racism, Zinn repeated his accusation in a subsequent chapter. In chapter 5, "A Kind of Revolution," Zinn wrote:

> Jefferson tried his best, as an enlightened, thoughtful individual might. But the structure of American society, the power of the cotton plantation, the slave trade, the politics of unity between northern and southern elites, and the long culture of race prejudice in the colonies, as well as his own weaknesses—that combination of practical need and ideological fixation—kept Jefferson a slaveowner throughout his life.[21]

Historian David Greenberg, a professor of journalism and media studies at Rutgers University, wrote a highly critical 2013 analysis of Zinn's scholarship, entitled "Agit-Prof: Howard Zinn's Influential Mutilations of American History." Greenberg noted that since its 1980 publication, Zinn's textbook had sold over two million copies. He also commented that "as a faculty brat" in the 1980s, he was "enamored" with Zinn's history, thrilled by Zinn's "now-famous victims'-eye panorama of the American experience."[22] But Greenberg also noted that the radical Left's debunking of American history gained widespread academic acceptance in the 1970s amid the race riots that began in the mid-1960s and the anti-war protests that intensified in the 1970s. Greenberg pointed to Jonathan Wiener, a professor of history at the University of California, Irvine. Wiener, in 1989, published an academic article explaining how radical history strongly influenced by Marxism became institutionalized as the norm among academic historians.[23] Beginning in the late-1960s, in short order, curriculums in major universities across America began featuring courses in "African American History," "Woman's History," and "Hispanic History." These courses universally described the United States as a capitalist nation with a history of racism, sexism, and antagonism to immigrants that resulted in social and economic discrimination.

Coughlin and Higgins point out that those of us who believe in God and cherish the Constitution's extension of equal rights to all Americans, regardless of race, religion, or sex, are losing today's battle to preserve the nation Lincoln conceived and brought forth. Why? Because we fail to understand how the neo-Marxist Left dominates the Democratic Party today and uses techniques derived from the Hegelian dialectic to construct and drive the dominant narratives of our time: "Political correctness is the enforcement mechanism of the multicultural narrative that implements neo-Marxist objectives."[24]

Political warfare is fought on a battlefield that does not require guns and tanks. In combating neo-Marxist political warfare, we need to understand that the radical Left's battlefield is made of ideas, the tactics are dialectical, and the weapons are pseudoreality narratives. The revolution the radical Left is planning today does not require a foreign army attacking our shores. Today's enemy is an enemy fighting traditional values, and the revolution is a spiritual coup d'état, a Maoist cultural insurgency directed by the neo-Marxists who now control the Democratic Party. The crux of Coughlin and Higgins's political warfare analysis is that the radical Left in America today influences national public policy through carefully constructed neo-Marxist narratives "that mainstream and conservative leaders neither understand nor control."[25]

Language Perversion Techniques and Subjective Reality

The neo-Marxist narratives involve a perversion of language that the ancient Greek historians and philosophers understood. Let's now expand the passage quoted at the beginning of this chapter from Thucydides:

> The ordinary acceptation of words in their relation to things was changed as men thought fit. Reckless audacity came to be regarded as courageous loyalty to party, prudent hesitation as specious cowardice, moderation as a cloak for unmanly weakness, and to be clever in everything was to do naught in anything. Frantic impulsiveness was accounted a true man's part, but caution in deliberation a specious pretext for shirking. The hot-headed man was always trusted, his opponent suspected. He who succeeded in a plot was clever, and he who had detected one was still shrewder; on the other hand, he who made it his aim to have no need of such things was a disrupter of party and scared of his opponents. In a word, both he that got ahead of another who intended to do something evil and he that prompted to evil one who had never thought of it were alike commended.[26]

In this passage, Thucydides described a phenomenon that occurred during the Peloponnesian War (431–404 BC), in which the whole Hellenic world convulsed. In both Athens and Sparta, leaders of democratic factions were uniquely able to oppose ruling oligarchs. Because of the ongoing war, democratic factions in Athens desiring a revolution could bring in outside allies favorable to Sparta and vice versa. The same risk prevailed in Sparta. As both Athens and Sparta fell into revolution, the dire necessities of war pushed people to extreme measures. In one of the most widely quoted passages by modern sociologists, political scientists, philosophers, and ancient historians, Thucydides described how language became perverted as emotionally charged. Thucydides commented the severe hardships of war drove the factions to "still more extravagant lengths" with "the invention of new devices, both by the extreme ingenuity of their attacks and the monstrousness of their revenges."[27] Violent hostilities not typically experienced in peacetime led the revolutionaries to bend language to justify what we can imagine was anarchy.

As Thucydides scholar John Wilson pointed out, the Thucydides passage is typically rendered incorrectly as meaning the following: "They changed the usual meanings of words."[28] Translators and commentators typically compare what this passage describes to disinformation campaigns, political propaganda, and works of fiction like George Orwell's *1984*. The passage quoted above from book 3, 82, 4 of the *History of the Peloponnesian War* involves the internal dynamics of revolutions. Wilson correctly insists that what changes in factional political turmoil is not the meaning of words. Political parties gain a moral advantage by modifying the "*use of* the available descriptions"[29] to justify or otherwise make acceptable their extreme actions. By abandoning the pejorative connotation typically bestowed on immoral or otherwise outrageous acts, political actors substitute new morally positive designations "to make different value-judgments about the phenomenon described."[30] Wilson explained the phenomenon as follows:

> As Thucydides knew well, politicians and other wicked men are greatly assisted, not by enforced and arbitrary changes in the meanings of words (something no one would be persuaded by), but by more or less plausible redescriptions of phenomena within the existing vocabulary. We might write of the USSR "Political dissidents were considered mentally ill"; or of some liberal societies "To cause disorder and hurt people in the streets was regarded as a justifiable protest in the name of Liberty."[31]

For instance, the radical Left's goal in America today is not to change the meaning of anarchical violence. Instead, the radical Left aims to recharacterize Antifa's anarchical violence as morally justified. The goal is to trick an unthinking public into accepting the movement's extreme violence as justified. The language game tricks us into perceiving that destructive violence as just because their goal is just. Because Antifa wants to establish "social justice," we are supposed to understand that they must first destroy the evil capitalist, imperialist, colonial, and white-dominated society in which we live. Because they aim to destroy an evil fascist social structure, Antifa urban terrorists operate on a higher moral plane where their obvious anarchical violence is necessary, hence just and not deserving of criminal punishment. The point of this perversion of language is not to deny that Antifa's tactics call for extreme violence against perceived opponents but to portray their outrageous behavior as worthy of praise. The radical Left's destructive behavior typically outmaneuvers mainstream and conservative thinkers in an "information space" that traditionalists barely perceive exists. As Coughlin and Higgins pointed out: "The political rhetoric driving American politics runs along well-trodden paths sustaining a political framework from a by-gone era incapable of coming to terms with the political movements threatening our constitutional system today."[32]

Contemporary politics demonstrate that we are already far down the path to losing our constitutionally protected rights. In June 2020, during the presidential election cycle, the FBI in Washington, DC, "took a knee" and raised their fists to demonstrate their solidarity with these Black Lives Matter Maoist revolutionaries marching through the streets of the capital.[33] The FBI stood by and watched while BLM occupied a street across from the White House, renamed the street "Black Lives Matter Plaza," and proceeded to vandalize one of the most sacred Christian churches in America, St. John's Church on Lafayette Square.[34] Since James Madison, every sitting U.S. president has attended services since that church opened in 1816.

Then, in Portland, Oregon, the FBI refused to investigate Antifa urban terrorists who looted, burned, and rioted night after night in the city's downtown streets during the 2020 presidential election cycle. In further disrespect for the rule of law, state and local prosecutors and judges in Portland, many of whom George Soros funded, allowed those few Antifa anarchists who were apprehended and arrested by law enforcement to be released back onto the streets without bail. In August 2020, Multnomah County District Attorney Mike Schmidt announced that he would not prosecute most of the approximately 550 rioters arrested in Portland, Oregon, since May 29.[35] Why not? Because Schmidt said the Antifa rioters were "deeply frustrated with what they perceive to be structural inequalities in our basic social fabric"[36]—causes that had political favor in a town dominated politically by the radical Left. As neo-Marxist insurgents, BLM and Antifa radical Left activists understand how to use "cultural level narratives to power down into the political space where fidelity to the narrative will result in non-enforcement of law that, over time, becomes institutionalized."[37] The image of federal, state, and local law enforcement authorities standing by and allowing Antifa and BLM criminal arsonists and looters to destroy American cities is reminiscent of German police standing by and watching as mobs of Nazi thugs destroyed Jewish property, burned synagogues, ransacked and looted Jewish homes, and beat helpless Jews in cities throughout Nazi Germany on Kristallnacht (Night of Broken Glass) on November 9–10, 1938.

In sharp contrast, the FBI characterized the protest at the Capitol on January 6, 2020, as an insurrection. The FBI argued that Donald Trump supporters stormed Congress to prevent then-Vice President Mike Pence from presiding over a bicameral session of Congress to follow the constitutional procedures of counting electoral college votes to certify the presidential election. Characterizing the January 6 protest as a move to overthrow the government, the FBI has hunted down, arrested, and indicted Trump supporters with breaching the Capitol while refusing to investigate seriously whether voter fraud cheated Trump of reelection.[38] The MSM (mainstream media) consistently maintained the narrative that President Trump "falsely claimed" that he, and not Joe Biden, won the presidential election held on November 3, 2020.[39]

Again, Coughlin and Higgins noted that what "is popularly called 'fake news' and the 'deep-state' are better understood as **propaganda** and the **counter-state**."[40] They explained the point as follows:

> Transitioning to a political warfare analysis, one begins to discern methods, processes, and directionality that terms like "fake news" and "deep-state" do not capture. By their nature, media terms like "fake news" and "deep-state" ensure that analysis always remains on the surface of events. Our national aversion to recognizing threats beyond the strictly military, **especially ideological threats in the political warfare arena**, has long been recognized by America's foes as an exploitable strategic level vulnerability.[41]

Coughlin and Higgins continued as follows:

> The Left uses dialectically determined political warfare concepts to drive a core set of narratives that inter-operate at the tactical level, while integrating at the strategic. Narratives are associated with the pseudorealities (or second realities) they seek to establish and enforce. **They are called narratives because they are stories—fictions—that seek to supplant the real with the unreal**. These narratives are directional, they have velocity, and are always oriented on a target.[42]

At the beginning of this chapter, the quotation from German philosopher Josef Pieper emphasizes an aspect of language perversion subtly distinct from Thucydides. Pieper, a prominent Catholic theologian who understood the importance of Thomas Aquinas in advancing principles of natural law, appreciated from his personal experience of living through the Nazi rule that the abuse of language was required to advance intolerant totalitarian political purposes. In his short but precisely argued book, *Abuse of Language—Abuse of Power*, Pieper returned to Plato to explain the following:

> Plato's literary activity extended over fifty years, and time and again he asked himself anew: What is it that makes the sophists so dangerous? Toward the end he wrote one more dialogue, the *Sophist*, in which he added a new element to his answer: "The sophists," he [Plato] says, "fabricate a fictitious reality." That the existential realm of man could be taken over by pseudorealities whose fictitious nature threatens to become indiscernible is truly a depressing thought. And yet this Platonic nightmare, I hold, possesses an alarming contemporary relevance. For the general public is being reduced to a state where people not only are unable to find out about the truth but also become unable even to *search* for the truth because they are satisfied with deception and trickery that have determined their convictions, satisfied with a fictitious reality created by design through the abuse of language. This, says Plato, is the worst thing that the sophists are capable of wreaking upon mankind by their corruption of the word.[43]

As understood by Pieper, what we are experiencing today as the radical Left's neo-Marxist narratives is that revolutionaries create pseudorealities to reframe our perception of reality so they can gain power. To destroy America, neo-Marxist revolutionaries rewrite American history to vilify the prevalent political culture in which we live. Coughlin and Higgins described the neo-Marxist narrative tactics as follows:

> At their core, these narratives are not American. Rather, they are dialectically driven neo-Marxist memes that infuse mass line efforts operating at the cultural level intent on powering down into the political space.
>
> This furthers the Left's political warfare effort to impose conformance resulting in the non-enforcement of laws by those tasked with their oversight and enforcement. As these narratives transition into prevailing cultural memes, non-enforcement becomes institutionalized and enforced by an opposition that increasingly comes under the control of these narratives.[44]

Political warfare then functions as "a Maoist insurgency concept that recognizes the role **narratives** play in **overwhelming** rule of law societies."[45] The neo-Marxist Left constructs narratives "**so that it is easier for people to comply than to not**."[46] They characterize its politics as liberal or progressive for tactical reasons. As Coughlin and Higgins explained, a principal objective of the Left "**is to keep its agenda camouflaged in the old lexicon while escalating radicalized agendas that find cover under 'politics as usual' memes.**"[47] Neo-Marxist "mass line" narratives amplified by the leftist mainstream media augments these neo-Marxist pseudoreality narratives to create a dialectical paradox in which "the highly ideological thrust of the Left's ambitions **are made to sound normal while mainstream defenses of America sound shrill, rigid, and even ideological.**"[48]

Neo-Marxist Critical Theory

The ideological roots of today's revolutionary Left derive from neo-Marxist critical theory as advanced by various modern political thinkers ranging from Antonio Gramsci to Herbert Marcuse. Subsequent chapters will analyze the ideological evolution of today's neo-Marxism. For our purposes here, we reference Helen Pluckrose and James Lindsay's 2020 book *Cynical Theories: How Activist Scholarship Made Everything about Race, Gender, and Identity—and Why This Harms Everybody*. Pluckrose and Lindsay expanded on Pieper's concern by explaining that the radical Left's embrace of language manipulation results from a postmodern conviction that objective reality does not exist. Consider, for instance, the following excerpt:

> Cultural constructivism is not the belief that reality is *literally* created by cultural beliefs—it doesn't argue, for instance, that when we erroneously believed the Sun went around the Earth, our beliefs had any influence over the solar system and its dynamics. Instead, it is the position that humans are so tied into their cultural frameworks that all truth or knowledge claims are merely representations of those frameworks—we have decided that "it is true" or "it is known" that the Earth goes round the Sun *because of the way we establish truth in our current culture*. That is, although reality doesn't change in accordance with our beliefs, what *does* change is what we are able to regard as true (or false—or "crazy") about reality. If we belonged to a culture that produced and legitimated knowledge differently, within that cultural paradigm it might be "true" that, say, the Sun goes round the Earth. Those who would be regarded as "crazy" to disagree would change accordingly.[49]

The neo-Marxist Left rejects the proposition that there are "real truths about an objective reality 'out there' and that we can come to know them."[50] Pluckrose and Lindsay correctly understand that this neo-Marxist cultural confusion about reality necessitates the radical Left's rejection of Enlightenment thinking so central to Judeo-Christian ethics. Instead, the belief that all reality results from subjective personal experience shaped by cultural beliefs put identity politics at the center of the radical Left's rejection of traditional American values. Once the "mass line" narrative is established in the space of mass media, political correctness takes over as an enforcement mechanism to implant neo-Marxist objectives into the popular political culture. Republican Party politicians today tend to "shrink from Constitutional principles for fear of being accused of racism, sexism, homophobia, etc."[51]—a tactic the radical Left utilizes to marginalize supporters of traditional American values. By subordinating traditional American values to the public policy outcomes that neo-Marxist narratives are designed to propagate, Republican leaders end up "**subordinating those principles to neo-Marxist narratives**."[52] Coughlin and Higgins continued, explaining how political correctness operates to turn GOP politicians into pawns of the neo-Marxist political warfare strategy:

> By submitting to these narratives, establishment Republicans first become pliant, and then obedient to the Left, accommodating it through **"words that work" that create the illusion of opposition while signaling surrender in the information battle space**. In that role, regardless of the mandates that got them elected, establishment

> Republicans will defend the issues that got them elected in deliberately under-inclusive manners that conditions those issues for dialectical negation while demoralizing their base. What Republicans demoralize, the Left then disenfranchises. In this role, **establishment Republicans become the defeat mechanism of the Left.**[53]

Coughlin and Higgins stressed that a strategic understanding of the neo-Marxist Left demands recognizing that it is dialectically driven. The neo-Marxist Left executes tactics of negation through a rewriting of American history that involves demonizing traditional American political values along a Hegelian arc. The goal of the Hegelian dialectic is to negate traditional American values so as to perpetuate the type of "hope and change" themes Barack Obama used as his 2008 campaign themes. In propagating those themes, Obama masked the reality that "hope and change" were neo-Marxist revolutionary codewords for ending capitalism and destroying the United States.

Now, let's return to the subject of "social justice" and neo-Marxist critical theory. "The obsession with language is at the heart of postmodern thinking and key to its methods," Pluckrose and Lindsay correctly observed.[54] The cultural relativism of the neo-Marxist Left rejects "the commonsense idea that words refer straightforwardly to things in the real world."[55] Instead, words are subjective, given a "commonsense" or consensus meaning only within the context of culture. Since the neo-Marxist Left views modern American culture as inherently corrupt, personal meanings attributed to words have greater power in expressing and defining personal realities. Pluckrose and Lindsay explained as follows:

> In this understanding, language operates hierarchically through binaries, always placing one element above another to make meaning. For example, "man" is defined in opposition to "woman" and taken to be superior.[56]

Thus, "critical theory" becomes a code word for viewing and "deconstructing" reality from the perspective of this neo-Marxist subjective truth. "White privilege" becomes a key concern because critical theory begins by accusing the dominant cultural identity of America as being "white, male, wealthy, and Western." This benefits white people unjustly because "society was already set up for their benefit."[57] From this follows the "social justice theory" aims to elevate the cultural importance of the subjective reality of oppressed minorities. "If knowledge is a construct of power, which functions through ways of talking about things, knowledge can be changed and power structures toppled by changing the way we talk about things," Pluckrose and Lindsay wrote. "Thus, applied postmodernism focuses on controlling discourses, especially by problematizing language and imagery it deems Theoretically harmful. This means that it looks for and then highlights ways in which the oppressed problems they assume exist in society manifest themselves, sometimes quite subtly, in order to 'make oppression visible.'"[58]

Coughlin and Higgins stressed that radical Left narratives embody socially enforceable speech codes by design. They explained the following:

> "You can't say this" until one day, you cannot even say you exist. This is neither latent nor theoretical. In a complete negation of a biological fact, you cannot declare yourself to be a man (if you are a man) or a woman (if you are a woman) because that is genderism.
>
> The fact of being born an American, living in America, you cannot say you are American because that is racism. You cannot defend the Constitution on college campuses because that is white privilege.[59]

Coughlin and Higgins stressed that the "**very way we have come to speak of these issues renders them incomprehensible because that is what narratives are designed to do.**"[60] Today, the average American is bewildered because we fail to comprehend Mao Tse-tung's perspective in 1949. Mao viewed the rise of Marxism worldwide as a historical necessity whose inevitability was sure, not a subject open for debate or revision by reactionary thinking. Mao felt he was giving birth to a new reality of social justice in a world without class or race divisions. He saw his mission as "working hard and creating conditions for the natural elimination of classes, state authority, and political parties so that mankind will enter the era of universal fraternity."[61] Pluckrose and Lindsay observed that "the intense scrutiny of language and development of ever stricter rules for terminology pertaining to identity often known as *political correctness* came to a head in the 1990s and has again become pertinent since the mid-2010s."[62]

"Social Democrats" and the Neo-Marxist Stealth Plan

In 2013, New Zealander Trevor Loudon published a comprehensive new 689-page volume entitled *The Enemies Within: Communists, Socialists and Progressives in the U.S. Congress*[63] to accompany his 668-page 2011 book, *Barack Obama and the Enemies Within.*[64] In both volumes, Loudon proved himself to be among the foremost experts in the world investigating and reporting upon the penetration of neo-Marxists masquerading as democratic socialists or progressives in the U.S. Congress. Loudon made clear these congressional neo-Marxists portray themselves as liberals to mask their actual radical attachment to the dialectic view of revolutionary historical inevitability aimed at destroying the Constitution.

Loudon documented how the Democratic Socialists of America (DSA) formed a coalition of former Trotskyite, new-Left activists; Socialist Party; and Communist Party members in 1983. "Democratic Socialists of America is now the U.S.'s largest Marxist organization and its moderate name has allowed it to infiltrate other parties, including the New Party, the Working Families Party, the Greens, and the Democratic Party," Loudon noted.[65]

In 1996, when Barack Obama first ran for office, running for the Illinois State Senate as the Democratic Party candidate, the Chicago Democratic Socialists of America and the New Party endorsed him. The New Party, formed by the Democratic Socialists of America and the Association of Community Organizations for Reform Now (ACORN), was the U.S.'s largest radical organization. Before attending Harvard Law School, Obama worked with ACORN as a community organizer.[66] Loudon made clear the Democratic Socialists of America played a significant role with Senator Bernie Sanders in forming the Congressional Progressive Caucus (CPC) in 1991. At that time, the openly socialist Sanders served in Congress as an Independent senator from Vermont. In his 2013 book, Loudon detailed the neo-Marxist backgrounds of the more than seventy members of the U.S. House of Representatives who were members of the CPC.[67] Loudon stressed that the legislative agenda of the Democratic Socialists of America is identical to that of the Communist Party USA (CPUSA), "but the word 'Democratic' in the DSA's name enables it to penetrate organizations that wouldn't accept more open communists."[68]

Louden detailed congressional profiles of members of Congress in 2013, providing extensive evidence of radical leftist ties in the backgrounds of top Democratic Party U.S. senators Barbara Boxer (CA), Dick Durbin (IL), Tom Harkin (IA), Barbara Mikulski (MD), Elizabeth Warren (MA), Ed Markey (MA), Debbie Stabenow (MI), Al Franken (MN), Sherrod Brown (OH), Ron Wyden (OR), Jeff Merkley (OR), Patty Murray (WA), and Tammy Baldwin (WI). In the House of Representatives, Loudon profiled the radical Left background of Democratic Party representatives Nancy Pelosi (CA), Louis Gutierrez (IL), John Conyers, Jr. (MI),

Charles Rangel (NY), Marcy Kaptur (OH), Peter DeFazio (OR), Sheila Jackson Lee (TX), Jim McDermott (WA), and dozens more. What makes Loudon's profiles of the radical associations of Democratic Party members of Congress impressive is his extensive research. Loudon's documentation for each identified member of Congress included footnoted discussions, news clips, website screen captures, and quotations from published sources that leave no doubt about the authenticity and accuracy of his allegations.

Loudon's painstaking research affirmed an important point Coughlin and Higgins make:

> Analysis of the Left that fails to account for the narrative impact of terms like Democratic Socialism will fail because they are under-inclusive to the activities and events that these terms bring into play, not the least because **so few are aware of the hard association of "Democratic Socialism" with Marxist-Leninism**.
>
> At the same time, well-worn terms with American political pedigrees like "liberal" serve as foils that mask socialist agendas through narratives that limit political analysis to what an anachronistic political lexicon permits.[69]

As we noted earlier, Coughlin and Higgins stressed that a principal objective of the radical Left is to hide its revolutionary purposes in the old lexicon of liberal or progressive politics while escalating radicalized agendas that find cover under politics as usual.

Representative Alexandria Ocasio-Cortez has self-identified as a "democrat socialist," though the Democrat Socialists of America website brags that "Bronx Congresswoman Alexandria Ocasio-Cortez, best known as AOC, is DSA's foremost socialist superstar."[70] The DSA website continued: "Today—with over 12 million Twitter followers, her picture on the December cover of Vanity Fair, and mass cultural appeal to the teens and the not-yet political—she continues to use her unasked-for celebrity to build support for a democrat socialist agenda."[71] Yet, in interviews, AOC downplays her neo-Marxist agenda by likening her view of democratic socialism to Scandinavian social democracy. "So when millennials talk about concepts like democratic socialism, we're not talking about these kinds of 'Red Scare' boogeyman," AOC explained in a 2019 interview with Business Insider. "We're talking about countries and systems that already exist that have already been proven to be successful in the modern world." She insisted her view of democratic socialism was exhibited by her support of a single-payer health care system that covers all forms of health care. "We're talking about single-payer health care that has already been successful in many different models, from Finland to Canada to the UK," she said. She emphasized that her platform includes guaranteeing Americans a living wage that maintains "basic levels of dignity so that no person in America is too poor to live," Ocasio-Cortez said. "That's what democratic socialism means in 2018, and not this kind of McCarthyism Red Scare of a past era."[72]

The DSA takes pains to distinguish the organization from a political party. The DSA does not register with the Federal Elections Commission. Instead, the DSA is a nonprofit registered as a 501(c)4 organization. Rather than admit the DSA's goal is to eradicate capitalism, DSA proclaims the need to "democratize" capitalism. "Socialism is about democratizing the family to get rid of patriarchal relations; democratizing the political sphere to get genuine participatory democracy; democratizing the schools by challenging the hierarchical relationship between the teachers of the school and the students of the school," insisted Jared Abbott, a member of DSA's national steering committee. "Socialism is the democratization of all areas of life, included but not limited to the economy."[73] Few remember that the Russian Social-Democratic Workers' Party, formed in Minsk in 1898, a party to which Vladimir Lenin belonged, was the predecessor to the Communist Party of the Soviet Union.[74]

A Communist Warns America

In June 1953, Bella Dodd, a card-carrying CPUSA member in the 1930s and 1940s, testified to the House Un-American Activities Committee (HUAC), explaining why she left the Communist Party.[75] Her testimony was particularly significant for her revelations describing how the CPUSA "masked its Marxist agenda in language that made it acceptable to Americans."[76] Dodd was a Communist in her twenties during the Great Depression through her middle age in the post–World War II era. Dodd eventually rose to become a high-level member of the CPUSA. She understood how Communism worked as a revolutionary methodology in practice. She also knew from the inside how deviously the CPUSA disguised its message to make Communism acceptable to Americans. In the 1920s, the general American public rejected Marxism despite the appeal of the Russian Revolution to a generation of American liberal intellectuals of that era. By the 1940s, Dodd understood that the strategy of the CPUSA had come to concurring from within America, mainly by advancing American socialism under "social justice" themes and by taking over the Democratic Party. Her warnings bear remembering once again today.

Marxism: A Secular Religion

Dodd testified that she had been a member of the national committee of the CPUSA from 1944 to 1948. She explained to the committee that "communism is a way of life."[77] She testified the following:

> It [Communism] is a whole philosophy of being. If you believe in communism, then everything you do, you do with this philosophy. If once you lose that philosophy, you have to rethink your every single act and every statement you make.[78]

Indoctrination into the CPUSA for Dodd was a quasi-religious process. She explained:

> Communism is like a religion. President Eisenhower said that the other day, but it is a religion without a God. If you believe strongly in communism, it is your duty to bring it into every phase of your life. If you are a member of the American Association of University Professors, if you are a member of the association of your specialty such as a member of the mathematical association, it is your duty to bring the party line into those organizations. If you are a member of a fraternity, you are supposed to bring it into the fraternity, into any group where there is the privilege of discussion. If you are a teacher, you are supposed to live by the principles of Marxism and Leninism.[79]

Dodd told HUAC outright that the United States "is being prepared for revolution." She elaborated that the "strategy" of the Communist Party was "world revolution."[80] Communists in the United States, even in the 1930s and 1940s, pursued these goals with zeal, intolerant of any disagreement.

"There is only one academic freedom to them [the Communists], that is loyalty to the Communist Party," she said. "There is no room for a difference of opinion."[81] She insisted Communists attacked those who opposed them with "high-sounding words" that were in reality "general smear words" and "emotional words," such that in the 1940s, the Communists called their enemies "fascists" and in the 1950s, "McCarthyites." She detailed that these "are words which have no definition, and first you create a sense of fear and hatred and then you apply this word to everyone against you."[82] Dodd understood how important taking control of language was to the success of Communism. She pointed out that "they [the Communists] took the anti-Fascist slogan and made themselves the protagonists of antifascism. They did the same thing with the word 'democracy.' It became very difficult to oppose them because they posed everything in terms of the word 'democracy.'"[83]

The Attack on God and the Constitution

She expressed alarm that "if you go through the catalogs of various colleges of America, you find from the period of 1925 to about 1948 or 1949 that most of the colleges, for instance, have dropped all their courses on ethics and religion; you will find most of the colleges dropped their courses—even the law schools dropped their courses—on constitutional law."[84] She asked, "If your law schools drop their courses on constitutional law, how much more do the liberal arts colleges do it?"[85] A few moments later in her testimony, she returned to the point: "You will be interested in noting the catalogs about ethics, courses on religion, courses on the Bible; they have practically been dropped out of the college curricula. It is a method of despiritualizing the American people."[86]

She acknowledged that "the first enemy of the Communist is a belief in the fact that you are created by a Divine Creator." She insisted that Communists "have to get rid" of God "before anything else." Why? "If they [Communists] can wipe that out [belief in God], then it is easy, because if you don't believe in a God, all you believe in is better material advancement, and the Communists promise greater material advancement for all."[87] She explained how Communist indoctrination begins by eliminating God in the nursery schools:

> In the nursery schools, you begin by affecting the children by emphasizing material values. You eliminate, for instance, from the nursery school rhymes and anything that has to do with religion. At Christmas you deal with Christmas as a pagan holiday. You choose the rhymes, choose the activities, and you follow the educational philosophy that says the child is just a blank page. He learns only by doing. You adopt that philosophy and implement it.[88]

The Important Role Teachers Play Indoctrinating American Youth

She received a doctor of jurisprudence degree from New York University in 1927 and was admitted to the New York bar in 1931. She graduated from

Hunter College in New York City in 1925 and returned there to teach courses in the political science and economics departments from 1926 to 1938. In her June 1953 testimony to HUAC, she openly admitted to using her teaching position to indoctrinate students into Communism.

> There is no doubt in my mind that I influenced students. I was teaching economics; I was teaching political science, history. These are subjects which are very easily influenced by a Marxist-Leninist approach. I was teaching during the period of the depression, and during that period the Communists said the reason for the depression was the breakdown in the capitalist system and the only thing which would obviate any future depressions would be elimination of the system. Change the system, and you would have no more depressions. Unfortunately, there were no other answers being given at the time. The Communist answer was the easiest answer to give. It was easy to just push the students in that direction.[89]

Dodd acknowledged that when she went into the classroom, she was entirely a Communist and that it was impossible to teach objectively. She explained it was impossible for a Communist to "divide himself," so that even when she went into the classroom, she was a Communist "primarily" because it was "impossible" for her "to divide" herself. "You can't tear yourself apart," she explained.[90] As a teacher, she clearly understood the importance of her role in indoctrinating students. In her summation, he returned to her earlier theme:

> Well, as I said before, communism is a way of life, and it is almost like a religion. It affects your attitude toward your students, toward your government, affects your attitude toward things that are happening day by day. Most Communist college professors begin by being very much interested in their students, and if they have a Communist philosophy, they pass it on. Many of them try to influence their students to become Communists. Any number of students have become Communists because they admired a professor who was going in that direction. Then he functions within all the other organizations on campus in affecting their thinking, the question of choosing books for the library, the question of establishing curricula for the college.[91]

In response to questioning from the committee, Dodd responded that teachers are desired by the Communist cause because "the Communists know that the old people living in America today are not going to make the revolution." She stressed Communists "count on the young people, and those who control the youth are the people who control the future of this country."[92] One of Dodd's most essential points came in this discussion of the Communist plan to take over the United States by indoctrinating the youth of America in the schools. "I certainly believe the American people have got to stop fooling around with just fighting communism in the abstract," she insisted. "They [the American people] have got to know what the thing means, why they are against it, and how to fight it."[93]

Propaganda and the Communist Perversion of Language

On November 16, 1953, Dodd testified again before HUAC in Philadelphia.[94] While much of Dodd's testimony in Philadelphia was a repeat of her testimony in Ohio, she added several crucial points. "I was told by Gil Green, chairman of the party in New York State, that if ever communism came to America it would…come under a label palatable to the American people," she revealed. She asked Green to explain what he meant. "He said 'It might be liberty or democracy or something of that kind.'" Dodd elaborated. "In other words, they will hide themselves under labels which the American people will think are their own."[95] She continued as follows:

> They [Communists] will use words with a definition which you and I do not use. For instance, they regard themselves as the most democratic. I was always told that the American form of democracy is only a limited democracy. The most perfect democracy is the democracy of the Communist movement and of the Soviet Union, so when they use the word "democracy" they are obviously not using the same terms that we are using. The word is the same but the meaning is different.[96]

Later in her testimony, Dodd picked up this point again. "The Communist cause is highly geared to propaganda. They understand it even better than Dr. Goebbels did. Propaganda is the most effective weapon in the hands of the Communists in beclouding the minds of American citizens."[97]

Regarding the importance of language, Alexander Trachtenberg exerted an impactful influence over Dodd's thinking. Born to a Russian Jewish family in Odessa in 1885, Trachtenberg served in the Russian army during the Russo-Japanese War (1904–1905). He escaped the pogroms against the Jews in 1905 and 1906 to flee via Hamburg to America later that year. In

Russia, Trachtenberg was a dedicated socialist who turned Communist. In the United States, he founded International Publishers and devoted himself to publishing Marxist-Leninist texts. In the United States, he rose to hold a position as a CPUSA's Central Control Committee member. In her 1954 book *School of Darkness*, Dodd recalled that "Trachtenberg once said to me that when communism came to America it would come under the label of 'progressive democracy.'" Trachtenberg added that when it came, it would come "in labels acceptable to the American people."[98] In a lecture she gave at Fordham University in 1953, Dodd referred to Trachtenberg at greater length. She explained that Trachtenberg said the following at the 1944 Communist Party's National Convention at Madison Square Garden, which she attended:

> When we get ready to take the United States, we will not do it under the label of Communism; we will not take it under the label of Socialism. These labels are unpleasant to the American people, and have been smeared too much. We will take the United States under the labels we have made very lovable; we will take it under liberalism, under progressivism, under democracy, but take it we will.[99]

The Marxist Party Line

Dodd stressed in her testimony that Communist propaganda had an orthodoxy imposed by the Communist International, an organization known as the "Comintern." The Comintern, founded in 1919 in an international meeting of Communist revolutionaries, served through the early 1940s as Moscow's directorate for controlling the world Communist movement. In her Columbus testimony before HUAC, Dodd explained that the policy directives from the Comintern shifted as Russia's interests as a nation-state changed. She explained the following:

> There is no doubt, at first, the Third International, the Comintern, which was in existence at that time, laid down the policy for all the world Communist Parties. For instance, the seventh world congress of the Comintern laid down the policy of the united front, laying down the anti-Fascist, united-front tactic of fighting the Fascists.
>
> Then when the Soviet-Nazi pact was formed, we had to have a new line of approach which was, everything which would strengthen the Soviet Union was good for the working class all over the world—even unity with the Nazis.

> Of course, when the Soviet Union was attacked by the Nazis, there was the slogan of saving democracy. Then the United States, France, England, China, and the Soviet Union became the great democracies.
>
> When in 1945, the policy in Russia was changed—at that time the Comintern had been abolished as a concession, I think, to the United States—because the United States said, "All right, we will have co-existence, but we don't want any Comintern directing the Communist Party in the United States." Then in 1945, the Soviet Union changed its line, which was not announced to the entire world, but came in the form of the Duclos letter to the Communist Party of the United States. No tactics for United States Communists from 1929 on were made by the Communist Party of the United States.[100]

The "Duclos letter" refers to an article Jacques Duclos, the leader of the Communist group in the French National Assembly, published in April 1945. The Duclos letter repudiated a decision made by Earl Browder, then the head of the CPUSA, to abolish the CPUSA in the spirit of the Tehran Conference at the end of World War II. Browder's position had been that at the Tehran Conference, Joseph Stalin had agreed that communism and capitalism would coexist after the defeat of Nazi Germany. American Communists at that time took the Duclos letter as the official statement of the Soviet Union, given that the Comintern had been disbanded.[101] In her testimony, Dodd expanded on the importance of the Duclos letter:

> In the spring of 1945, when the tremendous change in the party line took place because of the Duclos letter sent from France to the United States which said we American Communists had better stop playing the democracy game, stop working so closely with the liberals and democrats and get back to the job of preparing for revolution, at that time, I was a delegate to the convention [of the CPUSA] in 1945. I was elected again to the national committee, and remained on the national committee until 1948, when the new convention, of course, failed to elect me, because I had gotten into difficulties with the party in the interim.[102]

Dodd's disillusionment with Communism began after World War II when she realized the Soviet Union was less about establishing a Communist utopia around the world than about the Soviet Union playing power politics internationally to establish global hegemony for Moscow. She continued her testimony as follows:

> We were against repression, against war, against fascism, and the Communist Party takes our best interests and uses them against us by twisting us into a program which they want us to follow.
>
> Take, for instance, the whole question of antifascism. The Communist Party in this country set itself up as the one organization that was fighting fascism. Very few other organizations gave them a battle for that, and so the Americans got to feeling, "These are the anti-Fascists."
>
> We only learn now, after reading the documents captured by the American soldiers in Germany, that throughout the time the Communists were calling themselves "anti-Fascists," they were working with the German high brass while Hitler was in power. They were meeting to decide on the division of Europe. When Molotov [Soviet foreign minister under Stalin] said the Soviet-Nazi pact was written in blood, he didn't mean the blood of the Soviet Union, but he meant the blood of the Polish people, of the Czechoslovakian people.[103]

In this vein, Dodd made one additional important revelation. Her testimony continued as follows:

> I was teaching at Hunter College from 1926 to 1938. In 1935, I stood up before the faculty, and the students, and made a speech which I will never forget. It was entitled, "Fascism Means War." I was going on the assumption that Fascists and Communists were two different things. I didn't know then what I know now, that every drop of crude oil used by the Fascists in Italy to drop bombs on Abyssinia was sold to them by the Soviet Union.[104]

Modern historians with access to newly available Russian archives on World War II have analyzed Stalin's foreign policy that explains Dodd's disillusionment in a new light. Sean McMeekin, a history professor at Bard College, in his 2021 book *Stalin's War*, argued that the ultimate aim of Stalin's foreign policy was "the weakening of capitalist regimes by any means necessary and the concomitant global expansion of Communism."[105] McMeekin noted that another example of this policy can be observed in Moscow's reaction to the Nazi invasion of France. McMeekin explained, for instance, that Soviet officials were supportive of the German invasion of France and the Low Countries. McMeekin wrote the following:

> The Comintern line laid down in Moscow even instructed French men and women—via both print propaganda and the soon-notorious radio

> broadcasts of French Communist Party (PCF) leader Maurice Thorez—not to resist the Germans, however absurd this sounded to more patriotic party members (many hundreds of whom, including twenty-one of the PCF's seventy-three parliamentary deputies, tore up their party cards in disgust).[106]

Henry Kissinger turned his doctoral thesis at Harvard into his first book published in 1957, *A World Restored.*[107] In this work, Kissinger focused on the efforts Klemens von Metternich, the Austrian Empire's foreign minister, expended to establish a stable European international setting in 1812, after the defeat of Napoleon in Russia. Kissinger attributed Metternich's skills as a diplomat to the establishment of the political equilibrium among the various European nation-states that created peace in Europe until 1914 and the outbreak of the First World War. Metternich relied on a balance of power to establish this equilibrium. Balance of power is a concept in international relations known to Thucydides in explaining the outbreak of the Peloponnesian War between Athens and Greece (431–404 BC). A balance of power involves an equilibrium between various nation-states where no one nation-state becomes sufficiently strong militarily to begin contemplating war to dominate neighboring nation-states. Kissinger attributed Metternich's political acumen and diplomatic skill with having established the political equilibrium that formed peace between nations in Europe for over a century. A complimentary term "sphere of influence" emerged in international politics in the 1880s when nations like England and Germany began extending their colonial reach into Asia and Africa.

The relevance of these terms to the discussion here is that while Karl Marx and Friedrich Engels expected a worldwide revolution to overthrow capitalism to develop out of the European revolutions of 1848, the first state to adopt Communism was Russia in 1917. Again, Lenin was disappointed the Russian Revolution did not trigger a worldwide revolution to overthrow capitalism. Instead, Russia adopted a revised Marxist-Leninist Communist ideology as the ruling principle of Russia as a nation-state. While the United States can claim a sphere of influence, for instance, over the Western Hemisphere, Russia as a nation-state claims a sphere of influence over Eastern Europe generally, and countries like Ukraine in particular. The point is not to be confused. Just because a country like Russia or China is Communist does not mean Russia and China have quit acting like nation-states. When acting like a nation-state, Russia and China can make policy decisions that do not further the interests of advancing

Communism worldwide. An example that makes this point is the Sino-Soviet border conflict that brought China and Russia to the brink of war in March 1969.

The HUAC questioned Dodd over whether she became disillusioned when she saw policy dictates coming from Moscow to the CPUSA that rationalized Russian foreign policy actions in terms of Russia's balance-of-power or sphere-of-influence politics instead of different foreign policy actions justified in terms of promoting a worldwide Communist revolution. In the lead-up to World War II, Stalin's decision in 1939 to enter into a nonaggression pact with Hitler disturbed Communist sympathizers worldwide. Dodd explained she dealt with the issue by distinguishing between Russia's strategy as the leader of a worldwide Communist revolution and Russia's tactics as a nation-state. "In a period in which the Soviet Union changes its foreign policy, as for instance during the time of the Stalin-Hitler pact, the tactics in the United States were different than they would be at a time when the United States was in alliance with the Soviet Union," she explained in her Philadelphia testimony. "The tactics should and are constantly being changed. The strategy is always the same and the Communist does not lose sight of the fact that the strategy is the same. The ultimate objective is a Soviet world."[108]

In her testimony in Columbus, Ohio, Dodd explained how the tactics changed again when Hitler invaded Russia in June 1941. "Take, for instance the question—we used to have the American League Against War and Fascism," she clarified. "We were against war and fascism. We were almost a superpacifist group. We picketed the White House for peace. Then came the invasion of the Soviet Union. Overnight, we had to change the name for—the league's name."[109] She described how little time it took the CPUSA to make the shift. "I was chairman of a trade-union committee for peace," she said. "I led a lot of women down there, and we picketed the White House for peace. Then suddenly we were told we had to be for war. It took us at least 2 months to wash out the old idea and put in the new one."[110]

Why Dodd Became a Communist

Dodd explained that in the early 1930s she visited Italy and Germany, and she was "distressed" by what she saw of fascism. "On the campus in Germany, I saw young men fighting with fists, guns, rocks," and she came back to the United States a confirmed anti-fascist. "When I got back, we were deep in the depression," she testified. "Immediately after

I got back, the banks closed. I stood on 42nd Street and watched the Bowery Savings Bank close and watched the line of people scared stiff as to what was going to happen to them."[111] The Communists in 1932 and 1933 introduced legislation to create social security, and Dodd felt "these things were right."[112] When Earl Browder, then head of the CPUSA, told Dodd he was pleased she would fight fascism, Dodd shook his hand and went along. Only later did she become disillusioned when she realized the Communist Party "uses these slogans, these generalizations, in order to break down their resistance, and ultimately they are tied in with the Communist movement."[113] She joined the Communist Party because she was against racial discrimination, repression, war, and fascism. Dodd succinctly summarized why she became a Communist in her second round of HUAC testimony. "In 1932 they [the CPUSA] first approached me on the question of uniting in the fight against fascism, and since I had been to Germany and seen the terrible things they could do, I fell for the propaganda line of the Communists," she said.[114]

William Z. Foster and Why Communism Is Inevitable in America

In her Philadelphia HUAC testimony, Dodd focused on the theme that Communism would take over America inevitably as if a matter of destiny. She explained that William Z. Foster, who served as CPUSA general secretary from 1945 to 1957, said precisely that in his 1949 book *The Twilight of World Capitalism*: "Communism is inevitable in America."[115] She commented that Foster dedicated the book to his grandson, whom he predicted would live in a Communist America. Dodd went on to explain that in the book's chapter called "The Advent of Socialist Man," Foster wrote the following:

> Man will free himself, under socialism, from the burden of weakness and disease that has nursed him for so long and which is such a distressing feature of present-day society. Man, too, for the first time disregarding foolish religious taboos, will boldly solve the population problems, both in respect to the size of his own individual family and that of the number of people in the nations generally.[116]

Foster argued that the Communists, once in power worldwide, would use eugenics to solve the global population problem. He wrote:

> The vital matter of the evolution of mankind is not one that can any longer be left to chance, especially a capitalist society is now having

such a negative effect on the development of the species. The law of natural selection, which built the marvelous complexities of plant and animal species, no longer can work spontaneously. Now the evolution of the human species must be done artificially, by the conscious action of man himself.[117]

Dodd affirmed Communists felt that killing one hundred million people "would be a good thing." She concluded, "There is no doubt in my mind that this [Communism] is a program for reorganizing and rebuilding mankind, according to their own peculiar pattern."[118] Foster was a member of the 1920s national committee of the American Civil Liberties Association. In 1932, he wrote a book entitled *Toward Soviet America*[119] that defined his vision for creating a Communist utopia in the United States.

In a Moscow article with the dateline of September 1, 1961, the *New York Times* reported Foster had died in a Moscow sanitorium at the age of eighty. He was receiving medical treatment for a stroke that he suffered in 1957. Hoping to be allowed to travel to the Soviet Union for medical treatment, he went to court in 1959 to lift his indictment under the Smith Act for conspiring to teach and advocate the destruction of the United States government. His medical condition had prevented the U.S. Justice Department from bringing him to trial. The State Department twice denied him permission to leave the United States before relenting in December 1960 and issuing him a passport. The *New York Times* obituary noted that on his eightieth birthday, February 25, 1961, Russian Premier Nikita Khrushchev visited Foster in the Moscow medical facility where he was convalescing.[120]

The Communist Plan to Exploit Race

In her 1954 book, Dodd disclosed that in 1946 at a December CPUSA national committee meeting, Foster furthered a plan to exploit blacks to promote a Communist revolution in the United States. Here is how Dodd described the Stalin/Foster plan:

> The sessions of the December [1946] National Committee were notable for their long-winded, long-spun-out, and fantastic justification of the line of "self-determination of the Negro in the black belt." Only the intelligence and patience of Negro leaders in America have made possible resistance to this mischievous theory which was contrived by Stalin

> and was now unleashed by [William Z.] Foster. Briefly told, it is the theory that the Negroes in the South form a nation, a subjugated nation with the desire to become a free one, and that the Communists are to give them all assistance. The Party proposed to develop the national aspirations of the Negro people so they would rise up and establish themselves as a nation with the right to secede from the United States. It was a theory not for the benefit of the Negroes but to spur strife, and to use the American Negro in the world communist propaganda campaign to win over the colored people of the world. Ultimately, the Communists proposed to use them as instruments in the revolution to come in the United States.[121]

The callous manipulation of African Americans at the heart of this scheme exposes the duplicity of the CPUSA's supposed sympathy for the oppression experienced by people of color in this country. The idea to exploit racial unrest to cause a Communist revolution originated with Stalin. In 1913, Stalin published a book entitled *Marxism and the National Question*.[122] In that book, Stalin moved away from Marx's idea that a workers' revolt based on class conflicts would produce a worldwide Communist revolution, rising and taking the wealth of the capitalists to share equally. As anti-Communist expert Trevor Loudon explained, "before revolutionaries can integrate all nations into a global socialist super-state, existing nations must be broken down and fractured along class and racial lines."[123]

Stalin realized that to accomplish the goal of the worldwide Communist revolution, Communist operatives needed to proceed nation by nation, exploiting in each state the ethnic and racial tensions appropriate to that particular national setting. "In essence, Stalin believed revolutionaries should destroy targeted nations by encouraging ethnic or racial minorities to work toward a separate state, to secede or break away from their existing country," Loudon summarized. "In modern times, this has been extended to campaigns for bilingualism, separate justice systems, reparations for slavery, land confiscations, and so on." Thus, Stalin's innovation was to press the issue that each state targeted for a Communist revolution needed to proceed through "national questions."[124]

Stalin understood that ethnic and racial divisions, not class divisions, were the fertile ground to cause the nation-state to become irreparably divided. Loudon pointed out that Communist revolutions have promoted national question-type policies worldwide. In Ireland, the Communist Party played on the Protestant-Catholic divide. In Scotland, Communists formed the Scottish National Party to help break up the United Kingdom.

In France and Spain, Communists backed the Basque separatist movement. In Canada, Communists agitated for a separate French-speaking state in Quebec. In the United States, Communists began working to radicalize the southern black population in the late 1920s.[125]

With the publication of *Marxism and the National Question* in 1913, Stalin shifted the focus of the international Communist movement to nation-states, arguing that nations are "historically constituted communities of people"[126] typically characterized by a common language, economic cohesion, and a distinct geographical location. While class mobility was possible in countries like the United States, Stalin understood that people are much more wedded to their culture and religion and cannot change their race.[127] In 1928, the Sixth Congress of the Communist International (Comintern) meeting in Moscow passed a resolution that supported Stalin on the "Black National Question" by endorsing the creation of a Black Belt–separate nation being formed in the United States with the slogan of the "Right of Self-Determination for the Negroes."[128]

Stalin believed that racial tensions within the United States were more pivotal than class tensions to produce a Communist revolution. Bella Dodd was right. Stalin had embraced the idea of creating within the United States the separate Black Belt Republic out of the southern states of Florida, Georgia, Alabama, Tennessee, and North and South Carolina.

In the 1920s, Harry Haywood championed Stalin's idea in the United States. Haywood was one of the few black Communists in the 1920s and a member of the African Blood Brotherhood (ABB), the first black group that joined the CPUSA. Haywood studied at the International Lenin School in Moscow in the mid-1920s, where he explored how African American oppression could be used to trigger a revolution in the United States. Haywood submitted his "Resolution on the Negro Question," proposing his Black Belt Republic concept, to the Sixth Congress of the Comintern in 1928. Stalin embraced Haywood's Black Belt Republic as a promising solution to the "Negro Question." He declared black self-determination to be a priority of the international Communist community, and he ordered the CPUSA to eliminate racism from their ranks.[129]

Foster's 1954 book *The Negro People in American History*[130] clarifies that he agreed that America's most vulnerable issue with the potential to trigger a Marxist revolution was slavery and the subsequent history of racial discrimination in the United States. Here is how Foster, in the preface to his book, described the condition of African Americans. In the very first sentence of the preface, he claimed that during the "three-and-a-half centuries since the first English colonies were planted along the Atlantic Coast, the landowner and industrialist rulers of this country, to further their own greed, have committed many monstrous crimes against the growing American people." Next, Foster noted how whites "barbarously stripped the Indians of their lands, broke up their social institutions, and slaughtered them." But he reserved his greatest disdain for the way white Americans have treated black Americans. Foster wrote the following as the preface's second paragraph:

> But the worst of all the crimes of expanding capitalism in this country has been the centuries-long outrage it has perpetrated, and continues to perpetuate, against the Negro people. To satisfy the greed of an arrogant landed aristocracy, the Negroes were stolen from their African homeland and compelled to submit, generation after generation, to a chattel slavery which was a measureless tragedy to them and a shame to our nation. And after the Negroes were emancipated, in the course of the great revolution of 1861-1865, they were forced into a semi-slavery which still persists. During three generations of "freedom," the Negroes have been lynched, pillaged, Jim Crowed, and generally mistreated as being less than human, in order to fatten the profits of insatiable capitalist exploiters. The most shameful pages of American history are those dealing with the exploitation and oppression of the Negro masses.[131]

Haywood's idea never caught on, mainly because of the large numbers of African Americans leaving the south during the Great Depression to move to northern cities where they could seek industrial jobs. In 1934, the CPUSA dropped the idea, realizing that creating a separate black nation in the Black Belt of southern states was no longer a viable plan.[132] In his 1954 book, Foster gave up the call to develop an African American secession movement. Commenting that the African American fight "against gross injustice and oppression has become an issue of major importance in the growing worldwide struggle of the oppressed colonial peoples for national liberation," Foster continued as follows: "During the course of their long, bitter uphill struggle the American Negro people have welded themselves literally into a nation."[133] Trevor Loudon noted that after World War II, American Communists shifted their strategy to agitating for full civil rights for southern blacks. He documented the various organizations for civil rights that the Communists helped establish. These organizations included the African Negro Labor Congress, the League of Struggle for Negro Rights, the International Labor Defense, the National

Negro Congress, the Civil Rights Congress, the Negro Labor Victory Committee, and the Southern Negro Youth Congress. "The civil rights movement was necessary and just," Loudon commented. "But it was riddled with communists from top to bottom. The goal was first to liberate the blacks from Jim Crow, then utilize their growing political power to push for socialist change—increasingly through the Democratic Party—then to push on to socialism."[134]

The importance of Bella Dodd's testimony on the CPUSA's treatment of the race issue was to warn America that the Communists had no genuine sympathy for African Americans in the United States. But the Communists found the race issue useful in their determination to foster a revolution in this country.

Party Discipline and Dodd's Disillusionment with Communism

Dodd explained the CPUSA operates as a rigid ideological system that tolerates no deviation from the party line of the moment. She was called before the party's control commission three times from 1945 to 1947. She described the CPUSA control commission as a "government within a government." She elaborated: "They [the CPUSA] have their own court system whereby a person violating the Communist Party code is brought for trial and punishment is meted out to him just as it would be in an open court, only this is a private court."[135] Dodd noted this was a time when she was "very upset by things that were going on" within the CPUSA. But the accusations against her were vague. "They called me on the carpet for something I said in a unit meeting," she said. "Another time they tried to inquire into certain personal affairs, and each time I was not cleared but was told to come to a meeting at a certain hour and I was made to wait until I was psychologically conditioned and disturbed, and a lot of questions were asked of me."[136] Finally, the CPUSA expelled Dodd. "My whole attitude toward my country while I was in the party was that my country was run by a group of people who were very interested in profits and were selfish and the only thing that would save this country would be the establishment of a Communist society," she summed up.[137]

Through World War II, Dodd woke up to the reality the CPUSA was a political branch of the Soviet government aimed at destroying capitalism within the United States. As noted earlier, Coughlin and Higgins understood that we Americans have a blind spot in our "national aversion to recognizing threats beyond the strictly military, especially our aversion to ideological threats in the political warfare arena."[138] They emphasized that "our lack of situational awareness" of ideological warfare "constitutes a great threat to national security." Why neo-Marxism has taken such an ideological hold on millennials and Gen Z remains a puzzle this book is resolved to solve. When neo-Marxists control the Pentagon and the U.S. Department of Justice, we must wake up to a crisis as dangerous to our freedom and independence as a thermonuclear war with Russia or China. Perhaps the most crucial part of Dodd's testimony was her warning that the American people must stop fighting neo-Marxism in the abstract. She was right. We must understand what neo-Marxism means, but we must also understand how to fight it.

The Neo-Marxist Plan to Take Over the Democratic Party

In the 1930s, the Communists in the United States developed a stealth plan to take over the Democratic Party. Jack Kawano was a young longshore leader who joined the Communist Party in Hawaii in the 1920s. Through the post–World War II period, Kawano played a role in the International Longshore and Warehouse Union (ILWU) and the Democratic Party in Hawaii. On February 10, 1951, he wrote a letter to Hawaii's territorial Subversive Activities Committee, in which he admitted to having joined the Communist Party. In the letter, Kawano explained why he initially felt that the Communist Party's objectives were consistent with his aims for the ILWU. "I did not think it was harmful to the union as long as the Communists were willing to assist me in bringing up the living standards of the workingman because they led me to believe that the basic existence of the Communist Party was primarily to promote the best interests of the workingman," he wrote. "I decided to quit the Communist Party because I found that the primary purpose of the Communist Party was not for the best interests of the workingman but to dupe the members of the union for purposes other than strictly trade-union matters."[139]

On July 6, 1951, Kawano testified before the House Un-American Affairs Committee (HUAC) in Washington, DC. Kawano made clear that in 1948, the Communist Party decided to infiltrate and take over the Democratic Party. He explained in his HUAC testimony that the plan was for "[t]he Communist Party, through the ILWU and other organizations will, join the Democratic Party." Next, the Communist Party would "take over leadership of it [the Democratic Party] by getting the majority of convention delegates elected who were Communists, Communist sympathizers, or at least union men." Kawano continued his testimony by explaining that Hawaii's Communist Party had decided to go underground, preferring to gain power through a stealth takeover of Hawaii's Democratic Party. "With enough infiltration, we could control the Democratic Party of Hawaii," Kawano explained. His testimony left no doubt that the Communist Party in Hawaii had decided to go underground by rebranding their identities as members of Hawaii's Democratic Party. Kawano noted how nearly victorious the Hawaii Communists were:

> I believe that the influence of the Communist Party in the Democratic Party of Hawaii is very strong, and if it were not for the few liberals in the Democratic Party who are strongly anti-Communist but at the same time command the respect of many laboring people and union members, and who are fighting Communists in the Democratic Party, the Democratic Party of Hawaii would be controlled by the Communist Party. These few liberals are having a tough time trying to keep the control of the Democratic Party out of the hands of people influenced by Communists.[140]

Paul Kengor, PhD, is a political science professor at Grove City College in Pennsylvania and an expert on Communist infiltration into America. In his 2012 book *The Communist: Frank Marshall Davis—The Untold Story of Barack Obama's Mentor*, Kengor documented that Davis abruptly decided to move from Chicago to Honolulu, Hawaii, at the urge of singer Paul Robeson, who like Davis was also a Communist. Here is how Kengor related the story:

> "I had also talked with Paul Robeson," he [Frank Marshall Davis] added, "who the previous year had appeared there [in Hawaii] in a series of concerts sponsored by the International Longshoremen's and Warehousemen's Union (ILWU), the most powerful labor organization in the territory. Paul enthusiastically supported our pending trip." Frank then added two more very revealing names: "I also wrote to Harry Bridges, head of the ILWU, whom I had met at the Lincoln School. He suggested I get in touch with Koji Ariyoshi, editor of the *Honolulu Record*, a newspaper that was generally similar to the *Chicago Star*."[141]

Kengor noted that Bridges and Ariyoshi, like Robeson and Davis, were secret members of the CPUSA. The ILWU, *Chicago Star*, and *Honolulu Record* were all either CPUSA organizations or were manipulated by the CPUSA "to further the Soviet/communist agenda."[142] Kengor also noted that on September 4, 1948, before Davis decided suddenly to move to Hawaii, the *Chicago Star* announced that the newspaper had been sold to the Progressive Publishing Co. and renamed the *Illinois Standard.* One of the new board members to the *Illinois Standard* was Harry Canter, "whose family would mentor David Axelrod, the man who would get Barack Obama elected president."[143] In 2008, Axelrod served as the manager of Obama's presidential campaign. Kengor further documented that, in his first piece he wrote for the *Honolulu Record,* Davis hailed Robeson, arguing that the USSR had abolished racism.[144]

In his 1951 sworn testimony to HUAC, Jack Kawano explained that the Hawaiian Communist Party, at an executive meeting in 1948, decided to instruct its members to sell out their stock in the competing newspaper, the *Hawaii Star,* and transfer it to the *Honolulu Record.* He explained that the first issue of the *Honolulu Record* came out on August 8, 1948, about the same time Davis moved from Chicago to Honolulu. Kawano explained: "As they did with the *Hawaii Star,* the *Honolulu Record* got all the help from the ILWU through the Communists in it. However, it was a lot easier to hustle subscriptions and ads for this paper, because it was not concentrated for the alien Japanese and could be accepted by all who read the English language."[145]

Kengor's research confirmed that as the Hawaiian Communist Party "went underground" in the post–World War II era, its Communist members "infiltrated the Democratic party, the start of a long march by American communists."[146] He commented that the Communists who infiltrated the Democratic Party in Hawaii continued "to masquerade as 'progressives,' except this time from within the Democratic Party." He concluded that the decision in the late 1940s for the CPUSA to move its members by stealth into the Democratic Party in Hawaii "arguably helped foster a tectonic shift within the Democratic Party, moving it away from the party of JFK, Harry Truman, and (at one time) even Ronald Reagan, to the party of Ted Kennedy, Nancy Pelosi, and Barack Obama."[147]

Summing up, Kengor wrote the following:

> The FBI file reported details from an informant, provided in April 1950, saying that "members of the subversive element in Honolulu were concentrating their efforts on infiltration of the Democratic Party through control of Precinct Clubs and organizations." These communist subversives were pushing "their candidates in these Precinct Club elections." According to the informant, on April 6, 1950, one such candidate, Frank Marshall Davis, was elected "assistant secretary and delegate" to the Territorial Democratic Convention in his particular Precinct Club—the Third Precinct of the Fifth District. Frank, in fact,

> attended that convention on April 30, 1950. The Reds' infiltration and internal subversion of the Democratic Party were on. And it would be as a "Democrat" that Frank would one day influence a future Democratic Party president [Barack Obama].[148]

In *The Communist*, Kengor reprinted as "Figure 1" the summary page from Frank Marshall Davis's six-hundred-page FBI file, including his Communist Party number: CP #47544.[149] Kengor's note under the "Figure 1" FBI summary page indicates Kengor chose to publish this one page from Frank Marshall Davis's extensive FBI file because the page listed Davis's Communist Party number. Kenger obviously wanted to leave no doubt that Frank Marshall Davis was a committed Communist during his lifetime. When running for president in 2008, Barack Obama minimized Davis's Communist ties. In his autobiography, *Dreams from My Father*, Obama discusses the influence Frank Marshall Davis had upon him when he was growing up in Hawaii. But Obama introduces Davis only by his first name, "Frank." Obama neglects to mention Davis's Communist past. Instead, he introduces Davis only as "a poet named Frank who lived in a dilapidated house in a run-down section of Waikiki."[150] Obama only hints about Davis's leftist past by mentioning that "Frank" was "a contemporary of Richard Wright and Langston Hughes during his years in Chicago."[151] But then, if we examine the way the MSM has tried since 2008 to deny Barack Obama's radical past, we get an insight into how the neo-Marxist MSM designs cover-up narratives by demonizing those who dare expose inconvenient political realities as "conspiracy theorists."

The Alice Palmer Saga

In 1995, Obama saw his opening to run for elected office when Illinois state senator Alice Palmer decided to run for U.S. Congress the following year, in the November 1996 election. Palmer went out of her way to name Obama as her hand-picked successor. Palmer had her eye on higher office, namely, the congressional seat Mel Reynolds was vacating. In 1995, Reynolds resigned from the U.S. House of Representatives after a state court convicted him of sexual misconduct with a sixteen-year-old campaign volunteer. Reynolds served two-and-one-half years for the crime and was subsequently sentenced to another six-and-one-half-year prison term on federal corruption charges, including wire fraud and bank fraud. President Bill Clinton commuted Reynolds's prison term only hours before Clinton left office.[152]

In 1986, Alice Palmer, as the editor of the *Black Press Review*, was the only African American to cover the Twenty-Seventh Congress of the Communist Party of the Soviet Union meeting in Russia. On June 19, 1986, the *People's Daily World*, an overtly Communist newspaper, wrote an article profiling Palmer's trip to Russia.[153] The article quoted Palmer as believing the Soviets could double their wealth and productive power by the end of the twentieth century. The article also quoted Palmer saying that the Soviet Union had "a comprehensive affirmative action program, which they have stuck to religiously—if I can use that word—since 1917." When Palmer visited the Soviet Union for the Twenty-Seventh Congress of the Communist Party, Russia was approximately two years away from withdrawing its military from Afghanistan in failure and three years away from the fall of the Berlin Wall.[154]

To get Obama's state senate race off to a good start, Palmer arranged a function for a few influential liberals in the district at the Hyde Park home of Bill Ayers and Bernardine Dohrn. Ayers and Dohrn were active members of the radical "New Left" organization Students for a Democratic Society (SDS). After SDS began collapsing in 1969, Ayers cofounded the Weather Underground. The FBI describes the Weather Underground as a revolutionary group "inspired by communist ideologies and embracing violence and crime as a way to protest the Vietnam War. racism, and other left-wing aims."[155]

In 1976, the Weather Underground claimed credit for twenty-nine bombings, and in subsequent years Weather Underground anarchists bombed several public buildings, including police stations, the U.S. Capitol, and the Pentagon.[156] Dohrn, also a member of the Weather Underground, was, like Ayers, on the FBI's most wanted list before she and Ayers each went into hiding for several years as fugitives eluding justice. In arranging the meeting at the home of Ayers and Dohrn in 1995, Palmer sought to introduce Obama to likely campaign supporters and contributors.[157] This meeting led to the quip that "Barack Obama started his political career in Bill Ayers's living room."[158]

Dr. Quentin Young, a prominent Chicago physician who attended the informal get-together for Obama at the Ayers-Dohrn home, remembered Palmer and Obama being at the gathering. Young told Politico.com that Obama and Ayers were "friends."[159] In 1995, a Chicago-based blogger named Maria Warren, writing in her progressive liberal blog called *Musings & Migraines*, reported watching Obama give "a standard, innocuous little talk" in the living room of Ayers and his wife.[160] Warren said Ayers and

Dohrn introduced Obama to the Hyde Park community as "the best thing since sliced bread."[161] Palmer would never have introduced Obama to the Hyde Park political community at the Ayers-Dohrn home unless she saw an affinity between Ayers and Dohrn's radical leftist history, her history of openly professed Communism, and the politics of Obama.

There is a bitter end to the story of Alice Palmer. In 1995, Obama had no intention of letting Palmer's defeat in the special election derail his political ambitions. Instead of stepping aside in deference to Palmer, Obama decided to fight Palmer for the nomination. He hired a fellow Harvard Law School alumnus to be his gunslinger and challenged the legitimacy of the signatures Palmer got on petitions to put her name on the ballot. Once he set on this strategy, Obama kept challenging petitions until he succeeded in getting all four of his Democratic primary rivals forced off the ballot. In 2007, the *Chicago Tribune* wrote that "a close examination of Obama's first campaign puts a hard edge on the image he has honed throughout his political career." The *Tribune* article noted, "The man now running for president on a message of giving a voice to the voiceless first entered public life not by leveling the playing field, but by clearing it."[162] Obama stepped on the Chicago political stage with a pure power play the most seasoned Richard Daley–machine operative would have to appreciate, even if the strategy required Harvard-trained lawyers, instead of Al Capone-recruited thugs, to bring it to fruition.

Not surprisingly, in 2008, Alice Palmer showed up to campaign for Hillary Clinton in the Indiana primary.[163]

Barack Obama and Bill Ayers

In February 2008, months before Obama was the Democratic Party's presidential nominee, Ben Smith at Politico.com began covering up Obama's relationship with Bill Ayers. On February 26, 2008, Smith penned an article in Politico.com claiming that David Axelrod, identified as Obama's "chief strategist," asserted that Obama and Ayers barely knew one another. Here is how Smith reported his interview with Axelrod on the subject: "'Bill Ayers lives in his [Obama's] neighborhood [Hyde Park in Chicago],' he [Axelrod] said. 'They're certainly friendly, they know each other, as anyone whose kids go to school together.'" Smith accepted uncritically Axelrod's insistence that Obama disapproved of Ayers's 1960s participation in the Weather Underground revolutionary bombings. Axelrod created the narrative that Obama barely knew Ayers. But in doing so, Axelrod completely ignored the role Ayers had played in launching Obama's political career by holding that introductory fundraiser at his Hyde Park apartment to help fund Obama's run for Alice Palmer's seat in the state legislature.[164]

During the 2008 presidential campaign, conservative author Stanley Kurtz, a senior fellow at the Ethics and Public Policy Center, published several well-documented Obama exposés detailing Obama's radical past as a community organizer in Chicago and his close association with Bill Ayers. In a *Wall Street Journal* opinion piece published on September 23, 2008, Kurtz produced extensive documentation that Obama had worked with Ayers in heading an educational foundation Ayers created. "Despite having authored two autobiographies, Barack Obama has never written about his most important executive experience," Kurtz wrote. "From 1995 to 1999, he [Obama] led an education foundation called the Chicago Annenberg Challenge (CAC) and remained on the board until 2001. The group poured more than $100 million into the hands of community organizers and radical education activists." Kurtz explained that the CAC was "the brainchild" of Bill Ayers. In early 1995, Obama became the first chairman of the CAC board, while Ayers cochaired the foundation's other body, the "Collaborative." Kurtz did his research in the archives of former Chicago Mayor Richard Daley. The Daley archives contained CAC board meeting minutes and documentation on CAC-funded and rejected groups. "The Daley archives show that Mr. Obama and Mr. Ayers worked as a team to advance the CAC agenda," Kurtz wrote.[165]

In response to Kurtz's questions, the Obama campaign issued a statement claiming that Ayers had no involvement in Obama's recruitment to the CAC board. The Obama campaign insisted Deborah Leff and Patricia Albjerg Graham (presidents of other foundations) had recruited Obama. "Yet the archives show that, along with Ms. Leff and Ms. Graham, Mr. Ayers was one of a working group of five who assembled the initial board in 1994," he noted. "Mr. Ayers founded CAC and was its guiding spirit. No one would have been appointed the CAC chairman without his approval." Kurtz documented that the CAC's agenda "flowed from Mr. Ayers's educational philosophy which called for infusing students and their parents with a radical political commitment, and which downplayed achievement tests in favor of activism."

Kurtz pointed to Ayers's published writings in which Ayers insisted that teachers "should be community organizers dedicated to provoking resistance to American racism and oppression." He quoted an interview Ayers gave about the same time he was forming CAC, in which Ayers stated, "I'm a radical, Leftist, small 'c' communist." Kurtz concluded that

"CAC translated Mr. Ayers's radicalism into practice." And "instead of funding schools directly, [the CAC] required schools to affiliate with 'external partners,' which actually got the money." Kurtz also noted that Ayers's supporters were also trying to minimize his radical political activism, claiming Ayers has redeemed himself with public-spirited education work. "That claim is hard to swallow if you understand that he [Ayers] views his education work as an effort to stoke resistance to an oppressive American system. He likes to stress that he learned of his first teaching job while in jail for a draft-board sit-in. For Mr. Ayers, teaching and his 1960s radicalism are two sides of the same coin."[166]

On October 9, 2008, in the last full month of the 2008 presidential campaign, the leftist, Poynter Institute–owned PolitiFact.com engaged in a disinformation tactic to provide Obama cover on this issue. PolitiFact's tactic was to offer an alternative explanation after Republican presidential candidate Senator John McCain ran television campaigns claiming, "Ayers and Obama ran a radical education foundation together." PolitiFact.com tried to redirect the story away from Obama's genuine relationship with Ayers. PolitiFact.com wrote the following:

> Obama served on the foundation [the CAC's] volunteer board from its inception in 1995 through its dissolution in 2001, and was chair for the first four years. So an argument can be made that he ran it, though an executive director handled day-to-day operations.
>
> Ayers, who received his doctorate in education from Columbia University in 1987 and is now a professor at the University of Illinois at Chicago, was active in getting the foundation up and running. He and two other activists led the effort to secure the grant from Annenberg, and he worked without pay in the early months of 1995, prior to the board's hiring of an executive director, to help the foundation get incorporated and formulate its bylaws, said Ken Rolling, who was the foundation's only executive director. Ayers went on to become a member of the "collaborative," an advisory group that advised the board of directors and the staff.
>
> However, Ayers "was never on the board of the Chicago Annenberg Challenge," and he "never made a decision programmatically or had a vote," Rolling said. "He (Ayers) was at board meetings—which, by the way, were open—as a guest," Rolling said. "That is not anything near Bill Ayers and Barack Obama running the Chicago Annenberg Challenge."[167]

PolitiFact also challenged Kurtz's opinion by arguing that "Ayers' views on education, though certainly reform-oriented and left-of-center, are not considered anywhere near as radical as his Vietnam-era views on war. And even if they were, there was a long list of individuals involved with the Chicago Annenberg Challenge whose positions provided them far more authority over its direction that Ayers' advisory role gave him."[168]

In his 2010 book *Radical-in-Chief: Barack Obama and the Untold Story of American Socialism*,[169] Kurtz pointed out that his investigative journalism during 2008 revealed Obama's radical past not only with Bill Ayers but with ACORN and with his hate-America pastor, Reverend Jeremiah Wright. "During the Ayers uproar of 2008, the Obama campaign took aggressive steps to discredit me, even attempting to block my appearance on Milt Rosenberg's respected Chicago radio program," Kurtz wrote. "Later in the campaign, when I wrote about Obama's still poorly understood links to the ACORN-controlled 'New Party,' the Obama campaign attacked me again."[170] He noted that while he was proud "to have had some small part in the 2008 presidential campaign," he was confident "the mainstream press had quite caught the drift of my central argument."[171] Kurtz stated his central argument as follows:

> Although William Ayers's history as a Weather Underground terrorist is a worthy and important issue in and of itself, it has never been the most important aspect of the Ayers-Obama link. What's particularly significant about Obama's ties with this unrepentant terrorist is less Ayers's terrorism than the lack of repentance. Since coming out of hiding, Ayers has certainly smoothed out his rhetoric. Yet he's never truly abandoned his radical views. So the real problem is that Obama had a political alliance with someone as radical as Ayers *in the present*. And Obama's Ayers tie is only one of a great many other such radical links. That Ayers's terrorist past makes him notorious only helps to shed light on the much broader phenomenon of Obama's hard-left political alliances. That was my argument during the campaign.[172]

Kurtz commented that while he "published extensively on additional ties between Obama and various radical groups right up through election day, the mainstream press effectively circled the wagons and refused to follow up."[173] Kurtz experienced firsthand the degree to which the MSM in the United States has become a propaganda arm for the neo-Marxist agenda. The owners, publishers, and editors of once-proud MSM outlets, including the *New York Times*, the *Washington Post*, and the ABC, NBC, and CBS newsrooms, refuse to allow reporters to write any story that could cast the neo-Marxist agenda in a negative light. Instead, the MSM has become a disinformation propaganda machine dedicated to finding a counter-story or an alternative explanation to cast doubt on honest reporting on neo-Marxist ideology, politicians, and thought leaders. Those raised to understand that real investigative journalists wrote only fact-based stores they had researched thoroughly and documented deeply are puzzled. Why has the neo-Marxist MSM been so successful in convincing the American public that honest investigative reporters like Kurtz are peddling "fake news" when everything Kurtz wrote about Obama was true? Answering that question is one of the main objectives of this book.

The Weather Underground

In 2008, when Barack Obama ran for president the first time, he and Bill Ayers downplayed their long-time working relationship and friendship in Chicago. Ayers was clearly trying to distance himself from Communism when he called himself a "small-'c' communist." At the same time, Obama said Ayers was just "a guy who lives in my neighborhood [Hyde Park in Chicago], not somebody who I exchange ideas with on a regular basis."[174] The point in this subsection is that Bill Ayers was a violent revolutionary in 1969 when he helped found SDS. Rather than regret his bombing activities, Ayers remained unrepentant. "I don't regret setting bombs," Ayers told the *New York Times* in 2001, in an interview for his newly published book *Fugitive Days*. "I feel we didn't do enough."[175] Ayers tried to take that statement back in a new afterword to the 2009 paperback edition of *Fugitive Days*. "I regretted the deaths of our beloved comrades and wrote about the subsequent and contested Weather decisions to engage in purely symbolic actions," Ayers wrote, referencing the Weather Underground bombings in which he admitted he had participated. "But I killed no one, and I harmed no one, and I didn't regret for a minute resisting the murderous assault on Viet Nam with every ounce of my being." He continued, saying the Weather Underground was not strong or effective enough to stop the Vietnam War in which he claimed over a thousand people a week were being annihilated. He admitted celebrating when the United States was defeated. "This was a shameful, murderous, illegal war carried out by my government for over a decade," he wrote. "I didn't do enough to stop it, and I don't know anyone who did."[176]

That is the point here. Ayers admitted that his violent acts as a founding member of the Weather Underground were revolutionary. In 1974,

Bernardine Dohrn, Ayers, and other Weather Underground members published the 156-page book *Prairie Fire: The Politics of Revolutionary Anti-Imperialism*.[177] This book, published while Dohrn and Ayers were fugitives, served as the Weather Underground's "ideological manifesto."[178] The book's title borrowed a line from Mao—"a single spark can start a prairie fire."[179] Ayers wrote the first draft and won a bitter internal battle to reject a rewrite emphasizing the traditional Marxist concept of promoting revolution by stirring working-class tensions. The book, from the start, "was Bill Ayers's baby."[180]

In an introductory letter to *Prairie Fire* addressed to "Sisters and Brothers," signed May 9, 1974, Dohrn and Ayers expressed the following:

> Our movement urgently needs a concrete analysis of the particular conditions of our time and place. We need strategy. We need to battle for a correct ideology and win people over. In this way we create the conditions for the development of a successful revolutionary movement and party. We need a revolutionary communist party in order to lead the struggle, give coherence and direction to the fight, seize power and build the new society. Getting from here to there is a process of coming together in a disciplined way around ideology and strategy, developing an analysis of our real conditions, mobilizing a base among the US people, building principled relationships to Third World struggle, and accumulating practice in struggle against US imperialism.[181]

The Weather Underground's 156-page manual *Prairie Fire*, printed in 1974, promoted waging a guerrilla people's war of national liberation in the United States. The battle cry of *Prairie Fire* reads as follows:

> We are a guerrilla organization. We are communist women and men, underground in the United States for more than four years. We are deeply affected by the historic events of our time in the struggle against US imperialism.
>
> Our intention is to disrupt the empire...to incapacitate it, to put pressure on the cracks, to make it hard to carry out its bloody functioning against the people of the world, to join the world struggle, to attack from the inside.
>
> Our intention is to engage the enemy...to wear away at him, to harass him, to isolate him, to expose every weakness, to pounce, to reveal his vulnerability.

> Our intention is to encourage the people…to provoke leaps in confidence and consciousness, to stir the imagination, to popularize power, to agitate, to organize, to join in every way possible the people's day-to-day struggles.
>
> Our intention is to forge an underground…a clandestine political organization engaged in every form of struggle, protected from the eyes and weapons of the state, a base against repression, to accumulate lessons, experience and constant practice, a base from which to attack.
>
> The only path to the final defeat of imperialism and the building of socialism is revolutionary war. Revolution is the most powerful resource of the people. To wait, to not prepare for the fight, is to seriously mislead about what kind of fierce struggle lies ahead.[182]

Statements like this appearing throughout *Prairie Fire* clarify that "Ayers declares himself to be a communist, and announces that his group's bombing campaign was intended to start a violent revolution to overthrow the American government."[183] What was evident in 2008, when Obama was running for president, as it should be now, "Ayers is just as politically radical now as he was back then."[184] Ayers has never renounced his Weather Underground bombing activities or his call for a revolutionary overthrow of the U.S. government. That Ayers has chosen to devote his mature years to being a professor of education indicates not that Ayers has dropped his revolutionary aspirations but that he shares Bella Dodd's awareness of the importance of indoctrinating youth into Communism for the revolution to occur.

In analyzing *Prairie Fire* carefully today, we need to clarify some additional key points. From the book's title to the methodology of fighting a people's war, *Prairie Fire* calls for a Maoist insurgency in the United States. Ayers's version of *Prairie Fire* justifies his revolutionary violence as opposition to U.S. imperialism in Vietnam—this theme, which we will see in the next chapter, was a shift in Marxist ideology achieved by Mao's decision to wage a "people's liberation war" in Vietnam. With Vietnam primarily a peasant society, Mao understood there was no industrial working class to revolt against capitalism. But with the United States replacing France in what was essentially the continuation of a colonial war, class conflict could easily be replaced by the "national question" of fighting United States imperialism. But what Ayers suggested in writing *Prairie Fire* was that at its root, the Communist revolution was aimed at racism—the oppression of blacks in the United States and the oppression of Asians in Vietnam.

Page 2 of *Prairie Fire* makes clear the Weather Underground took its inspiration from the struggle of African Americans: "We are a part of a wave of revolution sparked by the Black liberation struggle, by the death of Che [Guevara] in Bolivia in 1967, and by people's war in Vietnam."[185] Page 2 elaborated this theme as follows:

> In our own hemisphere, Che Guevara urged that we "create two, three, many Vietnams" to destroy US imperialism by cutting it off in the Third World tentacle by tentacle, and opening another front within the US itself. At home, the struggle and insurrection of the Black liberation movement heightened our commitment to fight alongside the determined enemies of the empire.[186]

A careful examination of the *Prairie Fire* text makes clear the word "racism" appears fifty-seven times, rivaling the number of times the word "Vietnam" occurs. In *Prairie Fire*, Ayers argued that "people now see that imperialism is warlike, with an economy based on the arms race."[187] He stressed that people also "understand corporate greed: the criminal policies of ITT, United Fruit, Standard Oil, Gulf Oil, Dow Chemical, Chase Manhattan, Safeway, and Honeywell."[188] So, for Ayers, the Vietnam resistance to U.S. imperialism was still reducible to the ultimate evil of capitalism. Yet "opposition to racism" is how Ayers framed the argument, focusing on the situation of African Americans in the United States. Ayers stressed the following:

> <u>Opposition to racism.</u> The spirit of resistance inside the US was rekindled by Black people. The power and strategy of the civil rights movement, SNCC [Student Nonviolent Coordinating Committee], Malcolm X, and the Black Panther Party affected all other rebellion. They created a form of struggle called direct action: awoke a common identity, history and dignity for Black people as a colonized and oppressed people within the US: drew out and revealed the enemy through a series of just and undeniable demands such as the vote, equal education, the right to self-defense, and an end to Jim Crow. The police, the troops, the sheriffs, the mass arrests and assassinations were the official response. The Black movement was pushed forward into a revolutionary movement for political power, open rebellion and confrontation with the racism of white people and the racism of institutions.[189]

Later in *Prairie Fire*, Ayers wrote the following: "Racism is the main and most consistent weapon for holding back the revolutionary struggle.

Skin color will be a brand to turn proletarians against one another until this brand is decisively rejected by white folks. The oppressed nation of Black people is the leading anti-imperialist force in our country."[190] The political unrest in the United States began over the issue of race. Protest activity in the United States started with the rise of the civil rights movement in the 1950s. Martin Luther King Jr. and his brand of nonviolent civil disobedience intensified civil rights protesting into the 1960s. The wave of summer race riots that began with the Watts Riots in Los Angeles in 1965 and the Hough Riots in Cleveland in 1966 transformed protest activity into violence. The student protests that began in the 1950s and 1960s were mainly in sympathy with the civil rights movement before student protests turned into anti-war demonstrations in the late 1960s and early 1970s.

Bryan Burrough, in his 2015 book *Days of Rage: America's Radical Underground, the FBI, and the Forgotten Age of Revolutionary Violence*, stressed how the support of the black liberation movement was pivotal to the formation of the Weather Underground. At the 1969 SDS convention at the Chicago Coliseum, Revolutionary Youth Movement (RYM) supporters expelled the Progressive Labor Party over this issue. "The turning point came on Friday night, when a delegate from the Black Panthers took the microphone and read a statement that condemned PL [Progressive Labor] as 'counterrevolutionary traitors' who, if their ideological positions did not change, 'would be dealt with as such.'"[191] Burroughs commented this statement "amounted to an ultimatum from the Panthers, whose approval every SDS leader sought like lost gold."[192] When RYM members shouted the Black Panther slogan, "Power to the People!" the Progressive Labor members shouted back, "Power to the Workers!" Finally, after throwing the Progressive Labor members out of SDS, Dohrn led the RYM caucus out of the auditorium shouting, "Power to the People!" and "Ho, Ho, Ho Chi Minh!"[193]

Burroughs quoted former SDS leader Cathy Wilkerson who recalled that SDS leaders adored black Americans even more than they adored Che Guevara. "I think in our hearts what all of us wanted to be was a Black Panther," Wilkerson said.[194] Burrough also quoted "JJ" John Jacobs, who, like Mark Rudd, gained fame within the SDS movement for his participation in the 1968 student takeover of the Columbia University administration building. "Wars like Vietnam came and went, but it was only the brewing revolution of American blacks, JJ prophesied, that had the potential to destroy the country," Burroughs wrote.[195] He called it "a myth" that the radical violence that started in the 1970s was a protest against the Vietnam War.[196] "In fact, while members of this new underground [radicals like the Weather Underground committed to using violence] were vehemently antiwar, the war itself was seldom their primary focus," Burroughs wrote. He quoted Howard Machtinger, one of the Weather Underground's early leaders. "We were happy to draw new members who were antiwar," Machtinger said. "But this was never about the war."[197] "What the underground movement was truly about—what it was always about—was the plight of black Americans," Burroughs stressed.[198]

Conclusion: The Battle for the Soul of America

We cannot afford to close our eyes and think we will win by repeating comfortable platitudes of traditional American values. Critical theory and social justice ideology are rapidly becoming our mainstream culture. The language and thinking of critical theory and social justice ideology are intentionally dense. But the neo-Marxist social justice ideas are powerful, as bizarre as they may initially seem. Cultural Maoism motivates the radical Left intent to capture control of our institutions as part of the extreme Left's goal of destroying capitalism and taking down the United States Constitution. At the moment, critical thinking and social justice ideology are winning.

Today, neo-Marxists control our most prestigious institutions of higher learning, the well-established beacons of our mainstream media, and the backbone of our law enforcement and justice systems. Today, neo-Marxist ideology controls the federal government from the presidency of the United States to Congress through virtually every agency in the massive DC bureaucracy and much of the federal judiciary. Today, cultural Maoists control the "cancel culture" enforced by politically correct mainstream media. We cannot afford to persist with comfortable establishment thinking, hoping that the bizarre nature of neo-Marxist social justice critical theory will cause its demise. We must comprehend Coughlin and Higgins's admonition fully:

> **A strategic understanding of the Left recognizes that it is dialectically driven**. As such, the Left is a teleologically informed movement that executes through history and thought, along an arc, with a trajectory. It is Hegelian. It defines everything that "is" as fuel for "becoming" in a dialectical process that compels it to negate. — "Change"

"Perpetual Revolution." — Analysis of the Left that does not account for the dialectic will fail.[199]

They continued:

This is how the Left should be understood. Hence, it would be a mistake to treat the historical elements of this assessment as little more than background material. Assessing the Left as if Hegel and Marx simply provide interesting historical context to today's events is the failure to recognize that **for the Left, Marx was yesterday and Hegel the day before**. Between the two, they are the source code of today's Left.[200]

Understanding the radical Left's dialectical materialism involves conceptualizing neo-Marxist ideology and Maoist cultural insurgency tactics as if they were computer malware. Like computer malware, neo-Marxist ideology and Maoist cultural insurgency are intellectual malware that infects our brains and causes them to malfunction. We must not lose this battle for the soul of America because we failed to understand the ideological basis upon which the neo-Marxists and cultural Maoists, who have been planning the destruction of America for decades, have constructed their new reality. We are just now engaged on the political warfare battlefield of what is perhaps the most severe challenge to liberty in human history. To beat this ultimate challenge to freedom, we will have to learn how to think differently. Counterinsurgency tactics begin with exposing the Left's lies in this age of disinformation. But proclaiming truth, while a necessary first step, is not enough, not when the neo-Marxists and cultural Maoists control city councils and school boards throughout the nation.

If we lose this ideological-driven political war here, in the United States, there will be nowhere else in the world to go to find any semblance of individual liberty.

CHAPTER 2

Cultural Maoism

As Marcuse recognized, Mao executed Marx's strategy.
—Stephen Coughlin and Richard Higgins,
Re-Remembering the Mis-Remembered Left, 2019[201]

Young comrades who have just joined the Party and have not read Marxism-Leninism may not yet understand this truth. They must understand this truth before they can have a correct world outlook. They must understand that all mankind have to go through the process of eliminating classes, state authority, and party; the question is only one of time and conditions. The Communists in the world are more intelligent than the bourgeoisie in that respect. They understand the law governing the existence and development of things. They understand dialectics and thus see farther ahead.
—Mao Tse-tung, 1949[202]

Today's radical neo-Marxist Left seeks to destroy America by implementing the Hegelian dialectical ideology of critical justice theory with the operational plan of a Maoist cultural insurgency. The battlefield is one of words and ideas, not armies and weapons. The tactics of the Left are the insurgency strategies Mao developed during the Chinese revolution. Mao refined these tactics through the Great Leap Forward and the Cultural Revolution. In the process, Mao recast Marx's hypothesis that workers and economic class warfare would create the world Communist revolution. Instead, Mao realized that cultural warfare was the real trigger capable of bringing about the worldwide revolution that Marx envisioned to end capitalism.

This chapter details the human tragedy of Mao's rise to power in China. The radical Left in America has adopted the tactics of cultural Maoism to destroy the United States of America, despite the disastrous consequences Maoism has had for the Chinese people. Together with the previous chapter, this chapter sets the stage for the subsequent deep dive the next chapters will take into the history of phenomenology and political philosophy that has given rise to critical theory and social justice ideology. In the next chapter, we will dissect the political philosophy beginning with Kant and Hegel, to start an investigation of worldview (*Weltanschauung*) that produced today's anarchy.

How Mao Captured the Lead in the World Communist Revolution

Communism came to China soon after the Russian Revolution. In 1919, Lenin formed the Comintern. In 1920, Grigorii Voytinskii, a Comintern agent, arrived in China. In 1921, the Chinese Communist Party (CCP) began to take shape in Beijing and Shanghai. Mao Tse-tung first emerged as the Chinese Communist Party's local secretary at the party's branch in Hunan, a landlocked province in south-central China that was Mao's birthplace and childhood home. In the early 1920s, the Soviet Union urged the CCP to merge with Sun Yat-sen's Chinese nationalist Kuomintang (KMT) movement.

Frank Dikötter, a professor of humanities at the University of Hong Kong and a former professor of China's modern history at the University of London, noted that "Stalin placed little faith in Mao and his peasant soldiers."[203] The cooperation of the CCP with the KMT ended in 1926 when Generalissimo Chiang Kai-shek, the leader of the KMT army, succeeded in a war aimed at the warlords of central China. But after Japan invaded China, Stalin once again forced Mao "into the arms of his sworn enemy,"[204] demanding that Mao form a united front with the KMT to fight the Japanese.

Mao's Long March

The Japanese overran Manchuria in 1931 and made it a puppet state called Manchukuo. In 1936, the KMT still exerted a loose form of control over two-thirds of the population of China. Warlords still controlled much of China, and there was no land reform. In the late 1930s, Mao developed a strategy of changing the Communist goal in China from a workers' revolution to a peasant revolution as the first step toward a socialist revolution. Mao evolved a strategy of operating from a stable base while harassing government troops by guerilla tactics. In October 1934, some one hundred thousand people broke through the KMT armies in south Jiangxi and began the "long march" some six thousand miles to the northwest province of Shaanxi (Shensi), a landlocked province in northwest China. Despite the KMT's military victory over the Communists, historian Anna Maria Cienciala commented that Mao's long march and the arrival of survivors in Shaanxi "signified the survival of Mao's brand of communism in a secure base. Here, it could gather forces and, by waging a guerrilla war against Japan, lay the groundwork for its later conquest of China."[205] Cienciala further observed the following:

> Also, the Long March provided a heroic myth for Chinese communists in the future, much as Valley Forge had done for Americans. It deepened the communists' sense of destiny. Finally, it provided the leaders of future communist China. Of the few hundred top PRC leaders that still lived in the 1980s and those still alive [in the] early 1990s, some 90 percent were/are veterans of that odyssey.[206]

At home in Shaanxi, his birthplace province, Mao's brand of Communism had a secure base. In Shaanxi, Mao created a counter-state opposed to the Chinese nationalist KMT party. From Shaanxi, Mao would ultimately overthrow Sun Yat-sen's KMT and Chiang Kai-shek, a lieutenant to Sun Yat-sen in the KMT revolution and the KMT party leader of the Republic of China (ROC) from 1928 to 1949.

Mao Establishes the People's Republic of China (PRC)

In the summer of 1946, civil war broke out between Mao's People's Liberation Army (PLA) and Chiang Kai-shek's nationalist KMT. In April 1948, Mao's PLA crossed the Yangtze River, the KMT's last line of defense against the PLA attacking Nanking and Shanghai. On October 1, 1949, Mao proclaimed the creation of the People's Republic of China from Beijing (Peking), China's old capital city with more than a three-thousand-year history. On December 7, 1949, the KMT fled to Formosa (Taiwan) in what is known as the Great Retreat. In Taiwan, Chiang Kai-shek set up a "Free China" government in exile.[207]

Stalin sent airplanes, arms, and advisers to the Kuomintang, but all Mao got from Stalin during World War II was "a planeload of propaganda leaflets."[208] Dikötter explained the relationship between Stalin and Mao as follows:

> Mao was a peasant, a caveman Marxist, Stalin determined after reading translations of the Chinese leader's writings, which he dismissed as 'feudal.' That there was a rebellious and stubborn streak in Mao was clear; his victory over Chiang Kai-shek, forced to retreat all the way to Taiwan, would have been difficult to explain otherwise. But pride and independence were precisely what troubled Stalin so deeply, prone as he was to seeing enemies everywhere.[209]

But Mao led his CCP to victory over Chiang Kai-shek, and he fought the United States to a stalemate in Korea. If Stalin was complex, so was Mao. Dikötter explained as follows:

> After Stalin's death [in 1953] Mao finally saw a chance to secure independence from the Kremlin and claim leadership of the socialist camp. The Chairman naturally assumed he was the leading light of communism, which was about to crush capitalism, making him the historical pivot around which the universe revolved. Had he not led his men to victory, bringing a second October Revolution to a quarter of the world? Stalin could not even claim to have presided over the Bolshevik revolution; still less could Nikita Khrushchev, the man who soon took charge in Moscow.[210]

But once in power after the defeat of Chiang Kai-shek, Mao modeled his leadership style after Stalin, ruling China in the same ironhanded manner with which Stalin had ruled Russia.

Mao and the Tragedy of Liberation

In his 2013 book *The Tragedy of Liberation*, covering Mao's revolution from 1945 to 1957, Frank Dikötter acknowledged Mao's success as a revolutionary directing the Chinese Communist Party's "liberation movement." But Dikötter also noted the subsequent "tragedy of liberation" that resulted when Marx tried to govern China with his Maoist brand of Marxism-Leninism.[211] Dikötter noted that Mao-imposed land reform followed liberation, leading to a wave of violence and terror across China. Dikötter wrote:

> Violence was an indispensable feature of land distribution, implicating a majority in the murder of a carefully designated minority. Work

> teams were given quotas of people who had to be denounced, humiliated, beaten, dispossessed and then killed by the villagers, who were assembled in their hundreds in an atmosphere charged with hatred. In a pact sealed in blood between the party and the poor, close to 2 million so-called "landlords," often hardly any better off than their neighbors, were liquidated.[212]

Dikötter detailed the extreme nature of the violence in which people were burned alive, dismembered, shot, or throttled to death. "Some children were slaughtered as 'little landlords.'"[213]

Less than a year after liberation, Mao laid down the Great Terror, designed to eliminate enemies of the party. Entire villages were razed to the ground. Schoolchildren as young as six were accused of spying and were tortured to death. By the end of 1951, close to two million people had been murdered, sometimes during public rallies in stadiums.[214] In 1951, Mao turned on former government officials, and over a million were sacked from their jobs.[215] In 1952, Mao attacked entrepreneurs. In more than two months, some six hundred entrepreneurs, business owners, and shopkeepers killed themselves in Shanghai alone.[216] Mao's policy of collectivization of farming proved devastating, with the PRC admitting in 1954 that farmers had a third less food to eat compared to the years before liberation. Virtually everyone in the countryside was on a desperation diet.[217] In 1957, Mao turned against intellectuals, sending half a million to the gulag. Dikötter commented that Mao's campaign against intellectuals "was the culmination of a series of drives by the party to eliminate all opposition, whether it came from ethnic minorities, religious groups, farmers, artisans, entrepreneurs, industrialists, teachers, and scholars or doubters within the ranks of the party itself."[218]

Mao's Great Leap Forward and China's Mass Starvation

> How can we conceptualize the 36 million people who starved to death?... The Great Famine makes all of China's other famines pale in comparison....
>
> Cannibalism was no longer exceptional. Ancient annals report cases of families exchanging children to consume during severe famines, but during the Great Famine, some families resorted to eating their own children. I met people who had eaten human flesh, and heard them describe its taste. Reliable evidence indicates there were thousands of cases of cannibalism throughout China at that time.... It is a tragedy

> unprecedented in world history for tens of millions of people to starve to death and to resort to cannibalism during a period of normal climate patterns with no wars or epidemics....
>
> The basic reason why tens of millions of people in China starved to death was totalitarianism.
>
> Yang Jisheng, describing Mao's Great Leap Forward, *Tombstone: The Great Chinese Famine 1958–1962*, 2008[219]

As we noted before, Marxist-Leninist-Maoist ideologies are powerful in creating revolutions, but these same principles are disastrous when Communists try to run a country after gaining power. In his 2010 book, *Mao's Great Famine: The History of China's Most Devastating Catastrophe, 1958–1962*, Dikötter made clear that in those years, China "descended into hell" under Mao's "Great Leap Forward."[220] The Great Leap Forward was Mao's plan to overtake Great Britain economically in fifteen years. Here is how Dikötter described the reality of the Great Leap Forward:

> Instead of following the Soviet model of development, which leaned heavily towards industry alone, China would "walk on two legs": the peasant masses were mobilized to transform both agriculture and industry at the same time, converting a backward economy into a modern communist society of plenty for all. In the pursuit of a utopian paradise, everything was collectivized, as villagers were herded together in giant communes which heralded the advent of communism. People in the countryside were robbed of their work, their homes, their land, their belongings and their livelihood. Food, distributed by the spoonful in collective canteens according to merit, became a weapon to force people to follow the party's every dictate. Irrigation campaigns forced up to half the villagers to work for weeks on end on giant water-conservancy projects, often far from home, without adequate food and rest. The experiment ended in the greatest catastrophe the country had ever known, destroying tens of millions of lives.[221]

In researching newly opened Chinese archives, Dikötter estimated that "at least 45 million people died unnecessarily [in China] between 1958 and 1962 [as a result of Mao's Great Leap Forward]."[222]

In his 2008 book on the Great Leap Forward, *Tombstone: The Great Chinese Famine 1958–1962*, Yang Jisheng described in vivid terms the mass starvation those policies caused. Land reform stripped peasants of the traditional farms they had lived on for centuries. Communes forced people into communal kitchens, which eventually ran out of food. Collectivization forced peasant farmers into government-controlled collective farming disasters. He explained why he felt totalitarianism caused the mass starvation:

> The regime considered no cost or coercion too great in making the realization of Communist ideals the supreme goal of the entire populace. The peasants bore the chief burden of realizing these ideals; they shouldered the cost of industrialization, of subsidizing the cities, and of the extravagant habits of officials at every level. Most of this cost was imposed through the state monopoly for purchasing and marketing. Peasants were obliged to sell their produce to the government at prices that did not cover their costs. With official priority placed on feeding the burgeoning urban population and importing machinery in exchange for grain exports, grain was all but snatched from peasant mouths.[223]

Jisheng commented that the inadequacy of the grain left after the peasants sold their "surplus" to the government at prices below costs was one of the reasons why so many millions starved to death.[224] The PRC brutally suppressed political dissent while running a highly centralized planned economy that resulted in "an abuse of executive power exceeding that of the Soviet Union or of any of China's emperors, controlling politics, the economy, culture and ideology, and every aspect of daily life."[225] The Communist "dictatorship's coercive power penetrated every corner of even the most remote village, to every member of every family, into the minds and entrails of every individual."[226] The PRC blamed the mass starvation on political deviants on the Right. Jisheng reported that statistics from the 1962 reexamination and rehabilitation programs of the Socialist Education Movement resulted in targeting between three and four million cadres and party members targeted for criticism and designated as "right-deviating opportunists."[227] Starvation surged in 1959, reaching a peak in 1960 and continuing into 1961.[228] Jisheng observed the following:

> Whatever Mao said was the "directive from the highest level." Regarding his directives, the rule was, "When you understand them, carry them out; when you don't understand them, carry them out anyway, and while carrying them out gain a better understanding of them."[229]

Jisheng's judgment on Mao's rule was unforgiving, but he took Mao to be the extreme example of what Communism creates. He wrote:

> Totalitarianism is the most backward, barbaric, and inhumane of all systems in the modern world. The deaths of tens of millions of innocent people during the three-year famine rang the death knell for this system, as the Socialist Education Movement and Cultural Revolution that rose in response to it only managed to push beyond all possibility of redemption.[230]

Page after page, Jisheng detailed the brutality of Mao's rule. Communist cadres in the Great Leap Forward, foreshadowing the Red Guards of the Cultural Revolution, showed no mercy. Cadre-inflicted punishments on villagers "included being beaten while suspended in midair, forced into protracted kneeling, paraded through the streets, deprived of food, exposed to the cold or the sun, and having one's ears or fingers cut off."[231] He commented that the replacement of capitalism by socialism and the ultimate progression to Communism became "objective law." Under Mao, China's intellectuals embraced this theory and instilled it in their students from elementary school to the universities. As Jisheng summarized, "Any means employed in removing obstacles to Communism were considered a service to heaven's decree."[232]

Mao's Great Leap Forward and Stalin's Collectivization Comparisons

Mao's devastating Great Leap Forward is reminiscent of Stalin's farm collectivization of the 1930s, in which millions of peasants were forced off their farms and into state farms. In 1932, at Stalin's urging, the Soviet Politburo, the elite leadership of the Soviet Communist Party, made a series of decisions that deepened the famine in the Ukrainian countryside. Anne Applebaum, a staff writer at *The Atlantic* and a fellow at the SNF Agora Institute at Johns Hopkins University, described how Stalin imposed famine on Ukraine to punish Ukrainian peasants who resisted Moscow's rule. She wrote:

> Despite the shortages, the state demanded not just grain, but all available food. At the height of the crisis, organized teams of policemen and local Party activists, motivated by hunger, fear, and a decade of hateful propaganda, entered peasant households and took everything edible: potatoes, beets, squash, beans, peas, and farm animals. At the same time, a cordon was drawn around the Ukrainian republic to prevent escape. The result was catastrophic: At least 5 million people perished of

> hunger all across the Soviet Union. Among them were nearly 4 million Ukrainians who died not because of neglect or crop failure, but because they had been deliberately deprived of food.[233]

The collectivization movement, an equal disaster under both Stalin in Russia and Mao in China, resulted primarily because of the Communist insistence on the collective ownership of the means of production. Yet, the forced movement of peasant farmers from their traditional small farms into large-scale collective farming operations, while ideologically driven, in practice failed miserably to produce the abundance promised.

Press Apologists for Stalin and Mao

Neither the Ukrainian famine nor the broader Soviet famine was ever officially recognized by the USSR. Stalin was able to hide the Ukrainian famine from the world in large part due to the journalists like Walter Duranty, the *New York Times*'s Moscow correspondent from 1922 to 1936. Duranty complied with Moscow censors to remain in the Soviet state's good graces. As Applebaum explained, members of the Moscow press corps required the state's permission to live and work within Russia. Without the official stamp of the Soviet press department, the central telegraph office would refuse to send their dispatches to their newspapers abroad.

Duranty was willingly compliant in the Soviet cover-up of the Ukrainian famine not out of an ideological preference that favored Communism but as a show of good faith to Moscow, which provided him a luxurious and remarkably decadent lifestyle. As Applebaum pointed out, the Soviet regime made sure Duranty had a large flat in Moscow, the services of a car, and the availability of a mistress. He had the best access of any correspondent in Moscow and received coveted interviews from Stalin twice. His dispatches made him one of the most influential journalists of the time. In 1932, his series of articles on the successes of Stalin's farm collectivization program and his five-year plans won Duranty a Pulitzer Prize.

At the height of his fame, Duranty lived a high life of drugs, alcohol, and the most glitzy and expensive nightclubs New York City offered. In exchange for this, he sang Stalin's praises. S. J. Taylor, in her brilliant 1990 biography of Duranty, *Stalin's Apologist: Walter Duranty: The New York Times's Man in Moscow*, detailed that in exchange for money, celebrity status at the Metropol Hotel in Moscow, women, drugs, jazz, and fame, Duranty became Stalin's chief apologist. Taylor explained as follows:

> As Fascism rose in Europe and Japanese Imperialism threatened the East, the Western powers sank deeper into the quagmire of the Great Depression, unable, it seemed at the time, to protect themselves from these forces. Against this background, Duranty touted the accomplishments of Stalin's Five-Year Plan, ushering in what would come to be called "the Red Decade." His stubborn chronicle of Soviet achievements made him the doyen of left-leaning Westerners who believed that what was happening inside Soviet Russia held the key to the future for the world.[234]

Duranty attributed his success in Russia to his having made the right bets. He pointed to a column he wrote on January 18, 1923, to argue he was the first to single out Stalin as the next leader of the Soviet Union after the death of Lenin.[235] "Stalin is one of the most remarkable men in Russia, and perhaps the most influential figure here today," Duranty wrote in that early column.[236] On Christmas Day 1933, the last time Duranty saw Stalin, "the dictator said to him the following, a quote Duranty put in practically every book he wrote afterward."[237] Here is what Stalin said:

> You have done a good job in your reporting the USSR, though you are not a Marxist, because you tell the truth about our country and try to understand it and to explain it to your readers. I might say that you bet on our horse to win when others thought it had no chance and I am sure you have not lost by it.[238]

Taylor was not sure those words were Stalin's or Duranty's version of what Stalin said. But she was sure "the sentiments were no doubt those of the Georgian dictator."[239] Taylor understood Duranty bet on Stalin because Duranty thought Stalin was in tune with the direction of history:

> By putting his faith on the iron determination of the Bolsheviks to bend the fate of the nation to their will, Duranty had come out a winner. He was arguably the best-known foreign correspondent in the world, a central figure in the new dialogue between East and West, the star of the international social circuit. By putting his money on Stalin, he had climbed from anonymity to celebrity, the recognized world authority on Soviet Russia. You might say that Walter Duranty was "dizzy with success."[240]

Taylor posed a crucial question. Some four decades later, when the truth about Stalin's devastating rule began to come out, the question arose:

"How did Stalin manage to conceal the greatest man-made disaster in modern history, when perhaps as many as ten million men, women, and children were allowed to die by slow starvation as a result of their refusal to conform to Stalin's plan to collectivize agriculture?"[241] Taylor clearly understood how important Duranty was to covering up Stalin's mass murder. She titled her book *Stalin's Apologist*, adding a subtitle (*Walter Duranty: The New York Times's Man in Moscow*) to stress the newspaper's complicity in the cover-up.

Gareth Jones, a twenty-seven-year-old Welshman who had studied Russian, French, and German at Cambridge University, and had worked as a private secretary to former British prime minister David Lloyd George, journeyed to Russia on a visa and began visiting rural Ukrainian villages in 1932 and 1933. Jones witnessed the Ukrainian famine firsthand and began filing press reports on the disaster.[242] Jones announced his findings first in a press conference in Berlin, then at a lecture at Chatham House in London. Finally, the *Manchester Guardian* published a story with Jones's dispatches at the end of March 1933.[243]

The newspaper had published earlier accounts by Malcolm Muggeridge, the only other person to report on the famine in Ukraine. Muggeridge arrived in Moscow in September 1932 with his wife, a niece of prominent British socialist Beatrice Webb. Kitty Muggeridge arrived in Moscow pregnant with their second child, having left their son behind at school in England. Muggeridge had made arrangements to string for the *Manchester Guardian* as a temporary financial arrangement to support himself and his family. Muggeridge's real purpose in coming to the Soviet Union was to join in the great effort of "building socialism." He planned to relinquish British citizenship to become a citizen of the new Soviet state.[244]

Muggeridge's disillusionment began when he started looking for an apartment. Unlike other correspondents in Moscow, Muggeridge decided to live like the common Muscovites since he planned to become one. But all he could find were rooms that "invariably turned out to be a part of a room, with, at best, the possibility of hanging a blanket to curtain off the portion offered us, and the use of corporate cooking and washing facilities…an impossible arrangement."[245] Muggeridge began writing stories for the *Guardian*, pointing to the problems of collectivization. Then he bought a train ticket and set off for Kiev in Ukraine. With that train trip traveling through Ukraine, Muggeridge witnessed the horror of Stalin's utopia.[246] In a series of articles the *Guardian* published in March 1933, Muggeridge confirmed the widespread famine through his eyewitness accounts. The peasant population was starving. Muggeridge documented this, writing the following in a British Embassy dispatch to the newspaper dated March 22, 1933: "I mean starving in its absolute sense; not undernourished as, for instance, most Oriental peasants...and some unemployed workers in Europe, but having had for weeks nothing to eat. 'We have nothing. They have taken everything away.'"[247]

Muggeridge left the Soviet Union an embittered idealist. He returned to England by way of Berlin, where he "watched the Nazis march along the *Unter den Linden* [boulevard in the center of Berlin] and realized, of course, they're [K]omsomols [All-Union Leninist Young Communist League], the same people, the same faces. It's the same show."[248] In England, there was skepticism about the truth of Muggeridge's reports. "His wife's eminent 'Aunt Bo,' Beatrice Webb, called his coverage a hysterical tirade."[249] For his efforts, the *Manchester Guardian* fired Muggeridge, who subsequently had trouble finding work. To their dismay, Muggeridge and Jones found what others who attempted to report on the Ukrainian famine had learned. Western editors favored the Russian revolution and Stalin's leadership following Lenin. The public in the United States and Great Britain were largely uninformed about Russia but willing to believe reporters like Walter Duranty, who were nothing more than propagandists for Stalin.

In a dispatch to the *New York Times* on March 31, 1933, Duranty took the lead in downplaying Jones's reports. Duranty acknowledged some mismanagement of collective farming, but he attributed it to the project's novelty. Duranty agreed that there had been "serious food shortages" in Ukraine. Still, he insisted, "There is no actual starvation or deaths from starvation but there is widespread mortality from diseases due to malnutrition, especially in the Ukraine, Northern Caucasus, and Lower Volga."[250] Duranty justified Stalin ideologically to the point of excusing the mass starvation Stalin's experiment in collective farming caused. On March 31, 1933, Duranty wrote a story published in the *New York Times* with the title "Russians Hungry but Not Starving." Here is what Duranty wrote in that article:

> But—to put it bluntly—you can't make an omelet without breaking eggs, and the Bolshevik leaders are just as indifferent to the casualties that may be involved in their drive toward socialism as any General during the World War who ordered a costly attack in order to show his superiors that he and his division possessed the proper soldierly spirit.

> In fact, the Bolsheviki are more indifferent because they are animated by fanatical conviction.[251]

Taylor commented that Duranty "had little patience"[252] with Gareth Jones. Taylor went on to observe that Duranty dismissed Jones's claim that the Soviet Union was "on the verge of a terrific smash" by insisting that the prediction amounted to "nothing more than a new twist to an old prediction."[253] Taylor further explained that Duranty claimed there would be no smash, arguing that "the young Jones, like his earlier predecessors, was indulging himself in wishful thinking."[254] Taylor explained Jones's reaction as follows:

> But Jones pitied the journalists who had been turned "into masters of euphemism and understatement." Hence, "they give 'famine' the polite name of 'food shortage,' and 'starving to death' is softened to read as 'wide-spread mortality from diseases due to malnutrition." It was an uncompromising statement [that Jones wrote in a reply letter to Duranty, published in the *New York Times* on May 13, 1933], one that showed integrity and courage, but Jones was up against an establishment larger than Duranty.[255]

Taylor summed up the episode as follows: "'Throwing down Jones' signaled one of the sorriest periods of reportage in the history of the free press, one in which Walter Duranty led the way—with others in the pack not all that far behind."[256]

Before we depart from Duranty, we need to mention one more curious aspect of his life. Duranty had a sexual and opium-smoking relationship with the occultist Aleister Crowley (1875–1947). S. J. Taylor, the respected scholar whose definitive biography of Duranty we have been quoting, chronicled that relationship in her book *Stalin's Apologist*, published by Oxford University Press, a top university press.[257] After Duranty graduated in classics with honors from Emmanuel College at Cambridge in England, he for several years "beat a path back and forth from New York to Marseilles to Paris, experimenting with a fly-by-night sort of existence he found exhilarating."[258] Taylor noted that Duranty and Crowley cemented their relationship because of "the pair's common interest in smoking opium and in a woman, said to be a former artist's model [Jane Cheron], who represented to Crowley throughout his life the epitome of the Scarlet Woman [the Whore of Babylon, Revelation 17:4], Crowley's ideal of femininity."[259] Taylor suggested Duranty, Crowley, and Jane Cheron were involved in a sexual, opium-laced ménage à trois.[260] Taylor also pointed out that Crowley commonly referred to himself as "Beast 666," a reference to the Antichrist predicted in the book of Revelation (Revelation 13:18) that had been his mother's pet name for him.[261] In his 2020 book *The Devil and Karl Marx*, Professor Paul Kengor pointed out that Crowley, "The Wickedest Man in the World," also known as the "Great Beast," had a strong influence on modern Satanism, a theme we will see throughout this book associated with Marxism.[262] "Crowley performed all sorts of strange magic, or 'magick,' if not black magic, and crowned that with macabre other-worldly sexual perversity, especially shocking for his time at the turn of the nineteenth to the twentieth century," Kengor wrote.[263] Kengor contemplated several of the bizarre scenes Taylor recounts, including one pagan-like "ritualistic happening" in which Crowley "received" Duranty's semen.[264] Kengor expressed his disgust as follows:

> This was sick stuff. Certainly demented. The ritualistic element smacks of not only blasphemy but certainly a form of pagan activity (perhaps even bordering on the demonic). Imagine this behavior from the *New York Times*' feted Pulitzer winner. One of the top reporters in the world, soiled by the Great Beast, his strange political bedfellow. Perhaps it was fitting private behavior for a man who would lie to the world about the deliberate starvation of millions of people by a murderous communist tyrant [Stalin] in the Kremlin.[265]

On March 7, 2020, in the *Daily Mail* in London, S. J. Taylor published an article entitled "The British Playboy Who Was Stalin's Stooge: How War Reporter Walter Duranty Covered Up a Kremlin-Created Famine That Killed Millions and Allowed the Left to Continue Worshiping a Mass Murderer." In that article, she explained that Duranty married Crowley's discarded mistress, Jane Cheron, who conveniently possessed a "small fortune."[266] While Cheron succumbed to her opium addiction, Taylor reported that Duranty managed "to wean himself off the drug."

In the same article, she gave the following graphic description of Stalin's genocide against the "kulaks," a group of prosperous peasants that Stalin scapegoated as the cause for the failure of his first Five-Year Plan for collective farming that was the genesis of the Ukrainian famine of 1932–33. Taylor explained as follows:

> Classed as farmers who owned as many as three cows, some chickens and a few acres of land for an average family of seven, they [the Kulaks] were

> targeted for extinction and called "bloodsuckers" or "vermin." Three years before the actual famine, there was a widespread deportation of as many as five million kulaks to Siberia. One of the few records kept of "the liquidation of the kulaks as a class" was a report from the Soviet secret police, the NKVD [People's Commissariat for Internal Affairs]. Deportees were stripped of their shoes and clothes, crowded into carriages and dropped in Siberia. Once there, they were abandoned without shelter in extreme cold and ordered to build dwellings. Many did so by working almost around the clock, without sleep so they wouldn't freeze to death. Inevitably, most died—their numbers replenished by the arrival of new deportees.[267]

She continued:

> Ironically, those who were deported turned out to be the "lucky ones." Those left behind were fated to become the victims of slow death by starvation in the famine. The symptoms of starvation are harrowing. There is a brooding for nourishment, a psychological obsession, which leads to involuntary movement of the jaws, as if chewing. The gums turn white, the skin grey, suggesting a disease more like leprosy than hunger. There is an unnatural aging that causes even children to look old. As the body shrinks, the eyes become large and unfocused, bulging and immobile. Children's bodies swell and their stomachs distend hugely. Festering sores appear, and the diarrhoea associated with starvation begins. As the body consumes itself, there are sometimes hallucinations and other symptoms of madness. Once this stage begins, cannibalism is frequent. In Ukraine, there were many reports of parents eating their own children.[268]

Taylor added a postscript to the *Daily Mail* article stating that the *New York Times* had never rescinded Duranty's Pulitzer Prize. Although the newspaper conceded that Duranty's work, "measured by today's standards for foreign reporting, falls dangerously short," there was "not clear and convincing evidence of deliberate deception."[269]

Mao's Repeat of Stalin's Mass Famine

In his book *Tombstone*, Jisheng described the mass starvation in China during Mao's Great Leap Forward in terms almost identical to how Taylor described the famine in Ukraine under Stalin's failed first Five-Year Plan:

> Starvation was a prolonged agony. The grain was gone, the wild herbs had all been eaten, even the bark had been stripped from the trees, and bird droppings, rat, and cotton batting were used to fill stomachs. In the kaolin clay fields, starving people chewed on the clay as they dug it. The corpses of the dead, famine victims seeking refuge from other villages, even one's own family members, became food for the desperate.[270]

Jisheng reports the suppression of information about the mass starvation caused by Mao's Great Leap Forward was equally severe. "At that time and in the decades to follow, China's books, newspapers, and official documents assiduously covered up this massive human tragedy," he explained. "Officials sealed their lips and falsified statistics, and the authorities ordered the destruction of all data reporting the depletion of China's population by tens of millions."[271] Refugees who escaped to Hong Kong and Chinese family members living overseas tried to spread the news of the calamity. To discredit these reports, the Chinese government labeled the few piecemeal articles published in Western sources as "vicious attacks" and "slanderous rumors."[272]

Launching a massive cover-up operation, Mao's government invited "friends of China" to visit and see for themselves. "The government meticulously planned every step of a visitor's itinerary, including which places he would visit, the people with whom he could come into contact, and the lines people should recite when receiving the guests," Jisheng wrote. "Foreign guests were kept segregated from ordinary people, and well-fed and well-clothed individuals were sometimes put on display."[273] China's suppression efforts generated China apologists. Felix Greene, a British journalist, published the 1964 book *A Curtain of Ignorance: How the American Public Has Been Misinformed about China* based on a 1960 trip through China. He downplayed reports of mass starvation, alleging a press biased against Chinese Communism had misinformed Americans about Chairman Mao.[274]

American journalist Edgar Snow would be precisely the type of journalist China would want to cover Xi Jinping's regime today. In 1937, Snow authored an international bestseller *Red Star Over China* that featured extended private interviews with CCP leaders, including Mao. In that book, Snow wrote that the Chinese Communist movement sought "to awaken [China's millions] to a belief in human rights, to combat the timidity, passiveness, and static faiths of Taoism and Confucianism, to educate, to persuade and, I have no doubt, at times to beleaguer and coerce them to fight for 'the reign of the people'—a new vision in rural China—

to fight for a life of justice, equality, freedom, and human dignity."[275] In an invited six-month visit to China in 1960, Snow wrote *The Other Side of the River: Red China Today*, in which he denied the existence of famine and starvation. In that book, Snow wrote: "I diligently searched, without success, for starving people or beggars to photograph....I must assert that I saw no starving people in China, nothing that looked like old-time famine...that I do not believe there is famine in China at this writing."[276] One reason Greene and Snow saw no mass starvation was that Mao's public security bureaus controlled all postal communications, holding back all letters mailed out of the locality. As Jisheng noted: "Entire villages were placed under lockdown, and refugees who were caught attempting to escape were paraded through the streets, flogged, or otherwise punished as 'vagrants.'"[277]

Khrushchev's Secret Speech

Dikötter noted that "Mao, who had modeled himself on Stalin, felt personally threatened by deStalinisation."[278] In a secret speech on February 25, 1956, "that shook the socialist camp to the core, Khrushchev had demolished the reputation of his predecessor Stalin, detailing the horrors of his rule and attacking the cult of personality."[279] The occasion was the Twentieth Congress of the Communist Party of the Soviet Union, when Khrushchev assembled a secret session in the Grand Kremlin Palace, the Moscow residence of the Russian tsars. In a four-hour speech delivered without interruption, Khrushchev detailed Stalin's purges that involved the torture and execution of some wholly innocent party loyalists.[280] Then, in 1958, Khrushchev proposed "peaceful coexistence" with the West, a concept Mao viewed as a betrayal of the principles of revolutionary Communism. Parenthetically, what Khrushchev demonstrated was that Marxism-Leninism might have successfully put the Communists in power. Still, by pursuing a policy to reduce Stalin's importance, Khrushchev was abandoning leadership of a global Communist revolution to protect Russia's interests as a nation-state. With Khrushchev's attack on Stalin, Mao saw a risk to his power as the head of China, another nation-state, and an opportunity to launch a second revolution in his country. The move, Mao calculated, would both preserve his power as head of state in China and advance the country over Russia as the leader of the global Communist revolution that he, as a dialectically trained Marxist-Leninist, felt was inevitable. Dikötter analyzed Mao's thinking as follows:

> In communist parlance, after the socialist transformation of the ownership of the means of production had been completed, a new revolution was required to stamp out once and for all the remnants of bourgeois culture, from private thoughts to private markets. Just as the transition from capitalism to socialism required a revolution, the transition from socialism to communism demanded a revolution too: Mao called it the Cultural Revolution.[281]

By launching the Cultural Revolution, Mao caused a fundamental reexamination of the global Communist revolutionary movement. Again, Dikötter's analysis illuminated the point:

> The Great Proletarian Cultural Revolution was the second stage in the history of the international communist movement, safeguarding the dictatorship of the proletariat against revisionism. The foundation piles of the communist future were being driven in China, as the Chairman guided the oppressed and downtrodden people of the world toward freedom. Mao was the one who inherited, defended and developed Marxism-Leninism into a new stage, that of Marxism-Leninism-Mao Zedong Thought.[282]

But while the Cultural Revolution may have secured cultural Maoism a position in advancing dialectical Marxism-Leninism to a new level, the Cultural Revolution was a disaster to China's well-being as a nation-state. The Cultural Revolution wrote a new chapter adding the principles of cultural Maoism and tactics of Maoist insurgency into the global Marxist-Leninist revolutionary movement. But the Cultural Revolution added to the misery of the Great Leap Forward, characterizing Mao's rule of China as head of state to be comparable to the suffering of Russia under Stalin's rule.

The Sino-Soviet split that occurred in the fallout from Khrushchev's 1956 secret speech involved the breaking of relations between the PRC and the USSR over Mao's doctrinal differences with Khrushchev's determination to pursue a policy of peaceful coexistence with the Dwight D. Eisenhower administration. Mao accused Khrushchev of abandoning the goal of achieving worldwide Communism, claiming instead that China had now taken over the lead in the Marxist-Leninist ambition to produce Communist revolutions aimed at destroying capitalism in all countries around the globe, including the United States. In 1997, Roderick MacFarquhar, the Leroy B. Williams Research Professor of History and

Political Science at Harvard University, published *The Origins of the Cultural Revolution*. In that book, MacFarquhar observed that the 1956 Hungarian revolution, which Khrushchev's secret speech triggered, prompted Mao to challenge whether Khrushchev was competent to set the ideological guidelines for the world Communist movement. "By 1960, Beijing and Moscow were engaged in bitter polemics over a range of national and international issues, and Khrushchev abruptly withdrew thousands of Soviet technical-assistance personnel," MacFarquhar wrote. "During the early 1960s, as relations worsened, Mao pondered how to avert a similar betrayal of the revolution in China."[283]

Mao ramped up China's involvement in the world revolutionary struggle of international Communism, filling the vacuum created by Khrushchev's thaw in relations with the United States. Mao also decided he needed an offensive strategy in China to ward off the internal rivals positioned and ready to use Khrushchev's attack on Stalin to launch a similar attack on Mao.

China's Cultural Revolution and the Red Guards' Tactics of Shaming

In May 1966, Mao Tse-tung launched the Great Proletarian Cultural Revolution, described as "a decade-long period of political strife and social chaos caused by Mao Zedong's bid to use the Chinese masses to reassert his control over the Communist party."[284] The Red Guards, a youthful student-based paramilitary social movement organized by the CCP, was the vanguard of the Cultural Revolution. Mao's decision to launch the Cultural Revolution is today "widely interpreted as an attempt to destroy his enemies by unleashing the people on the party and urging them to purify its ranks."[285] Roderick MacFarquhar offered another explanation for Mao's decision to unleash the Cultural Revolution. In 2016, MacFarquhar observed the following:

> First, no Mao, no Cultural Revolution. One needs a supreme leader with a cult so pervasive that he can act with little danger of being questioned. Second, the supreme leader must sense danger so great—either to the system or to himself or to both—that he must take extraordinary measures to ward it off. Mao did not launch a cultural revolution in the 1950s, because he was only beginning to develop his obsession with the concept of revisionism, i.e. Soviet "abandonment" of Leninist doctrine. And while Khrushchev's denunciation of Stalin in 1956 may have

> caused Mao to fear that his own doctrines might be abandoned after his death, it was only when Khrushchev was dismissed in 1964 that he may have begun to fear that his colleagues might unseat him even before his death.[286]

So, in an attempt to reinvigorate China's Communist revolution of 1945–1949, Mao unleashed the mobs of Red Guards.

The Red Guards consisted of thousands of Chinese youths clad in military fatigues. Mobs of Red Guard youths waving their Little Red Books of Chairman Mao's quotations caused chaos throughout China. The Cultural Revolution in China ended up as a civil war between the generations. The Red Guards roamed the streets of major cities, closed universities, destroyed churches, burned libraries, and toppled historical statues and monuments. The Red Guards did not hesitate to ransack private homes to eliminate the Four Olds—old ideas, old customs, old habits, and old culture. Gangs of students and Red Guards attacked people wearing "bourgeois clothes" on the street, tore down "imperialist signs," and drove party officials to suicide.[287] The Chinese Cultural Revolution involved a "Maoist inspired rejection of all cultural values and institutions associated with everything old or elderly represented an attempt to destroy Confucian family life and traditional disciplinary systems in favor of a collectivized communist society."[288]

In the end, the Cultural Revolution "crippled China's economy, ruined millions of lives, and threw China into ten years of turmoil, bloodshed, hunger, and starvation."[289] In his 2019 book *Agents of Disorder: Inside China's Cultural Revolution*, Andrew Walder, a professor of sociology at Stanford University, noted that when the dust finally cleared in 1969, close to 1.6 million people had died. These deaths resulted from the upheaval and suppression campaigns that ravaged China in the most violent first three years of China's ten-year-long Cultural Revolution. In the summer of 1966, the PRC was approaching its seventeenth anniversary after taking power in a two-decade guerrilla insurgency against Japan and a three-year civil war against the KMT and the ROC. Walder concluded that Mao decided to set the Cultural Revolution in motion "to foment rebellion against his own party-state as a means to halt the bureaucratization that afflicted virtually all regimes modeled after the Soviet Union. The ultimate result, by 1969, was a new state structure built on a hierarchy of 'revolutionary committees' composed of rebel activists, selected veteran officials, and military officers who, in most regions, exercised real control."[290]

Chinese author Yang Jisheng, in his 2016 book *The World Turned Upside Down: A History of the Chinese Cultural Revolution*, also commented on the intense suffering and misery the Chinese people experienced:

> The Cultural Revolution produced millions of unjust cases and unnatural deaths affecting more than one hundred million people to varying degrees. Since most of the official data remains classified, there is no way of ascertaining exactly how many people fell victim to the Cultural Revolution. Even so, what can be unambiguously stated is that it was catastrophic for China in terms of the human toll, immense cultural destruction, and economic loss.[291]

Jisheng brilliantly observed that Mao's cult of personality was at the heart of the Cultural Revolution. After seventeen years of relentless bombardment by Mao's unique version of Marxism, Jisheng observed that sympathy for the oppressed and the exploited at the center of Mao's Marxist ideology "inspired tens of millions of people to sacrifice everything for the cause." He commented that Mao's Marxist ideology "became religion, and Mao its high priest." He then painted the following picture: "Waving his hand from the gate tower of Tiananmen Square at mass rallies, Mao aroused surges of ardor that dwarfed a papal appearance at the Vatican."[292]

Frank Dikötter, in his 2016 book *The Cultural Revolution: A People's History, 1962–1976*, detailed the Red Guards rampage in Shanghai at the start of the Cultural Revolution. Red Guards destroyed thousands of books from the Zikawei Library, a scholarly repository of over two hundred thousand volumes the Jesuits started in 1847.[293] The Red Guards demolished eighteen monuments of historical and religious importance in only a few days. The destroyed monuments included the tomb of Xu Guangqi (1562–1633), the city's first Christian convert, the Longhua Pagoda, the oldest temple in Shanghai, and the Confucius Temple, an ancient temple complex located in a public park.[294] The Red Guards' search of private homes seized counter-revolutionary items including articles of worship, luxury items, reactionary literature, foreign books, concealed weapons, hidden gold, foreign currency, signs of a decadent lifestyle, portraits of Chiang Kai-shek, old land deeds, documents from the nationalist era, and signs of underground activities or incriminating evidence of links with enemies of the regime.[295] In various Chinese cities, piles of plundered loot heaped with works of art, musical instruments, furniture, watches, nationalist flags, kilos of gold, and mounds of jewelry, including silver rings, bracelets, necklaces, and earrings.[296] The Red Guard roaming mobs left many piles of irreplicable values to rot, including rare books, ancient calligraphy scrolls, and valuable paintings.[297] They melted down many priceless bronzes in foundries and sold them on the black market. Antique porcelain was smashed to pieces.[298] Cemeteries, particularly those belonging to foreigners, were vandalized. Headstones were smashed, crosses were broken, and memorial plaques and inscriptions were obliterated with cement or smeared with paint.[299]

Black Lives Matter (BLM) and the Red Guards Comparisons

Doug Bandow, a senior fellow at the Cato Institute and a former special assistant to President Ronald Reagan, described the Red Guards' chaos during Mao's Cultural Revolution as follows:

> The images of the Cultural Revolution remain indelible more than a half century later. People beaten to death. Crowds of automatons waving red books and chanting in unison. Accomplished professionals sitting wearing dunce caps while being harangued by baying crowds. Demands for confessions of manifold ideological crimes. People fired, discredited, exiled, and impoverished by an ideological crazy and politically manipulated mob. The normal, responsible, professional, and sensible being sent to be reeducated in the crazed ideological ruminations of a self-absorbed dictator. An entire generation gone mad, without education or work while passionately oppressing neighbors and governors at the behest of the Red Emperor determined to reassert control of the people's revolution while living in luxury in Beijing's Zhongnanhai compound.[300]

Parenthetically, Bandow commented, his description of the Red Guards' terror during the Cultural Revolution "sounds a lot like academia today."[301] Bandow expanded on this theme by stressing that the cancel culture views ideas disagreeing with its radical Left ideology as evidence of depravity, immorality, indecency, and even insanity. He explained this perception as follows:

> So self-righteous mobs demand that anyone with unpopular thoughts be denied publication, disciplined by employers and professional associations, and fired from their jobs. Those targeted are expected to engage in the online version of self-criticism sessions during the Cultural Revolution. Apologies and acknowledgment of heresies from progressivism are the bare minimum acceptable. Weepy promises to resolutely

adhere to the most radical left-wing agendas in the future are expected. Of course, reeducation, directed by well-compensated, mostly white professionals who make a living selling such nonsense as "white guilt" and "white fragility" is mandatory. Even then, those deemed as insufficiently obsequious are targeted for personal destruction.[302]

But the radical Left has pushed back strong, for instance, against any claim that the Black Lives Matter (BLM) movement is a repeat of China's Cultural Revolution. Tao Peng, PhD, a senior columnist for the Taiwan-sympathetic Chinese-language newspaper *World Journal* in New York, has insisted in print that BLM is not conducting an "American Cultural Revolution." Peng explained the following in an editorial for the Center for International Relations published in the online journal *International Affairs Forum* in May 2020. Peng argued the following:

> The BLM movement can be regarded as a cultural "revolutionary" movement, but it is not a Cultural Revolution in the sense of China's Cultural Revolution. The revolt is a bottom-to-top social movement that renews the resistance and the liquidation of long-standing cultural and structural (or systemic) racial discrimination in the United States and Western societies, requiring historical figures related to apartheid and discrimination to be re-evaluated. The uprising wants to establish an ideal society where individuals will not be discriminated against because of race.
>
> The BLM movement has been deeply inspired by the African American People's Rights Movement, the Black Power Movement, the black feminist movement in the 1980s, Pan-Africanism, the anti-apartheid movement, hip-hop, the LGBT rights movement, and the Wall Street occupation movement, which has been called the "New Civil Rights Movement." The movement originated in the African American community and protested against violence and systematic discrimination against black people. BLM protests also oppose broader issues such as racial induction, violent law enforcement, and racial inequality in the U.S. criminal justice system.[303]

As Coughlin and Higgins pointed out, a media compliant to the progressive agenda, even media from a supposedly conservative or politically neutral stance, internalizes neo-Marxist values or dares not oppose radical Left movements like BLM for fear of being called racist. We should not be surprised to find media branded as "fake news" as reporting that dares to challenge the radical Left's politically correct agenda. Ironically, Peng argued BLM does not resemble the Red Guards in China's Cultural Revolution by identifying the united front of multiple neo-Marxist organizations that support BLM. As we will discuss later in this chapter, creating a united front to back a radical Left movement like BLM is one of the critical tactics and distinguishing characteristics of Maoist insurgency.

Lenin, Stalin, and Mao: Revolution Followed by a Reign of Terror

Like Lenin and Stalin, Mao never apologized for the catastrophic misery he caused among the people he ruled. Mao's failures governing China concerned him when Khrushchev decided, in 1956, to reveal the true horror to the Russian people of Stalin's rule. But, as we noted earlier, in the wake of Khrushchev's secret speech, Mao refused to admit he too failed to make Communism work. Instead, Mao launched the Cultural Revolution to discipline the Chinese people even more severely into respectful silence. In the United States, Khrushchev's 1956 speech also disturbed William Z. Foster. While Foster came around to admit that Stalin's many mistakes and errors were "appalling," he continued to support Stalin and his brand of Communist rule in Russia. Ultimately, Foster reduced himself to a very predictable rationalization, arguing that Stalin "consistently followed a correct general political line…and he has performed great services in the rapidly advancing Russian and World Revolution."[304]

In the late 1990s, a book first published in France, *The Black Book of Communism: Crimes, Terror, Repression,*[305] swept Europe on its way to becoming an international sensation. The 858-page book documented that wherever Communism gained power, the Marxist-Leninist-Maoist governments committed horrific crimes, including terror, torture, censorship, suppression of dissent, famine, deportations, and massacres—all resulting in millions of deaths. The authors also credited Khrushchev's 1956 secret speech as a turning point. "For the first time, a high-ranking Communist leader had officially acknowledged, albeit only as a tactical concession, that the regime that assumed power in 1917 had undergone a criminal 'deviation.'"[306] The authors acknowledged that Khrushchev's complex motivations for delivering the secret speech included advancing his career after Stalin's deaths. Those listening to Khrushchev's speech were stunned by what they were hearing. *The Black Book of Communism* authors stressed that the delegates listened in absolute silence. The first secretary of the Russian Communist Party, Khrushchev, "systematically dismantled the image of the 'little father of the peoples,' of the 'genius Stalin,' who for thirty years had been the hero of world Communism."[307]

In his 2007 book *Lenin, Stalin, and Hitler: The Age of Social Catastrophe*, historian Robert Gellately presented a perceptive analysis of Lenin. He described Lenin as "the most intransigent practitioner of Russian Marxism in the prerevolutionary period."[308] Gellately defined Lenin's power politics in historical terms. "It was precisely his will [Lenin's] to power that drove on the doubters among fellow Bolsheviks in 1917. Without a hint of moral scruple or sense of national loyalty, Lenin desperately hoped for Russia's defeat in the First World War and ridiculed fellow Bolsheviks who thought they should defend their country."[309] When the 1917 revolution came, Lenin was in Switzerland. Emboldened that the tsars had been toppled, Lenin returned to his homeland. "He was determined to destroy what remained of the old social and political order in Russia and intent on killing any chance that the new Russia would become a liberal democracy," Gellately explained.[310]

Gellately noted that Lenin, as "the foundation of Soviet Communism," was "the key advocate of establishing the one-party state, the concentration camps, and the terror." He stressed that within days of the October Revolution of 1917, Lenin insisted that civil rights had to be curtailed. Weeks later, Lenin pushed for creating a new secret police force (the Cheka).[311] Lenin had little sympathy for the common people, including peasant farmers and the industrial working class. He felt that if left to their own devices, workers would merely want better wages—trade union demands that would preclude the need for a real revolution. Here is how Gellately summed up his analysis of Lenin and Leninism:

> Leninism was based on the idea that professional revolutionaries would form an avant-garde or vanguard party and rule in the name of the proletariat. They would not waste time on the "sham" of liberal democracy, which they regarded as nothing more than the government of the hated bourgeoisie. Getting rid of the absolute monarchy and replacing it with a constitutional system was merely a prelude to a more authentic revolution. None of this was going to happen without bloodshed and Lenin took it as self-evident that the class struggle meant civil war. He was convinced that Communism had to be forced through violently. His followers were elitist to the core and assured of their own superiority. They took it upon themselves to create a new world from top to bottom.[312]

Gellately argued that Stalin was Lenin's logical heir: "Stalin justified every zigzag in policy, every twist of the screws, every dose of terror, by tracing it to some statement or other that Lenin had made."[313] He took exception with Khrushchev's 1956 secret speech only because Khrushchev "trotted out the myth of Lenin the noble and good to save the 'inner truths' of Communism from association with what were belatedly recognized as 'Stalinist evils.'"[314] The truth, he insisted, as made clear by then-newly opened Soviet archives, revealed Lenin "to be the most extreme of the radicals, and the leader who pressed for terror as much as, and probably more than, anyone."[315] Gellately's well-documented analysis forces us to come to terms with the reality that Marxist-Leninist-Maoist ideologies share the characteristic of being psychologically powerful perversions of language that have proven to be highly successful in toppling the existing order. What precedes the revolution are promises of utopia. What follows the revolution is a living Communist hell. Lenin, Stalin, and Mao used terror, imprisonment, and murder to exert authoritarian control over their populations. In the reality of the Communist state, millions more under Stalin and Mao starved to death in failed schemes to eliminate private property.

As Jisheng pointed out about Mao's China, there is no possibility of resistance under totalitarianism. He emphasized the following:

> For the most part, people submitted; the exceptional people who opposed the system were usually crushed by it. In the face of a rigid political system, individual power was all but nonexistent. The system was like a casting mold; no matter how hard the metal, once it was melted and poured into that mold, it came out the same shape as everything else. Regardless of what kind of person went into the totalitarian system, all came out as conjoined twins facing in opposite directions: either despot or slave, depending on their position respective to those above or below them.[316]

Jisheng stressed that the CCP established "an ironclad system of social control that included an impermeable organizational structure, a household registration system, food rationing, and controls on population movement."[317] A disarmed population had no chance to succeed in a rebellion against the CCP and Mao's rule. "From 1958 to 1962, the government maintained a military strength of more than four million," Jisheng wrote. "These armed forces were well equipped and prepared to deal with both foreign aggression and domestic strife. It was impossible for citizens to contend with the might of government armed forces."[318]

The Maoist Concept of Insurgency

Thomas A. Marks, PhD, the head of War and Conflict Studies (WACS) at the College of International Security Affairs (CISA) of the National Defense University (NDU), has devoted his career to studying the Maoist concept of political warfare. A West Point graduate, Dr. Marks specialized in counterinsurgency tactics, formerly serving as the Oppenheimer Chair of Warfighting Strategy at Marine Corps University in Quantico, Virginia.[319] In his 2007 book *Maoist People's War in Post-Vietnam Asia*, he formalized Mao's ideological blueprint for seizing state power. "What Mao did was to recognize that the solution to the challenge of seizing state power lay in forming a counter-state, an alternative infrastructure grounded in the same 'nation in arms' as had come to characterize conventional warfare but a nation created from scratch," he stressed.[320]

Marks argued that if the Japanese had not invaded and occupied China in World War II, there "would not have been a Maoist insurgency."[321] He reasoned that the Japanese invasion so weakened the KMT resources that the KMT military "was no longer able to muster the power that had previously proved quite sufficient to crush the communists."[322] He emphasized this point as follows:

> It is not an overstatement to posit that without the Japanese invasion, there might well have been no Mao. The collapse of the KMT in the 1945–49 civil war was an anti-climax. The Nationalist cause was mortally wounded before the battle was joined.[323]

Marks also argued that Mao's actual people's war framework developed in the guerrilla warfare he launched against the Japanese. In the process, Mao redefined Communist revolutionary theory, giving birth to the Maoist insurgency strategy of political warfare. He explained the point as follows:

> Let us look at this more carefully. By perfecting the notion of the clandestine party of revolutionaries, Lenin removed the Marxian revolution from its position as a course of action open only to advanced capitalist societies and placed it within the realm of possibility for any state, provided a revolutionary situation existed and a revolutionary party could guide the population toward consciousness. Mao took this lesson and applied it to China, producing a movement far more grounded in the masses than anything Lenin envisioned. Mao thus demonstrated the

need for revolutionaries to bend Marxism to their particular situation, rather than attempting to fit the situation to Marxism.[324]

He observed that Mao's most significant contribution was to recognize that in China there was no working class available to participate in the revolutionary movement. In China, the overwhelming majority of the population, the peasantry, bore a relationship to the dominant class similar to the traditional Marxist assumption of class conflict in a capitalist society between the proletariat and the bourgeoisie. Marks correctly understood that there was "insufficient human material in the urban centers of proletarian concentration to build a potent movement" in Mao's China.[325] The peasantry was where the bodies were.

Conrad Brandt, then a fellow of the Russian Research Center at Harvard, together with then Harvard University history professors Benjamin I. Schwartz and John King Fairbank, in their 1952 book *A Documentary History of Chinese Communism*, agreed with Marks's analysis. These authors also noted that Chinese society was marked by "bifurcation into two groups—the mass of peasantry and the upper classes." They stated this observation directly: "It does not require a Marxist to make a class analysis of this social structure; the Confucian classics long ago divided the Chinese people into scholars, farmers, artisans, and merchants—an ideological device whereby the officials smuggled themselves into the top position under the category of 'scholars,' much as the CCP today assumes the top position by identifying itself with the 'proletariat.'"[326] These authors commented that Chinese society has always been "structurally elitist," with those with learning, wealth, and power constituting "a small minority, quite distinct from the ignorant, poor, and powerless mass of the Chinese people."[327] Brandt, Schwartz, and Fairbank agreed with Marks that "the immediate and obvious circumstance in the rise of the Communists has without doubt been the debility and the collapse of the Kuomintang government." They commented that the demise of the KMT "gave the CCP a rapid victory, almost by default."[328]

Marks noted the Japanese invasion of China in 1937 "threatened to wipe out Chinese society," such that "all classes faced the issue of survival."[329] The need to resist Japan became a struggle against Japanese imperialism that took priority, and "since this was a struggle of the Chinese people as a whole, the entire Chinese population could be viewed as a revolutionary class."[330] Mao realized that mobilizing the Chinese people against Japanese imperialism required a united front. Thus, Mao made concessions not involving key ideological issues of principle. Marks understood that Mao's accommodations broadened the goal of a "workers' and peasants' republic" to include all allied elements in a "people's republic."[331] While participating in this united front throughout World War II, Mao directed the CCP to "proselytize, to win over to its way of thinking 'the middle forces.'"[332] This strategy enabled Mao to create the mass organization that ultimately allowed him to defeat the Kuomintang. Marks quoted Mao explaining the tactic as follows:

> All correct leadership is necessarily from the masses, to the masses. This means: take the ideas of the masses (scattered and unsystematic ideas) and concentrate them (through study turn them into concentrated and systematic ideas), then go to the masses and propagate and explain these ideas until the masses embrace them as their own, hold fast to them and translate them into action, and test the correctness of these ideas in such action. Then once again go to the masses so that the ideas are preserved in an endless spiral, with the ideas becoming more correct, more vital and richer each time. Such is the Marxist-Leninist theory of knowledge, or methodology.[333]

Marks stressed that Mao transformed Marxist-Leninist theory into a war against imperialism, with imperialism viewed "as a higher form of capitalism." When the United States entered the Vietnam War, Mao realized "the situation in Asia ripe for revolution had been transformed by America's assumption of the Japanese imperial role."[334] Mao moved to position American imperialist aggression as the new enemy, shifting the focus from capitalism per se to imperialism. Thus, in an anti-imperialist united front, Mao motivated Communist parties throughout Asia "to rally all anti-imperialist patriotic forces, including the national bourgeoisie and all patriotic persons.[335] He commented that America's entry into the Vietnam War was thus not a setback for Mao but a boon that Mao saw as the next stage in the historical decline of capitalism. America became the target of a worldwide Communist revolution that Mao now led. Moreover, Mao had developed his methods for grabbing power into a sophisticated political warfare model that transformed the guerrilla war against Japan into the sophisticated multilevel insurgency methodology described in the points articulated at the start of this chapter subsection.

Let's contemplate two additional observations before moving on from this chapter subsection. First, perhaps the most disturbing and tragic irony of Mao's successful insurgency in China involved the peasants. Without the peasants' support, Mao would have failed. Once in power, Mao and his top party comrades assumed China's elite class for themselves. Under Mao's rule, the peasants discovered they were the first victims of the totalitarian state Mao's brand of Communism created.

Yang Jisheng, in his book *Tombstone*, tells a heartbreaking story of his father during the Great Leap Forward. In April 1969, while he was away at school, a childhood friend told Jisheng that his father was dying of starvation. Jisheng collected a three-day ration of 1.5 kilos of rice from the school canteen and rushed home. Arriving there, he found "utter destitution." The elm tree in front of their home was now nothing more than a trunk stripped of the bark that was eaten when there was no more food. There was nothing edible in the house, not even a grain of rice, and his father was a skeleton, lying in bed, immobilized by starvation. "I boiled congee from the rice I'd brought and took it to my father's bed, but he was no longer able to swallow," Jisheng wrote.[336] Three days later, his father died. "I grieved deeply over my father's death, but never thought to blame the government," he admitted. "I harbored no doubts regarding the party's propaganda about the accomplishments of the 'Great Leap Forward' or advantages of the people's communes. I believed that what was happening in my home village was isolated, and that my father's death was merely one family's tragedy."[337]

Jisheng realized the truth during the Cultural Revolution when the governor of the province where his father lived told Jisheng that some three hundred thousand people had starved to death during the three years of hardship in that province. "Only then did I realize that my family's tragedy was not unique."[338] He never placed a tombstone for his father because he recalled that in 1958, "many of the village's tombstones had been dismantled for irrigation projects or as bases for smelting ovens in the steelmaking campaign during the Great Leap Forward."[339] Other tombstones had been laid out on roadways. "I did erect a tombstone for my father, in my heart, and this book is made up of the words I carved into that tombstone," he wrote. "Even after I leave this life, these heartfelt words will remain behind in libraries throughout the world."[340] That Jisheng did not recognize that what killed his father was one incident in ongoing mass starvation is testament to the power of ideology to block out unwelcome truths, aided by an ideologically driven, government-controlled media that refuses to publish anything harmful to those in power at the time.

Second, as Coughlin and Higgins have observed, since 1972, the year President Richard Nixon went to China, opening up the West to Chinese influence, America has been on notice that the American radical Left has adopted the neo-Marxist political warfare model as refined by Maoist cultural insurgency tactics to seek America's negation.[341] As discussed in the previous chapter, while the Weather Underground opposed American military intervention in Vietnam, the group's primary message was black liberation at home. In 2021, historian Roxanne Dunbar-Ortiz published a new book entitled *Not "A Nation of Immigrants": Settler Colonialism, White Supremacy, and a History of Exclusion*.[342] In her radical Left critical theory assessment, Dunbar-Ortiz characterized United States history as a continuous extension of the settler colonialism that slaughtered the indigenous peoples and imported slaves from Africa. Dunbar-Ortiz portrayed "a nation of immigrants" as "a mid-twentieth-century revisionist origin story"[343] that is "generally used to counter xenophobic fears."[344] She was sharply critical of John F. Kennedy's 1958 book *A Nation of Immigrants* that she hints "liberal historian" Arthur Schlesinger Jr. first suggested.[345] For Dunbar-Ortiz, the "nation of immigrants" is a metaphor designed to mask American genocide, white supremacy, and slavery. She believed these themes established an equal ground for racism in the United States and imperialism abroad. For her, as for the Weather Underground, racism is the theme that ties together the Black Panther movement in the United States and the people's liberation struggle in Vietnam. Here is how she dismissed Kennedy:

> The idea of the United States as a nation of immigrants was hatched in the late 1950s, and while Kennedy was its ambassador, it came to reflect the US ruling-class response to the challenges of the post–World War II anticolonial national liberation movements, as well as civil and human rights social movements domestically.[346]

Thus, Dunbar-Ortiz gives us a deeper insight into why the "hate America" radical Left in this country has no problem with the Maoist extension of Stalin's "National Question" to explain the unity of theme within a neo-Marxist organization like the Weather Underground. For the Weather Underground, the U.S. war in Vietnam was simply the extension of white supremacy and racism against blacks projected onto people of color in Asia.

Two Russian Communist Defectors Warn America

Two Russian intelligence agents who defected, one in 1961 and the other in 1970, revealed to U.S. intelligence the deceptive plans of the Soviet Union to destroy the United States without firing a shot. Both defectors insisted the Communist Party in Russia has not changed its primary goal of causing a worldwide Communist revolution since the time of Lenin.

Anatoliy Golitsyn and the Perestroika Deception

> **Question**: For 34 years, Golitsyn has remained in hiding. He is never seen in public; his whereabouts are a closely guarded secret.... Is Golitsyn's secrecy a reflection of his prudence, or of paranoia?
>
> **Answer**: Golitsyn was condemned to death in 1962, after Semichastniy, then head of the KGB, had formally asked the party [Russian Communist Party] for its approval that he should be liquidated.... In the *Perestroika Deception*, Golitsyn clearly acknowledges that his life is in danger. If this is so, it proves he is a living threat to the Soviet strategists—since he has released the essence of their long-range strategy. Incidentally, Golitsyn explains that a strategy differs from a policy in the following respect: Whereas a policy is overt, a strategy contains within it a *secret maneuver or dimension* which is not revealed, the purpose of which is to ensure the realization of the strategy.
>
> Christopher Story, Interview, 1995[347]

In December 1961, Anatoliy Golitsyn, a KGB major who worked in the KGB's strategic planning department, defected with his family to the United States in Helsinki, Finland. Golitsyn joined the Soviet army in 1944 and was assigned to a military counterintelligence unit. After World War II, he was transferred to the KGB's First Chief Directorate, where he ran operations against the United States. The CIA arranged to fly Golitsyn to the United States, where James Jesus Angleton, the CIA's counterintelligence director, debriefed him. Angleton came to trust Golitsyn, although there were doubters with the CIA. Golitsyn provided Angleton clues to the identity of a secret mole Angleton suspected the KGB had planted within the CIA's counterintelligence division. Golitsyn's working knowledge of Soviet intelligence guided Angleton to identify and remove a prime suspect, Peter Karlow, a career officer in the CIA's Technical Service Division.[348] Golitsyn further solidified his worth with Angleton by providing the names of several Soviet spies operating in the West.[349] Golitsyn confirmed that British intelligence officer Kim Philby was a double agent working for the KGB.[350] But, most importantly, Golitsyn confirmed what Angleton suspected was true, namely, that the Soviet Union had not changed since the death of Stalin. Angleton, as CIA head of counterintelligence, suspected that Khrushchev's talk about "peaceful coexistence" was an elaborate disinformation ploy to deceive the West.[351]

Golitsyn brought with him a potentially game-changing message that confirmed Angleton's suspicions. Golitsyn warned the United States that the KGB, since 1959, had engaged in a massive disinformation campaign to convince the West that Russia was moving away from Communism. In a book completed in 1980 and published in 1984, entitled *New Lies for Old: An Ex-KGB Officer Warns How Communist Deception Threatens the Survival of the West*, Golitsyn explained the Russian deception strategy as follows:

> The conclusion was reached that, if the factors that had previously served to forge a degree of Western cohesion—that is, communist ideological militancy and monolithic unity—were to be perceived by the West, respectively, as moderating and disintegrating and if, despite an increase in the bloc's actual strength, an image was to be successfully projected of a bloc weakened by economic, political, and ideological disarray, then the Western response to communist policy would be feebler and less coordinated; actual Western tendencies toward disintegration might be provoked and encouraged, thereby creating conditions for a change in the balance of power in favor of the communist bloc.[352]

Alexander Shelepin, a Russian politician and member of the Politburo whom Khrushchev appointed as KGB chairman in 1958, devised a long-term strategy for Communism to achieve worldwide dominance. "After the end of the Second World War, the threat of monolithic, Stalinist communism drove the West into military and political alliances, such as NATO [North Atlantic Treaty Organization], SEATO [Southeast Asia Treaty Organization], and the Bagdad pact [Middle East Treaty Organization, METO, that Iran, Iraq, Pakistan, Turkey, and the UK developed in 1955], and into other forms of military, political, economic, and security collaboration," Golitsyn wrote.[353] He also identified the factors that tended to undermine Western unity. These included moderation in official Soviet policy, emphasis on the conflicting national interests of Communist parties at the expense of ideological solidarity, and the dissolution of the Comintern in 1943, which led Western observers to believe Russia had abandoned worldwide Communist subversion. The split between Stalin and Josip Tito in Yugoslavia in 1948 showed that not all consequences were adverse. "Open defiance of Stalin had sent Tito's prestige soaring in his own country and throughout the world," Golitsyn noted. "Independence of the Soviet Union had enabled Yugoslavia to obtain substantial economic and military assistance from the West and to acquire the beginnings of political influence in the Third World and with West European socialist parties. Moreover, Tito had demonstrated in 1957–58 that, despite the Western support he had received, he remained a faithful Leninist willing to work wholeheartedly with the other leaders of the bloc."[354]

Shelepin realized "spurious splits and independence in the communist world could be used to ease Western pressure and to obtain increased Western economic and even military aid for individual communist countries while the world balance of power was being shifted inconspicuously in communist favor."[355] Golitsyn stressed the importance of the Bilderberg Group that he described as a "group of distinguished Western statesmen and commentators" who were studying "the possibilities of a Sino-Soviet split, the likely consequences of such a split for the communist bloc, and the ways it might be exploited for the benefit of the west."[356] The Bilderberg Group's first conference was in 1954, at the Bilderberg Hotel in Oosterbeek, Netherlands. The annual invitation-only, off-the-record meeting involves elite government and business leaders whose original interests were to foster dialogue between the United States and Europe. Since Communist strategists studying the Bilderberg papers realized the West "half expected and ardently desired the disintegration of the communist bloc," Shelepin came to understand that projecting to the world a fictitious disintegration of the Communist bloc would be advantageous, "provided always that it was accompanied in parallel by an actual, but partially concealed, implementation of the long-range policy of strengthening the bloc and changing the world balance of power in its favor."[357] Golitsyn analyzed the utility of Khrushchev's 1957 secret speech as follows:

> Khrushchev had demonstrated in 1957 how misrepresentation of the Stalinist issue could be used to his own advantage in the struggle for power. The artificial revival of the dead issues related to Stalinism was the obvious and logical means of displaying convincing but spurious differences between different communist leaders or powers.[358]

Golitsyn argued that Stalin's negativity toward Mao during and after World War II was feigned, as was Mao's inaccurate statement, after the dissolution of the Comintern, that Russia had given China no assistance or advice since the Seventh Congress in 1935. Golitsyn reasoned the

Stalin-Mao rift was an engineered disinformation campaign designed to cloak the close cooperation Russia gave Mao in defeating the Kuomintang army and subverting Chiang Kai-shek's nationalist government. Still, Golitsyn acknowledged that China in the 1950s was not a Soviet satellite. Unresolved issues continued to divide the two countries. The extent of Soviet infiltration and control over the Chinese Communist Party and Mao's government was small compared with Eastern European countries. The most disagreement arose over the Korean War. Golitsyn commented that Stalin decided to embark on that conflict without fully taking Mao into his confidence. Then, when the war started to go wrong for the Communists, Mao was at first reluctant to come to Stalin's aid. Golitsyn argued Mao agreed to send "volunteers" to fight in Korea only after "severe Soviet pressure had been brought to bear."[359]

With Stalin dead, Soviet relations with China steadily improved. But by 1959, Shelepin and Khrushchev realized the utility of creating the appearance of a Sino-Soviet split, much as Stalin's misrepresentation of Mao's movement as "a relatively harmless agrarian reform movement" had concealed the extent of Soviet aid to the Chinese Communists in the final years of the civil war.[360] Golitsyn stressed that the Sino-Soviet duality strategy produced the effect on the West that Communist strategists intended, and it brought Russia substantial dividends. "For example, had it not been for General [Charles] de Gaulle's belief in the sincerity of Soviet interest in détente and his confidence in the authenticity of the Sino-Soviet split, it is more than doubtful that he would have gone as far as he did in his dealings with the Soviet Union, his recognition of Communist China, and his withdrawal of France from its military commitments to NATO."[361]

Golitsyn described the fake Sino-Soviet split as an example of what he called a "scissors strategy." At the final stroke, the scissor blades close, apparent duality in Russian and Chinese policies will disappear, and the Communist strategy "will develop logically into the 'strategy of one clenched fist'" to provide the driving force for a world federation of Communist states to form.[362] In a passage of *New Lies for Old*, written some four decades ago, Golitsyn described Shelepin's disinformation strategy's anticipated outcome in terms eerily sounding like what is happening today in the United States under the presidency of Joe Biden. Here's how Golitsyn described the Communist end game when the clenched-fist strategy takes over and becomes operative:

> At that point the shift in the political and military balance would be plain for all to see. Convergence would not be between two equal parties,

> but would be on terms dictated by the communist bloc. The argument for accommodation with the overwhelming strength of communism would be virtually unanswerable. Pressures would build up for changes in the American political and economic system on the lines indicated in [Andrei] Sakharov's treatise. Traditional conservatives would be isolated and driven toward extremism. They might become victims of a new McCarthyism of the left. The Soviet dissidents who are now extolled as heroes of the resistance to Soviet communism would play an active part in arguing for convergence. Their potential supporters would be confronted with a choice of forsaking their idols or acknowledging the legitimacy of the new Soviet regime.[363]

In *New Lies for Old*, Golitsyn portrayed Soviet nuclear scientist Andrei Sakharov as a willing participant in the Soviet disinformation campaign. Golitsyn singled out the argument Sakharov made in his writings to promote the concept of "convergence" between Communist and non-Communist systems. Golitsyn commented that Western convergence theorists "unwittingly and naively" accept the disinformation message, "namely that the influence of communist ideology is in decline, that communist regimes are coming closer to the Western model, and that there are serious possibilities of further changes in them that will prove favorable to Western interests."[364] He stressed that it is "inconceivable that, if he [Sakharov] were seriously at odds with the regime and therefore a security risk, he would have been given the opportunities he has had to maintain contact with Western friends and colleagues."[365] Golitsyn pointed out that even when Sakharov was in exile in Gorky, Sakharov continued to convey his views through intermediaries and correspondence. "The only conclusion consistent with these facts is that Sakharov is still a loyal servant of his regime, whose role is now that of a senior disinformation spokesman for the Soviet strategists," Golitsyn insisted.[366]

Golitsyn's description of the new world order under a unified Russian federation of Communist states is a grim reminder of the totalitarianism at the heart of Marxist-Leninist theory. He explained the following:

> In the new worldwide communist federation the present different brands of communism would disappear, to be replaced by a uniform, rigorous brand of Leninism. The process would be painful. Concessions made in the name of economic and political reform would be withdrawn. Religious and intellectual dissent would be suppressed. Nationalism and other forms of genuine opposition would be crushed. Those who

> had taken advantage of détente to establish friendly Western contacts would be rebuked or persecuted like those Soviet officers who worked with the allies during the Second World War. In the new communist states—for example in France, Italy, and the Third World—the "alienated classes" would be reeducated. Show trials of "imperialist agents" would be staged. Action would be taken against nationalist and social democratic leaders, party activists, former civil servants, officers, and priests. The last vestiges of private enterprise and ownership would be obliterated. Nationalization of industry, finance, and agriculture would be completed. In fact, all the totalitarian features familiar from the early stages of the Soviet revolution and the postwar Stalinist years in Eastern Europe might be expected to reappear, especially in those countries newly won for communism. Unchallenged and unchallengeable, a true communist monolith would dominate the world.[367]

Christopher Story, a highly credible British author who advised the government on intelligence and economic matters, assisted Golitsyn in publishing his second book, *The Perestroika Deception: The World's Slide Towards the "Second October Revolution,"* in 1995.[368] Like Angleton, Story championed Golitsyn. "Golitsyn is probably the most important Soviet defector ever to have reached the West," Story said in a 1995 interview. "The reason for this is that he revealed the details of a long-range deception strategy of which the West previously had no knowledge."[369] *The Perestroika Deception* is a compilation of memoranda Golitsyn wrote for the CIA. Leonid Brezhnev first proposed the policy of perestroika, or "restructuring" in English. During the administration of President George H. W. Bush, Mikhail Gorbachev implemented the policy represented to the West as the "liberalization" of Communism in Russia. Golitsyn consistently warned the CIA that the perestroika was a central strategy in the deception campaign Shelepin designed in his dozens of memoranda to the CIA.

In August 1985, Golitsyn wrote a memo to the CIA entitled "The Danger for the West: An Assessment of the Rise of Mikhail Gorbachev, the Role of 'Liberalization' in Soviet Strategy, and Its Grave Implications for the West." In that memo, he warned that the Soviet policy of liberalization had been in preparation for the past two decades under the direction of Shelepin and Yuri Andropov, the Soviet leader who followed the eighteen-year rule of Brezhnev, holding power from November 1982 until his death in February 1984. Gorbachev assumed control in March 1985. "Gorbachev was selected as the 'new generation' representative because of his decisiveness, his demeanor and, above all, because he has been well groomed for implementing the 'liberalization strategy,'" Golitsyn wrote in the month Gorbachev came to power. "Another factor favoring his selection was his non-involvement in Stalin's repression."[370] In the same memo, Golitsyn warned there were no valid grounds for favorable illusions or any euphoria in the West over Gorbachev's appointment and the coming "liberalization." He stressed the "liberalization" would be initiated, guided, and controlled by the KGB and the Russian Communist Party apparatus.[371] In a memo he wrote to the CIA in September 1988, Golitsyn cautioned the following: "By emphasizing the alleged instability of Gorbachev's position and the fragility of 'perestroika,' the operations are designed to induce an American underestimate of Soviet political strength, to create a favorable climate for Gorbachev's negotiations with American leaders and to entice them into adopting an ultimately suicidal policy of support for and engagement in 'perestroika.'"[372]

Author Mark Riebling, in his 1994 book *Wedge: The Secret War between the FBI and CIA*, devoted considerable attention to the controversy Golitsyn's defection and subsequent revelations caused within both the CIA and FBI. Riebling pointed out that in 1982, Golitsyn submitted a top-secret manuscript to the CIA in which he anticipated the end of Gorbachev's rule. In the memo, Golitsyn made nearly two hundred detailed predictions specifying the nature of the disinformation campaign he knew the KGB was about to launch.[373] That memo, transformed into book form, is the book Golitsyn published in 1984, *New Lies for Old*. Golitsyn predicted Brezhnev would be followed by "a younger man with a more liberal image," who would initiate "changes that would have been beyond the imagination of Marx or the practical reach of Lenin and unthinkable to Stalin."[374] He explained that the coming liberalization "would be spectacular and impressive. Formal pronouncements might be made about a reduction in the Communist Party's role; its monopoly would be apparently curtailed."[375] He foresaw that the "KGB would be reformed. Dissidents at home would be amnestied; those in exile abroad would be allowed to take up positions in the government. Sakharov might be included in some capacity in the government."[376] He envisioned that political clubs "would be opened to nonmembers of the Communist party. Leading dissidents might form one or more alternative political parties. Censorship would be relaxed; controversial books, plays, films, and art would be published, performed, and exhibited."[377] He even anticipated that the "demolition of the Berlin Wall might even be contemplated."[378]

In total, Riebling counted 194 predictions Golitsyn made in 1982. Of these, Riebling noted 46 were not falsifiable in 1994 when his book *Wedge* went to press. Of Golitsyn's falsifiable predictions, Riebling reported that 139 of 148 had been fulfilled by the end of 1993 for an accuracy rate of nearly 94 percent. Among Golitsyn's fulfilled predictions, Riebling included foreseeing correctly the reemergence of Solidarity in Poland, the creation of a newly independent government in Romania, and a Soviet repudiation of the Afghanistan invasion.[379] Riebling noted that "Golitsyn's case was deductive, based on pattern-recognition and abstract principles; he had no transcript of a secret session in which Gorbachov said he would do these things."[380] Thus, Riebling concluded that many within the CIA and the FBI, in general, refused to take Golitsyn's predictions seriously. Riebling commented that questions about Golitsyn limited Angleton's ability to prove his suspicions about KGB's penetration of a mole into the CIA, false defectors, and possible KGB complicity in the JFK assassination. "The result had been an increase in FBI-CIA tensions, an interagency feud over Golitsyn, a decrease in Angleton's popularity at both agencies, the decentralization of his CI [counterintelligence] staff, and then his outright dismissal," Riebling wrote.[381] He concluded that the CIA fell short in predicting Gorbachev's reforms because "the American intelligence community had chosen not to listen."[382] Yet, given the accuracy of Golitsyn's predictions, we would be ill-advised today to discount his warnings. Golitsyn insisted that perestroika was a KGB-devised disinformation campaign designed to deceive the West and destroy the United States by removing the fear of Soviet Russia as an enemy.

Yuri Bezmenov and the Four Stages of Ideological Subversion

Born in 1939, Yuri Bezmenov grew up in Stalinist Russia during World War II. His father was an officer of the general staff of the Soviet army, responsible for the inspection of Soviet military forces stationed on foreign soil in places like Mongolia, Cuba, and various Eastern European countries. When he was seventeen, Bezmenov entered the Institute of Oriental Languages, a part of Moscow State University under the KGB's direction and control. In 1963, he spent two years in India working as a public relations officer for Soviet Refineries Constructions.

In 1965, Bezmenov was called back to Moscow, where he began working as a Soviet journalist for RIA Novosti, a Russian state-owned news agency. He worked out of the Soviet embassy in that job, disseminating KGB propaganda through RIA Novosti. In 1970, Russian KGB officer Bezmenov defected to the West through Canada. In 1984, he published a book, *Love Letter to America*,[383] under the pen name of Tomas David Schuman. In that book, Bezmenov outlined the four stages the KGB utilized as techniques of ideological subversion. In the United States, Bezmenov gave a series of lectures and interviews in which he explained the four stages of a Marxist subversion of a country.[384] While Bezmenov was fairly consistent in how he described the four stages in his book and various lectures, he tended to blur some lines, at times seeming to blend together various of the four stages. Presented here is a synthesis of Bezmenov's four stages constructed so as to convey his meaning more precisely.

Stage One: Demoralization

The first stage involves demoralizing the target society with psychological warfare designed to attack the moral fiber of the population. Ideological subversion messages make the target country's population feel guilty for divisive issues like racial discrimination and unequal rights for women. Attacks on God and the family bring into question the fundamental social structures and beliefs that traditionally have given people purpose through a foundation of moral values that promote productive and fulfilling lifestyles. Bezmenov used "demoralization" in two subtly different ways. First, a population questioning its values induces confusion and a sense of unease. Second, a demoralized population becomes "de-moral" in that traditional values are challenged and abandoned. In the following quotes, Bezmenov explained the various ideological subversion techniques the KGB uses to demoralize countries like the United States.

- "Let's start with the first stage of Demoralization. It takes about 15 to 20 years to demoralize a nation. Why that many (or few)? Simple: this is the minimum number of years needed to 'educate' one generation of students in a target country (America, for example) and expose them to the ideology of the subverter."[385]
- It takes about fifteen to twenty years to demoralize a nation, the minimum number of years needed to "educate" one generation of students in a target country. "To be successful, the process of subversion at the stage of demoralization must be always and only a two-way street, which means that the target nation must be made a recipient—passive or active—of the ideas of the subverter."[386] In other words, Marxism-Leninism ideology is being pumped

into at least three generations of American students without being challenged. (You can see the result in) most of the people who graduated in the '60s. Drop-outs or half-baked intellectuals are now occupying the positions of power in the government, civil service, business, mass media, and educational system. You are stuck with them. You cannot change their mind even if you expose them to authentic information.

- "This process has many names: psychological warfare, ideological aggression, propaganda warfare, etc. The KGB calls it 'Active Measures,' which are more important and dangerous than classic espionage—James Bond style.[387] The purpose of this process is to change your perception of reality to such an extent, that even despite an abundance of information and evidence about the danger of Communism, you are unable to come to sensible conclusions in your own interests and in the interests of your nation. One of the main tactics in this process is to develop, establish and consistently enforce a set of 'double standards.'"
- "The main emphasis of the KGB is not in the area of intelligence at all…only about 15% of time, money, and manpower is spent on espionage as such. The other 85% is a slow process, which we call either ideological subversion…. What it basically means is to change the perception of reality of every American, to such an extent, that despite the abundance of information, no one is able to come to sensible conclusions."[388]
- "A person who was demoralized is unable to assess true information. The facts tell nothing to him. Even if I shower him with information with the authentic proof, with documents, with pictures, even if I take him by force to the Soviet Union and show him [a] concentration camp, he will refuse to believe it, until he is going to receive a kick in his fat bottom."[389]
- "To demoralize America's protective forces it is enough to make your kids call the police 'pigs' and 'fascists' for a decade, disband police agencies watching over subverters and radicals by calling them 'spies' (that is exactly what [the] American Union of Civil Liberties [ACLU] did), stage campaign after campaign of discreditation and 'investigations' of the 'wrongdoings' of the police, and in 20 years you arrive at the present situation, when the majority of civilian population of this nation is virtually without

civil laws or protection from murderers, lunatics, criminals, etc. Can you now expect your police and civil authorities to protect you and your family in case of terrorist attack or a major civil disturbance?"[390]

- "Marxist-Leninist ideology coated in various indigenous 'social theories' have greatly contributed to the process of American family break-up. The trend recently is changing in the opposite direction, but many generations of Americans, brought up in broken families, are already adults lacking one of the most vital qualities for the survival of a nation—loyalty. A child who has not learned to be loyal to his family will hardly make a loyal citizen. Such [a] child may grow into [an] adult who is loyal to the State though. The USSR example is rather revealing in this case."[391]
- "In the struggle for the 'final victory of Communism,' the goal of the subverter is to substitute, as slowly and painlessly as possible, the concept of loyalty for nation with loyalty to the 'Big Brother' welfare state, who gives everything and is able to take everything, including personal freedom—from every citizen. If that objective is successfully achieved, the subverter does not need any nuclear warheads and tanks and may not even need the physical military invasion. All that will be needed is to 'elect' a 'progressive thinking' president who will be voted to power by Americans, who have been addicted to welfare and 'security' as defined by Soviet [Marxist] subverters."[392]
- "Racial and ethnic interrelations is one of the most vulnerable areas for demoralization. There is not a single Communist country where racial groups are 'equal' and enjoy as much freedom to develop themselves culturally and economically as in America. Actually, there are not too many 'capitalist' countries where ethnic minorities have it as good as in the USA. I have been to many countries of the world and I can state to you, my dear Americans, that your society is the least discriminatory. The Communist 'solution' for racial problem(s) is 'final': they simply murder those who are different and stubbornly insist on remaining silent."[393]

Stage Two: Destabilization

Once the target population has been demoralized, the expectation is that people will implement destructive policies, such as defunding the police. These ill-conceived policies increase crime, people feel less secure, and society becomes less economically productive. Society becomes destabilized because demoralized populations act irrationally. Counterproductive public policies cause mass fear and economic misery as the country loses its psychological sense of balance. Again, Bezmenov explained as follows:

- "Here the efforts of [the] subverter narrow down to the 'essentials': the internal power structures of a target nation; the nation's foreign relations; economy and 'social fiber.' If the preceding stage of *demoralization* is successful, the subverter no longer has to bother about your ideas and your life. Now he gets to the 'spinal cord' of your country and helps *you* to bring your own society into the state of *destabilization*. That may take from 2 to 5 years, depending on the maturity of a nation and its ability to mobilize for resistance."[394]
- "The first symptom of instability is expressed as the desire of the population to bring to power those politicians and parties who are charismatic, act like good 'caretakers' and promise more 'security'—not from external and foreign enemies, but rather, job 'security,' 'free' social services and other 'pleasure strokes' provided by 'Big Brother.' By concentrating the attention of a nation on short-term solutions and 'improvements,' such irresponsible politicians simply procrastinate on facing 'the moment of truth,' when the nation will have to pay a much higher price for the main and basic problem—bringing [the] country back to stability and restoring the moral fiber."[395]

Stage Three: Crisis

A destabilized society is open to violent, revolutionary anarchy, as evidenced in the United States by groups like Black Lives Matter and Antifa. Leftist radicals begin operating in the open, with the full support of mass media as they take over positions in communities as law enforcement prosecutors, city councils, and boards of education. On the state and national scene, neo-Marxists and Maoists come forward with "progressive" policies that further throw the society into chaos, as demonstrated by the increasing use of mail-in voting and the efforts to characterize voter ID requirements as techniques designed to suppress minority voting. Bezmenov pointed to Central American countries racked by revolutionary violence and coup d'états as radical activists take over governmental positions and authorize emergency powers for themselves as the society moves toward civil war. Again, Bezmenov explained as follows:

- "It may take only 2 to 6 months, to bring America to the same situation which now exists South of the border in Central America."[396]
- "At this third stage of subversion, you will have all your American 'radicals' and Soviet 'sleeper' agents springing into action, trying to 'seize power as quickly and ruthlessly as possible."[397]
- "If all the previous stages of Soviet subversion have been successfully completed by that time, most Americans will be so totally confused that they may even *welcome* some 'strong' leaders who 'know how to talk to the Russians.' Chances are these leaders will be elected and given almost unlimited 'emergency powers.'"[398]
- "A forceful change of the U.S. system may or may not be accomplished through a civil war or internal revolution, and a physical *military* invasion by the USSR may not even have to take place at all. But change it will be, and rather a drastic one, with all the familiar attributes of Soviet 'progress' being instituted such as *nationalization* of vital industries, the reduction of the 'private sector' of the economy to the bare minimum, the redistribution of wealth and a massive propaganda campaign by the newly 'elected' government to 'explain' and justify the reforms."[399]

Stage Four: Normalization

In stage four, normalization, the target society capitulates to Communism. The Russian military may even be called into the target nation to reintroduce strict law and order. The fourth stage assumes the new Communist government has nationalized vital industries, reduced the economy's private sector to a minimum, redistributed wealth, and eliminated private property. The newly "elected" Communist government has also engaged in a massive propaganda effort to explain and justify progressive reforms. Now, in the fourth stage, a submissive population submits to totalitarian subjugation to the new world order of Marx, Lenin, and Mao. Bezmenov explained as follows:

- "This is when my dear friends, you will start seeing 'friendly' Soviet soldiers in the streets of our cities working together with American soldiers and the 'new' police force to 'restore law and order.' Very soon your yesterday's American socialist radicals and *do-gooders* who were working hard to bring 'progress' to their own country will find themselves *in prisons* and hastily built concentration camps. Many of them will be *executed*, quietly or publicly. Why? Simple: The Soviet 'liberators' will have no further use for the 'disturbers.' The 'useful idiots' will have completed their work. From then on, the New Order will need *stability* and *new morality*. No more 'grass roots' movements. No more criticism of the State. The Press will obediently censor itself. In fact, this censorship is already existing *now*, imposed by the so-called U.S. 'liberals' and socialist do-gooders. You will now have the opportunity to 'enjoy' the same life as the Vietnamese, Cambodians, Angolans, and Nicaraguans, betrayed by you enjoy *now*. This state of social '*normalization*' may last forever, that is—your lifetime and the lifetimes of you[r] children and grandchildren."[400]

Bezmenov's expertise with the KGB was in propaganda. Thus, the most convincingly elaborated of his four stages of ideological subversion is the first stage, involving what he conceptualized as "demoralizing" the population. The value for the discussion in this chapter of Bezmenov's analysis is that he conceptualized ideological subversion as a psychological process of political warfare. There is one additional Bezmenov quotation that merits consideration:

> In the files were people who were doomed to execution, there were names of pro-Soviet journalists with whom I was personally friendly. [Pro Soviet?] Yes, they were idealistically minded leftists who made several visits to the USSR. And yet the KGB decided that come revolution or drastic changes in political structure...they will have to go. [Why?] Because they know too much. Simply, because, you see, the useful idiots, the leftists who are idealistically believing in the beauty of Soviet Socialist or Communist or whatever system, when they get disillusioned, they become the worst enemies... No, they serve purpose only at the stage of destabilization of a nation. For example, your leftists in the United States, all these professors and these beautiful civil rights

> defenders, they are instrumental in the process of subversion only to destabilize a nation. When their job is completed, they are not needed anymore. They know too much. Some of them, when they get disillusioned, when they see that Marxist-Leninist come to power. Obviously, they get offended, they think that they will come to power. That will never happen, of course. They will be lined up against a wall and shot.[401]

Suppose there was any doubt that neo-Marxists and cultural Maoists who engage in political warfare have lost their belief in God. In that case, Bezmenov's quotations make clear that winning takes the place of morals in their secular religion where deception and lying become standard methods to propagate and proselytize their radical Left "truth-telling" narratives. His quotations also clarify that Communists cannot win until they first destroy. Communists demonstrated in the twentieth century that when they gain power, what follows is economic ruin, mass starvation, genocide, loss of individual freedom, and repression of dissent. These outcomes should not be a surprise. The momentum of a political movement that comes to power through deception designed to produce demoralization, destabilization, and crisis does not suddenly transform into goodness and light once the insurgency succeeds.

Stalin and Hitler's Rise to Power

Another Russian defector has helped illuminate the true nature of Communism. Vladimir Bogdanovich Rezun, known in the West by his pen name, Viktor Suvorov, defected to the United Kingdom in 1978. His father, a committed Bolshevik born in Ukraine, fought for the Soviet army in World War II. Suvorov considers himself Ukrainian even though his mother was Russian and he was born in Barabash, a small rural town in western Russia near the Sea of Japan. In 1968, Suvorov graduated from the Frunze High Command Army School in Kiev. He pointed out that the military school in Kiev trained intelligence operatives. Instead of four years, it took Suvorov three, and he graduated with honors. He served as a tank platoon commander in the Soviet army, participating in the 1968 Soviet invasion of Czechoslovakia. In 1970, the GRU, the military intelligence counterpart to the KGB, recruited him. The Soviet army sent him to study at the Soviet Army Academy, the top-secret military academy in the Soviet Union. After graduation, he went to Geneva, which he described as "the world capital of espionage."[402] In Geneva, he served as attaché of the USSR Permanent Mission to the United Nations. Despite that official title, Suvorov spent four years in Geneva processing intelligence information. After his defection, now residing in the United Kingdom, Suvorov wrote a series of very influential books exposing the true nature of Stalin and Communism in World War II.

Suvorov broke on the international scene in 1988, with the publication in France of his first book, *Icebreaker: Who Started the Second World War?*[403] Almost immediately, the book became an international sensation over Suvorov's controversial contention that Stalin would have invaded Hitler in 1941 or 1942 if Hitler had not first invaded Russia. He maintained that Stalin wanted Hitler to destroy capitalism in Europe by starting a world war amongst the Western nations and argued that Stalin saw Hitler as an "icebreaker" clearing the way for world Communism.[404] Although the English edition of *Icebreaker*, published in London in 1990, quickly sold out, the publisher, for reasons never explained to Suvorov, refused to print further editions. Suvorov's thesis was so damaging to Stalin's reputation and the future of Communism as a world revolutionary movement that *Icebreaker* prompted a massive counterintelligence effort by Moscow to suppress the book. Suvorov explained as follows:

> It quickly became apparent that the Western academic community was as reluctant as the Communist propaganda apparatus to accept my new interpretation of the cause of World War II. Instead of confronting my arguments the way the Soviets did, my Western opponents chose a different kind of confrontation—silence.[405]

Despite the cold reception Western media and academics gave Suvorov, he persisted, writing several books that prefigured a revision of World War II history after opening various previously classified Russian archives. "The primary reason for my decision to defect to the West in 1978 was to make my discoveries available to the Russian people and the world public," he wrote. The secret he brought to the United Kingdom was that "the Soviet version of the history of World War II was a lie and concealed the USSR's responsibility for planning the start of the war."[406]

Particularly relevant to the discussion in this chapter is an argument Suvorov made in his 2008 book, *The Chief Culprit: Stalin's Grand Design to Start World War II*, about the role Stalin played in 1932–1933, the years Hitler rose to power as chancellor in Germany. Suvorov began by stressing that Hitler and Stalin were both leftists. Suvorov made this point in the first paragraph of the preface to *The Chief Culprit*:

> Hitler had a red flag. And Stalin had a red flag. Hitler ruled in the name of the workers' class, his party was called the workers' party. Stalin also ruled in the name of the workers' class; his power system officially bore the title of "dictatorship of the proletariat." Hitler hated democracy and struggled against it. Stalin hated democracy and struggled against it. Hitler was building socialism. And Stalin was building socialism. Under the title of socialism Hitler saw a classless society. And Stalin, under the title of socialism, saw a classless society. In the midst of the classless society built by Hitler, and in that built by Stalin, flourished slavery in the truest sense of the word.[407]

One of the most significant distortions of political history is the Left's characterization of fascism as a political ideology and movement on the political Right. This misunderstanding pervades Western universities and journalism. In German, the Nazi party was named Nationalsozialistische Deutsche Arbeiterpartei (NSDAP), translated into English as the National Socialist German Workers' Party. Hitler never disavowed being a socialist modeled after Mussolini.[408]

Before World War I, Mussolini began his career as a journalist member of the Italian Socialist Party (PSI), writing for the Italian socialist newspaper *Avanti!* He coined the term "fascist" in 1919 to describe his socialist movement in Italy. In 1921, Mussolini formed the Partito Nazionale Fascista (in English, "National Fascist Party"). The term "fascist" derived from a symbol of ancient imperial Rome, formed by an ax, with its blade protruding, surrounded by a bundle of rods. The words fascist and fascism derive from *fascis*, a third declension Latin noun meaning "bundle."[409] Mussolini aspired to remake Italy into the glory of the ancient Roman imperial empire. Hitler modeled the rise of the Nazi party in Germany to the rise of Mussolini and his Italian Fascist Party.[410]

Hitler and the NSDAP in Germany initially called themselves "National Socialists," not "Nazis." Joseph Goebbels first used the term "Nazi" in 1926, in a publication called *Der Nazi-Sozi* [*The Nazi-Sozi*], used as an abbreviation of "National Socialism."[411] Fascism and communism are both totalitarian ideologies and movements that began on the political Left. But characterizing any historical political party or political movement on a Left-to-Right spectrum is a difficult exercise. In popular parlance, "liberal" was the common designation of the political Left in the United States, a term that has been increasingly replaced with the more politically acceptable term "progressive." In traditional political philosophy, however, "liberalism" is a conservative ideology that values the rights of citizens and the consent of the governed. British philosophers Thomas Hobbes (1588–1679) and John Locke (1632–1704) are commonly regarded as the "fathers of liberalism."[412]

In 1932, Hitler's National Socialists' Workers Party faced a deep financial crisis. Here is how Suvorov explained the predicament:

> Goebbels wrote in his diary: "All hope has disappeared.... There is not a pfennig in our cash boxes.... Nobody gives us credit.... We are on our last breath." Goebbels's entry on December 23, 1932, said: "I am overwhelmed by a terrible feeling of loneliness, which borders on a sense of total loss! The year 1932 was a sequence of one misfortune after another. It should be erased completely.... We have no prospects, no hopes left." That terrible position the Nazis found themselves in was no secret to outside observers. By New Year's Eve, the influential newspaper *Frankfurter Zeitung* was already rejoicing at the "disintegration of the NSDAP myth." Harold Laski, one of the leading intellectuals of the English left, was assured that: "The day when the National Socialists presented a lethal danger has passed.... If we discount chance, it is not so improbable that Hitler will finish his career as an old man in some Bavarian village, telling tales to his friends in the evenings in some beer hall, about how he once almost orchestrated a takeover in the German Reich."[413]

Suvorov noted that at the end of 1932, Hitler's time was up, and despite being the most popular political figure in Germany, he was deep in debt and running out of money. "German National Socialism faced doom until Hitler was saved by Stalin," Suvorov explained. "Comrade Stalin did not just save Hitler; he handed him the keys to power."[414] In the German federal election held on November 6, 1932, the NSDAP got 11,705,000 votes, compared to 7,231,000 votes for the Socialist Democrats and 5,971,000 for the Communist Party. Hitler won the election, but the NSDAP did not have the absolute majority required to take power. Combined, the Social Democrats and Communist Party had more votes.

Suvorov explained that Germany's fate was in the hands of the Communist Party in this situation. "If the Communists sided with the Social Democrats, Nazism would perish and never again resurface," he wrote. "If the Communists turned against the Social Democrats, Social Democracy would crumble."[415] Suvorov correctly pointed out that for the Communists, siding with the Social Democrats would mean defeating Hitler. For the Communist Party, siding with the Social Democrats was a very appealing option because siding with them would raise the Communist Party to a position of sharing power. If the Communist Party took the second option and went against the Social Democrats, Hitler would take power. "The consequences of such a move were very predictable: Hitler, having come to power, would throw both Social Democrats and Communists into concentration camps," Suvorov continued. "If the German Communists went against the Social Democrats, they would be sentencing to death both themselves and the Social Democrats."[416] Stalin ordered the German Communists to take the second option, refusing to form a bloc with the Social Democrats.

Suvorov noted the German Communists kept repeating, after their Moscow masters, the disinformation that Social Democrats were even more dangerous than the Nazis. Suvorov explained as follows:

> German Communists leaders told the workers: We are Communists, struggling against capitalism and fascism, while the Social Democrats are acting as protectors of capitalism, and are becoming de facto allies of the fascists. Therefore, the Social Democrats are really nothing more than a "left wing" of fascism, or they are "social fascists," a party which conducts a policy of "hidden fascism" that is more dangerous than Nazi policy. The peace-loving policy of the Social Democrats prevents war; therefore it prevents revolution and, ultimately, prevents the victory of the Working Class, while the Nazi policy enhances the chances for war and revolution and, ultimately, the victory of the Working Class.[417]

Suvorov commented that from this "bizarre dialectic," the German Communists concluded that Hitler's party had to carry out their main attack on the Social Democrats since they were the most dangerous enemy, which "still retained some influence over the worker class and hindered an effective war on capitalism."[418] Suvorov stressed that Hitler came to power "as a result of this perverted ideological mind game."[419] He observed that the German Communists should have joined a coalition with the Social Democrats out of an instinct for self-preparation. But "Stalin intervened and opened the way for Hitler."[420]

Once the Nazis came to power, Stalin worked tirelessly to push Hitler into war. Stalin understood that a war between Germany and democratic Europe had issued Hitler a death sentence, but only after England, France, and Germany exhausted their economic capital and their strength as they had done in World War I. "The struggle between Hitler and the Western democracies would create the moment for a 'mighty strike' from the East and bring forth world revolution on the bayonets of the Red Army," Suvorov wrote, elucidating Stalin's calculations.[421] In his earlier book, *Icebreaker*, Suvorov detailed that Lenin saw the utility of the capitalist nations going to war to exhaust their resources during World War I. Still, Lenin also understood a second world war in Europe. "Perhaps I am mistaken, but having read much of what Hitler wrote, I have certainly found no indications that in 1916 Adolf Schickelgruber [Hitler] was dreaming of the Second World War," Suvorov wrote. "But Lenin was. What is more, he was laying down the need for such a war as a theoretical base for the building of socialism throughout the world.[422] Suvorov stressed that "for Lenin, as for Marx, world revolution remained the guiding star." Lenin's calculation in 1918 was precisely the same as Stalin's in 1939. Here is how Suvorov summed up the calculation Stalin shared with Lenin: "Let Germany fight in the West, let Germany and the Western allies exhaust themselves one after the other to the greatest extent possible; we ourselves shall help Germany at any price to exhaust herself to the very limit, and then act."[423] In 1932–1933, Stalin was willing to sacrifice the German Communist Party if it meant Germany would begin World War II in the West.

Golitsyn warned the West that the political logic derived from Communism was fundamentally different than calculations that derived from liberal political philosophy and capitalism. In his foreword to *The Perestroika Deception*, Golitsyn explained the intrinsic long-term thinking of Communist strategy. He explained the distinction as follows:

> There is a marked difference between the American and the Communist use of the term "strategy." Americans tend to think of strategy in short-range terms in relation to presidential election campaigns, in football or baseball games or in such instances as the "strategy of stone-walling" during the Watergate investigations. For Russian Communists on the other hand, strategy is a grand design or general Party line which governs the Party's actions over a long period and contains one or more special maneuvers designed to help the Party achieve its ultimate objectives—the seizure of power in Russia in 1917, the subsequent expansion of the Communist camp and the final world-wide victory of Communism.[424]

In the buildup to World War II, Stalin's calculations clarify that he was willing to sacrifice the Russian-supported Communist Party in Germany. Why? Because Stalin aimed to start World War II, even though he realized after the disaster of World War I that millions of Russians would die in a second such global conflict. His goal was to destroy the capitalist West as a prelude to ushering in the worldwide Communist revolution that he and Lenin believed was inevitable. Golitsyn understood, like the ancient Chinese general Sun Tzu, that disinformation is not to be avoided because deception is morally wrong or evil. He began *The Perestroika Deception* by quoting Sun Tzu's admonition: "All warfare is based on deception."[425]

But to return to Henry Kissinger's study of Metternich that we discussed in the previous chapter, Russia is also a nation-state with a sphere of influence extending over Eastern Europe and parts of Asia, including Mongolia. China is a nation-state. While China does not contend with Russia's ambitions over Ukraine, Russia does not compete with China's ambitions over Taiwan. While world government is an ancient ambition extending back to Alexander the Great and Julius Caesar, no nation yet in human history has succeeded with the aspiration. If Golitsyn is correct that China and Russia cooperate today to perpetuate the Perestroika deception, which of the two governments is ultimately in control after the anticipated worldwide Communist revolution happens? Or, like Stalin in 1932–1933, calculated to cause the ultimate demise of Hitler, does Vladmir Putin plan Xi Jinping's demise, or is Xi planning Putin's demise? As Golitsyn understood all too well, the game of deception politics is tricky. We will continue to ask: Does Putin's endgame include a disinformation campaign that Russia is concurrently running on China? Or does Xi's endgame turn on a disinformation campaign that he may be running concurrently on Putin?

Conclusion: An American Communist Dies in Moscow

Let's conclude this chapter by first examining William Z. Foster's 1949 book *The Twilight of World Capitalism*. In this book, Foster expressed absolute certainty that capitalism would be destroyed. But he died in 1961 with his dream unfulfilled, lying in a Moscow hospital, avoiding Smith Act prosecution in the United States only by his prolonged illness. He ended his life in Moscow in 1961, with his dream unfulfilled. "As Marx and Engels forecast a century ago, world capitalism is doomed," he wrote in 1949. "Once progressive, it has now become, because of its own inner contradictions, a reactionary social system, a cancer on the body of humanity."[426] He insisted that capitalism is "historically slated to go, and go it will, regardless of its desperate struggles to survive."[427] He was confident "the elimination of world capitalism and the establishment of socialism" were "the broad steps needed to enable humanity to pass on to higher levels of civilization."[428] Foster left no doubt about what he saw as our inevitable future. He wrote:

> It will be a great day when mankind can finally write "The End" to the capitalist system. The peoples of the earth, with the workers in the lead, will not fail to accomplish this historic task.[429]

Mao's quotation from 1949, cited at the start of this chapter, demonstrates that he shared Foster's confidence that Communism would inevitably triumph over capitalism.

In 1949, on his way to defeating the nationalists in China and Foster leading the fight for Communism in America, Mao believed that the Hegelian dialectic was a scientific law that would replace the necessity for religion. "A profound development in recent decades has been the accelerated decline of religion," Foster wrote in his 1949 book. "This is all tied in with the developing decay of the world capitalist system."[430] Foster once again explained the logic behind these statements in terms of the Hegelian dialectic. He continued:

> Primitive man found the source of his religion in his crude efforts to understand the world, to explain his own existence, and to work out a moral code to govern himself. Religion undertook to answer these deep questions for him with its metaphysical explanations. But as man's knowledge, eventually grown into science, advanced, his need for religion with its "miracles" and "revelations," has progressively diminished. Consequently, his gods and devils, his heavens and hells have tended to retreat into the psychological distance, not without making a maximum resistance, however. They have sunk faster and faster into the vague, the generalized, and the remote.[431]

Foster was confident that in the rational working out of history, the need for religion would soon pass from the human scene. He continued:

> Eventually, man, in his intellectual advance, will arrive at a fully scientific world, in which he will have a good working knowledge of the universe and of himself, and then, accordingly, he will finally altogether dispense with his gods and their imaginary eternal rewards and punishment.

Foster and Mao were both seduced by the certainty that resides within the logic of the Hegelian dialectic. As we will see in the next chapter, Hegel believed contradictions in the present social, political, and economic system inevitably must lead to the downfall of that system. Hegel believed that history moves along a trajectory leading to human utopia on earth. Thus, as Hegelians, Foster and Mao both aimed to destroy capitalism to achieve the next higher social, political, and economic system, namely socialism. The seductive power of the Hegelian dialectic has again bewitched the neo-Marxist radical Left in the United States. Leftist radicals believe today as a matter of secular faith that today's neo-Marist revolution will bring forth a glorious new world order, not the misery Communism has caused wherever Communists have gained power.

CHAPTER 3

The Seductive Logic of the Hegelian Dialectic

I almost hesitate to continue—the spectacle of a nihilist stripping himself to the nude is embarrassing. For Hegel betrays in so many words that being a man is not enough for him; and as he cannot be the divine Lord of history himself, he is going to achieve Herrschaft *[domination] as the sorcerer who will conjure up an image of history—a shape, a ghost—that is meant to eclipse the history of God's making.*

—**Eric Voegelin**, "On Hegel—A Study in Sorcery," 1972[432]

PROBING TO FIND THE ORIGIN of Marx's dialectical materialism, we are led to Hegel. Searching to find the source of Hegel's dialectic, we are led to Immanuel Kant. Thus, we start this chapter by examining how Kant's concepts of pure reason and the categorical imperative led him to envision the unfolding of history into perpetual peace.

Kant was a German philosopher born in Königsberg on April 22, 1724. At that time Königsberg was the capital of East Prussia, and the dominant language was German. He was raised by a family practicing a form of evangelical Lutheranism called Pietism. He attended college at the University of Königsberg, known as the Albertina, where he ultimately returned to teach philosophy until he retired in 1796 at the age of seventy-two. In his retirement, Kant displayed unmistakable signs of mental decline. He died on February 12, 1804, just shy of his eightieth birthday.[433] We will not attempt here an exhaustive discussion of Kant's many writings. Rather, we are going to focus on Kant's writings and ideas that directly influenced Hegel.

Kant and Transcendental Knowledge

Kant began the *Critique of Pure Reason* (initially published in 1781, revised in 1787)[434] with a discussion of human experience fundamental to Kant's metaphysics, phenomenology, and moral philosophy. "Experience is without doubt the first product that our understanding brings forth as it works on the raw material of sensible sensations," he wrote as the first sentence to his introduction, section 1, entitled "The Idea of Transcendental Philosophy."[435] Kant started by puzzling how we know anything, and he acknowledged that experience is the starting point for understanding. But he wrote the *Critique of Pure Reason* essentially to refute empiricists like Scottish philosopher David Hume (1711–1776), who insisted that all human knowledge is subjective because what we know is a function of what we experience. Everyone has unique senses and unique experiences. But Kant found the empiricist argument impossible to accept. If all human knowledge is subjective, the scientific endeavor of Isaac Newton's mathematical physics would be impossible.

In this first paragraph, Kant quickly added that experience is not all that informs our understanding. He acknowledged that experience tells us "what is" but objected that experience can never tell us "that it must necessarily be thus and not otherwise."[436] Thus, Kant concluded that experience "gives us no true universality...which is so desirous of this kind of cognitions, is more stimulated than satisfied by it." Kant's metaphysics, phenomenology, and moral philosophy are predicated on his premise that the human consciousness functions through a higher innate knowledge of external reality that transcends our sensory experience. In other words, Kant contended human reason and understanding must serve to transcend experience with another method of knowing. He called this higher way of knowing "*a priori* cognitions," and he explained as follows:

> Now such universal cognitions, which at the same time have the character of inner necessity, must be clear and certain for themselves, independently of experience; hence one calls them *a priori* cognitions: whereas that which is merely borrowed from experience is, as it is put, cognized only *a posteriori*, or empirically.[437]

In his *Critique of Pure Reason*, Kant's jumping-off point reminds us of Plato's idealism and his discussion of "ideas" or "forms." In Book VII of the *Republic*, Plato explained his concept through the allegory of the cave. In that dialogue, Plato had Socrates introduce the cave allegory as follows:

> See human beings as though they were in an underground cavelike dwelling with its entrance, a long one, open to the light across the whole width of the cave. They are in it from childhood with their legs and necks in bonds so that they are fixed, seeing only in front of them, unable because of the bond to turn their heads all the way around. The light is from a fire burning far above and behind them. Between the fire and the prisoners there is a road above, along which see a wall, built like the partitions puppet-handlers set up in front of the human beings and over which they show the puppets.[438]

Socrates continued:

> Then also see along this wall human beings carrying all sorts of artifacts, which project above the wall, and statues of men and other animals wrought from stone, wood, and every kind of material; as is to be expected, some of the carriers utter sounds while others are silent.[439]

Kant, like Plato, assumed there was an understanding of the sensory experience that transcends the appearances we perceive. He explained this as a priori experience (i.e., the knowledge that precedes experience), permitting us to understand the experience in generalizable terms. Let's use René Descartes's image of a tree falling in the forest to make the point. If we see and hear the tree fall, we understand what we saw because we have an idea of what trees are, what death and decay are, and how the loud sound we hear connects to the impact the tree makes hitting the ground.

In the subsequent paragraphs of the introduction, Kant expanded this idea to suggest our a priori knowledge is different from experiential knowledge because we derive from our experience universal ideas and propositions about how things in the world have to be. He expressed this as follows:

> For if one removes from our experiences everything that belongs to the senses, there still remain certain original concepts and the judgments generated from them, which must have arisen entirely *a priori*, independently of experience, because they make one able to say more about the objects that appear to the senses than mere experience would teach, or at least make one believe that one can say this, and make assertions

> contain true universality and strict necessity, the likes of which merely empirical cognition can never afford.[440]

For Kant, this a priori knowledge is all-important because for human reason to understand the world, it demands more than a continuous sequence of sensory experiences. The human ability to reason involves making order out of what we experience. To him, discerning order from sensation demands comprehending how things have to be and how things could be different. He acknowledged his debt to Plato. "Likewise, Plato abandoned the world of the senses because it posed so many hindrances for the understanding and dared to go beyond it on the wings of the ideas, in the empty space of pure understanding."[441]

Next, Kant distinguished between analytic and synthetic judgments. He explained the distinction as follows: "Either the predicate *B* belongs to the subject *A* as something that is (covertly) contained in this concept *A*; or *B* lies entirely outside the concept *A*, though to be sure it stands in connection with it."[442] Kant identified the first category as analytic judgments that function much as tautologies. He specified that the second category involved synthetic judgments because the idea implied an experience that led to making the judgment. He illustrated this distinction with an example:

> [I]f I say: "All bodies are extended," then this is an analytic judgment. For I do not need to go outside the concept that I combine with the word "body" in order to find that extension is connected with it, but rather I need only to analyze that concept (i.e., become conscious of the manifold that I always think in it) in order to encounter this predicate therein; it is therefore an analytic judgment. On the contrary, if I say: "All bodies are heavy," then the predicate is something entirely different from that which I think in the mere concept of a body in general. The addition of such a predicate thus yields a synthetic judgment.[443]

From here, Kant puzzled at how analytic judgments and synthetic judgments interact. What follows is a crucial passage Kant wrote to demonstrate how the concept of "synthetic *a priori* judgments"[444] ties together his complex (and extended) philosophic writings. The passage is rather long and somewhat dense, but we must follow Kant's logic precisely to establish the groundwork from which to see how he influenced Hegel.

> If I am to go outside the concept *A* in order to cognize another *B* as combined with it, what is it on which I depend and through which the

> synthesis becomes possible, since I here do not have the advantage of looking around for it in the field of experience? Take the proposition: "Everything that happens has its cause." In the concept of something that happens, I think, to be sure, of an existence which was preceded by a time, etc., and from that analytic judgments can be drawn. But the concept of a cause indicates something different from the concept of something that happens, and is not contained in the later representation at all. How then do I come to say something quite different about that which happens in general, and to cognize the concept of cause as belonging to it even though not contained in it? What is the *X* here on which the understanding depends when it believes itself to discover beyond the concept of *A* predicate that is foreign to it and that is yet connected with it? It cannot be experience, for the principle that has been adduced adds the latter representations to the former not only with greater generality than experience can provide, but also with the expression of necessity, hence entirely *a priori* and from mere concepts. Now the entire final aim of our speculative *a priori* cognition rests on such synthetic, i.e., ampliative, principles; for the analytic ones are, to be sure, most important and necessary, but only for attaining that distinctness of concepts that is requisite for a secure and extended synthesis as a really new construction.[445]

Kant puzzled to understand how we form necessary statements that act as rules, or laws of nature—that is, "Everything that happens has a cause." His solution was to insist that we must apply a priori principles (analytic judgments) that involve logic, akin to mathematics, to our experience (synthetic judgments). We then can deduce how our experience must be perceived correctly (synthetic a priori judgments).

From this, Kant argued results "the idea of a special science, which could serve for the critique of pure reason."[446] Because pure cognition is absent from sensory experience, pure cognition is a priori (analytic). He elaborated as follows, explaining what the title of his book means:

> Now reason is the faculty that provides the principles of cognition *a priori*. Hence pure reason is that which contains the principles for cognizing something absolutely *a priori*. An organon of pure reason would be a sum of those principles in accordance with which all pure *a priori* cognitions can be acquired and actually brought about. The exhaustive application of such an organon would constitute a system of pure reason.[447]

Kant viewed this set of a priori analytic principles as hardwired into human consciousness, allowing us to operate in the realm of "transcendental cognition," in which pure reason dictates how to interpret our experiences in a meaningful way. For Kant, transcendental cognition is necessary a priori principles (like rules of logic or mathematics) such that our experiences are not only understandable but also meaningful. He thought that pure reason is a "critique" in that its function is negative—that is, "serving not for the amplification, but only for the purification of our reason, and for keeping it free of errors, by which a great deal is already won."[448] Pure reason allows us to deduce laws of nature that dictate what in human behavior is right (i.e., correct or moral behavior) and what is wrong (i.e., incorrect or immoral behavior). Thus, for Kant, metaphysics and the study of morality is a function of phenomenology, the study of perception. Pure reason dictates how the world must be correctly perceived and how we must act if we are to act correctly.

Regarding moral laws, Kant wrote the following: "What is an ideal to us, was to Plato an idea in the divine understanding."[449] God, for Kant, is pure reason. He continued the thought: "Without venturing to climb as high as that, however, we have to admit that human reason contains not only ideas but also ideals, which do not, to be sure, have a creative power like the **Platonic** idea, but still have **practical** power (as regulative principles) grounding the possibility of the perfection of certain **actions**."[450] He distinguished that moral concepts are not entirely pure concepts of reason, because they are grounded on something empirical (pleasure or displeasure). But because he saw freedom as "lawless," he saw the necessity for reason to provide moral rules.[451] He argued "we have in us no other standard for our actions than the conduct of this divine human being, with which we can compare ourselves, judging ourselves and thereby improving ourselves, even though we can never reach the standard."[452] Kant saw the realization of pure reason as a destiny the human race is programmed to advance toward through time. He ended the *Critique of Pure Reason* with a discussion of the history of pure reason. He saw the history of philosophy as an advancement in pure reason that he traced from Aristotle and Plato to more immediate philosophical predecessors like David Hume.

In concluding the *Critique of Pure Reason*, Kant invited the reader "to contribute his part to making this footpath into a highway, whether or not that which many centuries could not accomplish might not be attained even before the end of the present one: namely, to bring human reason to full satisfaction in that which has always, but until now vainly, occupied its lust for knowledge."[453] Should human beings ever understand the full organon of pure reason, we should advance to become divine beings—therefore, the goal Kant suggested in the quotation above is impossible. Yet, for Kant, the urge to advance toward the complete realization of pure reason is preordained by the synthetic a priori analytics God hardwired into human consciousness.

The Categorical Imperative

Kant applied the same idealistic a priori principles to his formulation of morals as he tried to explain our perception of reality. In his *Groundwork of the Metaphysics of Morals* (1797), Kant distinguished hypothetical imperatives from categorical imperatives. A hypothetical imperative is a rule of behavior that we only formulate after we encounter a particular experience.

As Christine Korsgaard, the Arthur Kingsley Porter Professor of Philosophy at Harvard University, explained in her introduction to Kant's *Groundwork of the Metaphysics of Morals*, a hypothetical imperative involves the principle "that whoever wills an end, in so far as he is rational, also wills the means to that end."[454] She further explained: "Since willing the means is conceptually contained in willing the end, if you will an end and yet fail to will the means to that end, you are guilty of a kind of practical contradiction."[455] For instance, if we want to be healthy, we should exercise.[456] But to formulate the moral problem as a metaphysical law, we must take the question to a higher, a priori level. Only then can we search for ethical principles that function as universal laws. Again, for a maxim to be a categorical imperative, Kant demanded a priori synthetic proposition that we can drive from pure reason to apply to the practical moral problem. To explain the transition from the hypothetical imperative, on which "popular moral philosophy" is based, to the categorical imperative, which Kant held to be the crux of the metaphysics of morals, he insisted there is only one categorical imperative: "act only according to that maxim through which you can at the same time will that it become a universal law."[457] The hypothetical imperative, for instance, that we should exercise if we want to be healthy does not rise to the level of a categorical imperative for Kant because it is a rule derived from habit (i.e., practical experience).

To achieve the level of a universal rule, Kant insisted the categorical imperative must be about experience. Hence, the categorical imperative must be synthetic. Still, it also must be a logically necessary a priori deduction. He also explained the categorical imperative by insisting that we must act "*as if the maxim of your action were to become by your will a* **universal law of nature**."[458] The maxim formulating the universal law of behavior must contain no logical contradiction to fulfill this rule. For example, he ruled out suicide to shorten a life "when its longer duration threatens more troubles than it promises agreeableness." Kant concluded that principle could never be a universal maxim because to destroy life "by means of the same feeling whose destination is to impel toward the furtherance of life would contradict itself and would therefore not subsist as nature." To fulfill the urge to live by compelling oneself to die is logically inconsistent, not a rule based on a priori synthetic proposition. Kant ruled out suicide as a categorical imperative on purely logical grounds, not because the consequences are undesirable. He excluded the maxim because killing oneself is logically inconsistent with the concept of wanting to live.[459]

Kant built to a second formulation of the categorical imperative by establishing that "a human being and in general every rational being *exists* as an end in itself, *not merely as a means* for the discretionary use for this or that will, but must in all its actions, whether directed to itself or also to other rational beings, always be considered *at the same time as an end*."[460] Kant scholar Allen W. Wood, a professor of philosophy emeritus at Stanford University, explained that Kant's respect for the dignity of all human beings grounded his understanding of the need for moral metaphysics to be grounded in universal, logically consistent propositions. Woods stressed that "Kant regards all rational beings as of equal worth and infers from this that the social inequalities between people, inequalities of honor, power, and above all of wealth, are fundamentally unjust."[461] In a pivotal section of the *Groundwork of the Metaphysics of Morals*, Kant argued that "[i]n the kingdom of ends everything either has a **price** or a **dignity**."[462] He explained that whatever has a price can be replaced by something else as an equivalent. What is above all price and has no equivalent replacement has "a dignity." [463]

Kant rejected the idea of negative freedom, contending that the freedom to act however one desires is a definition of lawlessness. He argued that free will demands autonomy, that is, "the property of the will of being a law to itself."[464] The autonomous will, by definition, avoids being subject to another. Thus, the autonomous will avoids allowing itself to be treated as a means to an end by another person. To remain autonomous, Kant maintained, means "the proposition, the will is in all its actions a law to itself, indicates only the principle, to act on no other maxim than that which can also have as object itself as a universal law." He defined this as "positive freedom." He concluded that since the formula for an autonomous will to operate is the same as the formula defining the categorical imperative, "a free will and a will under the moral laws are one and the same." In other words, he argued that an autonomous will must concede to pure reason in accepting the a priori synthetic propositions that compel moral laws to be logically consistent formulations. In his discussion of morality, Kant ended up at the same conclusion he reached in his discussion of phenomenology. Human beings, by our nature, are destined to advance in our understanding of a priori reason, a state that allows us to achieve the highest possible level of our existence, acting morally and living as free beings.

Perpetual Peace

In 1795, Kant wrote an essay entitled "Toward Perpetual Peace: A Philosophical Project." He explained that the ultimate destination of pure reason requires human beings to form republics that live perpetually in harmony, without the need for war. Kant formulated five rules or "preliminary articles" that he felt were necessary for nations to live at peace forever. The first article was this: "No treaty of peace shall be held to be such if it is made with a secret reservation of material for a future war." But he understood that though these articles were practical and necessary rules, they were not sufficient. For perpetual peace to have a chance of success, it depended upon nations consisting of citizens living moral lives. Like Thomas Hobbes, John Locke, and Jean-Jacques Rousseau, Kant imagined that the formation of states required a compact for people to leave the "state of nature." But even this was not sufficient if the nation-states created by civil society did not themselves resolve to live according to the rules of morality as defined by Kant's categorical-imperative logic. He wrote:

> In accordance with reason there is only one way that states in relation with one another can leave the lawless condition, which involves nothing but war; it is that, like individual human beings, they give up their savage (lawless) freedom, accommodate themselves to public coercive laws, and so form an (always growing) *state of nations* (*civitas gentium*) that would finally encompass all the nations of the earth.[465]

But Kant was practical enough to know that in 1795 the nation-states of Europe did not meet this condition. So, he proposed an intermediate step, acknowledging reality:

> But, in accordance with their idea [i.e., the idea of nation-states] of the right of nation, they do not all want this, thus rejecting *in hypothesi* what is correct *in thesi*; so (if all is not to be lost) in place of the positive idea *of a world republic* only the *negative* surrogate of a *league* that averts war, endures, and always expands can hold back the steam of hostile inclination that shies away from right, though with constant danger of its breaking out. (*Furor impius intus—fremit horridus ore cruento*. Virgil) [Within, impious rage—shall roar savagely with bloody mouth. *Aeneid* 1.294-6].[466]

Kant set as his "second definitive article for perpetual peace" the following resolve: "The right of nations shall be based on a federation of free states."[467] Thus, Kant envisioned the formation of a league of nations as a federation of states entering into a constitution similar to a civil constitution as independent states joined by their mutual determination to live together in peace:

> ...so there must be a league of a special kind, which can be called a *pacific league* (*foedus pacificum*) and what would distinguish it from a *peace pact* (*pactum pacis*) is that the later seeks to end only *one* war whereas the former seeks to end *all war* forever. This league does not look to acquiring any power of a state, but only to preserving and securing the *freedom* of a state itself and of other states in league with it, but without there being any need for them to subject themselves to public laws and coercion under them (as people in a state of nature must do).[468]

Kant envisioned this league of nations would be a federation of nation-states committed only to avoiding war:

> The practicality (objective reality) of this idea of a *federalism* that should gradually extend over all other states and so lead to perpetual peace can be shown. For if good fortune should ordain that a powerful and enlightened people can form itself into a republic (which by its nature must be inclined to perpetual peace), this would provide a focal point of federative union for other states, to attach themselves to it and so to secure a condition of freedom of states conformably with the idea of the right of nations; and by further alliances of this kind, it would gradually extend further and further.[469]

In the *Metaphysics of Morals*, written two years later (1797), Kant argued that we must act as if perpetual peace is achievable, adopting a maxim of working incessantly toward it. He clarified that forming a league of nations to establish perpetual peace is not a wish, but a duty established by the logic of morality. He made this point as follows:

> It can be said that establishing universal and lasting peace constitutes not merely a part of the doctrine of right but rather the entire final end of the doctrine of right within the limits of mere reason; for the condition of peace is alone that condition in which what is mine and what is yours for a multitude of human beings is secured under *laws* living in proximity to one another, hence those who are united under a constitution; but the rule for this constitution, as a norm for others, cannot be derived from the experience of those who have hitherto found it most to their advantage; it must, rather be derived a priori by reason from the ideal of a rightful association of human beings under public laws as such.[470]

As we will see later in this chapter, Woodrow Wilson's attempt to create the League of Nations at the end of World War I did not work out nearly as well as Kant had anticipated. Human beings may advance in science and technology through time. Still, Kant's confidence that we humans can grow in morals to live in utopia is unfounded.

Kant's confidence that human beings develop through time to actualize pure reason and realize the categorical imperative influenced Hegel. But Hegel's development of the dialectical process differed fundamentally from Kant's. Hegel, not Kant, is the father of today's neo-Marxist critical theory. Kant remains properly identified with the natural law and natural right political philosophy espoused by Aristotle and Plato. But as we set the stage to explore how Hegel's mysticism derived from Kant's idealism, let's first pause to identify essential takeaways from Immanuel Kant.

The first, and most important, is Kant's insistence that our understanding does not come simply from our experience of the exterior world. Kant is clear that what he calls a priori pure reason or transcendental idealism functions as a higher-level perception that allows us to perceive more deeply than simply seeing, hearing, or feeling. Transcendental idealism is, as it were, accessing the higher logic or meaning (i.e., in Plato's terminology, the "ideas" or "ideals" that allow us to make sense of our sensual experience). Thus, in the history of philosophy, Kant is categorized as an "idealist" instead of an "empiricist" like Hume. Yet Kant is not satisfied with the notion that our perception of external reality is unique to each of us. Yes, he argues that our experience of the external world through sense perception is subjective. But he also contends that the a priori ideas embedded in us by pure reason inform our higher perception of reality.

Hegel's Phenomenology of Spirit

Georg Wilhelm Friedrich Hegel was born in 1770 in Stuttgart, Germany. As a young man, Hegel worked as a tutor; then from 1808–1815, he worked as the headmaster and philosophy teacher at a gymnasium (high school) in Nuremberg. Hegel completed his first significant work, *The Phenomenology of Spirit*, in 1807, a work that established his stature as a critical philosophical thinker. In 1816, he took a chair in philosophy at the University of Heidelberg. Then in 1818, the University of Berlin offered him a chair in philosophy, the most prestigious position in the German philosophical world. In 1821, he published his major work in political philosophy, *Elements of the Philosophy of Right*, based on his lectures at Heidelberg. He enjoyed celebrity status in Berlin until he died in 1831.

Hegel followed Kant in advancing the German idealistic tradition, agreeing with Kant that a higher element is fundamental to the human sensual perception of the exterior world.[471] But where Kant felt our transcendental knowledge came from was a priori pure reason, Hegel felt that "spirit," a product of culture, was what shaped our experience and understanding of the exterior world. Hegel modified Kant's insistence that transcendental cognition proceeds from a priori pure reason. While reading Kant is difficult, reading Hegel is many times more difficult. Consider the following example. In these passages from part 4, entitled "Spirit," in the *Phenomenology of Spirit*, Hegel posited that spirit guides and shapes our perception of reality:

- Reason is spirit as the certainty of being all reality has been elevated to truth, and reason is, to oneself, conscious of itself as its world and of the world in itself.[472]
- Or, considered in terms of substance, this is the spiritual essence *existing-in-and-for-itself*, but which is not yet the consciousness of itself.—However, the essence *existing-in-and-for-itself*, which as consciousness is at the same time actual and which presents itself to itself is *spirit*.[473]
- Its spiritual *essence* has already been characterized as *ethical substance*, but spirit is *ethical actuality*. Spirit is the *self* of the actual consciousness which spirit confronts, or rather which confronts itself as an objective actual world, a world which has, for the self,

> just as much lost all significance as something alien, just as the self has lost all sense of being a dependent or independent being-for-itself separated from that world. Spirit is the *substance* and the universal self-equal, lasting essence—it is the unshakable and undissolved *ground* and *point of origin* for the doing of each and all—it is their *purpose* and *goal* as conceptualized in-itself of all self-consciousness.[474]

While Kant derived much of his philosophy by studying our consciousness of physical reality, Hegel shifted Kant's focus with his exploration of the "phenomenology of spirit." As Glenn Alexander Magee, a professor of philosophy and the chairman of the Department of Philosophy at Long Island University, pointed out in his 2010 book *The Hegel Dictionary*,[475] "spirit" is one of the most misunderstood terms in Hegel. Part of the confusion is that Hegel chose the German word *der Geist* (related to the English, "the ghost"), which brings to mind a supernatural phenomenon. Magee stressed that when Hegel is discussing "spirit," he has in mind "the unique form of consciousness possessed by human beings." Magee explained as follows:

> Unlike all other animals, human beings are capable of self-consciousness or self-awareness: we are the beings who are able to know ourselves. In common with other animals, we possess instincts and drives—but the difference is that we can reflect upon these, understand them and, to some extent, curb them. We are also capable of reacting against those drives, even disavowing or stifling them (as in the case of individuals who choose a life of voluntary celibacy). In fact, to a great extent human beings choose to be what they are—they choose their own nature through the act of self-understanding or self-discovery. In essential terms, this is what human freedom consists of.[476]

Hegel then stresses that for human beings, self-awareness (i.e., the achievement of a self-conscious spirit) takes time as we mature from small children, more or less in an animal state, to mature adults. Magee continued his explanation as follows:

> Maturation consists in large measure in the process of learning to think critically about ourselves, and achieving a degree of self-awareness. But all of this is also true for the human race as a whole. As a race we began, Hegel believes, in an infantile state where we were ruled by childish beliefs—myths and superstitions. We were actually the authors of these,

> but we were not self-conscious enough to realize it. Because we were unself-conscious, we lacked freedom for we could not see the degree to which we could change the ideas we lived by and therefore shape our own nature. For Hegel, history is in fact the story of our gradual achievement of self-consciousness, which is simultaneously the realization of our freedom, our capacity for self-determination. With this achievement, which truly occurs in the modern period, human Spirit is realized.[477]

Kant suggested human beings develop in history as our understanding of pure reason advances. But for Hegel, human advancement through history was driven by the spirit of the age such that our human nature matured the same way a child matures developing into an adult. The advancement of human freedom could not happen without history, any more than a child can become a mature adult without passing through the teenage years. He believed that history involved inevitable progress as the human spirit sought to self-actualize by working through contradictions in our social structures and cultures.[478] Spirit's final destination for Hegel was a truly free human being self-actualized by becoming fully self-conscious. In his introduction to his translation of Hegel's *Phenomenology of Spirit*, Terry Pinkard, a philosophy professor at Georgetown University, explained Hegel's theory that a fully actualized human being is as follows:

> If spirit were to shape the real flesh-and-blood lives of individuals into their true form, they would become what they really were: free and equal, united in friendship in the personal sphere and justice in the wider social and political sphere. Spirit as it is in itself would be equal and adequate to spirit as it appeared. If spirit does in fact require the kind of actual and not merely hypothetical recognition for which he had argued in "Self-Consciousness" [part 2 of *The Phenomenology of Spirit*], then the inquiry into the essence of spirit would have to turn to real history, not hypothetical accounts of how this might have happened.[479]

Hegel conceptualized spirit as being an objective force, often called Zeitgeist (in English, translated as the "spirit of the time"), a term that has come to be associated with Hegel. However, he did not use the word in his writings. The concept is that Zeitgeist, or the spirit of each age in history, orders our experience as our human culture through time develops. While Kant believed that human consciousness advances in time as our understanding of pure reason increases, Hegel believed human consciousness understood as a "communal consciousness or collection of cultural ideas, norms, and practices"[480] evolved into different, more advanced levels. Again, we turn to Magee and his *Hegel Dictionary* to appreciate Hegel's understanding of the "World Spirit," or in German, *der Weltgeist*:

> The many varieties of "Spirit" in Hegel are a source of great confusion, and in particular there are many misconceptions surrounding his use of "World Spirit." Spirit refers simply to humanity and its consciousness, which is unique in that it is capable of self-reflection. Hegel argues, in fact, that all forms of Spirit are in one way or another aiming at self-consciousness, which is only truly achieved in Absolute Spirit (art, religion and philosophy). Human consciousness, however, does not just suddenly appear on the scene already actualized. In fact, Spirit must develop itself over time: the achievement of human self-understanding is a long process, and history is the account of it. Thus, when Hegel looks at history he sees Spirit working within it as, in effect, its goal or final cause. When Hegel refers to Spirit as what moves history, he often terms it "World Spirit,"—but in fact there is little difference between the concepts of "Spirit" and "World Spirit." Hegel is often misunderstood as claiming that there is some kind of hypostatized, ghostly "spirit"—or God—acting in history to achieve its ends. When Hegel speaks this way, however, he speaks figuratively. All Hegel really claims is that there is an inner logic to history, and that it is the process of Spirit (or self-aware humanity) realizing itself.[481]

Kant is a philosopher in the original Greek understanding that philosophy is the pursuit and the love of wisdom. As we shall see next, philosophy professor Magee is right. Hegel is not a philosopher. He claims to have arrived at absolute knowledge, and he defines wisdom as knowing here and now what God knows eternally. As Magee wrote in his 2001 book, *Hegel and the Hermetic Tradition*, Hermeticism is fundamentally different from philosophy. "Hermeticists not only hold that God requires creation, they make a specific creature, man, play a crucial role in God's self-actualization. Hermeticism holds that man can know God, and that man's knowledge of God is necessary for God's own completion." Hegel not only claimed God needs us to self-actualize, but Hegel also claimed that God needs us to be God. He asserts to have the wisdom that without us and the dialectic's power to negate (*aufheben* in German), God would never be perfect.

World-Historical Individuals

> From the time he stepped out of his lecture hall in Jena in 1806 to gaze upon Napoleon, seeing in him a living manifestation of the universal merged with the particular in an individual, Hegel took it upon himself to form a new Volksreligion [people's religion] around which a unifying German people could form a nation state, believing as he did that the orientalism of Christianity had deprived Germany of its true metaphysic.
>
> Stephen Coughlin and Richard Higgins, *Re-Remembering the Mis-Remembered Left*, 2019[482]

Hegel saw history advance through the influence of "world-historical individuals," in German, "*die welthistorischen Individuen*." Hegel had figures like Alexander the Great, Caesar, and Napoleon in mind. As Magee pointed out in his *Hegel Dictionary*, in world-historical individuals, "private passions and projects happen to coincide with the universal aims of Spirit." Thus, Hegel conceptualized that the spirit uses world-historical individuals through "the cunning of history" to realize the universal aims of spirit.[483] In his *Lectures on the Philosophy of World History*, Hegel explained that one of the most crucial historical moments involved preserving the individual nation or state. But this is only a transitional state to what Hegel considered "the development, progress, and ascent of the spirit toward a higher concept of itself." Thus, world-historical figures are those who interrupt the spirit of a given nation-state because that nation-state's spirit "has exhausted itself and worked itself out to its conclusion."[484] Hegel elaborated as follows:

> But this [i.e., the ascent of the spirit to a higher concept of itself] is accompanied by the debasement, fragmentation, and destruction of the preceding mode of reality which had already developed its concept to the full. All this takes place to some extent automatically through the inner development of the Idea; yet, on the other hand, the Idea is itself the product of factors outside itself, and is implemented and brought to its realization by the actions of individuals. It is precisely at this point we encounter those great collusions between established and acknowledged duties, laws, and rights, on one hand, and new possibilities which conflict with the existing system and violate it or even destroy its very foundations and continued existence, on the other (although their content may well appear equally good and for the most part propitious, essen-

> tial, and necessary). These new possibilities then become part of history. They incorporate a universal of a different order from that on which the continued existence of a nation or state is based. For the universal they embody is a moment of the productive Idea itself, of that truth which works its way on its own realization.[485]

Here Hegel has explained that the creation and destruction of nation-states is the political manifestation of an a priori "Idea" at the heart of the world spirit. For Kant, the "ideas" were Platonic ideals, higher understandings of our sensory perceptions of external reality deriving from pure reason. For both Kant and Hegel, these "ideas" driving history have an a priori predetermined goal of achieving true freedom for all human beings. To Kant, this true freedom would be accomplished when all human beings live by the categorical imperative and achieve perpetual peace. But for Hegel, true freedom involves the realization of a completely autonomous, fully conscious self-awareness of ourselves and the reality in which we live. When Hegel wanted to explain what precisely this ultimate Idea of history is attempting to achieve, he turned to ancient Greece.

As political scientist Judith Shklar pointed out in her 1976 book *Freedom and Independence: A Study of the Political Ideas of Hegel's "Phenomenology of Mind,"* Hegel considered ancient Athens to have achieved the condition of "a free people in a harmonious community." Shklar explained that for Hegel there once existed in Athens a time where "I" and "we" were simultaneously at one. She commented that ancient Athens's "happy state" might never be consciously achieved, but it "hovers over" Hegel's writings as a beacon showing the destination toward which the world spirit aspires to attain.[486]

Georgetown professor and translator Terry Pinkard agreed with Shklar. In his introduction to his translation of Hegel's *Phenomenology of Spirit*, Pinkard wrote the following:

> In actualizing itself in terms of its concept, "spirit" sets itself up for changes in itself that it brings on itself as it shifts its concept of itself. Its concept of itself is not an ideal against which it measures itself but a statement of its true form, to which it tries to shape itself, and in its true form, spirit stands in a unity of I/You relations and I/We relations.... If spirit does in fact require the kind of actual and not merely hypothetical recognition for which he had argued in "Self-Consciousness" [part 4 of the *Phenomenology of Spirit*], then the inquiry into the essence of spirit

> would have to turn to real history, not hypothetical accounts of how this might have happened.
>
> So, Hegel argued, the existence of something that could be genuinely called "true spirit" was in fact the case for a brief period in the development of the ancient Greek shape of life, in which free and equal men (but notably not slaves and not women) met each other as free and equal in the polis, and the overall social order embodied the second-person virtue of justice.[487]

Returning to Hegel's *Lectures on the Philosophy of World History*, he next explained how world-historical individuals actualize the higher universal idea of history as the world spirit advances human beings closer to the realization of the "Absolute Idea," in German *die absolute Idee*. With the attainment of the absolute idea, Hegel posited that we will experience total self-awareness when we come to embrace the freedom in which the "I" and the "we" are united. He elaborated the role the world-historical figure plays in human advancement through time as follows:

> The great individuals of world history, therefore, are those who seize upon this higher universal and make it their own. It is they who realize the end appropriate to the higher concept of the spirit. To this extent, they may be called heroes. They do not find their aims and vocation in the calm and regular system of the present, in the hallowed order of things as they are. Indeed, their justification does not lie in the prevailing situation, for they draw their inspiration from another source, from that hidden spirit whose hour is near but which still lies beneath the surface and seeks to break out without yet having attained an existence in the present. For this spirit, the present world is but a shell which contains the wrong kind of kernel. It might, however, be objected that everything which deviates from the established order—whether intentions, aims, opinions, or so-called ideals—is likewise different from what is already there.[488]

Hegel next explained how the world spirit comes to possess world-historic individuals to advance the world spirit toward the absolute idea. He continued:

> Adventures of all kinds have such ideals, and their activities are based on attitudes which conflict with the present circumstances. But the fact that all such attitudes, sound reasons, or general principles differ from existing ones does not mean to say that they are justified. The only true

> ones are those whose content has been produced by the absolute power of the inner spirit itself in the course of its development; and world-historical individuals are those who have willed and accomplished not just the ends of their own imagination or personal opinions, but only those necessary and timely, and have an inner vision of what it is.[489]

Hegel saw Napoleon in person on October 13, 1806, when Napoleon entered Jena, Germany, after shattering the Prussians in the Battle of Jena. Hegel wrote a letter that day to his friend, the noted educator Friedrich Niethammer. In the letter, he clarified that seeing Napoleon in person gave him the experience of seeing the world spirit actualizing in the flesh. In this letter, his description of Napoleon is reminiscent of yet another passage in the Gospel of St. John. In John 1:14, we read of Jesus Christ in the following: "And the Word [i.e., is λογος, translated as "the word" in English] was made flesh, and dwelt among us, (and we beheld his glory, the glory as of the only begotten of the Father,) full of grace and truth." In his letter to Niethammer, Hegel described Napoleon as follows:

> I saw the Emperor [Napoleon]—this world-soul—riding out of the city on reconnaissance. It is indeed a wonderful sensation to see such an individual, who, concentrated here at a single point, astride a horse, reaches out over the world and masters it.[490]

When Hegel saw Napoleon in person, his bizarre political thinking crystallized at that moment of bedazzled observation. For us today, contemplating what Hegel experienced in this one moment is like seeing a snapshot of his entire political philosophy, explaining all the voluminous, "unparalleled scribblings of nonsense"[491] Hegel subsequently produced. When Hegel saw Napoleon, Hegel felt he saw embodied in Napoleon an archetypical "man of action," actualizing the world spirit driven to create a new order through waging war.

A Deep Dive into Hegel's Dialectical Mysticism

> Hegel is not a philosopher. He is no lover or seeker of wisdom—he believes he has found it.... Hegel's claim to have attained wisdom is completely contrary to the original Greek conception of philosophy as the love of wisdom, that is, the ongoing pursuit rather than the final possession of wisdom. His claim is, however, fully consistent with the ambitions of the Hermetic tradition, a current of thought that derives its name from the so-called *Hermetica* (or *Corpus Hermeticum*), a col-

lection of Greek and Latin treatises and dialogues written in the first or second centuries A.D. and probably containing ideas that are far older.

Glenn Alexander Magee, *Hegel and the Hermetic Tradition*, 2001[492]

As Coughlin and Higgins observed in the quotation at the beginning of this chapter, Hegel formed a new resolve from the moment he stepped out of his lecture hall in Jena in 1806 to see Napoleon. Coughlin and Higgins argued Hegel took it upon himself to form a new *Volksreligion*, a "people's religion," around which a unifying German people could unify into a nation-state. The Holy Roman Empire ended with the abdication of Emperor Francis II during the Napoleonic Wars in 1806, the same year in which Hegel saw Napoleon in person. Subsequently, Germany became a confederation of states until it unified into the German Empire in 1871, when the princes of the German states met at the Palace of Versailles outside Paris to proclaim Wilhelm I of Prussia as the German emperor following Germany's defeat of Napoleon III in the Franco-Prussian War. Frederick II, also known as Frederick the Great, was the king of Prussia until he died in 1786. He was instrumental in the rise of Prussia to dominate over the confederation of German states. Frederick II rose to prominence during the three Silesian Wars in which Prussia, under Frederick, defeated Hapsburg Austria under Archduchess Maria Theresa. During the Silesian Wars, Austria was second to Prussia among the most powerful states in the German Confederation. In 1806, Hegel and his poet-philosopher friend Friedrich Hölderlin agreed that the future of Germany depended upon creating this *Volksreligion* "wholly independent of the alien, imported orientalism of Christianity."[493] Hegel perceived the emergence of a unified German empire under Prussian leadership as essential if Germany were to emerge at the end of the nineteenth century as a dominant European power. As Professor Magee explained in his 2001 book *Hegel and the Hermetic Tradition*, Hegel's project after 1806 was to create specifically German metaphysics. Magee elaborated:

> On the initial page of the preface to the first edition of the *Science of Logic* [first published between 1812 and 1816], Hegel implies that he intends to provide Germany with its own metaphysics: "If it is remarkable when a nation has become indifferent to its constitutional theory, to its national sentiments, its ethical customs and virtues, it is certainly no less remarkable when a nation loses its metaphysics, when the spirit which contemplates its own pure essence is no longer a present reality

in the life of the nation." In the introduction to the *Science of Logic*, Hegel contrasts his book to "former metaphysics." In the introduction to the *Encyclopedia Logic*, Hegel writes that "Speculative Logic contains the older logic and metaphysics; it preserves the same forms of thought, laws, objects, but it develops and transforms them with further categories."[494]

Magee explained that Hegel's metaphysics involved not only his concept of God, but also "what it means to be and an account of the highest individual being."[495] He concluded that Hegel's metaphysical formula reduced to the following: "The Eternal = Truth = *Logos* = Absolute Idea = God."[496] He insisted that for Hegel, all these—the eternal, truth, logos, the absolute idea, and God—"*must* be knowable."[497] Hegel insisted that "stressing man's finitude and God's unknowability is contrary to the Christian faith."[498] In his *Lectures on the Philosophy of Religion*, Hegel stated, "I declare such a point of view to be directly opposed to the whole nature of the Christian religion, according to which we should *know* God *cognitively*, God's nature and essence, and should esteem this cognition above all else."[499] Magee correctly concluded that Hegel opposed both Kant and traditional Christianity with these views. Magee wrote:

> In making such claims, Hegel is not simply attacking longstanding religious views about man's relationship to God, he is also opposing the Kantian philosophy. Hegel's claim that we *can* know the thing-in-itself is the major reason why so many "tough-minded" philosophers seem to regard him as slightly mad.[500]

As noted by his quotation at the beginning of this chapter section, Magee concluded Hegel is not a philosopher. "By the end of the *Phenomenology [of Spirit]*, Hegel claims to have arrived at Absolute Knowledge, which he identifies with wisdom."[501] But, as Magee has pointed out, the claim to have attained wisdom is "completely contrary to the original Greek conception of philosophy as the love of wisdom, that is, the ongoing pursuit rather than the final possession of wisdom."[502] However, Hegel's claim was "fully consistent with the ambitions of Hermetic thought."[503] Magee pointed out that the legendary author of these works is Hermes Trismegistus ("Thrice-Greatest Hermes"). He also noted that the Hermetic tradition developed into alchemy and Kabbalism and is sometimes called theosophy, or esotericism, or less precisely, as mysticism or occultism. Hermeticism is fundamentally different from philosophy. "Hermeticists not only hold that God requires creation, they make a specific creature, man, play a crucial role in God's self-actualization," Magee stressed in his book. "Hermeticism holds that man can know God, and that man's knowledge of God is necessary for god's own completion."[504] Hegel not only claimed that God needs us to self-actualize, but Hegel also claimed that God needs us to be God. Magee continued:

> Not only does Man wish to know God, but God too desires to be known by the most glorious of His creations, Man. In short, it is man's end to achieve knowledge of God (or "the wisdom of God," theosophy). In so doing, man realizes God's own need to be recognized. Man's knowledge of God becomes God's knowledge of himself. Thus the need for which the cosmos is created is the need for self-knowledge, attained through recognition.[505]

Hegel's mysticism was at the heart of the metaphysics, the *Volksreligion*, that he aimed to create for Germany, the civilization he believed was capable of driving toward utopia. In this new *Volksreligion* (though metaphysic, cosmology, or theosophy may be more precise terminology here), Hegel saw the state bestriding the land.[506] In the *Lectures on the Philosophy of History*, Hegel identified the state with "the Divine Idea as it exists on Earth." He wrote the following:

> In the history of the World, only those peoples can come under our notice which form a state. For it must be understood that this latter is the realization of Freedom, i.e., of the absolute final aim, and that it exists for its own sake. It must further be understood that all the worth which the human being possesses—all spiritual reality, he possesses only through the State. For his spiritual reality consists in this, that his own essence—Reason—is objectively present to him, that it possesses objective immediate existence for him. Thus only is he fully conscious; thus only is he a partaker of morality—of a just and moral social and political life. For Truth is the Unity of the universal and subjective Will; and the Universal is to be found in the State, in its laws, its universal and rational arrangements. The State is the Divine Idea as it exists on Earth.[507]

Hegel continued, emphasizing the state acts for the community virtually as a secular religion functioning as the only way that we can experience true freedom on earth:

> We have in it, therefore, the object of History in a more definite shape than before; that in which Freedom obtains objectivity, and lives in the enjoyment of this objectivity. For Law is the objectivity of Spirit; volition in its true form. Only that will which obeys the law, is free: for it obeys itself—it is independent and so free. When the State or our country constitutes a community of existence; when the subjective will of man submits to laws—the contradiction between Liberty and Necessity vanishes.[508]

The state imbued with these God-like attributes exercised supreme right over the individual. In the *Philosophy of Right*, Hegel made clear the extent of the state's authority over the individual was unlimited:

> The state is absolutely rational inasmuch as it is the actuality of the substantial will which it possesses in the particular self-consciousness once that consciousness has been raised to consciousness of its universality. This substantial unity is an absolute unmoved end in itself, in which freedom comes into its supreme right. On the other hand this final end has supreme right against the individual, whose supreme duty is to be a member of the state.[509]

While Hegel understood it was not prudential during his lifetime to be anti-Christian in Germany, he came to view his concept that the world spirit created and destroyed nation-states in near-religious terms. He became convinced the future of Germany, and especially the bond among the German people, constituted a *Volksreligion*, a "people's religion" on the road to realizing God's fulfillment on earth. Hegel saw the "Holy Spirit" as God's earthly presence. For Hegel, Germany was the world-historic preeminent nation that would actualize God through the action of the German *Volk*. Hegel became convinced that the world spirit had destined a utopian future for Germany. He believed this utopian German future would emerge from the mystical bond that would unite the German *Volk* through a *Volksreligion* derived not from the life of Jesus Christ but through a truly German man of action that he identified as Frederick the Great.

Hegel envisioned this new, uniquely German *Volksreligion* as arising through the world spirit by acting as the "Holy Spirit" of the divine Trinity moving through history as God's earthly presence. But for Hegel, the Holy Spirit operating as the world spirit would cause the destruction and creation of nation-states through dialectic action. This mystical concept was utterly divorced from Christianity's emphasis on Jesus Christ's crucifixion and resurrection as proof of his divinity. Traditional Christianity is about attaining salvation in the afterlife, and Hegel is about achieving heaven on earth. For Hegel, God as the Holy Spirit of the divine Trinity was the world spirit advancing through history. He thought the dialectic explained how God, as the Holy Spirit, was able to do this. He praised Frederick the Great for unifying the German people in the Seven Years' War, making Prussia "one of the great powers of Europe as a Protestant power."[510] Hegel quickly added that Frederick II's world-historic greatness was also that he was a "philosophical King—an altogether peculiar and unique phenomenon in modern times."[511] Thus, not only was Frederick II a world-historic individual on par with Napoleon, but Hegel also perceived him as the embodiment of Plato's "Philosopher King."

Hegel's insistence that the state had absolute rights over the individual is highly statist, in that Hegel saw the state as having totalitarian, centralized power over the citizenry. Catholic New Testament scholar and author Benedict Viviano, in an essay on the adoration of the magi, made the connection between Hegel and the statist nature of World War I, "a war that leveled the playing field for the left."[512] In that essay, Viviano wrote the following:

> In its classic form, Hegel's *Philosophy of History*, it concludes that Prussia is the present and permanent incarnation of the Holy Spirit and that it is God's will that Prussia should conquer and govern the world. Or so was understood. Such an understanding led to the First World War.[513]

Viviano was not alone in concluding Hegel viewed Prussia as the ultimate state. In his 1945 book *A History of Western Philosophy*, published a year after the World War II, British philosopher Bertrand Russell argued that although Hegel often criticized Kant, Hegel's "system could never have arisen if Kant's had not existed."[514] Russell continued as follows:

> His influence [Hegel's], though now diminishing, has been very great, not only or chiefly in Germany. At the end of the nineteenth century, the leading academic philosophers, both in America and in Great Britain, were largely Hegelians. Outside of pure philosophy, many Protestant theologians adopted his doctrines, and his philosophy of history has profoundly affected political theory. Marx, as everyone knows, was a disciple of Hegel in his youth, and retained in his own finished system some important Hegelian features. Even if (as I myself believe) almost all Hegel's doctrines are false, he still retains an importance which is not

> merely historical, as the best representative of a certain kind of philosophy which, in others, is less coherent and less comprehensible.[515]

Russell agreed that Hegel, in his youth, was "much attracted to mysticism, and his later views may be regarded, to some extent, as an intellectualizing of what had first appeared to him as mystic insight."[516] Russell noted that Hegel "was in later life a patriotic Prussian, a loyal servant of the State, who comfortably enjoyed his philosophical pre-eminence; but in his youth he despised Prussia and admired Napoleon, to the extent of rejoicing at the French victory at Jena." [517] He concluded his introductory remarks on Hegel by commenting that "Hegel's philosophy is very difficult—he is, I should say, the hardest to understand of all the great philosophers."[518]

Russell noted that Hegel, in philosophizing about history, had in mind men such as Theodoric the Great, Charlemagne, Frederick Barbarossa, Martin Luther, and Frederick the Great. Russell insisted that Hegel was to be interpreted "in light of their exploits, and in light of the then recent humiliation of Germany by Napoleon."[519] He noted that Hegel glorified Germany to such an extent that "one might expect to find it [Germany] as the final embodiment of the Absolute Idea."[520] But that was not Hegel's view. He continued to explain that Hegel believed America would be the land of the future, where Hegel wrote that "the burden of the world's history shall reveal itself."[521] But Russell found that this would be problematic for Hegel:

> If it were suggested to him [to Hegel] that the attribution of America to world history might be the development of a society without extreme poverty, he would not be interested. On the contrary, he says that, as yet, there is no real State in America, because a real State requires a division of classes into rich and poor.[522]

Here, Russell made a characteristically astute observation: "Nations, in Hegel, play the part that classes play in Marx." He continued:

> The principle of historical development, he says, is national genius. In every age, there is some one nation which is charged with the mission of carrying the world through the stage of the dialectic that it has reached. In our age, of course, this nation is Germany.[523]

Russell quipped that for Hegel, everything important takes the form of war.

> But in addition to nations, we must also take account of world-historical individuals; these are men in whose aims are embodied the dialectical transitions that are due to take place in their time. These men are heroes, and may justifiably contravene ordinary moral rules. Alexander, Caesar, and Napoleon are given as examples. I doubt whether, in Hegel's opinion, a man could be a "hero" without being a military conqueror.[524]

Russell conceded that as a mature adult, Hegel understood that "in the times after the Reformation [Martin Luther and the split from Roman Catholicism], the political weakness and disunity of Germany was deplored, and the gradual rise of Prussia was welcomed as making Germany strong under Protestant leadership."[525]

Eric Voegelin was a political scientist born in Cologne, Germany, in 1901. As a result of the Anschluss in 1938, Voegelin and his wife fled Vienna. He was a prolific writer who considered Hegel instrumental in developing the philosophy of what he called "political religions" that led to the totalitarianism of the twentieth century. In an essay published in 1971 entitled "On Hegel—A Study in Sorcery," Voegelin characterized Hegel as a "Messiah" of the early nineteenth century whose "megalomania" left so deep an impact on the so-called modern age that we have been accustomed to his madness.

Voegelin detailed Hegel's particular madness as consisting of existential insecurity, anxiety, and especially a *libido dominandi*, translated as the "will to power."[526] Stephen Coughlin and Richard Higgins picked up on Voegelin's theme in their book. They commented that the *libido dominandi* was the driving force in Hegel's understanding of the dialect. They also commented that Hegel's reconstruction of reality resonated for them philosopher Josef Pieper's pseudoreality.[527] Coughlin and Higgins continued:

> Recognizing the **statism** behind Hegel's vision of a new Teutonic cosmology, while at the same time understanding the interplay of Hegel's "men of action," god, and the state, **one begins to recognize the archetype form (the template) of modern authoritarian rule and governance that demands absolute fidelity to the Hegelian state and its leaders**.[528]

Coughlin and Higgins argued Hegel's *Volksreligion* did produce a certain "man of action" who would lead Germany to a destined future. But the world-historic figure was not Frederick the Great as Hegel had imagined. It was Adolf Hitler arising to power in 1933 who promised to lead a master race of Aryans in the Thousand-Year Reich. The Hitlerian statist *Volksreligion* culminated in the 1935 *Triumph of the Will* Nazi propaganda film that Leni Riefenstahl wrote, edited, and produced of the 1934 Nazi Party Congress in Nuremberg, Germany.

Coughlin and Higgins note Hitler's rise to power as a "man of action" who "would lead a master race of Aryans to a 'Thousand Year Reich'" is consistent with Hegel's vision of "a new Teutonic cosmology" that, in turn, is consistent with Voegelin's *libido dominandi* (the will to power)."[529] This discussion resonates with the 1935 Leni Riefenstahl German Nazi propaganda film, *Triumph of the Will* (*Triumph des Willens*) that helped propel Hitler to power. Coughlin and Higgins noted that Hitler was not the last. The "New Soviet Man" postulated by Communist ideology helped propel Lenin and Stalin to "men of action" status."[530] The torch passed to Castro, and "the model devolved to Hugo Chavez and his ruination of Venezuela."[531] Again, note that Hegelian totalitarianism has been, since the twentieth century, a characteristic of the political Left. Again, this defies the traditional politically correct insistence that Hitler's fascism in Nazi Germany was a movement on the political Right.

Coughlin and Higgins agreed with Magee that Hegel's phenomenology involved a mysticism that created a Pieper-like pseudoreality. They focused on the particular meaning Hegel gave to "science," in German, *die Wissenschaft*. Magee pointed out that one of Hegel's terms for his philosophy was "science." The full title of Hegel's first major work, *The Phenomenology of Spirit* (1807), was *System of Science: First Part, The Phenomenology of Spirit*. Magee argued that *Wissenschaft* is derived from *Wissen*, which means simply "knowledge."[532] Magee also stressed that Jacob Boehme (1575–1624) significantly influenced Hegel. Boehme was a shoemaker in Goerlitz, Lusatia, on the border with Bohemia. He had a mystical vision in 1600 that lasted about fifteen minutes. In 1612, Boehme wrote a book called *Aurora oder Morgenröte im Aufgang*, translated in English as *Aurora: Dawn Rising*, a book Magee noted was Boehme's first attempt to explain the revelation he had received years earlier. Magee thought Boehme's book was "largely a work of theosophy," understood as "an attempt not only to know the nature of God but to attain divine wisdom itself."[533] He speculated that Hegel could have encountered Boehme's work as early as the mid-to-late 1790s.[534] If so, Hegel may have realized his magical moment seeing Napoleon in person in 1806 bore a striking resemblance to Boehme's mystical fifteen minutes in 1600.

Magee stressed that Boehme believed "that God develops or realizes himself through creation, and that considered separately from creation God is 'not yet' God." Magee explained as follows:

> It is out of a desire to confront himself or to achieve self-consciousness that God expresses himself as nature. In one of his later works, Boehme wrote 'No thing can be revealed to itself without opposition.' In other words, in order for God to become the truly realized God he must oppose an 'other' to himself, through which he comes to be. This process of God expressing himself in creation and achieving self-awareness reaches completion with man.[535]

Coughlin and Higgins point out that Voegelin recognized the alchemy in Hegel's *Wissenschaft*, labeling it sorcery. "For Voegelin, the sorcerer is the 'imaginator' who first creates than imposes 'a second reality,'" thereby creating a Josef Pieper–pseudoreality.[536] Coughlin and Higgins also note that Bertrand Russell held "the same jaundiced view of Hegel's schema."[537]

In the essay "Philosophy and Politics" that Russell published in his 1950 book *Unpopular Essays*, Russell expanded his criticism of Hegel.

> They [philosophers] have professed to discover a formula of progress, showing that the world was becoming gradually more and more to their liking. The recipe for a philosophy of this type is simple. The philosopher first decides which are the features of the existing world that give him pleasure, and which are the features that give him pain. He then, by a careful selection among facts, persuades himself that the universe is subject to a general law leading to an increase of what he finds pleasant and a decrease of what he finds unpleasant. Next, having formulated his law of progress, he turns on the public and says: "It is fated that the world must develop as I say; therefore those who wish to be on the winning side, and do not care to wage a fruitless war against the inevitable, will join my party." Those who oppose him are condemned as unphilosophic, unscientific, and out of date, while those who agree with him feel assured of victory, since the universe is on their side. At the same time the winning side, for reasons which remain somewhat obscure, is represented as the side of virtue.[538]

Russell next explained that Hegel's problem was that he constructed an elaborate philosophical system on how he wished philosophy would turn out.

> The man who first fully developed this point of view was Hegel. Hegel's philosophy is so odd that one would not have expected him to be able to get sane men to accept it, but he did. He set it out with so much obscurity that people thought it must be profound. It can quite easily be expounded lucidly in words of one syllable, but then its absurdity becomes obvious.[539]

A few paragraphs later, Russell wrote a biting, but accurate, assessment of Hegel's philosophy, emphasizing Hegel's departure from Kant: "It follows from his [Hegel's] metaphysic that true liberty consists in obedience to an arbitrary authority, that free speech is an evil, that absolute monarchy is good, that the Prussian State was the best existing at the time when he wrote, that war is good, and that an international organization for the peaceful settlement of disputes would be a misfortune."[540]

Russell further commented that most philosophy teachers in British and American universities were Hegelians when he was young. Thus, until he read Hegel, he supposed there must be some truth in his system. "I was cured, however, by discovering that everything he said on the philosophy of mathematics was plain nonsense," he wrote.[541] Still, he mused that Hegel had a "most curious" effect on Marx. Russell repeated his comments on Marx, noting again that Marx "took over some of his [Hegel's] more fanciful tenets, more particularly the belief that history develops according to a logical plan, and is concerned, like the purely abstract dialectic, to find ways of avoiding self-contradiction."[542] Russell added parenthetically that "[o]ver a large part of the earth's surface you will be liquidated if you question this dogma, and eminent Western men of science, who sympathize politically with Russia, show their sympathy by using the word 'contradiction' in ways that no self-respecting logician can approve."[543] Russell ended his commentary on Hegel by noting it was "something of an accident" that Hegel glorified Prussia. He said that Hegel, in his earlier years, ardently admired Napoleon. But he quipped that Hegel "only became a German patriot when he became an employee of the Prussian State."[544]

In *Unpopular Essays*, Russell prefaced his discussion of Hegel with an observation casting doubt on Hegel's central thesis that the logic of history demands we advance on an upward arc. He contemplated the following:

> Our own planet, in which philosophers are apt to take a parochial and excessive interest, was once too hot to support life, and will in time be too cold. After ages during which the earth produced harmless trilobites and butterflies, evolution progressed to the point at which it generated

> Neros, Genghis Khans, and Hitlers. This, however, is a passing nightmare; in time the earth will become again incapable of supporting life, and peace will return.
>
> But this purposeless see-saw, which is all that science has to offer, has not satisfied the philosophers. They have professed to discover a formula of progress, showing that the world was becoming gradually more and more to their liking.[545]

Russell suggested that once *Homo sapiens* showed up, our history has been filled with countless tyrants and a series of nearly continuous wars, going back to the earliest days of recorded history. One estimate is that over the past 3,400 years, humans have been entirely at peace for just 268 of them, approximately 8 percent of recorded history.[546] Russell estimated that organized wars began in Egypt some 6,000 years ago.[547] Through the years of the Cold War, we managed to avoid a nuclear holocaust. But today, Russia, China, and the United States appear to be doing their best to achieve first-strike capabilities with supersonic nuclear weapons. What assurance do we have that we will live through as short a time as the current decade without a nuclear holocaust that will constitute Earth's sixth great extinction?

In his book *Wisdom of the West*, Russell repeated the observation again, commenting that Hegel's "Absolute in politics seems to be the Kingdom of Prussia."[548] He expressed his fundamental disdain for Hegel's philosophy with his usual flair for insight and understatement:

> Again, the progression toward the Absolute in history provides an opportunity for some pretty crude nationalistic propaganda. It would appear that history had reached its ultimate stage in the Prussian state of Hegel's day. Such is the conclusion that Hegel reaches in the "Philosophy of History." It now appears that the great dialectician was here somewhat hasty in his deduction.[549]

Throughout his long life, Russell never wavered in his disdain for war. He published *Wisdom of the West* in 1959, fifteen years after the defeat of the Nazi Thousand-Year Reich in World War II. In 1959, Germany was a divided nation still suffering from the ravages of strategic bombing and victorious Allied military maneuvers on the ground. In the subsequent few sentences, Russell pointed out that Hegel's idea of progression toward the Absolute in history led him to favor a state "organized in a totalitarian manner."[550] He argued that for Hegel, the "development of spirit in history is above all the task of the Germans."[551] He insisted that Hegel "greatly values strife."[552] Thus, Hegel rejected Kant's conception of worldwide confederation. Russell compared Hegel to the ancient Greek philosopher Heraclitus, commenting that Hegel agreed with Heraclitus's dictum that war is the father of all. He concluded that Hegel believed that war is morally superior to peace because external enemies "were vital to the moral health of a nation."[553] On this matter, Russell said that Kant displayed greater insight than Hegel. "For our own times have shown that war will in the end lead to universal destruction," Russell wrote. "That would indeed amount to a dialectic consummation which must satisfy even the most orthodox Hegelian."[554]

Yet as Coughlin and Higgins pointed out, today's neo-Marxist Left is a "teleologically informed movement" that executes through thought and history, along an arc, driven by the trajectory of the Hegelian dialectic. Hegel defines everything that "is" as fuel for "becoming" in a dialectical process that compels negation. In Hegel, the arch of history only proceeds by destroying the politics and culture that exist today.[555] "Hope and Change," as Barack Obama pledged when first running for president in 2008, references the Hegelian dialectic that presumes a "perpetual revolution" to lead to a future utopia. Coughlin and Higgins cautioned us that any analysis of today's neo-Marxist Left that does not account for the dialectic will fail.[556] "There is no understanding the Left outside a recognition that it is dialectically informed and driven," they insist.[557] Terry Pinkard, in his translator's note to Hegel's *Phenomenology of Spirit*, commented that *aufheben*, a German verb that Hegel used frequently, carries two senses in different contexts, namely "to cancel" or "to preserve." While Hegel tells the reader that he intends to use the word in both senses, Pinkard concluded that in the context in which Hegel usually employed the term, he "most often clearly means 'cancel' or 'negate.'"[558]

Even among his contemporaries, Hegel had critics. German philosopher Arthur Schopenhauer (1788–1860) greatly admired Kant but despised the philosophy of Hegel. In 1839, Schopenhauer submitted an essay entitled "On the Basis of Morality" that was the single entry in a prize essay contest held by the Royal Danish Society of Scientific Studies. In this essay, Schopenhauer said the following about Hegel:

> Now if for this purpose [i.e., the purpose of seriously testing Hegel to see if Hegel's philosophy deserved praise] I were to say that the so-called philosophy of this fellow Hegel is a colossal piece of mystification which will yet provide posterity with an inexhaustible theme for laughter at

> our times, that it is a pseudo-philosophy paralyzing all mental powers, stifling all real thinking, and, by the most outrageous misuse of language, putting in its place the hollowest, most senseless, thoughtless, and, as is confirmed by its success, most stupefying verbiage, I should be quite right.[559]

Schopenhauer continued to say that Hegel's "pseudo-philosophy has as its central idea an absurd notion grasped from thin air, that it dispenses with reasons and consequents, in other words, is demonstrated by nothing, and itself does not prove or explain anything, that it lacks originality and is a mere parody of scholastic realism." He called Hegel's philosophy a "monster." He also ridiculed Hegel for his fundamental misunderstanding of Christianity.[560] The Royal Danish Society rejected Schopenhauer's essay because of his strident but accurate criticism of Hegel, a philosopher whom the Royal Danish Society considered a *summus philosophus* [i.e., a philosopher of the highest rank].

Marx and Satan: How Marx Weaponized Hegel

> It is essential at this point to state emphatically that Marx and his comrades, while anti-God, were not atheists, as present-day Marxists claim to be. That is, while they denounced and reviled God, *they hated a God in whom they believed.* They challenged not His existence, but His supremacy.
>
> Richard Wurmbrand, *Marx & Satan*, 1986[561]

Karl Marx (1818–1883) was born in Trier, Prussia, under the German Confederation. He studied at the University of Bonn and Berlin, where he became deeply involved in studying Hegel.

In 1843, when Karl was twenty-five years old, he married Jenny von Westphalen, a woman four years older than him, and who was raised in an aristocratic family. Karl met Jenny as a child in Trier, where they became close friends when he was a teenager. Karl and Jenny Marx had a troubled marriage. Of their seven children, two daughters killed themselves by drinking poison in suicide pacts. Three of their children died of malnutrition. In London, the Marx family lived in miserable poverty, mainly because Karl preferred to borrow money from family and friends and sent Jenny to do the same with her family and friends rather than work. He had an illegitimate child by a maid but said Friedrich Engels was the father—a lie that Engels repudiated on his deathbed. Karl sent the illegitimate son to live with foster parents, cutting off all contact with him.

Although they were married at a Protestant church in Kreuznach, Germany, Jenny turned against religion, as did Karl. None of his family, including his mother and father, attended. The only family member in attendance at the wedding on Jenny's side was her brother, Edgar. In London, Jenny left Karl twice, only to return both times. When Jenny died in London in December 1881, Karl did not attend the funeral. At that time, Karl was confined to bed, unable to move, and forbidden by his doctor to attend the funeral. Engels gave Jenny's eulogy at her grave, claiming she died in the full conviction of atheist materialism.[562]

Professor Paul Kengor, in his 2020 book *The Devil and Karl Marx: Communism's Long March of Death, Deception, and Infiltration*, gave a graphic description of Marx's refusal to work:

> It would have been nice if Karl had merely gotten a job. Naturally, those who suffered most from Marx's refusal to secure work was his family, which was destitute from his laziness. His wife and kids lacked money, food, a steady roof over their heads, and even medical attention. He demanded more and more from his parents, until they could no longer give more and insisted on some tough love for their selfish son.[563]

Kengor's description of Marx's personal traits was equally graphic:

> The landlord was also fed up with Marx's resistance to grooming. Karl drank too much, smoked too much, never exercised, and suffered from warts and boils from the lack of washing. He stunk. "Washing, grooming, and changing his lines are things he does rarely, and he likes to get drunk," stated a Prussian police-spy report. "He has no fixed times for going to sleep or waking up." As for the family apartment, "everything is broken down," busted, spilled, smashed, falling apart—from toys and chairs and dishes and cups to tables and tobacco pipes and on and on. "In a word," said the report, "everything is topsy-turvy.... To sit down becomes a thoroughly dangerous business." Quite literally, the chair you chose to sit upon in the Marx household could collapse.[564]

In 1843, Marx and his wife moved to Paris, where he began writing for various radical newspapers and met his longtime colleague and collaborator Friedrich Engels. Under pressure from the Prussian government over adverse reaction to his increasingly revolutionary political writings, Marx went to Brussels in 1845. Under increasing political pressure on the continent, he moved with his wife and children to London in 1849, where he stayed for the rest of his life. He lived there as a stateless resident in exile after the government of Great Britain denied him citizenship, and the Prussian government banned him from returning to Germany. For decades, he lived there, working out of the British Museum's Reading Room, developing a collaboration with Friedrich Engels, a German businessman and philosopher of politics and economics. Marx is best known for his 1848 pamphlet *The Communist Manifesto* (1848), which Engels coauthored, and his three-volume *Das Kapital* (1867–1883).

In 1843 and 1844, Marx wrote a manuscript known today as the *Critique of Hegel's Philosophy of Right* that remained unpublished in his lifetime, except for the introduction that was published in Paris in 1844.[565] In this work, Marx objected to Hegel's ultimate defense of a constitutional monarchy. Hegel followed Aristotle's *Politics* in arguing that a constitutional monarchy is the highest form of government. Aristotle developed this opinion from his study of constitutions, a study that is today lost. Aristotle introduced in book 4 of the *Politics* (at 1297b–1298a) the concept of checks and balances in which the three coequal branches of government—the executive, the legislative, and the judicial—made the emergence of a dictator less likely. He further concluded that binding the power of each branch of government by a constitution (*Politics* at 1298b) was essential to specify limits to the authority granted each branch of government, with particular emphasis on limiting the executive branch's power. Hegel's support of a constitutional monarchy as the best form of government was consistent with his conclusion that Frederick II was a world-historic figure for his advancement of Prussia in the movement to unify Germany.

In the *Philosophy of Right* (paragraph 273), Hegel characterized the development of the state to constitutional monarchy as "the achievement of the modern world, a world in which the substantial Idea has won the infinite form."[566] He continued to argue the development of the state to constitutional monarchy involved the "genuine formation of ethical life," that is, "the content of the whole course of world-history."[567] He further concluded that a constitutional monarchy was completed by the world of civil servants (*Beamtenwelt*), constituting a bureaucracy (*Beamtemstaat*) that functions as an administrative state applying dispassionate reason to implement the sovereign's decisions competently.[568]

While Marx follows in the Hegelian tradition, he broke sharply from Hegel on many vital points. In his treatise entitled "A Contribution to the Critique of Hegel's Philosophy of Right: Introduction" published in 1844, Marx severely criticized Hegel's attempt to remain in good graces with Germany's Lutheranism. Marx made his hatred of God and religion clear beyond doubt in this piece. In the third paragraph of this published introduction to Hegel's treatise, Marx launches into a diatribe against religion. "The foundation of irreligious criticism is this: man makes religion; religion does not make man," he wrote there. "Religion is, in fact, the self-consciousness and self-esteem of man who has either not yet gained himself or lost himself again."[569] The fourth paragraph contains one of Marx's most famous characterizations of religion as a tool of oppression:

> The wretchedness of religion is at once an expression of and a protest against real wretchedness. Religion is the sigh of the oppressed creature, the heart of a heartless world and the soul of soulless conditions. It is the opium of the people.[570]

The fifth paragraph advances this theme to call for the destruction of religion:

> The abolition of religion as the illusory happiness of the people is a demand for their true happiness. The call to abandon illusions about their condition is the call to abandon a condition which requires illusions. Thus, the critique of religion is the critique in embryo of the vale of tears of which religion is the halo.[571]

In the penultimate paragraph, he wrote: "The only practically possible emancipation of Germany is the emancipation based on the unique theory which holds that man is the supreme being for man." He claimed that the "emancipation of Germany is the emancipation of man." He asserted that the "head" of the emancipation is philosophy, and the "heart" is the proletariat. "Philosophy cannot be abolished without the abolition of the proletariat; the proletariat cannot be abolished without the actualization of philosophy," he insisted.[572] The German word that Marx used here for "abolition" was "*Aufhebung*," the noun form of the verb discussed earlier that Hegel used for "negation." Marx's point was that Germany had to negate (i.e., abolish or destroy) Lutheran Christianity to embrace the political philosophy of revolution. Even in 1844, as his mature revolutionary political philosophy was just developing, he imagined that class warfare would be the origin of the German revolution. "The proletariat is only beginning to appear in Germany as a result of the industrial revolution taking place," he wrote.[573]

Kengor noted that Marx and Engels viewed their first draft of the *Communist Manifesto* as if they were writing a revolutionary "catechism," provisionally entitled *Communist Confession of Faith*. But in November 1847, Engels wrote to Marx suggesting they should reconsider. "I believe we had better drop the catechism form and call the thing: *Communist Manifesto*."[574] Kengor argued that their Communism became their religion for Marx and Engels, and their manifesto "became their catechism—their bible."[575] Here Marx and Engels departed from the religious tradition of Kant and Hegel, who believed the culmination of history would involve the full actualization of God, which for Kant was "pure reason" and for Hegel was "the spirit." While Marx and Engels adopted Kant and Hegel's dialectic, they were careful to distinguish their version as "dialectic materialism." Kengor explained:

> Atheist communists and socialists have always mistakenly felt that the answers to man's miseries are found not in God (the existence of which they deny) but in economic materialism. It is so ironic that communists and socialists blast the wealthy for being allegedly obsessed with money and material things when, in fact, communists and socialists are obsessed with money and material things. But as most rich people learn, money does not buy happiness. Humans desire more than that. How profound that Jesus told Satan that man does not live on bread alone. As the two debated, the Living Bread told the tempter that man lives by every word from the mouth of God. Marx took not the side of Christ on that one. Of course, Marx rejected Christ in total. Communists are atheists after all.[576]

Kengor commented that Communists are secular utopians who seek heaven on earth, but for them, the goal is the earth without religion.[577]

Turning again to Bertrand Russell, he agreed that Marx's materialism is a crucial point that distinguishes Marx from Hegel. In his 1959 *Wisdom of the West*, Russell makes this exact point:

> While the Marxist account is Hegelian in method, it repudiates Hegel's insistence on the spiritual nature of the world. Marx said that Hegel had to be put upside down, and this he proceeded to do by adopting the materialist doctrines of the eighteenth century.[578]

Russell concluded that Marx's theory was, like Hegel's, also authoritarian. He conceded that dialectic materialism "is valuable in pointing to the importance of economic influences as molding the life of a society."[579]

But he felt Marx oversimplified his thinking in terms of this idea. Here's how Russell argued that Marx too was authoritarian:

> In the social field itself this [the oversimplification of explaining everything by dialectical materialism] provokes some rather odd consequences. For if you do not agree with the Marxist doctrine, you are deemed not to be on the side of progress. The term of distinction reserved for those who have not been visited by the new revelation is the word "reactionary." Literally, the inference is that you are working against progress, in a backward direction. The dialectical process, however, ensures that you will be eliminated in due course, for progress must win in the end. This, then, becomes the rationale for violent removal of non-conformist elements. There is a strong messianic streak in the political philosophy of Marxism. As the founder of an earlier creed had put it, he who is not with us is against us. This is clearly not the principle of a democratic doctrine.[580]

Russell stressed that this argument points out that Marx "was not only a political theorist, but also an agitator and revolutionary pamphleteer."[581] He commented that the tone of Marx's writings is often "one of indignation and ethical rectitude, which would seem to be quite logical if the dialectic is going to run its inevitable course in any case."[582] Here he reflected on Lenin's point that if the state will wither away anyway, "it is pointless to make a fuss about it before the event."[583] His point was that Marx was concerned about the here and now. Marx was impatient to let the dialectic work its course, especially if that took eons. Russell understood that Marx preached "the overthrow of the existing order by violent means." Marx expected this to happen in industrial Europe in 1848, when a series of republican revolts against European monarchies created widespread disruption in France, Germany, Italy, and the Austrian Empire. All these "revolutions" disappointed Marx by failing. Russell concluded that Marxism's great appeal and widespread influence are due to the religious character of its utopian prophecies and the revolutionary appeal in its program for action.[584]

Kengor correctly judged that Communists are typically atheists, but he qualified that Marx acknowledges God exists. Marx's mission was to war against God, not specifically deny God's existence. Kengor's view is that Marx's hatred of God drew him to side with Satan. Thus, Marx and Engels saw their *Communist Manifesto* as the replacement of God's law with the laws of dialectical materialism. They sought to change human nature fundamentally to eliminate the idea that our fulfillment is in God or that we are spiritual beings who seek satisfaction in an afterlife.

Reverend Richard Wurmbrand, a Lutheran minister whom Romanian Communists imprisoned and tortured from 1948 to 1964,[585] openly accused Marx of being a Satanist. In his 1986 book *Marx & Satan*, Wurmbrand rejected the idea that Marx's mission in life was to champion "the hungry, destitute, and oppressed here on earth."[586] Like many of Marx's critics, Wurmbrand began his analysis by quoting poetry Marx wrote in his youth praising Satan. He quoted the following lines from "The Player," one of Marx's early poems:

> The hellish vapors rise and fill the brain,
> Till I go mad and my heart is utterly changed.
> See this sword?
> The prince of darkness
> Sold it to me.
> For he beats the time and gives the signs.
> Ever more boldly I play the dance of death.

Wurmbrand commented that "these lines take on special significance when we learn that in the rites of higher initiation in the Satanist cult an 'enchanted' sword which ensures success is sold to the candidate. He pays for it by signing a covenant, with blood taken from his wrists, agreeing his sword will belong to Satan after death."[587] He insisted that Satanism remained central to the character of the mature Marx. Wurmbrand wrote:

> When no Creator is acknowledged, there is no one to give us commandments, or to whom we are accountable. Marx confirms this by stating, "Communists preach absolutely no morals." When the Soviets in their early years adopted the slogan, "Let us drive out the capitalists from earth and God from heaven," they were merely fulfilling the legacy of Karl Marx.[588]

Wurmbrand argued that another proof of Marx's Satanism was his association with avowed Satanists such as the French anarchist Pierre-Joseph Proudhon (1809–1865) and Russian anarchist Mikhail Bakunin (1814–1876). In his 1918 sympathetic biography of Karl Marx, Franz Mehring detailed Marx's association with Proudhon and Bakunin. He noted that the "Inner Satan" was Bakunin's "strength and weakness." In making this observation, Mehring commented that Bakunin's reference to his "Inner Satan" was Bakunin's "favorite expression."[589]

In *God and State*, an unfinished manuscript that remained unpublished in Bakunin's lifetime, Bakunin made his admiration of Satan clear. In his chapter 1 discussion of Adam and Eve in the biblical Garden of Eden, Bakunin portrayed Satan's role in tempting Eve to taste the forbidden fruit as follows:

> But here steps in Satan, the eternal rebel, the first freethinker and the emancipator of worlds. He makes man ashamed of his bestial ignorance and obedience; he emancipates him, stamps upon his brow the seal of liberty and humanity, in urging him to disobey and eat of the fruit of knowledge.[590]

Bakunin ridicules God's reaction, suggesting that God "flew into a terrible and ridiculous rage," and that God "cursed Satan, man, and the world created by himself, striking himself so to speak in his own creation, as children do when they get angry."[591] He continued, explaining that God was angry because Adam and Eve elevated themselves to godlike status by their disobedient act:

> God admitted that Satan was right; he recognized that the devil did not deceive Adam and Eve in promising them knowledge and liberty as a reward for the act of disobedience which he had induced them to commit; for, immediately they had eaten of the forbidden fruit, God himself said (see Bible): "Behold, the man is become as one of the gods, to know good and evil; prevent him, therefore, from eating of the fruit of eternal life, lest he become immortal like Ourselves."[592]

But here, Bakunin twists the Bible verse. Genesis 3:3 (King James Version) has Eve explaining to the Serpent: "But the fruit of the tree which is in the midst of the garden, God hath said, Ye shall not eat of it, neither shall ye touch it, lest ye die." In Genesis 3:4, the serpent responds to Eve: "And the serpent said unto the woman, Ye shall not surely die." In Genesis 3:5, the serpent continues with a seductive lie misrepresenting God's word: "For God doth know that in the day ye eat thereof, then your eyes shall be opened, and ye shall be as gods, knowing good and evil."

But in the indented Bakunin passage quoted immediately above, Bakunin misquotes Genesis 3:22. That passage reads: "And the Lord God said, 'Behold, the man is become as one of us, to know good and evil: and now, lest he put forth his hand, and take also of the tree of life, and eat, and live for ever." Genesis 3:22 is a difficult passage, yet it must be read in conjunction with the following 3:23. This reads: "Therefore the

Lord God sent him forth from the garden of Eden to till the ground from whence he was taken." For their disobedience, God expels Adam and Eve from the Garden of Eden. In Genesis 3:24, God places cherubim and a flaming sword at the entrance to the Garden of Eden "to keep the way of the tree of life." Adam and Eve are cast from the Garden of Eden because they have disobeyed God (i.e., partaken of evil). They are banned from the tree of life and now doomed to die. According to the New Testament, banned from the Garden of Eden, eternal life is only granted to those "born again" by the grace of Jesus, the Son of God, dying on the cross for our sins. Bakunin twists the story to make it sound like God's motivation was to prevent Adam and Eve from becoming gods.

Bakunin concluded his rendition of the Genesis story, insisting he had discerned the true understanding of Adam and Eve's actions:

> Let us disregard now the fabulous portion of this myth and consider its true meaning, which is very clear. Man has emancipated himself; he has separated himself from animality and constituted himself a man; he has begun his distinctively human history and development by an act of disobedience and science—that is, by *rebellion* and by *thought*.[593]

Bakunin prefigured Friedrich Nietzsche's 1886 book *Beyond Good and Evil*. Like Bakunin, Nietzsche believed "good" and "evil" are simply conventions, artifacts of a Christian religion designed to enslave believers. In part 4 of *Beyond Good and Evil*, epigram 129 reads: "The devil has the broadest perspective on God, which is why he keeps so far away from God: – the devil, that is, as the oldest friend of knowledge."[594] So too, Bakunin concluded: "Christianity is precisely the religion *par excellence*, because it exhibits and manifests, to the fullest extent, the very nature and essence of every religious system, which is *the imprisonment, enslavement, and annihilation of humanity for the benefit of divinity*."[595] Bakunin reversed Voltaire's famous saying on God. In the *Epistle to the Author of "The Three Imposters"* published in 1769, Voltaire proclaimed: "If God did not exist, it would be necessary to invent him."[596] Bakunin's version read: "*If God really existed, it would be necessary to abolish him*."[597] Bakunin's point is that true knowledge is only available to those who acknowledge that on earth Satan rules. For Marx and Bakunin, God exists, but for them God is the great deceiver.

Coughlin and Higgins argued that "from Marx to [Saul] Alinsky, Marxists make a point of professing enmity to God while swearing allegiance to Satin in some form."[598] They suggested that as "Marx was formulating his critical philosophy, he understood it to be a hostile nihilistic rebellion against God that envisioned the destruction of Western civilization."[599] Alinsky was a 1930s Communist who built his career organizing labor in Chicago. There he interpreted the street politics of class warfare into a set of community organizing rules that would allow radical leftists to destroy capitalism. Thus, in the 1960s, Alinsky turned from working with union organizers to working with leftist street radicals protesting for civil rights and against the Vietnam War. Alinsky began his seminal 1971 book *Rules for Radicals* with an acknowledgment to Lucifer:

> Lest we forget at least an over-the-shoulder
> acknowledgment to the very first radical: from all
> our legends, mythology, and history (and who is to
> know where mythology leaves
> off and history begins—
> or which is which), the first radical known to man
> who rebelled against the establishment and did it
> so effectively that he at least won his own kingdom
>
> —Lucifer.[600]

With his identification of Lucifer as a rebel, we can assume Alinsky intended for us to catch his obvious wink to Bakunin. The dedication to Lucifer remains so explosive yet today that newly published editions of *Rules for Radicals* frequently omit the testimonial to Lucifer altogether. Still, what Alinsky is saying is obvious. He embraces the dark side, modeling himself after the Prince of Darkness as if to say that fulfillment of his destiny demands rebelling against the established powers in the United States. In his rebellion, he bows down to Satan, identifying himself with Lucifer's goal in the biblical revolution—namely, to grab power from the hands of God to place himself on the heavenly throne.

In the March 1972 issue, *Playboy* published an interview with Alinsky two months before he died on June 12, 1972. In that interview, *Playboy* asked Alinsky about his beliefs in God.

> ***Playboy***: Having accepted your own mortality, do you believe in any kind of afterlife?
>
> **Alinsky**: Sometimes it seems to me that the question people should ask is not "Is there life after death?" but "Is there life after birth?" I don't know whether there's anything after this or not. I haven't seen the evi-

dence one way or the other and I don't think anybody else has either. But I know that man's obsession with the question comes out of his stubborn refusal to face up to his own mortality. Let's say that if there is an afterlife, and I have anything to say about it, I will unreservedly choose to go to hell.

Playboy: Why?

Alinsky: Hell would be heaven for me. All my life I've been with the have-nots. Over here, if you're a have-not, you're short of dough. If you're a have-not in hell, you're short of virtue. Once I get into hell, I'll start organizing the have-nots over there.

Playboy: Why them?

Alinsky: They're my kind of people.[601]

More than simply wanting to grab power, Marx and Engels's message embraced the principle of negation, *aufheben*, that Hegel made central to his understanding of how the dialectic advances through history. By the time Marx had finished writing his three-volume *Das Kapital*, he had formulated the need for the working-class proletariat to revolt from the bourgeois capitalists who were exploiting their labor. What Kant saw as pure reason leading to a league of nations, Hegel saw as an advance of the German people to unite in a new Prussian state that would dominate Europe. Marx and Engels saw a worldwide revolution of the proletariat that would destroy the existing capitalist basis of Western civilization. But even more, they envisioned the destruction of Western civilization itself as they attacked Christianity. They loathed the spiritual force that had propelled Europe out of the Dark Ages into the flourishing art and culture of the Renaissance. Coughlin and Higgins extended this insight into the destructive nature of Marxism. They explained the point as follows:

> From Marx to Alinsky, the worldview expressed here is one of people who would rather be rulers in Hell than subjects in Heaven. When analyzing the Left today, the hate-filled nihilist drive for destruction should always be understood as a paired set with Voegelin's *libido dominandi* (will to power) that should never be left out of any analysis of the Left. "Why do they want to destroy?" "Because that's what they want to do?" "Why?" "Because they want to." "Why?" "There is no 'why,' they just are. Nothing follows."[602]

Marx's central thesis aimed to apply Hegel's *Aufheben* to destroy God by destroying Western civilization. "His soul [Marx's] was no longer true to God (Marx indeed had become a committed atheist by this point) but was now true to Lucifer," Kengor wrote. "Admirers of Marx will surely want to dispute that, given their fealty to their beloved founding father, for whom they make excuses for everything. Nevertheless, there is no debating the man's misery and his shaking his fist at God."[603]

Referencing the *Black Book of Communism*, Kengor continued: "The communist culture of death has been prolific. Whether by bullet, by starvation, by exposure to the elements, by war and terror against internal citizens and 'enemies' of the state, or by whatever means. How many victims? Truly only God knows."[604] The fundamental contradiction of communism is to presume that a theory that is aimed at destroying could result in a utopia. We have observed that both Stalin's Russia and Mao's China have demonstrated that communism is an effective ideology allowing a small group to stage a coup d'état overthrowing the established order. But once in power, Communist ideology is incapable of producing the promised results. Instead, the cadre staging the coup d'état continues destroying because the logic of their ideology is incapable of breaking from *Aufhebung*. Thus, the revolution once in power turns to abolishing, destroying, and negating their own.

Sergey Nechayev (1847–1882) was a Russian Communist revolutionary who wrote the pamphlet entitled *Catechism of a Revolutionary*[605] in 1869. In this influential pamphlet, Nechayev listed the "duties of the revolutionist toward himself." The second duty listed made clear Nechayev understood the dialectical necessity to destroy the existing order:

> The revolutionist knows that in the very depths of his being, not only in words but also in deeds, he has broken all the bonds which tie him to the civil order with all its laws, moralities, and customs, and with all its generally accepted conventions. He is their implacable enemy, and if he continues to live with them it is only in order to destroy them more speedily.[606]

The sixth duty is equally vivid:

> Tyrannical toward himself, he must be tyrannical toward others. All the gentle and enervating sentiments of kinship, love, friendship, gratitude, and even honor must be suppressed in him and give place to the cold and single-minded passion for revolution. For him, there exists only one

> pleasure, one consolation, one reward, one satisfaction—the success of the revolution. Night and day he must have but one thought, one aim—merciless destruction. Striving cold-bloodedly and indefatigably toward this end, he must be prepared to destroy himself and to destroy with his own hands everything that stands in the path of the revolution.[607]

He died on December 3, 1882, at the age of thirty-five in a Russian prison for the murder of a fellow student, though his real crimes were political. In prison, he was Tsar Alexander II's special prisoner, with weekly special reports of his prison activities going directly to the tsar. One of his revolutionary goals was to assassinate Tsar Alexander, which the revolutionaries accomplished on March 13, 1881, as Tsar Alexander was riding through the streets of St. Petersburg.[608] In 1969, the Black Panther Party republished his *Catechism of a Revolutionary*.

Ironically for Marx, when a Communist revolution finally came, it was not in the industrializing Europe of 1848 but in peasant Russia in 1917. In his 2017 book *The Russian Revolution: A New History*,[609] historian Sean McMeekin revealed substantial revisions of traditional analyses of the Russian revolution, primarily informed by access to Russian archives not previously open to scholars. McMeekin presented a well-documented and convincing case that Germany financed Lenin's return to Russia from exile in Switzerland. Germany's interest in Lenin stemmed from their hope that Lenin could capitalize on the fall of Tsar Nicholas II to get Russia to pull out of World War I. McMeekin noted that the founder of the Bolshevik Party, Lenin, was an "afterthought" in the 1905 revolution and "barely worth the attention of tsarist police agents until his return to Russia in April 1917, after an absence of nearly two decades."[610]

McMeekin put Lenin's role in the October 1917 revolution in perspective as follows: "Even then [when Lenin returned to Russia in April 1917], an out-of-touch Lenin would have had little impact on the political scene had he not been furnished with German funds to propagandize the Russian army at a time when Russia was at war on fronts stretching from the Baltic Sea to the Caspian, with more than 7 million men under arms."[611] He continued: "Lenin and the Bolsheviks played no role worth mentioning in the fall of the tsar, an unexpected gift of fate that, in mockery of Marxist pretensions of historical determinism, took them entirely by surprise."[612]

McMeekin's analysis affirmed historian Richard Pipes's then-controversial analysis in his 1990 book *The Russian Revolution*. His research confirmed Pipes's conclusion that what had happened in Red October 1917 in Russia was "not a mass movement from below, but a top-down coup d'état, the 'capture of governmental power by a small minority.'"[613] He understood that not only was Pipes's analysis of the Russian revolution correct, but the analysis also made clear that what had happened in Russia in 1917 had nothing to do with Marxist political theories. McMeekin emphasized that "far from being a product of social evolution, class struggle, economic development, or other inexorable historical forces foreseen in Marxist theory, the Russian Revolution was made 'by identifiable men pursuing their own advantages,' and was therefore 'properly subject to value judgment.'"[614]

McMeekin described the Bolsheviks' hostile takeover of the Russian army in 1917 as "an audacious, chancy, and close-run affair that was nearly thwarted at critical moments."[615] He commented that "had the statesmen thrown up by the February Revolution, above all Socialist Revolutionary orator and would-be strongman Alexander Kerensky, shown more competence and fortitude in suppressing Leninist agitation in the armies, the Bolsheviks would be no more remembered today than Europe's other socialist minority parties. Lenin would merit, at most, a footnote in the history of Russia, and of socialism."[616]

McMeekin stressed that rather than produce a Communist utopia on earth, the Russian revolution of 1917 led to the deaths of countless millions. The failure of Stalin's First Five-Year Plan, as we noted earlier, resulted in what "the Ukrainians now refer to as the Holodomor (hunger-extermination), Stalin's crash industrialization drive and the gulag network of murderous forced-labor camps that followed in its wake, or of the Great Terror that began in 1936, targeting not only 'enemies of the people' as in Lenin's time, but also (indeed especially) high-ranking Communist functionaries."[617] He confirmed the analysis in this book that sympathetic, sycophantic chroniclers covered up the reality of the specter of communism (the opening image in Marx and Engels's *Communist Manifesto*) and its resulting murderous horror. McMeekin wrote:

> For all the crude, reductive violence of their policies, the Bolsheviks were masters of propaganda, and they succeeded, with the aid of sympathetic chroniclers, such as John Reed, in electrifying millions around the world with the drama of their story. Reed's bestselling *Ten Days That Shook the World* (1919), a blend of reporting and propaganda beatified by Lenin himself (who wrote the introduction), painted flattering portraits of Lenin and Trotsky (less so of Stalin, who did not like the book) that influenced generations of readers, along with those who watched

> movies based on it, from Sergei Eisenstein's *October* (1929) to Warren Beatty's *Reds* (1981). That Reed was paid 1 million rubles by the Soviet government for writing this book, that he later recanted his earlier views after witnessing the misery of the Volga region on a boat tour, does not undermine his political importance. Like the "fellow travelers" who sang Stalin's praises after being taken on conducted tours of Soviet Russia in the 1930s, Reed saw what he wanted to see in the October Revolution, and he tapped into a huge market. Millions of foreign sympathizers, too, wanted to see their dreams of a better world realized in Communist Russia, even if few wanted to go there in person to experience it for themselves.[618]

Yet, McMeekin laments that "millennial Marxists" blind to the historical record of Communist mass starvation, political murders, gulags, and other forms of political imprisonment and torture, are positioning Marx "for a surprising comeback, as "younger historians revive the old dream of social revolution."[619]

The Rise of the Bureaucratic State

In the *Philosophy of Right*, Hegel devoted §287 through §297 to a discussion of the executive powers of the state. In these sections, he formulated the first theory of modern bureaucracy.[620] He conceptualized that making the bureaucracy a subcategory of the executive branch was consistent with Aristotle's division of government into three equal branches—the executive, the legislative, and the judicial—as we discussed earlier. Aristotle had not envisioned that the bureaucracy could expand to become the largest branch of government. Nor had Aristotle imagined that an unelected fourth branch of government could operate outside of the people's will.

Today, the massive federal government bureaucracy is capable of legislating (as our bureaucratic agencies promulgate rules and regulation through postings on the *Federal Register*) and determined to exercise judicial power (through administrative hearings aimed at withholding benefits or imposing fines for noncompliance). For Hegel, civil servants exist to transition the executive power from the universal to the particular. He instructed civil servants to govern concretely (§290). Therefore, he required that civil servants come from the middle class because the middle class embodies the educated intelligence and legal consciousness of the mass of the people (§297). He saw Russia as a country consisting of serfs at the bottom and rulers at the top. Thus, he believed Russia could not have civil servants because Russia had no middle class.

Hegel placed his discussion of administrative bureaucracy in his *Philosophy of Right* because he believed civil servants must administer morally and rationally. In the "Addition" to §297, he specified that the middle class was the class the civil servants belonged to because the middle class has a political consciousness and is the most conspicuously educated class. For these reasons, he concluded the middle class is the "mainstay of the state" as far as integrity (*Rechtlichkeit*, in English "legality") and intelligence are concerned.[621] For him, the Absolute Idea involved the manifestation through the historical dialectic of what Kant called "pure reason." Hegel expected the bureaucracy to operate according to "right"—that is, what Kant explained as "categorical imperatives." In Rousseau's terms, Hegel expected that civil servants would embody the common good as expressed by the "general will," avoiding the temptation to administer policy according to the whims of their subjective views—that is, ideology, personal motivations, or opportunities for gain.

German sociologist Max Weber (1864–1920) is the father of the modern bureaucratic management theory. Weber rationalized the bureaucratic role by specifying bureaucratic principles that included organizing civil servants and hierarchal rules that demanded bureaucrats be responsible and accountable for their actions. He expected civil servants would be career-oriented, recruited based on merit, and chosen through open competition, with their official conduct supervised according to strict rules of discipline. Like Hegel, Weber expected civil servants to be politically neutral and rule driven, not personally motivated. Like Hegel's civil servants, Weber expected bureaucrats to embody the application of reason to government administration.[622] Emeritus Professor Michael W. Jackson, an expert on Hegel, in a 1986 article "Bureaucracy in Hegel's Political Theory," argued Weber's account of bureaucracy lacked one major component of Hegel's bureaucracy. "Where they differ is in Hegel's insistence that the bureaucracy has a moral mission that defines its functional one," Jackson argued. "Commitment to that moral mission, according to Hegel, can be attained only through the continual development of ethical character as recommended by Aristotle and Kant. To meet Hegel's standard of bureaucracy, a government must be organized in a certain way to be functionally effective and efficient, but it must also be profoundly committed to the common good."[623]

Enter Woodrow Wilson

Fritz Sager, a professor of political science at the KPM Center for Public Management at the University of Bern and a visiting scholar at the Center for European Studies at Harvard University, published an insightful 2009 paper in *Public Administration Review*. With his senior research colleague Christian Rosser, Sager documented Hegel's influence on Max Weber and Woodrow Wilson.[624] Sager argued Weber's sociological analysis of the ideal bureaucracy, as expressed in Weber's book *Economy and Society* (published posthumously in 1921),[625] reinforced for American academics the principles of public administration advanced by Woodrow Wilson in his influential article "The Study of Administration" (1887).[626] Sager concluded that Wilson and Weber's theories on bureaucracy converged because Hegel was the common influence such that "Wilson's and Weber's administrative models may be ascribed to the Prussian tradition of public administration."[627] In other words, Hegel was the missing link between Weber and Wilson. Through American academics like Wilson, Weber's sociology and the tradition of Prussian public administration found their way into the study of public administration itself. Sager documented Hegel's influence on Wilson, noting that Hegel's *Philosophy of Right* appears in the working bibliographies in several works Wilson authored and published. Wilson's 1887 article served as the foundation for studying public administration in this country, earning him the designation as the "Father of Public Administration" in the United States.[628] With Hegelian confidence that civil servants would simply administer per the common good, Wilson launched upon America the rise of a bureaucratic state that by 2020 was capable of pulling off a neo-Marxist coup d'état aimed not just at ousting President Donald Trump but, more importantly, at overturning the Constitution. Today, the federal bureaucracy is dominated by woke civil servants determined to legislate and enforce their radical agenda through promulgating hearings, issuing fines, and initiating civil and criminal actions through the courts.

As Bertrand Russell observed, Hegel was the dominant philosophy among American professors at the turn of the nineteenth century, when Woodrow Wilson was a professor. In 1885, Wilson began his teaching career at Bryn Mawr College, a woman's college near Philadelphia. In 1902, the trustees promoted Wilson to be president of Princeton University. Ronald Pestritto, a political science professor at Hillsdale College, published a collection of Woodrow Wilson's essential political writings in 2005. Pestritto observed that Wilson's "view become intelligible in light of Hegel's doctrine," commenting that "by far the most important direction which Wilson's thought developed was in its adoption of Hegelianism."[629] Pestritto has argued that Hegel put "the German stamp on Wilson's administrative progressivism."[630]

Before examining a Wilson campaign quote, we need one final observation articulating Hegelian influence. In his book *Hegel and the Hermetic Tradition*, Professor Magee pointed out that Hegel rejected Sir Isaac Newton as a "depiction of a dead, mechanical system of externally related entities." Newton's mechanical view of the world differed from Hegel's organic view seeing the world "as a cosmos: an internally related organic whole," in which, for instance, he saw the earth's atmosphere, including the trade winds, as "a vast, living whole."[631] Coughlin and Higgins commented that Wilson's progressivism led him to view the U.S. Constitution in Hegelian terms, concluding that the Constitution was "a manifestation of the inferior science of Understanding that rendered it in dire need of being progressed—or more accurately, negated."[632] They noted that Wilson "prominently signaled the Hegelian nature of his agenda" when he campaigned for president in 1912, running on "The New Freedom." In his 1912 campaign speeches, Wilson proclaimed various versions of the following thoughts:

> The Constitution was founded on the law of gravitation. The government was to exist and move by virtue of the efficacy of "checks and balances." The trouble with the theory is that the government is not a machine, but a living thing. It falls not under the theory of the universe, but under the theory of organic life. It is accountable to Darwin, not to Newton. It is modified by its environment, necessitated by its tasks, shaped by the sheer pressure of life.[633]

Wilson repeated these ideas in his 1912 campaign, advancing his New Freedom concept. Wilson's New Freedom agenda called for employing "the power of government in behalf of social justice for all."[634] During his first term in office (1913–1917), Wilson pushed through his Democrat Party–controlled Congress banking regulations, antitrust legislation, and tariff reductions. In his 1912 speeches, Wilson reformulated the thought: "Living political constitutions must be Darwinian in structure and practice. Society is a living organism and must obey the laws of life, not of mechanics; it must develop."[635] The earliest mention of the Constitution as a "living" document traces to Woodrow Wilson's 1908 book, *Constitutional Government in the United States*. In that book, he wrote:

> Living political constitutions must be Darwinian in structure and in practice. Fortunately, the definitions and prescriptions of our constitutional law, though conceived in the Newtonian spirit and upon the Newtonian principle, are sufficiently broad and elastic to allow for the play of life and circumstance. Though they were Whig theorists, the men who framed the federal Constitution were also practical statesmen with an experienced eye for affairs and a quick practical sagacity in respect of the actual structure of government, and they have given us a thoroughly workable model. If it had in fact been a machine governed by mechanically automatic balances, it would have had no history; but it was not, and its history has been rich with the influences and personalities of the men who have conducted it and made it a living reality. The government of the United States has had a vital and normal organic growth and proved itself eminently adapted to express the changing temper and purposes of the American people from age to age. [636]

Coughlin and Higgins commented that Wilson's preference for Darwinian science and a living Constitution was ominous. They wrote:

> In transitioning America to a Hegelian state, a long-term dialectical negation of the Bill of Rights would quietly position the "rights endowed by the creator" [thesis] against "privileges granted by the state" [antithesis] in recognition that the unfolding Wilsonian state would become "the divine idea as it exists on earth"—i.e., god, at least in the Hegelian schema.
>
> **Beginning with Wilson, individual rights [that exist before the state and ahead of the state] would be pitted against group rights [conferred as state privileges] in an ongoing series of negations**. In the dialectical process of negation, "privileges granted by the state" are made antithetical to "rights endowed by a Creator." And make no mistake, this was the Wilsonian gambit.[637]

With this statement, Coughlin and Higgins echoed a point Russell made in his 1945 *History of Western Philosophy*. Russell wrote:

> The State is obviously valuable as a means: it protects us against thieves and murderers, it provides roads and schools, and so on. It may of course, also be bad as a means, for example by waging an unjust war. The real question we have to ask in connection with Hegel is not this, but whether the State is good *per se*, as an end: do the citizens exist for the sake of the State or the State for the sake of the citizens? Hegel holds

the former view; the liberal philosophy that comes from Locke holds the latter.[638]

Coughlin and Higgins conclude that from a Hegelian perspective, Wilson was "a man of action" who initiated the federal government's transformation "into a statist entity relying on scientized rationales."[639] They wrote with obvious distress: "Barely recognized to this day, the Constitution has yet to recover. It's not just that group rights are nowhere to be found in the Bill of Rights, group rights exist to negate the Bill of Rights."[640]

Coughlin and Higgins's reference to "scientize" appears similar to C. S. Lewis's attack on "scientism." By "scientism," we mean using science to replace religion as a source of authority in all questions, including morals. In his 1944 book *The Abolition of Man*, C. S. Lewis wrote that "[t]he serious magical endeavor and the serious scientific endeavor are twins."[641] John G. West, the director of the Seattle-based Discovery Institute and the former chair of the Department of Political Science and Geography at Seattle Pacific University, in an essay called "The Magician's Twin," analyzed precisely what C. S. Lewis meant. West noted that C. S. Lewis's observation might appear strange at first reading. He commented that science "is supposed to be the realm of the rational, the skeptical, and the objective," while magic is from "the domain of the dogmatic, the credulous, and the superstitious."[642] He explained that Lewis's view of "scientism" derived from his perception that magic and science are similar "in their ability to function as an alternative religion."[643] According to West, Lewis continued to specify that the second way magic and science are similar is "their encouragement of a stunning *lack* of skepticism."[644] And the third way magic and science are similar is that both share a "quest for power."[645]

Thus, in commenting that Woodrow Wilson's statism relied on "scientized rationales," Coughlin and Higgins remind us that Hegel's philosophy claims to have achieved a scientific certainty that the dialectic results in the advancement of spirit through history. Yet, as Magee demonstrated, the Hermetic roots of Hegel's philosophy put Hegel's thinking into the realm of the mystical. The point is that Woodrow Wilson argued that historicism demanded the Constitution be revised. Yet Wilson based this view on a near magical idea that by rewriting the Constitution to be in accordance with the times, we would be improving the Constitution. Coughlin and Higgins's point was that Wilson repeated Hegel's mistake by assuming the way Wilson wanted the Constitution to define human rights was the right way human rights should be defined. This "scientism" in Wilson's thinking is subtly intended to make us assume Wilson's leftist progressivism is in accordance with Hegel's concept of the "end of history" coming as the final stage of the dialectic achieving utopia.

Conclusion: Natural Right and History

In the introduction to his 1953 book *Natural Right and History*, political philosopher Leo Strauss commented on the opening passage to the Declaration of Independence: "We hold these truths to be self-evident, that all men are created equal, that they are endowed by their Creator with certain unalienable Rights, that among these are Life, Liberty, and the pursuit of Happiness."[646] Strauss continued to note that "about a generation ago," an American diplomat would say that "the natural and divine foundation of the rights of man...is self-evident to all Americans." He distinguished that "in Germany the very terms 'natural right' and 'humanity'" have become "almost incomprehensible." He stressed that by abandoning giving any "decisive importance to natural right...German thought has 'created the historical sense,' and thus was led eventually to unqualified relativism." He also emphasized that the "majority among the learned who still adhere to the principles of the Declaration of Independence interpret these principles not as expressions of natural right but as an ideal, if not as an ideology or a myth." He added that present-day social science "is dedicated to the proposition that all men are endowed by the evolutionary process or by a mysterious fate with many kinds of urges and aspirations, but certainly with no natural right."[647]

Strauss insisted that rejecting natural right was "tantamount to saying that all right is a positive right, and this means that what is right is determined exclusively by the legislators and the courts."[648] He distinguished between modern social scientists and philosophers like Aristotle and Plato. These ancient Greek philosophers judged that fixed standards of right and wrong determine human morality. Modern social scientists, Strauss insisted, consider that all statements of right and wrong in human behavior are "value judgments" determined by culture and subject to change through history. He singled out sociologist Max Weber as a prime example of value relativism. "I contend that Weber's thesis necessarily leads to nihilism or to the view that every preference, however evil, base, or insane, has to be judged before the tribunal of reason to be as legitimate as any other preference."[649] He viewed Kant's formulation of categorical imperatives as conclusive that Kant adhered to a theory of natural right, believing the moral imperatives operated as "absolutely binding rational norms."[650]

Strauss correctly viewed Hegel as outside the natural right tradition. For Strauss, Hegel belonged to a philosophical view that Strauss called "historicism." Strauss explained the distinction as follows:

> The fundamental premise of conventionalism [i.e., natural right philosophy] is, then, nothing other than the idea of philosophy as the attempt to grasp the eternal. The modern opponents of natural right reject precisely this idea. According to them, all human thought is historical and hence unable ever to grasp anything eternal. Whereas, according to the ancients, philosophizing means to leave the cave, according to our contemporaries all philosophizing essentially belongs to a "historical world," "culture," "civilization," "Weltanschauung," that is what Plato had called the cave. We shall call this view "historicism."[651]

While Strauss properly considered Hegel to be a historicist, he noted that Hegel believed his time was an absolute moment in history, "a moment in which the essential character of all thought becomes transparent."[652] Strauss elaborated on this concept: "Hegel had taught that every philosophy is the conceptual expression of the spirit of its time, and yet he maintained the absolute truth of his own system of philosophy by ascribing absolute character to his own time; he assumed that his own time was the end of history and hence the absolute moment."[653] Strauss argued that historicism "stands or falls by the denial of the solubility of the fundamental riddles."[654] Liberal relativism, Strauss maintained, arises not just from Weber-like assumptions that culture determines the values of the moment, but from "the natural right tradition of tolerance or in the notion that everyone has a natural right to the pursuit of happiness as he understands happiness."[655] He traced what today we know as neo-Marxist critical theory to liberal value relativism, which compels us "to be tolerant of every opinion about good or right, or to recognize all preferences or all 'civilizations' as equally respectful."[656] The end result is that value relativism leads to intolerance because for the liberal value relativist, the one absolute is the need to have "respect for diversity or individuality."[657]

Strauss objected to the notion of "progress" that abandoned universal principles for historical principles. Under the idea of progress, moral values were always as "principles fitting the particular age or particular nation, principles relative to the particular age or particular nation."[658] Strauss's classical theory of natural rights held that morals (i.e., absolute values) are the same today, unchanged through history, culture, or civilization. He took the philosophical importance of a belief in the divine seriously:

> Weber's own formulation of his categorical imperative was "Follow thy demon" or "Follow thy god or demon." It would be unfair to complain that Weber forgot the possibility of evil demons, although he may have been guilty of underestimating them. If he had thought only of good demons, he would have been forced to admit an objective criterion that would allow him to distinguish in principle between good and evil demons. His categorical imperative actually means "Follow thy demon, regardless of whether he is a good or evil demon." For there is an insoluble, deadly conflict between the various values among which man has to choose. What one man considers following God another will consider, with equal right, following the Devil. The categorical imperative has then to be formulated as follows: "Follow God or the Devil as you will, but, whichever choice you make, make it with all your heart, with all your soul, and with all your power." What is absolutely base is to follow one's appetites, passions, or self-interest and to be indifferent or lukewarm toward ideals or values, towards gods or devils.[659]

Fundamentally, Strauss's argument requires accepting that morality for human beings is unchanging through time. There is no Nietzschean "beyond good and evil." There is only good and evil. That moral values are absolute through time refutes Hegel's historicism, assuming we are morally imperfect today but will become morally perfected with the movement or the spirit (Hegel) through time. Strauss rejects Marxism because Marxism leaves individual appetites, passions, or desires—that is, personal preferences—to determine values. Marx's personal preference was a classless society where his needs would be provided as the state withered away. For Strauss, Marx's utopia exists "nowhere" on earth, never has, and never will.

CHAPTER 4

Identity Politics Bedlam

Mao did what Gramsci thought.
—**Arif Dirlik**, *"The Predicament of Marxist Revolutionary Consciousness," 1983*[660]

Marxist socialism thus faced a set of theoretical problems: Why had the predictions not come to pass? Even more pressing was the practical problem of impatience: If the proletarian masses were the material of revolution, why were they not revolting? The exploitation and alienation had *to be there—despite surface appearances—and it had to be being felt by capitalism's victims, the proletariat. So what was to be done about the decidedly non-revolutionary working class? After decades of waiting hopefully and pouncing on any sign of worker dissatisfaction and unrest, the plain fact was that the proletariat was not going to revolt any time soon.*
—**Stephen R. C. Hicks**, *Explaining Postmodernism, 2004*[661]

The Russian revolution of October 1917 and the success of Mao Zedong's Long March in 1934 both succeeded in establishing Communist regimes. But ironically, Lenin and Mao's success ended up as a significant setback for the theory of revolutionary dialectical materialism that Marx and Engels first articulated in the *Communist Manifesto*. In neither Russia nor China did revolutionary consciousness develop, as Marx had predicted, out of a class struggle in which the proletariat, identified as the workers of the world, would rise to overthrow the bourgeoisie, identified as the wealthy capitalist class owning the means of production. Stalin understood from Lenin's October 1917 revolution that a small cadre of disciplined, ideologically driven radicals could stage a successful coup d'état without first winning the mass support of the people. Mao's revolution was a peasant revolution in a largely rural country that lacked a dominant bourgeois-capitalist class or an exploited industrial working-class proletariat.

Gramsci's Long March

Antonio Gramsci (1891–1937) was an Italian Communist whom Mussolini imprisoned in 1926 for his revolutionary activities organizing workers in Turin, Italy. Gramsci spent the rest of his life, some twenty years, in Italian prisons. He is most famous for thirty-three *Prison Notebooks* that he meticulously composed while imprisoned. During his 1928 trial, the prosecutor cited words that allegedly came from Mussolini demanding, "we have to stop this brain from working for twenty years."[662] The notebooks cover various subjects, including Gramsci's reflection on Italian history, literature, and art going back to the Renaissance. While the notebooks bear no coherent structure, Gramsci's importance to developing Marxist ideology comes from his various scattered comments on clusters of themes that surrounded his thoughts on "hegemony," "common sense," and "culture." We will not attempt here any comprehensive discussion of his writings. Instead, this discussion will focus on the few key ideas Gramsci developed regarding the political theory of revolutions.

In his history of the Peloponnesian War (431–404 BC), Thucydides uses the term "hegemony" to designate the city in a leading position within the alliance of Greek city-states. Today's use of "hegemony" still identifies a situation in which one nation-state exercises international dominance in the military, economic, and diplomatic spheres. In the 1880s, Russian revolutionaries, particularly Georgi Plekhanov, argued "that the working class should form an alliance with the peasantry to overthrow the bourgeoisie, and described this alliance as one in which the workers would exercise 'hegemony' while the peasantry would be an ancillary force."[663] Lenin and the Bolsheviks attempted to put hegemony into practice with their program of forced land redistribution among the peasants. In his writings, Lenin's use of the term led to Gramsci's redefinition of the word in his prison notebooks. Gramsci used "hegemony" to designate the thought control the ruling class exerted over society by defining ruling class thought as "common sense." Thus, by shaping the language, meanings, and values of "common sense," the ruling class made subservient classes accept the values and culture of the ruling class unconsciously. His use of hegemony "stresses leadership's cultural, moral, and cognitive aspects."[664]

Gramsci explained his use of the term "common sense" as follows:

> Common Sense is not a single conception, identical in time and place. It is the "folklore" of philosophy, and like folklore, it appears in countless forms. The fundamental characteristic of common sense consists in its being a disjointed, incoherent, and inconsequential conception of the world that matches the character of the multitudes whose philosophy it is. Historically, the formation of a homogeneous social group is accompanied by the development of a "homogeneous"—that is, systematic—philosophy, in opposition to common sense. The main components of common sense are provided by religions—not only by the religion that happens to be dominant at a given time but also by previous religions, popular heretical movements, scientific concepts from the past, etc.[665]

Gramsci commented that common sense had been treated more extensively in French culture than in other cultures. He reasoned that this was due to the "popular-national" character of the French culture. "In France, more than elsewhere and because of historical conditions, the intellectuals tend to approach the people in order to guide it ideologically and keep it linked with the leading group." He continued:

> One should therefore be able to find in French literature a lot of useful material on common sense. The attitude of French philosophical culture toward "common sense" might even provide a model of hegemonic cultural construction. English and American culture might also offer many cures, but not in the same complete and organic sense as the French. "Common sense" has been treated in two ways: (1) it has been placed at the base of philosophy; (2) it has been criticized from the point of view of another philosophy. In reality, however, the result in each case has been to surmount one particular "common sense" in order to create another that is more compliant with the conception of the world of the leading group.[666]

Gramsci departed from Marx in that he disagreed that a ruling class is dominant because the ruling class consists of capitalists owning the means of production. In Gramsci's view, a ruling class is in control (i.e., exercises hegemony) through controlling the culture. He believed subservient classes accept the rule of the dominating classes willingly. He explained that common sense "is the conception of the world that is most widespread among the popular masses in a historical period."[667]

Gramsci realized that raising revolutionary consciousness was a "pre-revolutionary rather than a post-revolutionary requirement."[668] He further realized that culture and education were what raised a prerevolutionary consciousness. In other words, Mao, like Gramsci, understood that the development of a revolutionary consciousness had to precede a revolution. He also understood that the mass of peasants in China could develop revolutionary consciousness in a manner Marx had never considered. Mao and Gramsci both recognized that the development of a revolutionary consciousness did not require the presence of economic grievances resulting from class conflict generated by capitalist owners exploiting the labor of proletariat workers. Thus, Gramsci's emphasis on culture and education rather than economic class conflict redefined Marx's *Das Capital* formula for creating a revolution. In the process, Gramsci formed a bridge in revolutionary ideology linking Mao's emphasis on cultural issues to Marxist revolutionary aspirations, despite their noticeable ideological differences between Gramsci and Marx.

Gramsci also had a significant impact on the postmodernism movement of the late twentieth century, as well as on the Frankfurt School's development of critical philosophy. The Frankfurt School (i.e., a group of political intellectuals and writers) had their base of operations housed in the Institute for Social Research established at Goethe University in Frankfurt, Germany, in 1929, during the Weimar Republic (1918–1933). The postmodernists' embrace of subjective reality and relative values caused them to break from the eighteenth-century Enlightenment assumption of objective reality.[669] They questioned the importance of reason and the existence of objective truth. The postmodernists and the luminaries of the Frankfurt School shared an affinity to the psychological theories of Sigmund Freud, creating a natural affinity with Gramsci's emphasis on the importance of psychological reality in forming human consciousness.

With the Jewish intelligentsia escaping from Nazi Germany in the 1930s, the locus of the Frankfurt School shifted to Columbia University in New York City. In his 1986 definitive study, *The Frankfurt School: Its History, Theories, and Political Significance*, Rolf Wiggershaus, the historian of the Frankfurt School, described the evolution of the school as follows:

> The term "Frankfurt School" was a label first applied by outsiders in the 1960s, but [Theodor] Adorno in the end used it himself with obvious pride. To start with, it described a critical sociology which saw society as an antagonistic totality, and which had not excluded Hegel and Marx from its thinking, but rather saw itself as their heir. The label

> has, however, long since become more vague and all-embracing. Herbert Marcuse's media notoriety as an idol of rebellious students along with Marx, Mao Zedong and Ho Chi Minh gave the Frankfurt school a mythical status. In the early 1970s the American historian Martin Jay brought this myth back down to earth, back to its basis in historical fact, and made clear how multi-faceted the reality behind the label "Frankfurt School" was. But the label itself has long since become an indispensable part of the history of the influence of the ideas it represents, quite apart from the question of the extent to which we can speak of a "school" in the strict sense.[670]

Wiggershaus noted that from the publication of Max Horkheimer's essay on "Traditional and Critical Theory" in 1937, the term "critical theory" became "the main label used by the theoreticians of the Horkheimer group to describe themselves." In making this comment, his point was that the term "critical theory" was "a camouflage label" for "Marxist Theory." He continued to explain that "more than that, it expressed Horkheimer's and his associates' insistence on identifying themselves with the substance of Marxist theory as a principle and not in its orthodox form, a form obsessed with the critique of capitalist society as a system with an economic base and with a superstructure and ideology which were dependent on that base."[671] His point was that the critical Frankfurt School theoreticians like Marcuse did not have their origins in Marxism or the labor movement. Wiggershaus wrote: "The Critical Theorists themselves had their origins neither in Marxism nor in the labor movement."[672] Instead, Marcuse was influenced by postmodernist theory demonstrating "that capitalism was not merely an economic or a political crisis but a catastrophe for the human essence. What was required was therefore not just economic or political reform, but a total revolution."[673] He noted that Marcuse was deeply influenced by the young Marx after he read Marx's 1844 manuscripts.[674] Wiggershaus stressed that Marcuse led those Frankfurt School thinkers who came to see capitalism as an existential crisis in that capitalism produced alienation, blocking with an invisible barrier all paths humanity needed to travel to achieve "authentic human existence."[675] Thus, Frankfurt School thinkers like Herbert Marcuse, "reading the young Marx confirmed the fact that criticizing capitalist society was a matter of reflection on the true nature of humanity."[676] As a result, Frankfurt School thinkers like Marcuse tended to believe "[t]he substance of Marxist theory consisted of the specific criticism of alienated and alienating social conditions." For Marcuse, a revolution was needed not because capitalism oppressed workers, but because capitalism created one-dimensional alienated human beings.

Gramsci only became known to English-speaking readers through Quintin Hoare and Geoffrey Nowell Smith's book *Selections from the Prison Notebooks*, a book published on the eightieth anniversary of Gramsci's birth in 1971.[677] Yet his influence extended from the cultural Maoism of China's Cultural Revolution to the emphasis modern critical theory exhibits in various aspects of the "culture wars." His emphasis on the importance of cultural hegemony in forming a revolutionary consciousness is demonstrated today on university campuses across America. We see Gramsci's influence in all aspects of the critical race theory, critical gender theory, critical social justice theory, and so forth that drive today's neo-Marxist "identity politics." We will not be able to understand the *Weltanschauung* [worldview] of today's radical Left until we explore how Antonio Gramsci, the postmodernist movement, and the Frankfurt School morphed classical Marxism into today's critical theory.

Since the 1970s, as Gramsci's prison notebooks have become more available, his influence on Marxist ideology has been profound. Neo-Marxists have quietly morphed their emphasis from encouraging workers to revolt over economic class conflict issues to encouraging everyone living in capitalist systems to revolt because their lives were not authentic. After Marcuse, Marx's "Workers of the world revolt!" slogan morphed into today's culture war. Gramsci understood that workers in Western capitalist nations like the United States have generally agreed on all "common sense" cultural ideas. Until the 1970s, the United States had enjoyed broad consensus on the Judeo-Christian religious beliefs, the moral decrees of the Ten Commandments, and the principles of individual liberty defined by our founding documents. Gramsci "famously laid out a strategy for destroying Christianity and Western culture,"[678] arguing that instead of calling for a Communist revolution up front, what was needed first was a cultural war. Neo-Marxists since Gramsci have taken more seriously Mao's Cultural Revolution model. Gramsci's theories called for destroying capitalism not by a worker's revolt but by conducting a cultural war—a "long march through the institutions"[679] of the schools, the churches, and the media.

The Postmodernist Movement and the Rise of Subjective Reality

The seventeenth- and eighteenth-century Enlightenment is also known as "The Age of Reason." The Enlightenment was an intellectual and philosophical movement that followed significant advances in science. Enlightenment thinkers were confident the development of human reason would ensure continued progress in history. After World War II, the postmodernist era challenged the Enlightenment's confidence in human reason. With two world wars ravaging the twentieth century, postmodern thinkers questioned the value of absolute, objective knowledge and values that they concluded had resulted in the failed totalitarianism of Hitler, Mussolini, and Stalin.

Postmodernist thinkers see Immanuel Kant as "the decisive break with the Enlightenment and the first major step toward postmodernism."[680] As we have discussed, Kant's phenomenology presumes that our experience of reality is subjective. The inevitable conclusion of subjective perception is the realization we are capable of perceiving reality only insofar as our senses perceive reality. In other words, our personal experience of reality rules out the possibility that we will ever perceive reality as reality truly exists. In other words, just as a cat or a dog perceives reality differently from us, we humans each perceive reality differently. Not only do humans experience sensory variations, but we also differ in the cultural and other psychological screens that filter our personal sensory experiences to give us our unique perceptions of reality. In his 2004 book *Explaining Postmodernism*, Stephen Hicks, a philosophy professor at Rockford University, Illinois, explained Kant's postmodernism as follows:

> [Kant] held that the mind—and not reality—sets the terms for knowledge. And he held that reality conforms to reason, not vice versa. In the history of philosophy, Kant marks a fundamental shift from objectivity as the standard to subjectivity as the standard.[681]

Yet, Kant believed a priori synthetic perceptions that, like Plato's "ideas," act as hard-wired programs fixed in our brains that permit us to understand objectively the reality we perceived through our senses. Kant also believed a priori pure reason hard-wired our brains with a logic that produces categorical imperatives that allow us to judge human behavior with objectively true moral absolutes. Hicks explained as follows how Kant's particular reliance upon pure reason yet made his *Critique of*

Pure Reason the doorway through which postmodern thinking entered the world:

> Wait a minute, a defender of Kant may reply. Kant was hardly opposed to reason. After all, he favored rational consistency and he believed in universal principles. So what is anti-reason about that? The answer is that more fundamental to reason than consistency and universality is a connection to reality. Any thinker who concludes that in principle reason cannot know reality is not fundamentally an advocate of reason. That Kant was in favor of consistency and universality is of derivative and ultimately inconsequential significance. Consistency with no connection to reality is a game based on subjective rules. If the rules of the game have nothing to do with reality, then why should everyone play by the same rules. These were precisely the implications the post-modernists were to draw eventually.[682]

In other words, Hicks's point was that reason, for Kant, does not connect us to experience reality as it is. Instead, Hicks argued that Kant believed reason gives us the tools to imagine that our subjective perceptions of reality are objectively true perceptions. For postmodern thinkers, all perceptions of reality, including Kant's, are subjective. So too, all constructions of morality are subjective value judgments that are inherently relativistic, that is, nothing more than our personal opinions, predispositions, prejudices, or preferences. Humans are incapable of objectively perceiving reality for postmodern thinkers, and no absolute or universally true moral propositions exist.

Postwar French intellectuals and philosophers were instrumental in the development of postmodernist theory. In his 1979 book *The Postmodern Condition: A Report on Knowledge*,[683] Jean-François Lyotard (1924–1998) wrote a seminal treatise defining postmodernism. Lyotard railed against what he called "metanarratives," a concept similar to how Gramsci railed against hegemony based on commonsense stories about the world. In *The Postmodern Condition*, Lyotard explained his opposition to metanarratives as follows:

> Simplifying to the extreme, I define *postmodern* as incredulity toward metanarratives. This incredulity is undoubtedly a product of progress in the sciences: but that progress in turn presupposes it. To the obsolescence of the metanarrative apparatus of legitimation corresponds, most notably, the crisis of metaphysical philosophy and of the university insti-

> tution which in the past relied on it. The narrative function is losing its functors, its great hero, its great dangers, its great voyages, its great goal. It is being dispersed in clouds of narrative language elements—narrative, but also denotative, prescriptive, and so on. Conveyed within each cloud are pragmatic valencies specific to its kind. Each of us lives at the intersection of many of these. However, we do not necessarily establish stable language combinations, and the properties of the ones we do establish are not necessarily communicable.[684]

This passage proves that French intellectuals and philosophers can write prose equally dense as German phenomenologists like Kant and Hegel, perhaps only distinguished by a unique literary flair. Lyotard's point is that the metanarratives—the stories we tell to summarize crucial Enlightenment themes such as reason, science, and progress—created false intellectual assumptions that framed our perception of reality. By the term "metanarrative," Lyotard generally meant that any explanation based on the Enlightenment trusts in science and reason. In the next paragraph, Lyotard made clear he considers all metanarratives to be mere constructs of language, not of reality:

> Thus the society of the future falls less within the province of a Newtonian anthropology (such as structuralism or systems theory) than a pragmatics of language particles. There are many different language games—a heterogeneity of elements. They only give rise to institutions in patches—local determinism.[685]

The following paragraph contains Lyotard's complaint: namely, that decision makers (in Gramsci's terms, the dominant or ruling class) propagate these false metanarratives to gain the power to control our lives:

> The decision makers, however, attempt to manage these clouds of sociality according to input/output matrices, following a logic which implies that their elements are commensurable and that the whole is determinable. They allocate our lives for the growth of power. In matters of social justice and of scientific truth alike, the legitimation of that power is based on its optimizing the system's performance—efficiency. The application of this criterion to all of our games necessarily entails a certain level of terror, whether soft or hard: be operational (that is, commensurable) or disappear.[686]

Following the sequence of this argument, Lyotard explained how Marx was a captive to false metanarratives promising that material dialectical progress in history was inevitable:

> The logic of maximum performance is no doubt inconsistent in many ways, particularly with respect to contradiction in the socio-economic field: it demands both less work (to lower production costs) and more (to lessen the social burden of the idle population). But our incredulity is now such that we no longer expect salvation to rise from these inconsistencies, as did Marx.[687]

He commented that "the postmodern condition is as much a stranger to disenchantment as it is to the blind positivity of delegitimation." The postmodern condition then realizes that the Enlightenment narratives of reason, science, and progress were false narratives. The postmodern thinkers must learn to see Enlightenment narratives as nothing more than subjective language games. Thus, the postmodern thinker replaces disenchantment with the Enlightenment lie by embracing Gramsci's mission to get us to reexamine the common sense lies that imprison us.

Lyotard's postmodernism naturally led him to Vienna-born, Austrian-British philosopher Ludwig Wittgenstein (1889–1951), especially Wittgenstein's later thinking as expressed in his book *Philosophical Investigations*,[688] published posthumously in 1953. Later in his life, Wittgenstein came to reexamine the central thesis of his 1922 book published under the Latin title *Tractatus Logico-Philosophicus*[689] (*Logic-Philosophy Tract*, or translated as *Treatise*) that he wrote while serving in the Austro-Hungarian army in World War I. In the *Tractatus*, Wittgenstein attempted to formulate a set of propositions that would solve the problems of philosophy in a manner that is "unassailable and definitive."[690] But by the time he wrote the epigrams constituting *Philosophical Investigations*, Wittgenstein had come to adopt what was to become the central postmodernist assumption: namely, that all philosophical propositions, including statements about reality, are nothing more than subjective language constructions that he termed "language games."

In his book *Philosophical Investigations*, Wittgenstein embraced Kant's understanding that our perception of external reality is subjective to the extreme. Consider the following:

> Look at the blue of the sky and say to yourself "How blue the sky is!"—When you do it spontaneously—without philosophical intention—the

> idea never crosses your mind that this impression of colour belongs only to *you*. And you have no hesitation in exclaiming that to someone else. And if you point at anything as you say the words you point at the sky. I am saying: you have not the feeling of pointing-into-yourself, which often accompanies "naming the sensation" when one is thinking about "private language." Nor do you think that really you ought not to point to the color with your hand, but with your attention. (Consider what it means "to point to something with the attention.")[691]

Wittgenstein implied he has no idea what the other person sees. This paragraph aimed to demonstrate how we use a "language game" (i.e., the convention of attaching meaning to a word) to share our subjective perception of the blue sky with another person. We are not speaking a secret language because Wittgenstein assumed the other person has learned the "language game" attached to the word "blue." But he left open the possibility that the color "blue" the other person sees may not be identical to the color "blue" the person pointing to the sky sees. He worked this around to suggesting "word games" involve "language game" rules we utilize to draw our attention and the attention of others to objects and events in external reality.

Political scientist Walter Truett Anderson gave a lucid explanation of Lyotard's concept of metanarrative as follows:

> A metanarrative is a *story* of mythic proportions, a story big enough and meaningful enough to pull together philosophy and research and politics and art, relate them to one another, and—above all—to give them a unifying sense of direction. Lyotard cited as examples the Christian religious story of God's will being worked out on Earth, the Marxist political story of class conflict and revolution, and the Enlightenment's intellectual story of rational progress. (For Americans, Manifest Destiny was once a great metanarrative; for colonial powers, the theme of taking up "the white man's burden" served a similar purpose.) He proceeded to define the postmodern era as a time of "incredulity toward metanarratives"—all of them.[692]

Anderson explained that Lyotard did not mean people have ceased to believe in all stories, but that "stories aren't working so well anymore—in part because there are too many, and we all know it."[693] Anderson commented that Lyotard took "Yeats' famous 'center cannot hold' a step further." He explained that Lyotard perceived "we are exposed to a babble of diverse and contradictory fragments of stories, and the arts and sciences go their separate ways."[694] He suggested one way to understand this was to flip on the television and randomly change from channel to channel to hear the many diverse messages being broadcast simultaneously. "Consider the impact of a similar array of messages being beamed to every part of the world—people everywhere being bombarded by the sermons, the commercials, the vivid images of other people living quite different kinds of lives."[695] Anderson pointed out that we no longer live in premodern small towns and villages where people "lived within the context of a single coherent cultural package."[696] Instead, today we experience "culture shock," the "experience of coming into contact with other people with entirely different values and beliefs—the kind of experience that, in contemporary urban life, you're likely to have a couple of times before lunch."[697]

In postmodern thought, the conclusion drawn is that in a world where the objective perception of reality is impossible, there is no "absolute" meaning to any specific person's perception of reality. Reality means what it means to that person. From there, postmodern logic moves toward what we call today "identity politics," in other words, the idea that what I perceive as reality depends on who I am. Men do not necessarily perceive what women perceive. At a deeper level, a person may not perceive that he is male even if his physical body is masculine, nor may a person sense that she is female even if her physical body is female. Thus, the language dichotomy "he"/"she" and all related language loaded with a binary concept of gender and sex no longer work. We need "rules" (i.e., "language games") to permit language to be shared by others. Thus, we come up with "gender-neutral language rules."[698] One way to make writing gender-neutral is to use the plural forms "they/them." Thus, we would rewrite the above sentence: "People may not perceive that they are male even if their physical bodies are masculine, nor may people sense that they are female even if their physical bodies are female." But when the perceptions of reality are subjective, all ideas, values, conclusions—even logic and reason themselves—are relative, depending upon what each person thinks the words mean.

In their 2020 book *Cynical Theories: How Activist Scholarship Made Everything about Race, Gender, and Identity*, Helen Pluckrose and James Lindsay list two "inextricably linked core principles" of postmodernism as follows:

1. **The postmodern knowledge principle**: Radical skepticism about whether objective knowledge or truth is obtainable and a commitment to cultural constructivism.
2. **The postmodern political principle**: A belief that society is formed of systems of power and hierarchies, which decide what can be known and how.[699]

Pluckrose and Lindsay also identified four major themes of postmodernism:

1. **The blurring of boundaries**: The radical skepticism of the knowledge principle "results in a suspicion of all boundaries and categories that previous thinkers widely accepted as true." This blurring includes "not only the boundaries between objective and subjective and between truth and belief, but also those between science and the arts" (as in the writing of Jean-François Lyotard), "the natural and artificial" (e.g., writings of Jean Baudrillard[700] and Fredric Jameson[701]), "high and low culture" (Fredric Jameson), "man and other animals" (in Gilles Deleuze[702]), and "between different understandings of sexuality and gender as well as health and sickness (see especially [Michel] Foucault.)"[703]
2. *The power of language*: "Under postmodernism, many ideas that had previously been regarded as objectively true came to be seen as mere constructions of language. Foucault refers to them as 'discourses' that construct knowledge; Lyotard, expanding upon Wittgenstein, calls them 'language games' that legitimate knowledges. In postmodern thought, language is believed to have enormous power to control society and how we think and thus is inherently dangerous."[704]
3. *Cultural relativism*: "In postmodern theory, truth and knowledge are believed to have been constructed by the dominant discourses and language games that operate within a society." Because we are unable to step outside our own system and categories, "we have no vantage point from which to examine claims of truth and knowledge. The postmodern theory "insists that no one set of cultural norms can be said to be better than any other." Thus, for postmodernists, "any meaningful critique of a culture's values and ethics from within a different culture is impossible, since each culture operates under

different concepts of knowledge and speaks only from its own biases." Therefore, all such critique is "erroneous at best and a moral infraction at worst" since it presumes one's own culture to be superior.[705]

4. *The loss of the individual and the universal.* For postmodern thinkers, "the notion of an autonomous individual is a myth." The individual "is a product of powerful discourses and culturally constructed knowledge." "Equally, the concept of the universal—whether a biological universal about human nature; or an ethical universal, such as equal rights, freedoms, and opportunities for all individuals regardless of class, race, gender, or sexuality—is, at best, naïve." At worst, the attempt to form universal principles is "an attempt to enforce dominant discourses upon everyone." "The postmodernist view largely rejects both the smallest unit of society—the individual—and the largest—humanity—and instead focuses on small, local groups as the producers of knowledge, values, and discourses. Therefore, postmodernism focuses on sets of people who are understood to be positioned in the same way—by race, sex, or class, for example—and have the same experiences and perceptions due to this positioning."[706]

Rejecting the argument that postmodernism is dead, Pluckrose and Lindsay argued that we are now in the era of applied postmodernism. Today activist scholarship in the universities has morphed the fundamental concepts of postmodernism into the socialist ideas produced by the Frankfurt School to produce the culture war tenets of critical theory.[707]

Jean-Jacques Rousseau's famous phrase from his 1762 book *The Social Contract* resonates in the intellectual background of the political theories advanced by Hegel, Marx, Gramsci, and most postmodernist intellectuals. In that book, Rousseau wrote that "man is born free but is everywhere in chains."[708] Pluckrose and Lindsay note that throughout postmodern theory "runs the overtly left-wing idea that oppressive power structures constrain humanity and are to be deplored." They continued that the result is "an ethical imperative to deconstruct, challenge, problematize (find and exaggerate problems within), and resist all ways of thinking that support oppressive structures of power, the categories relevant to power structures, and the language that perpetuates them."[709] While not overtly Marxist, postmodern theory serves the neo-Marxist purpose to destroy existing culture as a prerevolutionary tactic.

Pluckrose and Lindsay stressed that advances in human freedom have not resulted from the dialectic of Hegel's "spirit" moving through history, Marx's emphasis on economic class oppression, Mao's cultural revolution, or the nihilism of postmodern theory. The advances in human freedom have come from the liberal tradition of political philosophers like Locke, Hobbes, and Hume. Political philosophers from this original liberal tradition formed the intellectual basis for Thomas Jefferson's famous preamble to the Declaration of Independence. Pluckrose and Lindsay argued the following:

> The gradual formation of liberal, secular democracy over the Enlightenment and the Modern periods was characterized by struggles against oppressive forces and the search for freedom. The battle against the hegemony of the Catholic Church was primarily an ethical and political conflict. The French Revolution opposed both church and monarchy. The American Revolution opposed British colonial rule and nonrepresentative government. Throughout these earlier periods, institutions like, first monarchical rule and slavery, then patriarchy and class systems, and finally enforced heterosexuality, colonialism, and racial segregation were challenged by *liberalism*—and overcome. Progress occurred fastest of all in the 1960s and 1970s, when racial and gender discrimination became illegal and homosexuality was decriminalized. This all occurred *before* postmodernism became influential. Postmodernism did not invent ethical opposition to oppressive power systems and hierarchies—in fact, much of the most significant social and ethical progress occurred during the preceding periods that it rejects and continues to be brought about by applying the methods of liberalism.[710]

Please note that by "liberalism," Pluckrose and Lindsay were not referring to the liberalism of recent Democratic Party politicians like Hubert Humphrey, but to the political philosophy of classically liberal seventeenth- and eighteenth-century philosophers like Hobbes, Locke, and Hume. In the 1960s and 1970s, Hubert Humphrey liberals remained in the liberal tradition of Hobbes, Locke, and Hume. Democratic Party politicians of that era wanted to protect individual freedoms they perceived God had bestowed as natural rights. Today's woke postmodern "liberals" do not believe in God, and they do not respect our right to object or disagree with their subjective "value judgments."

Algerian-French philosopher Jacques Derrida (1930–2004) is one more postmodern theorist who bears consideration. Derrida introduced the word "deconstruct," a concept central to how postmodern theory operates. In a series of three books he published in France in 1967—*Of Grammatology*,[711] *Writing and Difference*,[712] and *Speech and Phenomena*[713]—Derrida explained that the need for "deconstruction" occurs because the meaning of words used by any particular author must be established within the context of the words used by that specific writer. So, deconstruction for Derrida involved a tedious process of discerning the underlying meaning of a given text.[714] Applying his techniques of work analysis to determine meaning, Derrida argued that people tend to think in terms of binary oppositions (white/black, masculine/feminine, cause/effect, conscious/unconscious, presence/absence, speech/writing, etc.). As we shall see, critical theory adapts the postmodern idea of blurring boundaries to challenge these dichotomies. Pluckrose and Lindsay explained the importance of Derrida's deconstruction techniques as follows:

> In this understanding [i.e., Derrida's construct of binary oppositions], language operates hierarchically through binaries, always placing one element above another to make meaning. For example, "man" is defined in opposition to "woman" and taken to be superior. Additionally, for Derrida, the speaker's meaning has no more authority than the hearer's interpretation and thus intention cannot outweigh impact. Thus, if someone says that there are certain features of a culture that can generate problems, and I choose to interpret this statement as a dog whistle about the inferiority of that culture and take offense, there is no space in Derridean analysis to insist that my offense followed from a misunderstanding of what had been said.[715]

Finally, the binary oppositions must themselves be deconstructed to identify moral or political implications that imply power hierarchies that need to be rejected.

Serious students of postmodern theory have recognized that schizophrenia, customarily considered a psychological disorder, is the psychological state that best describes the subjective nature of postmodern reality. Catherine Prendergast, a professor of English at the University of Illinois at Urbana-Champaign, realized this in a 2008 article entitled "The Unexceptional Schizophrenic: A Post-Modern Introduction," published in the *Journal of Literary & Cultural Disability Studies*.[716] Prendergast noted that postmodern theory had destabilized the narratives of national progress, social order, and identity. She next commented that "crucial texts of postmodern theory have only achieved these destabilizations by holding one identity stable: that of the schizophrenic."[717] The Mayo Clinic defines schizophrenia as "a serious mental disorder in which people interpret reality abnormally." The medical center notes that schizophrenia "may result in some combination of hallucinations, delusions, and extremely disordered thinking and behavior that impairs daily functioning, and can be disabling."[718]

Prendergast cited the importance of the person with schizophrenia to Gilles Deleuze and Félix Guattari as typifying the "anti-Oedipus" postmodern hero, as described in their 1972 book *Anti-Oedipus: Capitalism and Schizophrenia*. Deleuze and Guattari insisted the following was true: "Far from having lost who knows what contact with life, the schizophrenic is closest to the beating heart of reality."[719] Prendergast explained why the schizophrenic holds such a place of honor in Deleuze and Guattari's book:

> The schizophrenic is imagined here [in the book *Anti-Oedipus: Capitalism and Schizophrenia*] to be immediately recognizable with a disorder visible, and yet, because not seen, at the same time invisible and outside the social order. So distanced from the public domain, the schizophrenic is ripe for appropriation by Deleuze and Guattari who find in this figure their anti-Oedipus.[720]

She continued to comment that it is "a peculiarly honorary position the schizophrenic holds for Deleuze and Guattari.[721] She also wrote earlier in the text: "Without schizophrenics, postmodernity would struggle to limn its boundaries, for the schizophrenic in postmodern theory marks the point of departure from the modern, the Oedipal, the referential, the old."[722] Prendergast concluded: "Reality is thus accessible to postmodern theory through the thought patterns of the schizophrenic."[723]

Postmodern theory assumes that since we must perceive external reality through our senses, human understanding of external reality must also be subjective. Yes, with the allegory of the cave, Plato acknowledged our experience of external reality is subjective. But both Plato and Kant insisted we have a higher a priori understanding of reality. For Kant our higher perception of reality involved synthetic a priori judgments forming transcendental ideas. For Plato, that higher a priori understanding was the Platonic ideas. Thus, both Plato and Kant would agree there is an objective element to external reality that limits or grounds our subjective understanding of that reality. Therefore, people who believe they can jump off a cliff and fly are most certainly going to kill themselves by trying. Psychiatry treats schizophrenia as abnormal behavior because schizophrenics fail to pick up the absolute element in the human perception of reality and the language conventions that we commonly use to discuss external reality.

Critical theory results in schizophrenic thinking because critical theory's underlying phenomenology derives from postmodern theory. Postmodern theory yields a hopelessly bizarre world even for French existentialists because precisely private languages and solipsism have us questioning whether there is any sure knowledge outside of our personal perception. Descartes's "I think, therefore I am"[724] transforms. We end up with a postmodern formulation: "I think, but I'm confused." The non-binary, idiosyncratically defined identities that critical theory generates would only work as imagined if the rules of external reality bent to our whims. As we saw with Hegel's mystical thinking, postmodern theory is fundamentally a mystical doctrine that permits each one of us to magically create the world for all.

The postmodern critique of the Enlightenment rails against reason and science because world wars ravaged the twentieth century. There is no doubt that reason and science since the Enlightenment have produced a world of increasing technological wonders—cellphones, personal computers, transportation of millions of people across continents via advanced commercial aviation, and so on. Yet, by presuming that the Enlightenment would also advance human nature to produce a race of Nietzschean *Übermensch*, we make a mistake assuming advances in technology would necessarily result in advanced human morality. What we are ending up producing is a postmodernist world of technological wonders populated by a woke generation that cannot tell us what a woman or a man is.

The Frankfurt School Rewrites Marx

On Sunday, June 22, 1924, an academic ceremony occasioned the opening of the Instituts für Sozialforschung (Institute for Social Research) in Frankfurt am Main, Germany. Carl Grünberg, a Marxist professor of law at the University of Vienna, established the Institute for Social Research as an adjunct to the Goethe University Frankfurt. Félix Weil, a committed Marxist who had received a doctoral degree from the University of Frankfurt, financed the Institute for Social Research through the resources of his father Hermann Weil, a wealthy grain merchant.

Wiggershaus, in his history of the Frankfurt School, noted that Hermann Weil came from a Jewish provincial mercantile family in Baden.[725] In 1890, when he was twenty-two years old, Weil went to

Argentina as an employee of a grain company in Amsterdam. In 1898, he established his own company that he then built into one of Argentina's largest grain enterprises with a worldwide business in the millions. During World War I, Hermann Weil advised Kaiser Wilhelm II that Germany could gain an advantage by sinking Allied grain freighters.[726] Wiggershaus commented that Hermann Weil was regarded as the "father of submarine warfare" for his role in World War I, but his advice only prolonged the war. Wiggershaus also commented that Félix Weil's goal was to establish an institute for Marxism, "hoping one day to hand it over to a victorious German soviet state."[727] Wiggershaus also commented that Grünberg created a unique situation, not only unique in Germany but also in the academic world. "Marxism and the history of the labor movement could now be studied at university level, and anyone who wished could take a doctorate on topics in these fields," Wiggershaus wrote. "There was a full Professor for Economic and Political Science in Frankfurt who openly embraced Marxism. There was an institute attached to the university whose work was specially dedicated to research into the labor movement and socialism from a Marxist point of view."[728]

On Grünberg's retirement in 1930, Marxist philosopher and sociologist Max Horkheimer received the nod to assume a newly created chair that incorporated the directorship of the Institute for Social Research with an appointment as a professor of social philosophy at Frankfurt University.[729] Horkheimer was born in Stuttgart, Germany, on February 14, 1895.

Horkheimer's father built the textile business established by Horkheimer's grandfather to the point where the Horkheimer family owned several textile factories in Zuffenhausen, near Stuttgart. At that time, Stuttgart was the capital of the Kingdom of Württemberg. Horkheimer came from a conservative Jewish family. According to plan, he left school in 1910 in his penultimate year to work as an apprentice in his father's business. In 1917, he was conscripted into the German army. An army medical exam found him "permanently unfit for service," and he observed the collapse of Germany and the November Revolution (1918) and the Spartacist Revolt (January 2019)[730] from a sanitorium bed in Munich. In the spring of 1919, after failing an army physical, Horkheimer enrolled in Munich University, where he studied psychology, philosophy, and economics. In 1925, he completed his doctoral studies with a dissertation on Kant. Wiggershaus explained that Horkheimer's primary concern was social injustice, the contrast between wealth and poverty. "Horkheimer was here able to draw on his own experience as the son of a millionaire, which protected him from any suspicion that he was merely harboring resentment," Wiggershaus wrote.[731]

On January 24, 1931, Horkheimer gave his inaugural lecture at the Institute for Social Research, entitled "Traditional and Critical Theory."[732] In that lecture, Horkheimer identified traditional theory with the Enlightenment reliance upon reason and science, an approach he argued had practical advances in the technological developments of the bourgeois period.[733] But he felt the exploitation of labor, and the resulting social injustice in 1930s Germany required "a radical reconsideration," not just of science, but of the human condition.[734] Wiggershaus explained Horkheimer's predicament as follows:

> Agreeing with Marx and Freud, Horkheimer also held that inequality, which had in the past been justified by its effectiveness as an instrument of progress, had no legitimacy in the conditions of the present day. It might appear that in earlier times achievements which accelerated material culture were only possible on the basis of a minority having significant privileges, while the majority had to make sacrifices. But at the present time it seemed to be the case that privileges awarded for not particularly brilliant achievements were obstructing the abolition of poverty, which was objectively possible.[735]

What Horkheimer aimed to achieve was the advancement of critical thinking that aimed at "emancipating" human beings through "an alteration of society as a whole."[736] He explained that critical thinking "is motivated today by the effort really to transcend the tension and to abolish the opposition between the individual's purposefulness, spontaneity, and rationality, and those work-process relationships on which society is built."[737] His point was similar to Gramsci's concepts of hegemony and common sense. For Horkheimer, critical thinking involved applying dialectical materialism to realizing how capitalism embodies injustice into working-class self-awareness through the cultural milieu in which we live. Horkheimer's dialectical thought process encompassed historical awareness and a vision that autonomous human beings could create a future utopia free of the enslavement of producing material goods. He explained this in his inaugural address as follows:

> In the historical form in which society has existed, however, the full measure of goods produced for man's enjoyment has, at any particular stage, been given directly only to a small group of men. Such a state

> of affairs has found expression in thought, too, and left its mark on philosophy and religion. But from the beginning the desire to bring the same enjoyment to the majority has stirred in the depths of men's hearts; despite all the material appropriateness of class organization, each of its forms has finally proved inadequate. Slaves, vassals, and citizens have cast off their yoke. This desire, too, has found expression in cultural creations.[738]

Horkheimer defined critical theory as the process of self-awareness increasing through the course of history, enabling us to understand our activities to recognize the contradictions that mark our existence. "The original fruitfulness of the bourgeois organization of the life process is thus transformed into a paralyzing barrenness, and men by their own toil keep in existence a reality which enslaves them in ever greater degree," he concluded.[739] He argued that unemployment, economic crises, militarization, and terrorist regimes, "in a word the whole condition of the masses," were not due to limited technological processes, "but to the circumstances of production which are no longer suitable to our time."[740] He argued that production was geared "to the power-backed claims of individuals while being concerned hardly at all with the life of the community."[741] He insisted this one-sided advantage to the powerful was "the inevitable result" of the "present property system" that he took to imply "that it is enough for individuals to look out for themselves."[742] As a result, the proletariat "have experience of meaninglessness in the form of continuing and increasing wretchedness and injustice in its own life."[743] What followed for Horkheimer was the realization that critical theory demanded forming "a dynamic unity with the oppressed class" to understand societal contradictions "not merely as an expression of the concrete historical situation, but also a force within it to stimulate change."[744]

Horkheimer explained to his institute audience the importance of their role in developing critical theory. As he saw it, the Marxist thinkers he attracted to the institute had a charge to revise Marxism to explain the proletariat was enslaved not by capitalism per se but by the capitalist culture that created mass consciousness in capitalist society. The function of the critical theory elite was to strive "for a state of affairs in which there will be no exploitation or oppression, in which an all-embracing subject, namely self-aware mankind, exists, and in which it is possible to speak of a unified theoretical creation and a thinking that transcends individuals."[745] Horkheimer had concluded that waiting for dialectical materialism to produce a revolutionary consciousness in the working-class proletariat was a waste of time. What was needed was a new elite of critical theory intellectuals equipped with the tools of social psychology, capable of identifying and articulating social injustice to stimulate the proletariat to a self-aware determination in order to overthrow the contradictions inherent in capitalism.

What was born out of Horkheimer's inaugural address was today's academic dominance of critical race theory, critical gender theory, queer theory, postcolonial theory, and intersectionality. Hegel relied on the dynamics of *Aufhebung* (i.e., negation) for the spirit to advance through world-historic figures. Horkheimer established that critical theory also demanded negation, the negation of cultural enslavement. He called upon the luminaries of his institute to follow what Jacques Derrida in 1967 would characterize as deconstructing the enslavement culture of capitalism. But additionally, Horkheimer's inaugural address hinted at the importance of applying social psychology to accomplish that task.

Erich Fromm Reads Sigmund Freud into Karl Marx

Erich Fromm was born in Frankfurt am Main on March 23, 1900. He was the only child of Orthodox Jewish parents who both came from the families of rabbis. In 1922, Fromm took his doctorate at the University of Heidelberg with a dissertation "On Jewish Law." In the 1920s, Fromm was deeply involved in Zionism under the influence of Rabbi Nehemiah Anton Nobel. Wiggershaus explained Fromm's Zionism as follows:

> This return to tradition took place in response to the fact that before the November Revolution in Germany [1918–1919], the great majority of the Jewish community had experienced only nominal equality at best, and even after the November Revolution the social situation of Jewish intellectuals was made extremely precarious by the growth of anti-Semitism. The return to tradition took various forms, among which were Zionism, Jewish settlement projects in Palestine or the USSR, practicing a Jewish lifestyle with kosher food and observance of the Sabbath and the feasts, or the modification of philosophical and other positions in the spirit of Jewish mysticism.[746]

Wiggershaus commented that Fromm "learned about psychoanalysis…through another Orthodox Jewish institution."[747] In 1924, Frieda Reichmann, a Jewish psychoanalyst, opened a private psychoanalytic sanatorium in Heidelberg. Fromm trained as a psychologist at Reichmann's institute. Then, in 1927, he opened his own private practice and married Reichmann. Wiggershaus also commented that Fromm's knowledge of religion and psychoanalysis, as well as his familiarity with Buddhism, Johann Bachofen (a Swiss jurist and anthropologist who was an early precursor of 1970s feminism), and Karl Marx, "meant that Fromm was able to go one step further than his humanist, Rabbinic models, [Rabbi Nehemiah Anton] Nobel and [Rabbi Salman Baruch] Rabinkow [a member of the Hasidic Chabad Lubavitch], and to become a socialist humanist who had freed himself from Orthodox Judaism."[748]

Fromm's contribution to critical theory was to "combine the Freudian theory of instinctual drives with Marx's class theory."[749] He simultaneously practiced as a psychoanalyst in Berlin, was a lecturer at the Frankfurt Institute of Psychoanalysis, and an assistant in social psychology at the Institute of Social Research. The Frankfurt Institute of Psychoanalysis set up offices at the Institute of Social Research. Wiggershaus noted that this positioning was "the first, even if only indirect, connection between psychoanalysis and a university, and it was followed in 1930 by the highly controversial award of the Goethe Prize to Freud, a public recognition of the founder of psychoanalysis by the city of Frankfurt."[750] Wiggershaus stressed that the "sharing of premises also led to an institutional link between psychoanalysis and historical-materialist social research."[751]

On February 16, 1929, Fromm was one of the speakers. His lecture, "The Application of Psychoanalysis to Sociology and Religious Studies," argued that both psychology and sociology were needed in critical theories. In the lecture, Fromm emphasized the connections "between the social development of humanity, particularly its economic and technical development and the development of its mental faculty, particularly the ego-organization of the human being."[752] At the end of the lecture, Fromm "sketched out the idea of an anti-metaphysical, historical anthropology"[753] in his effort to establish that psychology had a legitimate role to play in the investigation of sociological problems. Wiggershaus noted that at the end of his lecture, Fromm quoted the words of "one of the most brilliant sociologists." His quotation came from an 1845 book that Marx and Engels wrote entitled *The Holy Family*. The quote reads as follows: "History does nothing. It possesses no monstrous wealth, it fights no battles. It is man, genuinely living man, who does everything, who owns everything and who struggles."[754] Wiggershaus noted this passage shows Fromm emphasizing the humanism of the "Young Marx." He suggested this emphasis connected Fromm with Marxist thinkers like Hungarian Georg (György) Lukács (1885–1971), one of the founding members of the Frankfurt School. Lukács's writings had stressed the views of the "Young Marx" in tracing "all the phenomena of economics and sociology back to social relations between human beings, in order to unmask their fetishistic objectification and conceive of them as being the acts of human beings themselves, which had somehow escaped from human control."[755] In his 1923 book *History and Class Consciousness*,[756] Lukács advanced the idea that a Communist revolution needed a revolutionary vanguard to develop class consciousness among the workers. He conceptualized the vanguard of the revolutionary as a small dialectically created and ideologically advanced group of proletariat zealots to lead the revolution. This differed from Lenin's concept that the vanguard of the proletariat would be a small cadre of revolutionaries that would establish a dictatorship of the proletariat to change the ruling class from the bourgeoisie (capitalist owners) to the proletariat (socialist workers). Lukács agreed that Marx's great insight was revolution is economically motivated, in that "even production for the sake of production means nothing more than the *development of the productive energies of man, and hence the development of wealth of human nature as an end in itself*."[757] Lukács was influenced by Gramsci to consider that the real revolutionary goal was to attack capitalist culture, and he was influenced by Fromm to consider that capitalist culture had to be understood from a social psychological perspective.

In a chapter of *History and Class Consciousness* entitled "Reification and the Consciousness of the Proletariat," Lukács argued that "social relations between producers of commodities appear in capitalism under the guise of objective, calculable, properties of things ('value')."[758] "Reification" is the process of considering or representing something abstract, like "culture," in terms of the social psychological impact of traditions and practices that constitute culture. The word derives from the Latin word *res*, "thing" in English, such that reification is the process of expressing an abstract concept in terms of an actual entity or behavior. Thus, Lukács argued that capitalism's focus on producing material goods and services transforms the subjective reality of the participants, in this case, the proletariat or working class, into a commodity consciousness. He concluded that human beings in a capitalist economy experience alienation from themselves and others as they learn to comprehend themselves and their labor as commodities. He explained as follows: "*Subjectively*—where the market economy has been fully developed—a man's activity becomes estranged from himself, it turns into a commodity which, subject to the non-human objectivity of the natural laws of society, must go its own way independently of man just like any consumer article."[759] He elaborated: "If we follow the path taken by labor in its development from the handicraft via co-operation and manufacture to machine industry we can see a continuous trend towards greater rationalization, the progressive elimination of the qualitative, human, and individual attributes of the worker."[760]

As workers become subordinated by the machine, their intrinsic value becomes reified (i.e., worth so much money per hour). The value of a human being in a capitalist system becomes the hourly wage the person is paid for working. A worker is "free" when the worker "is freely able to take his labor-power to market and offer it for sale as a commodity 'belonging' to him, a thing that he 'possesses.'"[761] The worker's labor-power becomes the worker's "only possession."[762] Lukács concluded that a worker's "fate is typical of society as a whole in that this self-objectification, this transformation of a human function into a commodity reveals in all its starkness the dehumanized and dehumanizing function of the commodity relation."[763] Lukács believed that Fromm's emphasis on social psychological analysis was consistent with his own conclusion that a dialectically aware vanguard was necessary to address workers in a dehumanized capitalist culture to create an activist, revolutionary working-class consciousness.

In his affiliation with the Frankfurt School, Fromm's work became known as "radical Marxian social psychology."[764] Wiggershaus explained the importance of Fromm's thinking as follows:

> Fromm's central idea, which gave a class-theoretical edge to Freud, was that the power structure of class societies reproduces the infantile situation for those who are subjected to it. They experience their rulers as the powerful, the strong and the respected. Rebelling against them seems to be pointless, and seeking their protection and goodwill through love and submission appears to be rational. The idea of God demands a willingness, even from adults, to submit to father-figures and to view rulers in a transfiguring light.[765]

But Fromm ultimately parted ways from Lukács and the Frankfurt School over his embrace of Freudian psychology.

Yet, in 1930, the Institute for Social Research awarded Fromm a tenured position as its Social Psychology Section director. Fromm sent out 3,300 questionnaires featuring 241 items in a sociological exercise to measure working-class attitudes. But Wiggershaus felt the effort was pointless. He wrote:

> Information about the research on the working class is only available from the period after the Institute's flight from the Nazis, i.e., after the final proof that the German working class was powerless. However, on the basis of other works by Fromm from the same period and of the questionnaire itself, we can make reasonable conjectures about what Fromm expected from the research project, which he was responsible for drafting and initiating.[766]

Wiggershaus was equally dismissive of Fromm's sociological effort to take surveys:

> Would a social-psychological analysis of those who took part in the Russian Revolution or in the Munich or Hungarian Soviet Republics, for example, have shown that most of those who were involved were in favor of raising their children without corporal punishment, that they were in favor of married women having jobs, or that they held other views which proved that their attitudes were deeply anti-authoritarian? The fact that such questions spring to mind at once shows how absurd the idea was that an empirical research project, no matter how sophisticated, would be able to reveal the prospects for revolution.[767]

Wiggershaus noted that Fromm had concluded his study on the development of Christian doctrine "that Protestantism stood at the threshold of an era of society in which it was possible for the masses to take an active attitude," in contrast to the infantile-passive attitude of the Middle Ages.[768] In his essay "The Dogma of Christ," Fromm explained the Catholic Christianity of the Middle Ages as follows:

> This fantasy of the great pardoning mother is the optimal gratification which Catholic Christianity had to offer. The more the masses suffered, the more their real situation resembled that of the suffering Jesus, and the more the figure of the happy, suckling babe could, and must, appear alongside the figure of the suffering Jesus. But this also meant that men had to regress to a passive, infantile attitude. This position precluded active revolt; it was the psychic attitude corresponding to the man of hierarchically structured medieval society, a human being who found himself dependent on the rulers, who expected to secure from them his minimum sustenance, and for whom hunger was proof of his sins.[769]

Fromm saw the first Christians as "men and women, the poor, uneducated, oppressed masses of the Jewish people" who had a revolutionary attitude, much as he hoped he would find surveying the German working class in the Weimar Republic's Lutheran Germany. He characterized these first Christians as follows:

> In place of the increasing impossibility of altering their hopeless situation through realistic means, there developed the expectation that a change would occur in a very short time, at a moment's notice, and that these people would then find the happiness previously missed, but that the rich and nobility would be punished, in accordance with justice and the desires of the Christian masses. The first Christians were a brotherhood of socially and economically oppressed enthusiasts held together by hope and hatred.[770]

Fromm concluded the early Christians "were people who were tormented and despairing, full of hatred for their Jewish and pagan oppressors, with no prospect of effecting a better future."[771] He stressed that the Christian message "would allow them to project into fantasy all that reality had denied them [and] must have been extremely fascinating."[772]

Wiggershaus was dismissive of Fromm's attempt to view history in terms of Oedipal or other infantile psychological impulses, emphasizing that "the holding of revolutionary views" was no substitute "for engaging in a revolutionary struggle."[773] Wiggershaus continued:

> And didn't the fact that revolutionary struggles were not taking place [in early Christianity] mean that, in Fromm's eyes, the mere possession of revolutionary views was an adequate form of adaptation by workers to their objective social situation in the age of monopoly capitalism? There was a question whether the rationalization measures of the late 1920s, which eliminated many jobs, and the outbreak of the world economic crisis in 1929, tended to increase the sense of importance among wage-earners, rather than increasing their trust in the liberating progress of the productive forces. Even apart from this, the objective social situation was still marked by division into classes which in Fromm's eyes made a decisive contribution to reproducing the infantile situation among the masses.[774]

On the growing distance between Fromm and the Franklin School as Hitler came to power in the 1930s, Wiggershaus commented that "it was only a matter of time before someone like Fromm, who was convinced that fulfillment in life was possible for everyone, turned resolutely towards a messianic humanism which offered an ever-present escape from the endless chain of being and consciousness."[775] By introducing social psychology into Marxism, Fromm added a dimension to understanding Gramsci's concepts of hegemony and common sense and Lukács's emphasis on the culture of capitalist oppression. Cultural oppression involves not only patterns of behavior but also social psychology, a pattern of thinking that internalizes and conforms to the dictates of capitalist oppression.

But perhaps Fromm's ultimate mistake was to be a Freudian psychoanalyst. The hardline Marxists of the Freudian School, like Horkheimer and Lukács, considered Freudian psychology a failed pseudo-theory. Freudians believe that subconsciousness controls the way people act, which demands an analysis of infantile impulses and traumas. Marxists believe that the way people behave is dictated by their life circumstances, the most important of economic class distinctions that lead to bourgeoisie exploitation of labor in a capitalist system. As Dima Vorobiev, a former propaganda executive in the USSR (1980–1991), explained: "If Freud was right, there's little need in class struggle and proletarian revolutions. They can't change the way our childhood traumas impact our lives. All we need is to re-connect with the unconscious part of ourselves."[776]

At the same time that Fromm was moving closer to Freud, Lukács, a student of Martin Heidegger, was moving closer to understanding in economic terms the impact of the *Entfremdung* (in English, "alienation") that Heidegger expressed in his masterwork *Being and Time*.[777] Lukács concluded a Communist revolution was impossible until the capitalist culture itself was destroyed. A Communist revolution entailed negating the Enlightenment, destroying trust in reason and science, abolishing religion and all belief in God, and dismissing psychoanalytic theories that induced oppressed people to escape into fantasy salvation hopes and beliefs.

In the short but dramatic Hungarian Revolution from March 21, 1919, until August 1, 1919, the Hungarian Soviet Republic ruled. The influential foreign minister Béla Kun convinced Lukács to accept a position as the Hungarian deputy people's commissar for education and culture. He joined the Hungarian Communist Party, marking "his progression from being a cultural critic of bourgeois-capitalist society to becoming a Marxist." His cultural criticism of bourgeois-capitalist society "evolved into a cultural-revolutionary interpretation of radical communist change."[778] In the preface to his 1920 book *The Theory of the Novel*, Lukács wrote one of his more memorable passages, expressing the conclusions he reached during the outbreak of World War I:

> I arrived at more or less the following formulation: the Central Powers would probably defeat Russia; this might lead to the downfall of Tsarism; I had no objection to that. There was also some probability that the West would defeat Germany; if this led to the downfall of the Hohenzollerns and the Hapsburgs, I was once again in favor. But then the question arose: who was to save us from Western Civilization? (The prospect of final victory by the Germany of that time was to me nightmarish.)[779]

In his "Preface to the New Edition (1967)" of his 1923 book *History and Class Consciousness*, Lukács reflected that at the start of World War I, he felt the need for "a total break with every institution and mode of life stemming from the bourgeois world."[780]

In a 1970 article published in the year before he died, Lukács embraced the Frankfurt School's view that revolution demanded negating capitalist culture understood primarily in economic terms. He wrote:

> We now turn to the meaning of the communist transformation of society from the standpoint of culture. It means above all the end of the domination of the economy over the totality of life. It thereby means an end to the impossible and discordant relation between man and his labor, in which man is subjugated to the means of production and not the other way around. In the last analysis the communist social order means the *Aufhebung* of the economy as an end in itself. But because the structure of capitalism has so deeply penetrated the mental world of everyone living within it, this side of the transformation is only faintly perceived. This is all the more true because this side of the transformation, the *Aufhebung* of the economy is an end in itself, cannot express itself in the surface appearances of life after the seizure of power. Dominion over the economy—that is what the socialist economy is—means the *Aufhebung* of the autonomy of the economy.[781]

Lukács argued economic life under socialism would be free from "life under the hegemony of economic motives," those elements "which previously were accouterments at best now come to the fore: *the inner and outer life of man is dominated by human and no longer by economic motives and impulses*."[782] Later in the article, he expressed the thought again: "The *Aufhebung* of commodity relations enables men and cultural products, under which capitalism functioned entirely or primarily within economic relations, to recover their autonomous character."[783] He stressed that only through destruction could we achieve truly self-actualized, autonomous lives: "With the *Aufhebung* of human isolation and of anarchic individualism, human society will form an organic whole; its parts—individual members and products—will support and magnify each other in the service of the common goal—the idea of further human development."[784]

Coughlin and Higgins, in *Re-Remembering the Mis-Remembered Left*, commented that Lukács was invoking a purely Hegelian concept, "*aufheben der Kultur*" ("negate the culture"), calling for the negation of Western culture along dialectical lines using Hegelian forms of negation.[785] They expanded on this thought as follows:

> When saying "with the *Aufhebung* of human isolation and anarchic individualism, human society will form an organic whole," Lukács is conforming his concept of society to the Hegelian notion that particulars can only have meaning in the context of the Whole, which only manifests itself imperfectly until the end of history when the Whole fully manifests as Absolute Act. As such, individual identity only truly exists in the context of the Whole which the Vanguard of the Proletariat works diligently to facilitate.[786]

Coughlin and Higgins concluded that when read closely, Lukács's call for the "*Aufhebung* of the economy as an end in itself" makes clear that "Lukács was only interested in the destruction of the existing order." They stressed that consistent with Marx and Sergey Nechayev, "Lukács was driven by the same *libido dominandi*, the will to destroy."[787]

Horkheimer's inaugural address signaled a new direction in Marxist ideology. Having failed to create a German-Soviet state, both with the failure of the 1848 revolutions and the compromises made by Democratic Socialists to establish the Weimar Republic out of the November Revolution, Horkheimer ushered in a new round of revolutionary thought. Horkheimer and his Frankfurt School associates despaired that the dynamics of dialectical materialism would ever generate what Marx considered a historically inevitable workers' revolution against capitalism. Thus, Horkheimer and his Frankfurt School cohorts decided to appoint themselves the vanguard of the proletariat.

The Frankfurt School's real culprit, as Gramsci understood, was the culture of capitalism that enslaved workers into capitalist servitude. Yet, Horkheimer shifted the emphasis to explain that destroying Western civilization involved erasing the Enlightenment. No longer trusting faith in a benevolent God, the certainty of reason, and the material advances of science, the Frankfurt School embraced social psychology. Horkheimer and his associates agreed that Rousseau was right. Humans were born free, but Enlightenment acculturalization had subconsciously made workers obedient children to their parents by transferring the dependence infants had for parents to the authority workers conferred upon their capitalist masters.

By introducing social psychology into Marx, Fromm had shown the way, giving the green light to the importation of schizophrenic anti-Oedipal subconscious forces into the ego-driven rise of critical theory identity politics. Horkheimer advanced the project of transforming Descartes's famous formulation, "I think, therefore I am," into a neo-Marxist critical theory statement: "I think, therefore I am God." From the perspective of neo-Marxism and cultural Maoism, there is no need to be confused by the subjective experience of schizophrenic postmodernism. If all human experience and understanding are subjective, then each person is empowered to create their solipsistic universe, demanding all others respect who they are. The Hegelian *Aufhebung* built into the Marxian material dialectic requires that everyone deny and negate the enslaving culture of capitalism. Personal identity rather than Kant's a priori reason moved to center stage in Horkheimer's attack on capitalist culture as expressed by Western civilization.

Thus, in Horkheimer's formulation, the identity politics of critical theory was necessary to fill the phenomenological and psychological vacuum created by the attack on reason that was needed to destroy capitalist culture as expressed in Western civilization. All Marxism traces back to Hegel, and Hegel taught that God needed human beings to actualize God. Horkheimer suggested that to be "woke" is then to realize that we are each God unto ourselves, and as such, we have no reason to tolerate not even the slightest microaggression. To be woke is to be God in your own personal Garden of Eden, where only the woke are allowed to remain. To be woke is to live in your pseudoreality as if it were objective truth, universally true, and justifiably tolerant of no dissent. Thus, to sin against the woke is to deserve being cancelled.

Since the Frankfurt School opened its doors in 1930, neo-Marxists like Horkheimer and Lukács have diligently tried to fix the Marxist class warfare theory that failed to materialize. Horkheimer merged critical theory identity politics with Lukács's revisionist view arguing the vanguard of the revolution had a social psychological mission that needed to aim at creating a revolutionary class consciousness. Horkheimer and Lukács explained the proper techniques involved in negating capitalist culture.

For methods to negate any given culture, nothing worked as well as the deconstructive methodology of critical theory identity politics. Lukács also signaled to power-mad discontents that they, plus a small number of miscreants armed with the proper psychological techniques, could create revolutions by overthrowing economic systems, whether or not they had ever studied Marx.

Marx, Horkheimer, and Lukács also made abundantly clear that all future revolutionaries needed was a promise of utopia, where the revolutionaries would abolish evil capitalism so we would all be free. For those wanting more content to the promise of utopia, Horkheimer assured us we would be self-actualized and authentic when freed from the reified obsession with production of material goods under capitalism. Like genuine Marxists, Horkheimer and Lukács would not worry that where Marxists had managed to pull off a revolution, the aftermath was a nightmare. In Russia and China, the victorious vanguard of the revolution backed Stalin and Mao to commit genocide on the very proletariat that they had promised to elevate to utopia. Why give the description of utopia any detail, when the ultimate promise of self-actualization is to be whomever and whatever you want?

The Frankfurt School Flees Nazi Germany

On Monday, January 30, 1933, German President Paul von Hindenburg appointed Adolf Hitler as chancellor. On that same day, Hitler's Nazi SA, the *Sturmabteilung* (Nazi "Storm Division," i.e., "Storm Troopers"), moved into Horkheimer's house in Kronberg and converted it into a barracks. Horkheimer and his wife lived in a hotel near the railway station in Frankfurt after being warned of the Nazi's intentions. For the remainder of that semester, Horkheimer's chauffeur drove him from his apartment in Geneva once a week to give his lectures at the university in Frankfurt.

Then, on March 5, 1933, the elections for the Reichstag (Germany's parliament) took place. As Wiggershaus observed, the Nazis won 51.8 percent of the votes, enough for Hitler "to use it as a springboard for the continuing extension of Nazi rule—thanks to the compliance of the middle-class center parties, which legalized the Reichstag's self-destruction with the Enabling Act of 24 March."[788] On March 13, 1933, German police closed the Institute for Social Research in Frankfurt and searched the premises. In May, the Nazi Student League began using the institute's ground floor rooms.

For Horkheimer and the other principles of the institute, the exile to Geneva was provisional. With Nazism sweeping all over Europe, Horkheimer decided in 1934 to relocate the institute to Columbia University in New York City, accepting the university's offer to take over the building at 429 West 117th Street.[789] By 1938, most of the institute staff escaped Nazi Germany to rejoin the organization at Columbia. While Geneva remained the headquarters for the Société Internationale de Recherches Sociales, the New York branch became the academic center of the institute, which relabeled itself as the International Institute of Social Research (in English). After World War II, the New York institute dropped "International" from its title.[790]

In New York, Horkheimer had insisted that members of the institute refrain from active political involvement with politically organized groups among the émigrés. Wiggershaus explained:

> In the 1970s Jürgen Habermas asked Herbert Marcuse, "Did the Institute ever, let us say, take up a position in relation to the more strongly politically organized groups among the émigrés?" Marcuse replied, "That was strictly forbidden. Horkheimer insisted from the start that we were the guests of Columbia University, philosophers and academics." Even for those who were as fortunate, in spite of their misfortunes, as those who belonged to Horkheimer's circle, the trauma and insecurity of existence as a Jew was made very real by the flight from Nazi rule. But for Horkheimer's circle continuity was possible to an unusual extent. They merely intensified an activity they had practiced even in "normal" times—concentrating, as outsiders in society with social goals which were unacceptable to that society, on achieving recognition within the social and academic system. The directors of the Institute put all their efforts into being able to continue its academic work with as little disturbance as possible. In spite of a whole series of obstacles, this was surprisingly successful.[791]

In 1941, Horkheimer moved to Los Angeles. In June of that year, he and his wife moved into a bungalow in the Pacific Palisades, not far from Hollywood. There they settled into a growing community of exiles from Germany. His immediate neighbors were German novelists Thomas Mann and Lion Feuchtwanger. Wiggershaus explained the move to Los Angeles:

> A colony of German immigrants had formed in and around Hollywood. Most had come because of Hollywood—actors, writers and musicians

> who were working in the film industry, or hoping to. By giving nominal contracts to a whole series of writers—to [German novelist] Heinrich Mann, for instance—film companies such as MGM and Warner Brothers had made it possible for them to get visas and have a secure income, at least to begin with. For many of them, it was a case of "expulsion into paradise."[792]

Wiggershaus commented that Horkheimer and the others from the institute began arriving in the United States in 1934 when the Franklin D. Roosevelt administration was in its second year. In the first year in office, the Roosevelt administration "had made an impressive attempt" to minimize the effects of the Great Depression "by unconventional methods, under the label 'New Deal.'" There were hopes that the worst of the Great Depression was over. The Jewish emigrants from the Frankfurt School arrived "with a great deal of money" and at a time when the numbers of those escaping Nazi Germany were still small.[793] The Frankfurt Institute émigrés found the left-leaning Roosevelt administration "sympathetic towards intellectuals and prepared to entrust them with important tasks."

Horkheimer and Adorno Attack the Culture Industry

Theodor Wiesengrund Adorno was born in Frankfurt on September 11, 1903. His father, Oscar Wiesengrund, was a German Jew who converted to Protestantism around the time Theodor was born. Oscar Wiesengrund was the owner of a very successful wine wholesaling business established in Frankfurt in 1822. His mother, born Maria Cavelli-Adorno della Piana, was a Roman Catholic, descended from a French officer who had been a member of the Corsican nobility. Before her marriage, Maria had been a successful singer. Her sister, a well-known piano player, lived with the family. Wiggershaus noted that Adorno "had an extremely protected childhood and youth, marked above all by his two 'mothers' and by music. When he was sixteen, already a highly gifted high-school pupil, he began to study at the Hoch Conservatory at the same time. His teacher of composition was Bernhard Sekles, with whom Paul Hindemith had studied before the First World War."[794] The great tension in Adorno's life was his love of music and his desire to be a composer competing with his fascination with the German philosophical tradition that grew out of Kant and Hegel.

Adorno studied philosophy, psychology, and sociology at the Johann Wolfgang Goethe University in Frankfurt. In 1924, he took his doctorate with a dissertation on Edmund Husserl's phenomenology under the direction of the neo-Kantian Hans Cornelius. During the summer of 1924, Adorno met Viennese composer Alban Berg when Berg premiered his "Three Fragments from *Wozzeck*" in Frankfurt. In February 1925, Adorno moved to Vienna, where he immersed himself in the music of Arnold Schoenberg and Gustav Mahler. Wiggershaus noted that Adorno returned to Frankfurt in the summer of 1925, "apparently more suited to writing about music than composing it, feeling that he was not properly recognized by the Schoenberg circle, and unhappy with Vienna, which he accused of economic backwardness and cultural giddiness."[795] Wiggershaus further commented that while he had not entirely abandoned the plan to become a musician and a composer, he gained enthusiasm to pursue an academic career as a philosopher, possibly emphasizing aesthetics. "Nevertheless, his stay in Vienna had finally established the key role of the New Viennese Music for Adorno's aesthetic and philosophic thought," Wiggershaus wrote. "One of his most fundamental experiences continued to be the fact that a man like Schoenberg, who was only interested in culture and who believed in the monarchy and the nobility, had nevertheless managed to bring about a revolution in music."[796]

Adorno joined Horkheimer in Los Angeles in 1941. In 1944, Horkheimer and Adorno mimeographed a limited number of copies of what they initially titled *Philosophical Fragments*.[797] In 1947, Querido Verlag, then a leading European publisher of anti-fascist texts, published a substantially revised version in German, entitled *Dialectic of Enlightenment* (*Dialektik der Aufklärung*).[798] The book was an attempt to understand how the incredible barbarism of Nazi Germany was the culmination of the Enlightenment's Age of Reason, which dominated European intellectual and philosophical views in the seventeenth and eighteenth centuries. The Enlightenment aimed to lift humanity to a new, higher spiritual level of freedom through the advances in science. But for Horkheimer and Adorno, the Enlightenment was a failed project because it produced the grotesque horror of Hitler and Nazism. Horkheimer and Adorno could not comprehend why the German proletariat did not join the Communist Left in Germany to engage in a revolution that would have prevented Hitler from rising to power.

Even more puzzling to Horkheimer and Adorno, in 1933 Germany, when he assumed power, Hitler enjoyed the admiration of a significant percentage of the German population. Written while World War II was still raging in Europe, Horkheimer and Adorno explained that they wrote the *Dialectic of Enlightenment* to discover "why mankind, instead of entering a truly human condition, is sinking into a new kind of barbarism."[799] Their investigations concluded that the Enlightenment Age of Reason had self-destructed, based on the proposition that "social freedom is inseparable from enlightened thought."[800] In other words, Horkheimer and Adorno concluded that the dialectical extension of capitalism had not produced social freedom. But instead, the historical development of the Enlightenment had produced a culture of capitalist enslavement in Germany that the authors feared was developing rapidly in the United States.

The chapter of the *Dialectic of Enlightenment* that made the most significant impact on the Frankfurt School's development of neo-Marxism theory was entitled "The Cultural Industry: Enlightenment as Mass Deception." Here Horkheimer and Adorno explained that advanced capitalism as they experienced it in Germany and the United States opened their eyes to the "culture industry."[801] They reasoned that the loss of established religion's standard of objective truth and morality (i.e., "the last remnants of precapitalism") did not lead to "cultural chaos" in Hitler's Germany or the United States. Instead, "culture now impresses the same stamp on everything."[802] Horkheimer and Adorno explained as follows, writing about their experience in the United States:

> Films, radio and magazines make up a system which is uniform as a whole and in every part. Even the aesthetic activities of political opposites are one in their enthusiastic obedience to the rhythm of the iron system. The decorative industrial management buildings and exhibition centers in the authoritarian countries are much the same as anywhere else. The huge gleaming towers that shoot up everywhere are outward signs of the ingenious planning of international concerns, toward which the unleashed entrepreneurial system (whose monuments are a mass of gloomy houses and business premises in grimy, spiritless cities) was already hastening. Even now the older houses just outside the concrete city centers look like slums, and the new bungalows on the outskirts are at one with the flimsy structures of world fairs in their praise of technical progress and their built-in demand to be discarded after a short while like empty food cans.[803]

The point was that under advanced capitalism, "all mass culture is identical, and the lines of its artificial framework begin to show through."[804] They argued that the "people at the top" no longer conceal monopoly.[805]

Instead, as its violence becomes more open, its power grows. "Movies and radio no longer pretend to be art," they continued. "The truth that they are just business is made into an ideology in order to justify the rubbish they deliberately produce."[806]

Horkheimer and Adorno argued that the consumers of the culture industry were "workers and employees, the farmers and lower middle class. Capitalist production so confines them, body and soul, that they fall helpless victims to what is offered them."[807] Thus, the working class imprisons itself with the conspicuous consumption of goods not truly needed and the passing of idle time with amusements not designed to be uplifting. Eventually, under the influence of the culture industry, even language gets standardized:

> When German Fascists decide one day to launch a word—say "intolerable"—over the loudspeakers the next day the whole nation is saying "intolerable." By the same pattern, the nations against whom the weight of the German "blitzkrieg" was thrown took the word into their own jargon. The general repetition of names for measures to be taken by the authorities makes them, so to speak, familiar, just as the brand name on everybody's lips increased sales in the era of the free market. The blind and rapid spreading repetition of words with special designations links advertising with the totalitarian watchword.[808]

Horkheimer ended the chapter with the following:

> The way in which a girl accepts and keeps the obligatory date, the inflection on the telephone or in the most intimate situation, the choice of words in conversation, and the whole inner life as classified by the now somewhat devalued depth psychology, bear witness to man's attempt to make himself a proficient apparatus, similar (even in emotions) to the model served up by the culture industry. The most intimate reactions of human beings have been so thoroughly reified that the idea of anything specific to themselves now persists only as an utterly abstract notion: personality scarcely signifies anything more than shining white teeth and freedom from body odor and emotions. The triumph of advertising in the culture industry is that consumers feel compelled to buy and use its products even though they see through them.[809]

For Horkheimer and Adorno, examining the culture industry in advanced capitalist societies exposes the failure of the Enlightenment. The book explains why the Enlightenment principle that "social freedom is inseparable from enlightened thought" is a bankrupt lie. How could that principle be confirmed when the Enlightenment culminated in Hitler, the Holocaust, and World War II, the most devastating global war ever experienced on the planet? The Enlightenment required a culture industry because the actual product of the Enlightenment was not the triumph of reason. Instead of producing social freedom, the Enlightenment birthed capitalist enslavement through the standardization of material production, the diversion of television and cinema to keep people amused, and the lust for consumption that kept people satisfied with materialist goods.

Horkheimer and Adorno in the *Dialectic of Enlightenment* embraced a Gramsci-like conclusion that a Marxist working-class revolution failed to happen in the advanced industrial societies of Nazi Germany and the United States during World War II because the Enlightenment's Age of Reason failed to produce a superior, more ethical human being. For Horkheimer and Adorno, the Enlightenment resulted in a capitalist economic culture that allowed Hitler to turn Darwin's theory of evolution into eugenic master race hysteria. Horkheimer and Adorno fled Nazi Germany because Nazism mobilized the German people to target Jews as vermin worthy only of extermination. Horkheimer and Adorno feared they would experience the same fate in the United States if they failed to produce a true Communist revolution into this new nation to which they fled.

Marquis de Sade: Frankfurt School Hero

Needing a new, more powerful force to upend the culture of an advanced industrial society like the United States, Horkheimer and Adorno turned to sex. They devoted a chapter of the *Dialectic of Enlightenment* to Juliette, the evil hero of the Marquis de Sade's saga in which the virtuous sister, Justine, is destroyed. Appropriately, the chapter title, "Excursus II: Juliette or Enlightenment and Morality," subtly suggests that we can stay with the Enlightenment and its subjugation morality or liberate ourselves if we so choose. But liberation demands embracing Juliette's sexual revolution. To be liberated, we must mock Enlightenment reason and break the chains of its subjugation morality. Sade's Enlightenment dialectic posits Juliette's outrageous immorality against Justine's Enlightenment morality to demonstrate what Horkheimer and Adorno conclude is the ultimate, inevitable outcome of the Enlightenment's enslavement morality.[810] Justine comes to ruin because she is a slave to the Enlightenment morality she virtuously follows. Adorno and Horkheimer begin their treatment of Juliette with the following reflection on Kant:

> The conceptual apparatus determines the senses, even before perception occurs; *a priori*, the citizen sees the world as the matter from which he himself manufactures it. Intuitively, Kant foretold what Hollywood conspicuously put into practice: in the very process of production, images are pre-censored according to the norm of the understanding which will later govern their apprehension.[811]

In other words, because our perception of reality is subjective, the social reality (i.e., the culture we experience) must be a socially constructed reality. Truthfully, we have no idea what reality viewed as objective truth might be or how the liberated, self-actualized human might live. Horkheimer's point was that Kant's a priori synthetic judgment meant we have no choice but to live in a socially constructed reality, otherwise known as "culture," that the capitalist rulers created to hold in check the proletariat slaves, namely us. Thus, Horkheimer and Adorno concluded that the Marxist working-class revolution failed because the Enlightenment empowered capitalists to create an enslavement culture in which we would enslave ourselves. Subtly reading Freud into Marx, Horkheimer and Adorno unleashed libido, unbridled sexual energy (i.e., *eros*), to be their agent of destruction.

Horkheimer and Adorno argued that under Enlightenment thinking Kant's vision of pure reason building a utopia became "a mere systematic science"[812] that leveled down individuals into a democracy of socially defined categories:

> No one is other than what he has come to be: a useful, successful, or frustrated member of vocational and national groups. He is one among many representatives of his geographical, psychological and sociological type. Logic is democratic; in this respect the great have no advantage over the insignificant. The great are classed as important, and the insignificant as prospective objects for social relief. Science in general relates to nature and man only as the insurance company in particular relates to life and death. Whoever dies is unimportant: it is a question of ratio between accidents and the company's liabilities. Not individuality but the law of the majority recurs in the formula.[813]

Horkheimer and Adorno felt "Kant's work transcends experience as mere operation, and for that reason—in accordance with its own principles—is now condemned by the Enlightenment as dogmatic."[814] How could pure reason operating as science determine moral rules like Kant formulated in his categorical imperatives? The authors charged that Kant's reliance on the scientific method to determine truth "sealed its own nullity, for science is technical practice."[815] Science cannot reach beyond our subjective perceptions of reality, so science itself is culturally bound. "The moral teachings of the Enlightenment bear witness to a hopeless attempt to replace enfeebled religion with some reason for persisting in society when interest is absent," they concluded. Thus, they reasoned, Kant's moral doctrines are "propagandist and sentimental (even when they seem rigorous), or else they are merely *coups de main* [a sudden attack in force] by reason of the consciousness that morality itself is underivable—as in the case of Kant's recourse to ethical forces as a fact."[816]

Horkheimer and Adorno argued that the "root of Kantian optimism, according to which moral behavior is rational even if the mean and wretched would prevail, is actually an expression of horror at the thought of reversion to barbarism."[817] They rejected Kant's premise that a priori synthetic judgments can elevate our moral judgments from the subjective realm of our experiences to the absolute reality of categorical imperatives. If we live in a constructed reality experienced as culture, moral rules are nothing more than an artifact of the culture of capitalism that enslaved workers into capitalist servitude. "Liberated from the control of the same class which tied the nineteenth-century businessman to Kantian respect and mutual love, Fascism (which by its iron discipline saves its subject peoples the troubles of moral feelings) no longer needs to uphold any disciplines," they insisted.[818]

Horkheimer and Adorno contended that fascism is the logical result of Kantian morality, and enslavement of the working class is the goal of Enlightenment morality. In the chapter on the culture industry, the authors explain that the "less the culture industry has to promise, the less it can offer a meaningful explanation of life, and the emptier is the ideology it disseminates."[819] Again, they saw that the goal of the culture industry is domination:

> Value judgments are taken either as advertising or empty talk. Accordingly ideology has been made vague and noncommittal, and thus neither clearer nor weaker. Its very vagueness, its almost scientific aversion from committing itself to anything which cannot be verified, acts as an instrument of domination.[820]

Horkheimer and Adorno shock us by insisting Kant's *Critique of Pure Reason* led to Nietzsche's *Genealogy of Morals*. In Horkheimer and Adorno's view, the Marquis de Sade was the one person who had cracked the code explaining why the Enlightenment had led to a fascist totalitarian state. More specifically, they noted that Sade understood the capitalist enslavement culture as a "bourgeois individual freed from tutelage."[821] Their point is that Sade understood how the ruling class in advanced capitalist societies created a domination culture to enslave bourgeois and proletariat alike. To illustrate how domination "appears in a fascistically rationalized form" in a constructed reality where culture operates to subjugate, Horkheimer and Adorno quoted the lascivious Francavilla from Sade's *Juliette*:

> As Francavilla says at the court of King Ferdinand of Naples: "Religious chimeras must be replaced by the most extreme forms of terror. If the people are freed from fear of a future hell, as soon as it has vanished they will abandon themselves to anything. But if this chimerical fear is replaced by utterly relentless penal laws, which of course apply only to the people, then they alone will provoke unrest in the State; the discontented will be born only into the lowest class. What does the idea of a curb which they never experience themselves mean to the rich, if with this empty semblance they are able to preserve a justice that allows them to crush all those who live under their yoke? You will find no one in that class who would not submit to the worst tyranny so long as all others must suffer it."[822]

Horkheimer and Adorno quoted Sade's Francavilla a second time:

> The totalitarian State manipulates the people. Or, as Sade's Francavilla puts it: "The government must control the population, and must possess all the means necessary to exterminate them when afraid of them, or to increase their numbers when that seems desirable. There should never be any counterweight to the justice of government other than that of the interests or passions of those who govern…as we have said, have received from it only so much power as is requisite to reproduce their own."[823] Francavilla indicates the road that imperialism, the most terrible form of the *ratio*, has always taken: "Take its god from the people that you wish to subjugate, and then demoralize it; so long as it worships no other god than you, and has no other morals than your morals, you will always be its master…allow it in return the most extreme criminal license; punish it only when it turns upon you."[824]

To break the cycle of ruling class control, Horkheimer and Adorno felt Sade had explained the required methodology. To advance the discussion, they quoted from the particularly lascivious 1797 edition of Sade's companion novels *The New Justine* and *The Story of Juliette, Her Sister*, published as a single work that filled ten volumes and nearly 3,700 pages. The 1797 edition printed in Holland was the first illustrated edition of the Justine and Juliette saga, "adorned with a frontispiece and one hundred carefully wrought engravings," according to John Phillips, an emeritus professor of French literature and culture at London Metropolitan University.[825] Phillips described the illustrations as follows:

> All of these illustrations depict lewd scenes, including naked men, women, children, and sometimes animals engaging in orgiastic activity, in which flagellation and sodomy are dominant. The male organs are always erect and sometimes in the process of ejaculating. Most of the female figures are in the posture of passive and pleading victims. In *The New Justine* alone, there are 40 such illustrations. According to a contemporary newspaper article, these covered one-third of the pages of the novel. Though something of an exaggeration, this inflated perception of the number of engravings does nevertheless convey the impact of these volumes on the public of the time. Jean-Jacques Pauvert [Paris publisher prosecuted for publishing the Marquis de Sade in 1957] observes this was no less than "the greatest undertaking of print pornography ever accomplished."[826]

Horkheimer and Adorno realized that the individual living in the world created by the culture industry is only "seemingly free." That individual is "actually the product of its [the culture industry's] economic and social apparatus."[827] The authors elaborated this concept: "The bourgeois [i.e., capitalist] whose existence is split into a business and a private life, whose private life is split into keeping up his public image and intimacy, whose intimacy is split into the surly partnership of marriage and the bitter comfort of being quite alone, at odds with himself and everybody else, is already virtually a Nazi, replete with enthusiasm and abuse; or a modern city-dweller who can now only imagine friendship as a 'social contract': that is, as being in social contact with others with whom he has no inward contact."[828] They continued, making it very clear the capitalist enslavement culture works because the culture industry produces bourgeois and proletariat zombies alike who are only human in appearance:

> On the faces of private individuals and movie heroes put together according to the patterns on magazine covers vanishes a pretense in which no one now believes; the popularity of the hero models comes partly from a secret satisfaction that the effort to achieve individuation has at last been replaced by the effort to imitate, which is admittedly more breathless. It is idle to hope that this self-contradictory disintegrating "person" will not last for generations, that the system must collapse because of such a psychological split, or that the deceitful substitution of the stereotype for the individual will of itself become unbearable for mankind. Since Shakespeare's *Hamlet*, the unity of the personality has been seen through as a pretense. Synthetically produced physiognomies show that the people of today have already forgotten that there was ever a notion of what human life was. For centuries society has been preparing for Victor Mature and Mickey Rooney. By destroying they come to fulfill.[829]

In *Re-Remembering the Mis-Remembered Left*, Coughlin and Higgins commented that Sade's appeal for Horkheimer and Adorno comes from Sade's willingness to assault Enlightenment reason dialectically. Sade does so by confronting all personal familial and social relations with their antithetical forms. Horkheimer and Adorno celebrated Sade's libertine sexual wantonness that attacks the family, promotes incest, and encourages all sexual activities that generate pleasure without placing boundaries.[830] "There is a dialectical tension between the sisters as Justine is sweet, virtuous, faith-filled, faithful, in despair, is always getting brutalized, and dies a premature death while Juliette is an amoral, atheist, nymphomaniac and murderer who is successful and happy in life," Coughlin and Higgins note. "It is hard to explain the ugliness that Horkheimer envisions without entering into the sordid details Justine and Juliette experience in de Sade's universe."

We are tempted to feel sympathy for Justine's fate, but Horkheimer and Adorno rejected our sympathy as disgusting. They ended the chapter on Juliette with the question Nietzsche once posed himself: "Where do your greatest dangers lie?" Nietzsche's answer was "In compassion." They commented: "With his denial he redeemed the unshakable confidence in man that is constantly betrayed by every form of assurance that seeks only to console."[831] Why should we sympathize with those who have self-subjugated into capitalist slavery by embracing the synthetic reality the culture industry creates? Horkheimer and Adorno stated that *commiseratio* (in English, "compassion") is "*mala et inutilis*" (in English, "sick and useless") because compassion is the opposite of "manly prowess."[832] They explained that compassion is not consistent with Roman *virtus* (in English, "virtue") that "by way of the Medicis down to the efficiency required by the [Henry] Ford family, has always been the only true bourgeois [capitalist] value."[833] Horkheimer and Adorno pointed out that Sade and Nietzsche held in common a "doctrine of the sinfulness of compassion," agreeing that compassion was "an old bourgeois heritage," crafted by capitalists to show feigned sympathy to the powerless and weak proletariat.[834]

Coughlin and Higgins noted that Horkheimer and Adorno's "liberatingly tolerant world is that of de Sade's, which further advocates the destruction of families, and the promotion of incest, to satisfy statist demands for state control of children: they are the property of the state."[835] They saw Horkheimer and Adorno's hand in the Left's neo-Marxist social welfare agenda:

> Scratch just beneath the surface of many left-wing justifications for federal aid programs, push past the flowery language, and one can identify the Frankfurt archetype form based on de Sade. Such negating constructs can only function to undermine a culture. **It is a predatory, perverse and dark worldview that has, nonetheless informed narratives that resonate with political issues to this day.** It is made relevant by scientized claims of science from loathsome people. It is not American.[836]

For Horkheimer and Adorno, because the Enlightenment resulted in Hitler, the Holocaust, and World War II, they felt it necessary to negate the culture industry that was creating postwar America as early as 1944. Negating the Enlightenment through destroying American culture can be accomplished only through a purely Hegelian concept that, as Lukács realized, demands "*aufheben der Kultur*." Returning to the title of the book in German, *Dialektik der Aufklärung*, note that *Aufklärung* means "enlightenment," but it also signifies "sex education" in the form of an "awakening." The Frankfurt School may have parted ways from Fromm, but the influence of Freud lurks in the background. Horkheimer and Adorno's 1944 *Dialectic of Enlightenment* prefigures the work of Herbert Marcuse and the 1960s sexual revolution Marcuse championed in the United States. Under Horkheimer and Adorno's instruction, Marx's failed economic 1848 revolution was redeemed by the 1960s sexual revolution. This was the major enduring contribution of the Frankfurt School, as culminated by Herbert Marcuse.

The Authoritarian Personality and Anti-Semitism: Frankfurt School Villains

In 1950, Adorno and his colleagues at the University of California, Berkeley published a massive sociological study entitled *The Authoritarian Personality*.[837] The study involved the administration of a questionnaire to the University of California and University of Oregon students; specialized groups of San Quentin prison inmates; psychiatric clinic patients from Langley Porter Clinic of the University of California; men from the Alameda School for Merchant Marine Officers; and men from the U.S. Veterans Employment Services. In total, there were about 1,275 subjects.[838] In addition, subjects who scored in the lowest and highest twenty-fifth percentages were selected for more intensive clinical study. The researchers developed three statistical measures: an anti-Semitism scale (the A-S scale),[839] an ethnocentrism scale (E scale),[840] and a politico-economic conservatism scale (PEC scale). [841] The study's goal was to measure on a fascism scale (F scale) the tendency toward an authoritarian, anti-democratic personality that would be susceptible to anti-Semitic propaganda.

The precise context of Adorno's venture into the social sciences was the rise of fascism in Europe that brought Hitler and the Nazis to power in Germany and culminated with the genocidal murder of some six million Jews in the Holocaust. To understand the roots of modern critical theory, we are going to start by examining more closely the concluding chapter, "Elements of Anti-Semitism," in Horkheimer and Adorno's book *Dialectic of Enlightenment*. The admittedly dialectical analysis of the book is lacking in the *Authoritarian Personality*'s social psychology study. Yet, Adorno and the other Jews of the Frankfurt School who fled Nazi Germany wanted to understand what had gone wrong with a culture that had produced Goethe and Beethoven only to produce Hitler.

The *Authoritarian Personality* study leaves no doubt that Adorno viewed fascism as an extreme movement on the political Right. There is also no doubt Adorno presumed that right-wing fascism produced authoritarian personalities who conducted unthinkable genocide aimed at eradicating Jews from Europe. The last chapter clarifies the Marxist dialectic that convinced Adorno that Germany's culture, which once flourished with music, literature, and philosophy, contained an authoritarian quality compatible with the commission of barbaric acts of violence in willing acceptance of evil orders issued by governmental political authority exerted from above.

But turning to the final chapter of *Dialectic of Enlightenment*, we are disappointed.[842] Horkheimer and Adorno failed to serve up the same dialectic richness we saw in their condemnation of the culture industry or their embrace of the Marquis de Sade and Nietzsche as the ultimate repudiation of reason and science. At best, what Horkheimer and Adorno supplied as explanations are the obvious observations, such as the truth that anti-Semitism "is based on false projection."[843] Lacking is a dialectic explanation of how Enlightenment reason and science ended up as in the Holocaust. Toward the end of the chapter, they suggested that "the content of the Fascist program is so meaningless that, as a substitute for something better it can only be upheld by the desperate efforts of the deluded. Its horror lies in the fact that the lie is so obvious but persists."[844]

Yet, there is a hint in their discussion of anti-Semitism that Horkheimer and Adorno take seriously in their assertion that Sade, in his private sexual rebellion, found the key to break the hold of Enlightenment reason. After observing that anti-Semitism is based on a false projection, they considered that fascist anti-Semitism reflects the resulting paranoia.

> The actual paranoic has no choice but to obey the laws of his sickness. But in Fascism this behavior is made political; the object of the illness is deemed true to reality; and the mad system becomes the reasonable norm in the world and a deviation from it a neurosis. The mechanism which the totalitarian order uses is as old as civilization. The same sexual impulses which the human species suppressed have survived and prevailed—in individuals and in nations—by way of the mental conversion of the ambient world into a diabolical system. The blind murderer has always seen his victim as a persecutor against whom he must defend himself, and the strongest and weakest individuals have always felt their weakest neighbors to be an intolerable threat before they fell upon them to destroy them. Rationalization was a pretense, but at the same time inescapable. The person chosen as an enemy was already seen as an enemy.[845]

We return to Adorno's experiment in social psychology. The last paragraph of *The Authoritative Personality* admits the study found that the subjects in the United States did not exhibit "the extreme ethnocentric pattern" the researchers hypothesized would be associated with fascism.[846] Yet, Wiggershaus noted that Adorno expected this authoritarian personality to find a personality predisposition in the United States for fascism. "Since conservatives in the United States were seen as democrats and good

Americans just as much as liberals were, and after 1945 even more so than liberals, Adorno's distinction concealed a very European left-wing critique of the American way of life, of American civilization," Wiggershaus wrote. "As a critic of monopoly capitalism and the cultural industry, he [Adorno] was in fact forced to expect American civilization to produce a fresh rebellion against failed capitalism—that is, a fresh form of fascism."[847] Thus, the last sentence of *The Authoritarian Personality* concludes: "If fear and destructiveness are the major emotional sources of fascism, *eros* belongs mainly to democracy."[848]

In his introduction to the 2019 edition of *The Authoritarian Personality*, Adorno scholar Peter E. Gordon clarified that the Berkeley researchers expected to find a psychological type that would allow the F scale to identify potential fascists. He explained that "among the major achievements" of the study was the conclusion "the potential for fascism lies not at the periphery but at the very heart of modern experience."[849] Gordon continued:

> It [the Authoritarian Personality study] set out to demonstrate that fascism is something far deeper than a political form: it correlates with the psychological patterns of domination and submission that take shape in earliest childhood and later harden into a syndrome of attitudes regarding hierarchy, power, sexuality, and tradition. The psyche of a fascist is "authoritarian" in the sense that it attaches itself to figures of strength and disdains those it deems weak. It tends toward conventionalism, rigidity, and stereotypical thinking; it insists on a stark contrast between in-group and out-group, and it jealously patrols the boundaries between them. It is prone to obsession over rumors of immorality and conspiracy, and it represses with self-loathing the sexual licentiousness it projects onto others. In all these ways, fascism appears as the political manifestation of a *pre*-political disposition.[850]

Gordon next astutely commented that it was a mistake to assume fascism was necessarily a right-wing, ultra-conservative movement. He continued with the following:

> The authoritarian personality does not always turn explicitly fascist; its politics may remain dormant, only to emerge under certain social-historical conditions. This thesis offers an important corrective to those who prefer to see fascism as discontinuous with liberal-democratic political culture: fascism is not mysterious, and it is not something other-

> worldly or rare; it is the modern symptom of a psychopathology that is astonishingly widespread and threatens modern society from within.[851]

Horkheimer and Adorno, writing the *Dialectic of Enlightenment* in 1944 at the height of World War II in Europe, could not imagine that critical theory itself might turn into an authoritarian doctrine, producing true believers that are equally totalitarian to the Nazis.

Still, Gordon understood that for Horkheimer and Adorno, the reality of anti-Semitism had to be intrinsic to the development of fascism. Hence, the anti-Semitism scale had a one-third weight in their fascist scale. The A-S scale's weight was equal to the impact of their ethnocentrism scale and their politico-economic conservatism scale. The Adorno study of the authoritarian personality contained no Neo-Marxist or cultural Maoist scale, reflecting their bias that the political Left was incapable of authoritarian or totalitarian predispositions. Gordon continued:

> It should be obvious that the study of fascism and anti-Semitism was not unrelated to the personal biographies of the institute, nearly all of whom were of Jewish descent and whose careers were interrupted by the emergence of Nazism in Europe. Fascism was not only a topic of research; it was also an existential threat. But facts of personal identity can hardly account for the intellectual and political significance of this research. After all, fascism's spread across the continent and its potential for victory elsewhere confronted the European left with a devastating challenge to its theoretically grounded confidence in history; if the bourgeoisie was yielding to demagogues and the working class no longer proved reliable as the collective agent of emancipatory politics, then key precepts of historical materialism seemed to be thrown in doubt. One cannot understand the development of the Frankfurt School if one fails to appreciate its ongoing theoretical and empirical efforts to reckon with the rise of authoritarianism in the mid-twentieth century.[852]

Gordon was right. As one reads the *Dialectic of Enlightenment*, the traditional Marxist explanations for revolution are gone. Horkheimer and Adorno still clung to a certainty that the historical dialectic will prevail such that the capitalism they so obviously hate will be overthrown in a revolution. But strangely, the Marxist economic determinism is quietly replaced by a revolt against Enlightenment reason and science waged by the release of repressed erotic impulses. The Frankfurt School parted ways with Fromm because he had replaced Marx with Freud to explain the human psyche. But, strangely, Horkheimer and Adorno wrote the *Dialectic of Enlightenment* as if they were taking Freud to heart. The Marquis de Sade figures so prominently in the *Dialectic of Enlightenment.* So too, eros (in English, "love") appears in the last sentence to the nearly one thousand pages of *The Authoritarian Personality*. As noted, Horkheimer and Adorno prefigure Marcuse and the 1960s sexual revolution in the United States, subjects we will address in the next chapter. So, with the *Dialectic of Enlightenment*, Marx goes off stage, and Freud stands at the theater wings, ready to come on to play a leading role.

The Fascist Scale Morphs into a Right-Wing Authoritarian Scale

But Adorno with *The Authoritarian Personality* managed to establish in the public's mind that the Nazis were a right-wing extremist party, and that anti-Semitism was a right-wing extremist prejudice. In the 1960s, many former liberal commentators and social scientists "perceived the threat posed by communism."[853] Among the intellectuals so affected were Norman Podhoretz (former editor in chief of *Commentary* magazine), Daniel Bell (Harvard University socialist and expert on postindustrial society), and University of Chicago sociologist Edward Shils.[854] As early as 1954, Shils published an article insisting that there are authoritarians on both the political Left and the political Right.[855] "Would a C-scale [Communist scale] be very different from an F-scale [fascist scale]?" asked former journalist for the *Guardian* in London, Stuart Jeffries, in his 2016 book entitled *Grand Hyatt Abyss: The Lives of the Frankfurt School.* Jeffries pointed out that in the 1950s, the real opposition was between the liberal democracies and totalitarianism, be that fascist or Communist. "The Cold War had begun and so what was needed was not to understand the personality types that supported Hitler, but the personality types that supported Stalin and his successors and, quite possibly, to weed out those with communistic tendencies," Jeffries suggested.[856]

In 1981, Robert Altemeyer, then a professor of psychology at the University of Manitoba, Canada, adapted Adorno's F scale into a right-wing authoritarianism scale (RWA Scale).[857] Thus, the neo-Marxist left in the United States today views "Make America Great Again" (MAGA) nationalists as fascists, both because of their "America First" nationalism and because of their conservative politics supporting the Constitution and the Bill of Rights, including Second Amendment rights to bear arms. Altemeyer viewed his work as a corrective to Adorno's F scale, making it clear that social psychologists by the 1980s had associated fascists as bigoted right-wing extremists.

As noted in chapter 2, the Nazi party was officially titled Nationalsozialistische Deutsche Arbeiterpartei (in English, "National Socialist German Workers' Party"). The Nazis were a nationalist party promoting Germany, but more precisely, a national socialist party formed to advance the working class. At that time, there were two other major parties on the political Left in Germany:

1. the Sozialdemokratische Partei Deutschlands, SPD (in English, "Social Democratic Party of Germany"), Germany's more moderate, traditional socialist party; and
2. a separate German Communist party, Kommunistische Partei Deutschlands, KPD (in English, "Communist Party of Germany").

So, in 1933, the German conservative party coming out of the Weimar Republic was the Deutschnationale Volkspartei, DNVP (in English, "German National People's Party").

Also noted in chapter 2, Mussolini was a socialist politician before World War I who belonged to the Italian Socialist Party (PSI). The term "fascist" derived from a symbol of ancient imperial Rome, formed by an ax with its blade protruding and surrounded by a bundle of rods. Mussolini formed the Partito Nazionale Fascista (in English, "National Fascist Party") in 1921. Throughout the 1920s, Hitler was greatly influenced by Mussolini, going so far as to model his Nationalsozialistische Deutsche Arbeiterpartei after Mussolini's Partito Nazionale Fascista. When Hitler assumed power in 1933, he was initially happy to extend Otto von Bismarck's government-funded health care program to government employees and the elderly to provide socialized health care for the entire German population. He initiated the building of the Autobahn in 1933 to offer highspeed roadways to the public at government expense. He also launched a "Strength through Joy" program in 1933 to provide German workers affordable government-sponsored vacation packages and paid time off from work.[858] He promoted in 1937 the founding of Volkswagen (in English, "the people's car") to provide cheap manufactured vehicles that German families could afford. Hitler's version of national socialism was that government should provide a regulatory structure allowing international corporations to develop German businesses while at the same time providing a government-sponsored basic standard of living for the German population. The social democrats and the Communists in Germany sought to overthrow capitalism. The Communists wanted to abolish private property and capitalism to collectivize the ownership of the means of production and eliminate unequal distribution of goods and services. In a sense, Bill Maher is right: "fascism is when corporations become the government."[859]

But British historian Richard J. Evans, author of a trilogy on Nazi history, forced us to recognize what Horkheimer, Adorno, and the other leading Marxists of the Frankfurt School realized. We cannot fully understand either the Frankfurt School or the rise of Hitler without appreciating how central to his political ideology was his rabid anti-Semitism. Evaluating the importance of anti-Semitism to Hitler was a key reason Evans warned us that "it would be wrong to see Nazism as a form of, or an outgrowth from, socialism."[860] He explained:

> True, as some have pointed out, its [the Nazi party's] rhetoric was frequently egalitarian, it stressed the need to put common needs above the needs of the individual, and it often declared itself opposed to big business and international finance capital. Famously, too, antisemitism was once declared to be "the socialism of fools." But from the very beginning, Hitler declared himself implacably opposed to Social Democracy and, initially to a much smaller extent, Communism: after all, the "November traitors" who had signed the Armistice and later the Treaty of Versailles were not Communists at all, but the Social Democrats and their allies.[861]

Evans stressed that Hitler eschewed discussion of the Nazis as a political party, he "preferred on the whole to talk of the 'National Socialist movement,' just as the Social Democrats had talked of the 'workers' movement,' or, come to that, the feminists of the 'women's movement' and the apostles of prewar teenage rebellion of the 'youth movement.'"[862]

Evans explained that by "presenting itself as a 'movement,' National Socialism, like the labor movement, advertised its opposition to conventional politics and its intention to subvert and ultimately overthrow the system within which it was forced to work."[863] He explained that by replacing class with race, and the dictatorship of the proletariat with the dictatorship of the leader, "Nazism reversed the usual terms of socialist ideology."[864] He noted the "synthesis of right and left" was "neatly symbolized in the [Nazi] Party's flag, personally chosen by Hitler in mid-1920: the field was bright red, the color of socialism, with the swastika, the emblem of racist nationalism, outlined in black in the middle of a white circle at the center of the flag, so that the whole ensemble made a combination of black, white, and red, the colors of the official flag of the Bismarckian Empire."[865] Evans explained Hitler's principal targets were the Social Democrats and Jewish capitalists:

> By the end of the 1920s, Hitler's early emphasis on attacking Jewish capitalism had been modified to bring in "Marxism," or in other words Social Democracy, and Bolshevism as well. The cruelties of the civil war and "red terror" in Lenin's Russia were making an impact, and Hitler could use them to lend emphasis to common far-right views of the supposedly Jewish inspiration behind the revolutionary upheavals of 1918–19 in Munich. Nazism would also not have been possible, however, without the Communist threat; Hitler's anti-Bolshevism was the product of his anti-semitism and not the other way round. His principal political targets remained the Social Democrats and the vaguer specter of "Jewish capitalism."[866]

Yet, as Russian defector Viktor Suvorov reminded us in chapter 2, Hitler still had a red flag, as Stalin had a red flag. Hitler ruled in the name of the workers' class, as did Stalin. Hitler understood he needed Wall Street capital to lift Germany from the yoke of World War I reparation payments and from the economic depths of the Great Depression. He appreciated the value of German banks working with Wall Street banks. And he looked forward to the opportunities Wall Street afforded German corporations through the interlocking directorates major U.S. corporations desired to establish with their German corporate counterparts.

Horkheimer and Adorno turned on the United States precisely because the U.S. in the World War II–era was a decidedly capitalist country.

When World War II ended, Adorno and Horkheimer returned to Germany, where they witnessed the outlawing of the Nazi party. But during the postwar period, Germany embraced Jean Monnet and the dream of a European future that Germany might one day rule. In 1951, the Treaty of Paris created the European Coal and Steel Community (ECSC), and Europe was on the path to today's European Union. Suppose Hitler had the opportunity to be president today with Germany dominating the European Union, with abundant social welfare programs and virtually no Jews. The odds are good that Hitler would have accepted a similar deal with the West to have focused World War II on the East, seizing Poland to grab land, invading Ukraine to gain resources, and defeating Stalin to destroy Communism.

Conclusion: Schizophrenia, Value Relativism, and Identity Politics Bedlam

David Harvey, the Distinguished Professor of Anthropology at the City University of New York (CUNY) Graduate Center, in his 1989 book *The Condition of Postmodernity*, described postmodernism as the breakdown of the "Enlightenment project." He explained that the Enlightenment "took it as axiomatic that there was only one possible answer to any question. From this, it followed that the world could be controlled and rationally ordered if we could only picture and represent it rightly. But this presumed that there existed a single correct mode of representation which, if we could uncover it (and this was what scientific and mathematical endeavors were all about), would provide the means to Enlightenment ends."[867]

Jean-François Lyotard's emphasis on metanarratives undermined the Enlightenment's confidence in the certainty of reason and the advances in progress promised by science and technology. A postmodern condition in which no one of multiple competing worldviews can be determined to be the final word on objective reality empowers the schizophrenic as the cultural savant. Identity politics, in which each person's subjective experience is equally valid with other competing subjective experiences, elevates schizophrenia to the realm of morality and politics. As Gramsci pointed out, attacking the culture is the only way to undermine established orders, including capitalism. Thus, the Frankfurt School became determined to undermine establishment culture as their methodology of choice for destroying capitalism.

None of this is genuinely new. The ancient Greek pre-Socratic philosopher Heraclitus (535 BCE–475 BCE) was famous for arguing that the world is in constant flux, such that no one steps in the same river twice.[868] The ancient Greek sophist Gorgias of Leontini (483 BCE–375 BCE) "claimed that nothing exists and, even if it does exist, its nature cannot be understood and, even if it could, one is not able to communicate that understanding to another person."[869] Nietzsche, in his *Twilight of the Idols*, embraced Heraclitus's views explicitly, writing:

> With great deference I single out the name of *Heraclitus*. When other plebian philosophers rejected the evidence of the senses because these showed variety and variability, he rejected their evidence because it

> showed things as though they had duration and unity. Even Heraclitus did the senses an injustice. For these lie neither in the way the Eleatics believed, nor as he believed—they do not lie at all. What we *make* of their evidence inserts the lie, for example, the lie of unity, the lie of materiality, substance, duration.... "Reason" is the cause of our falsifying the evidence of the senses. In so far as the senses show becoming, passing away, change, the do not lie.... But Heraclitus will be permanently in the right to hold that being is an empty function. The "apparent" world is the only one: the "true world" is just *a lie added on*.... [870]

The Eleatics was a school of philosophy founded in the fifth century BC, whose chief proponents were Parmenides and Zeno. In addition to denying the validity of sense-experience, the Eleatics held that only a single, unchanging being existed and that becoming and change were illusions.[871] So, in a sense, the postmodernist movement is a throwback to the ancient Greek philosophy of Heraclitus and Gorgias.

In the Plato dialogue, *Gorgias*, Socrates confronted Gorgias on the subject of rhetoric. At a critical point in the dialogue, Gorgias revealed himself to be a value relativist when he argues to Socrates that an orator does not need to know the truth of actual matters. Instead, Gorgias maintained that an orator merely needs to have discovered some device of persuasion that will make one appear to understand those who themselves do not know (459c).[872] Socrates argued the natural law theory in contrast to the value relativism Gorgias has championed. Socrates distinguished that a physician understanding medicine knows the difference between the best foods for a body and the worst foods. But a cook, impersonating medicine, is not an expert in wholesome and bad foods, even if, through rhetoric, the cook persuades people not to listen to the physician's advice (465d).

Socrates refuted Gorgias's view of subjective reality: while the subjective construct reality may be the human condition, not all subjective constructs of reality work equally well. The Socratic challenge to postmodernism is that postmodernism conceptualizes schizophrenia and other types of mental disease not as aberrant or dysfunctional behavior but merely as different social constructs of reality that we must accept as legitimate. Socrates would object, arguing that schizophrenic constructs of reality are dysfunctional—that is, not productive to human growth, physical well-being, or intellectual development. The abandonment of the Enlightenment forces us to accept as normal the most confused and destructive among us who can only abolish, not create. In a world where Plato and Aristotle are scorned, the Marquis de Sade is free to rule.

CHAPTER 5

1960s Sex, Drugs, and Rock and Roll Intermezzo

Favorite sages included Herbert Marcuse, who, along with other members of the émigré Frankfurt school tried to marry Freud and Marx and Antonio Gramsci, the father of Italian communism, who invented the concept of "cultural hegemony."

—**Daniel Bell**, *Marxian Socialism in the United States*, 1952[873]

However, the main point about Marcuse's writing is not that he professes to be a Marxist despite clear evidence to the contrary, but that he seeks to provide a philosophical basis for a tendency already present in our civilization, which aims at destroying that civilization from within for the sake of an apocalypse of the New World of Happiness of which, in the nature of things, no description can be given.

—**Leszek Kołakowski**, *Breakdown*, 1978[874]

In the early 1930s, Reich coined the term "the sexual revolution" to describe the universe of happiness and love that would arise once people had shaken off their shackles, divesting the world of its punitive, prurient attitudes. He was undoubtedly naïve in this, as the French philosopher-historian Michel Foucault observes in The History of Sexuality. *If the orgasm is so powerful, Foucault asks, why is it that the vastly expanded sexual liberties of the intervening years have failed to dissolve capitalism or topple the patriarchy, despite all Reich's ardent predictions to the contrary?*

—**Olivia Laing**, "Wilhelm Reich," 2021[875]

On November 22, 1963, the day President John F. Kennedy was assassinated, the world changed. A postwar era mainly marked by peace and prosperity on our shores was tragically disrupted by a horrendous act of violence in one of the most murderous centuries in human history. The new president, Lyndon B. Johnson, first held his Vietnam meeting in the White House on November 24, 1963, the Sunday that JFK's body lay in state for public viewing in the Rotunda of the Capitol. "I am not going to lose Vietnam," Johnson said at that meeting. "I am not going to be the President who saw Southeast Asia go the way that China went."[876] Johnson signed Kennedy's National Security Action (NSA) Memorandum 273, leaving in the document the critical paragraph requiring the U.S. to begin withdrawing one thousand U.S. military personnel from South Vietnam by the end of 1963. Johnson, however, made a few changes to NSA Memorandum 273, specifically allowing U.S. Navy vessels to be involved in missions against North Vietnam. The alterations led to the Gulf of Tonkin incident in which three North Vietnamese torpedo boats attacked the U.S. Navy destroyer *Maddox* on August 2, 1964. LBJ leveraged the incident into the congressional Gulf of Tonkin Resolution that he subsequently utilized as constitutional authority, allowing the president to wage the Vietnam War.[877]

Civil Rights Protesters, 1960s Race Riots, and the Rise of the "New Left"

In June 1962, the Students for a Democratic Society (SDS) held its first convention. They adopted the Port Huron Statement that former civil rights Freedom Rider Tom Hayden had drafted. Kirkpatrick Sale documented the history of the SDS in a 753-page book entitled *SDS*. The subtitle of Sale's book read descriptively: *The Rise and Development of the Students for a Democratic Society, the Organization That Became the Major Expression of the American Left in the Sixties—Its Passage from Student Protest to Institutional Resistance, to Revolutionary Activism, and Its Ultimate Impact on American Politics and Life*.[878] Sale pointed out that the SDS students were not typical 1930s Communists steeped in the Marxist revolutionary theory based on the working class proletariat rising against capitalism. He explained that the SDS quickly became the home for "a new breed of activist, a younger, more alienated, more committed student" radicalized by Martin Luther King Jr.'s nonviolent civil disobedience and the escalation in Vietnam.[879]

> The new breed brought to SDS a new style and a new heritage. For the first time at an SDS meeting people smoked marijuana; Pancho Villa mustaches, those droopy Western-movie addenda that eventually became a New Left cliché, made their first appearance in quantity; blue workshirts, denim jackets, and boots were worn by both men and women. These were people generally raised outside of the East, many from the Midwest and Southwest, and their ruralistic dress reflected a different tradition, one more aligned to the frontier, more violent, more individualistic, more bare-knuckled and callus-handed, than that of the early SDSers. They were non-Jewish, nonintellectual, nonurban, from a nonprofessional class, and often without any family tradition of political involvement, much less radicalism.

The 1960s New Left movement was outside the 1920s and 1930s tradition of Eastern intellectuals who supported the Soviet Union through the 1950s. The youth comprising the majority of the 1960s New Left movement was largely uneducated in the history of socialism in America. Sale continued:

> They tended to be not only ignorant of the history of the left and its current half-life in New York City, but downright uninterested: they didn't know [David] Dellinger [pacifist, one of the Chicago Seven] from [John] Dillinger [Depression-era bank robber], [Bayard] Rustin [Freedom Riders, Southern Christian Leadership Conference civil rights leader] from [James] Reston [*New York Times* reporter], [Leon] Trotsky from [Noam] Chomsky, *Liberation* [New Left magazine] from *Liberator* [World War I–era socialist magazine], the Socialist Workers Party [Communist political party in the U.S. supporting Trotsky] from the Socialist Labor Party [socialist political party in the U.S.], and they really didn't care.[880]

Sale identified the New Left as a distinct tradition from the "Old Left" that traced back to the 1930s in America. Few of these student radicals had ever heard of socialist Rosa Luxemburg, a famous Polish-German Marxist revolutionary of the World War I era. Almost none had read Marx, Lenin, or Trotsky. Sale continued:

> Not that they were all simply "anti-intellectual," the phrase with which many of the old guard and more of the Old Left dismissed them; rather, they were generally without exposure to this kind of learning, being underclassmen from mediocre colleges or conservative state universities;

> they were nervous and often inarticulate in public debates with well-versed old guard radicals; and they emphasized "morals" and "values," action and bodies-on-the-line, honesty and courage, not ideology and theory an what they called "Old Leftism" and "all that thirties [1930s] horseshit. Their notions of politics had been formed *ab ovo* [In English, "from the egg," meaning "from the very beginning"] in the civil-rights struggle or with the impact of Vietnam escalation, so most of them had yet to make radical connections, to develop much beyond a moral view of race and war.

The 1960s radicals were primarily baby boomers, born in 1946 or the early 1950s, and most were teenagers whom the JFK assassination shocked into becoming politically aware. These radicals were a different breed than the upper-class New York City Communists who led the support of Stalin's Communism in the 1930s. These 1960s radicals did not come out of the World War I anarchist movement that led to the Espionage Act of 1917 and the Sedition Act of 1918. Nor were the socialists like Eugene V. Debs, who arose out of the early twentieth-century labor movement in the United States. These New Left student radicals bore more resemblance to the 1950s beatnik poets with their bongo drums in the Greenwich Village coffee shops than they did to the European café intellectuals that the Frankfurt School Marxists sought to influence. The Old Left adhered to a more orthodox Marxist interpretation, expecting the working class to lead an economic revolution against capitalism.

The first wave of the 1960s Old Left civil rights movement began before the JFK assassination when the baby boomers were still in high school. Consider the following: the Freedom Riders bus trips protesting segregated bus terminals in the South (1961); the segregationist actions of Alabama Governor George Wallace and his "Stand in the Schoolhouse Door" protest to block racial integration at the University of Alabama (1963); the racism of police chief Eugene "Bull" Connor using fire hoses and setting dogs against the lunch counter sit-in protests in Birmingham, Alabama (1963); and Martin Luther King Jr.'s "I Have a Dream" speech given on the steps of the Lincoln Memorial during the March on Washington (1963). After the JFK assassination, as the baby boomers began entering college, the intensity of the civil rights movement gained an added emotional dimension.

On Sunday, March 7, 1965, approximately six hundred civil rights marchers organized by Martin Luther King Jr. and the Southern Christian Leadership Council (SCLC) planned a massive protest march some fifty-four miles from Selma, Alabama, to the state capitol in Montgomery. State troopers armed with clubs, bullwhips, and tear gas rushed the protesters at the Edmund Pettus Bridge and beat them back to Selma. In the confrontation, future U.S. Congressman John Lewis suffered a skull fracture on a day that came to be known as "Bloody Sunday."[881] Television news rebroadcasts of the brutal scene on the Edmund Pettus Bridge brought national attention to the confrontation. On March 9, 1965, Martin Luther King Jr. led more than two thousand marchers, black and white, across the Edmund Pettus Bridge but found U.S. Highway 80 blocked by state troopers. King paused the workers and led them in prayer, which caused the state troopers to step aside. He, however, led the protesters back to Selma after deciding to respect a state injunction prohibiting the march.[882] Up until this time, Presidents Eisenhower and Kennedy could not pass various civil rights laws each had proposed. But after the JFK assassination, President Johnson declared the "Great Society" and was able to use the emotion from a martyred president to pass critical civil rights measures. On August 6, 1965, in the wake of the Selma marches, President Johnson signed the Voting Rights Act outlawing the discriminatory voting practices adopted in many southern states after the Civil War.

Following the assassination of Malcolm X on February 21, 1965, who was addressing the Organization of Afro-American Unity at the Audubon Ballroom in Washington Heights, New York, the civil rights movement took a militant turn. Black leaders like Stokely Carmichael championed the Black Power movement, while Bobby Seale and Huey Newton founded the Black Panther Party. In 1965, the season of annual summer race riots began. From August 11–16, 1965, a race riot broke out in the Watts neighborhood of Los Angeles. From July 18–24, 1966, a race riot occurred in the Hough neighborhood of Cleveland, Ohio. What became a regular summer occurrence saw significant race riots in cities throughout the United States, culminating in 110 riots that started on April 4, 1968, the night civil rights leader Martin Luther King Jr. was assassinated in Memphis, Tennessee.

On April 4, 1968, an assassin's bullet cut down Martin Luther King Jr. while standing on a balcony outside his second-floor room at the Lorraine Motel. Three months later, on June 6, 1968, the night he won the California Democratic Party's presidential primary, Senator Robert F. Kennedy was assassinated exiting a victory rally at the Ambassador Hotel in Los Angeles through the narrow corridor of a kitchen hallway. The assassinations of JFK, RFK, and MLK impacted the 1960s baby boomer students who saw the three as martyrs for freedom who had their lives cut short by racists and warmongers.

In 1965, the radicalized students who led the New Left movement were increasingly of draft age, and few were motivated to fight in Vietnam, a war they perceived as a colonial war in a little understood Southeast Asian nation. As LBJ began escalating U.S. military involvement in Vietnam, the nightly network news began broadcasting daily and weekly totals of battle casualties in a confusing, distant war. The president restricted the U.S. military to fight a limited war that, like the Korean War, was challenging to win. The Johnson administration defined the U.S. military role as supporting the South Vietnamese army. But truthfully, the Vietnam War was a civil war between Communist North Vietnam and their guerrilla Viet Cong forces and the South Vietnamese army under the command of largely inept South Vietnamese generals and corrupt politicians in Saigon (Ho Chi Minh City).

The student protests began in 1964, blending protests against racial discrimination with protests against the Vietnam War. On December 2, 1964, Mario Savio led a group of between 1,500 to 4,000 students to occupy Sproul Hall, the administration building of the University of California, Berkeley. This Free Speech Movement political action ended on December 4, 1964, when Alameda County deputy district attorney Edwin Meese III got permission from California Governor Edmund Brown Sr. to proceed with a mass arrest of the students. On April 23, 1968, student protests at Columbia University resulted in the student takeover and sit-in of Hamilton Hall, the building housing the university's administration. The students occupying Hamilton Hall held acting dean Henry S. Coleman hostage for twenty-four hours. In April 1969, protesting students took over Harvard College's administrative building, University Hall. The college protests against the Vietnam War culminated in the killings of four Kent State University students and the wounding of nine more by the Ohio National Guard on May 4, 1970.

While student protests aimed at ending racial discrimination and ending the Vietnam War, the subtext of the New Left student rebellion in the 1960s was free sex, free drugs (especially marijuana and LSD), and free rock and roll (that quickly became psychedelic). From August 15–18, 1969, an overflow of some four hundred thousand youths flocked to Max Yasgur's dairy farm in Bethel, New York, some forty miles southwest of Woodstock, New York. Woodstock became the 1960s symbolic protest with the hippie-clad, long-hair youths gathered at Yasgur's farm listening to three days of rock at a festival that massive rainfall and impossible traffic jams delayed deep into the night. The marijuana-riddled, LSD-laced celebration of rock music, free sex, and drugs ended on Monday, August 18, 1969, with two deaths from drug overdoses, two babies born, a lot of nudity, sex in the open, and general pandemonium. As the New Left protest movement progressed in the mid-1960s, it morphed into a sexual revolution that championed a countercultural movement aimed at the overthrow of capitalism.

Herbert Marcuse: "Father of the New Left"

Marcuse was born in Berlin, Germany, on July 19, 1898, to an upper-class Jewish family that prospered in business and was well-integrated into German society. He was drafted into the German army in 1916 but did not see action in World War I. The experience of the war and the failure of the German November Revolution of 1918 and the Spartacist Uprising in 1919 led Marcuse to begin studying Marxism. He entered Humboldt University in Berlin in 1919 but transferred to the University of Freiburg in 1920 to concentrate on German literature and take courses in philosophy, politics, and economics. He received his doctorate from the University of Freiberg in 1922 after submitting a doctoral dissertation entitled "*Der deutsche Künstlerroman*" (in English: "The German Artist-Novel"). His love of literature became an enduring theme in his writings. He frequently found refuge in the aesthetics of literature and art, emphasizing the liberating quality of the subconscious energy and flights of imagination required to produce significant works in both fields of endeavor. [883]

After completing his dissertation, he returned to Berlin, where his father provided him with an apartment and a share in a publishing and antiquarian book business. In 1927, Marcuse began reading Martin Heidegger's newly published *Being and Time*. The work so impressed Marcuse that he returned to Freiburg to study philosophy with Heidegger and Edmund Husserl, the philosopher to whom Heidegger had dedicated *Being and Time*. Under Heidegger's direction, Marcuse completed his habilitation thesis, *Hegel's Ontology and the Theory of Historicity* (1932). Marcuse parted ways with Heidegger over the latter's involvement in National Socialism. Heidegger joined the Nazi Party in 1933.

With the ascendency of Hitler to power in 1933, Marcuse inquired about seeking employment at the Institute for Social Research in

Frankfurt. Horkheimer hired Marcuse. Fearing a Nazi takeover of the institute, Horkheimer began planning to leave Germany. Marcuse never worked for the institute in Frankfurt since Horkheimer, who had already moved the institute's endowment to Holland, assigned Marcuse to work in the institute's branch in Geneva, Switzerland.

In July 1934, Marcuse and his wife fled to New York, where he worked for the institute's branch at Columbia University. Marcuse became a naturalized U.S. citizen in 1940. In 1942, he moved to Washington to serve as an intelligence analyst, first with the Office of War Information and then with the Office of Strategic Services (OSS), the predecessor to the CIA. After World War II, Marcuse stayed with the government for four years heading the State Department's Central European section of the Office of Intelligence Research, working to help implement the U.S. government's de-Nazification program in Germany. Marcuse maintained that his work for the government was motivated by his determination to struggle against fascism.

After leaving government service, Marcuse taught briefly at Columbia and Harvard before landing his first full-time faculty appointment as a professor of philosophy and politics at Brandeis University in 1954. Marcuse left Brandeis in 1965 after the university refused to extend his teaching contract. He wrote *One-Dimensional Man* at Brandeis and had Angela Davis and Abbie Hoffman as students. What caused the university not to renew Marcuse's contract was a fight over free speech on campus and his opposition to the war in Vietnam.[884]

The precipitating incident that caused Brandeis not to renew his teaching contract involved an address by anthropologist Kathleen Aberle during the 1962 Cuban missile crisis. Aberle closed a speech to students with the words, "Viva Fidel! Kennedy to hell!" Brandeis President Abram Sachar reprimanded Aberle for her "reckless" and "irresponsible" remarks. Marcuse was at the forefront of a campus move to reproach Sachar for stifling academic freedom, an action that cost Marcuse the tenured position he had coveted for years. During his final year at Brandeis, he became a vociferous critic of American policy in Vietnam. After the U.S. began intensive bombing of North Vietnam in February 1965, Marcuse gave a speech that sealed his departure. "When I came to this country in the Thirties, there was a spirit of hope in the air," he told a student assembly. "Now I detect a militarism and a repression that calls to mind the terror of Nazi Germany.[885]

After leaving Brandeis, Marcuse accepted a long-standing invitation for a faculty position at the University of California, San Diego, where he purchased a house on La Jolla's fashionable Cliffridge Avenue.[886] Angela Davis again studied with Marcuse in the one year she studied at the University of California, San Diego, pursuing graduate studies.[887] In June 1970, Marcuse's contract expired, and he was seventy-two, two years older than the mandatory retirement age at the University of California, San Diego. Again, controversy developed over him. Then-Governor Ronald Reagan demanded Marcuse's resignation from his teaching position. The American Legion offered to buy him out of his contract if he would retire, and the Ku Klux Klan (KKK) threatened to kill him.[888] The university allowed Marcuse to keep his office in the Humanities Building and continue teaching informally in a complicated settlement. But for a second time, a U.S. university refused to renew Marcuse's teaching contract.[889]

"Herbert Marcuse was not a famous man nor was his writing well known until late in his life," wrote George Katsiaficas, a student Marcuse mentored in San Diego. "When it became his fate to be blessed (or cursed) with public attention, fame quickly turned into notoriety, and he became more well-known than many people might now recall."[890] Katsiaficas was driving a taxi at night and active in the anti-war movement in Ocean Beach, San Diego, when he first met Marcuse. "To my present embarrassment, although I had heard of him, I had read none of his books nor heard him speak," Katsiaficas admitted.[891] Marcuse reached the pinnacle of his fame in 1968 when the student movement exploded throughout the United States and Europe. On April 11, 1968, Josef Bachmann, a far-right extremist, shot student activist Rudi Dutschke (famous for formulating the phrase "the long march into the institutions"), triggering the start of the West German student movement that produced mass student protests. The following month, May 1968, saw widespread civil unrest throughout France, resulting in mass demonstrations, general strikes, the occupation of universities and factories, and a breakdown of the French economy. In 1968, Marcuse and his wife traveled to Berlin, where they visited Rudi Dutschke in the hospital. "In 1968, students and young radicals the world over read and discussed the three M's: Marx, Mao, and Marcuse," Katsiaficas remembered.[892]

On July 29, 1979, ten days after his eighty-first birthday, Marcuse died after suffering a stroke on a trip to Germany as an honored guest of the Max Planck Society. The *New York Times* obituary noted that Marcuse's trip "afforded the retired professor an opportunity to pursue his lifelong passion for social and political analysis and to find what he felt was a more hospitable climate for his radical concepts than he had had in this country in recent years."[893] By 1979, the New Left movement had peaked and died. On April 30, 1975, the last Americans were airlifted out of Saigon in chaos as the city fell to Ho Chi Minh and the Communists. But the hated draft was over, and as the energy of the Vietnam War distanced into memory, the radical student protests ended. Once again, Marcuse had failed at prompting a revolution to abolish capitalism.

On March 12, 1974, in an interview with Bill Moyers broadcast on PBS, Marcuse's influence had already started to fade. Moyers began the interview by asking hard questions:

> **Mr. Moyers**: Dr. Marcuse, what happened to the student movement of the late 1960s?
>
> **Dr. Marcuse**: Well, I can tell you what did not happen to it. It isn't dead.
>
> **Mr. Moyers**: It isn't dead?
>
> **Dr. Marcuse**: It is not dead. I don't believe it is dead, and it will resurrect.
>
> **Mr. Moyers**: There's an eerie silence out there on the campuses.[894]

When Moyers pressed the issue, Marcuse explained he did not expect the student protests of the late-1960s and early 1970s to continue.

> **Mr. Moyers**: I wonder if you aren't speaking too exclusively of a small group, because a lot of the students that I talk and have met with—who have been very active in the late 1960s and early 1970s, relaxed the moment the draft ended as an interference on their personal lives. And I wonder if you aren't reading more into it.
>
> **Dr. Marcuse**: I may very well. On the other hand, whenever I can, I criticize the widespread notion that radical change has to start with the masses, or with the people. If you would remember history, it never did. Radical change always started with a very small minority, and mostly with a very small minority of intellectuals. And the masses came in when the economic and political conditions were ripe, and when their consciousness had been developed to the point that they felt now they had to take action. This point has certainly not been reached in this country.

> **Mr. Moyers**: You once believed that students were beginning a radical, historical transformation. I think that was your term for it. Do you still believe that?
>
> **Dr. Marcuse**: Yes, I still believe it. By the way, I never said the students, as a group, would replace the working class as the vehicle of change. I always considered the student movement as a preparatory movement in the development of consciousness.[895]

In 2014, when PBS broadcasted the Moyers interview, a Communist revolution had failed to succeed for the third time. The first time was in Germany when the November Revolution of 1918–1919 failed. The second time was also in Germany when Hitler rose to power in 1933, and Nazi fascism triumphed over German communism. The third time was in the 1970s, when the student counterrevolution fizzled away after the Vietnam draft ended.

Polish philosopher Leszek Kołakowski in volume 3 entitled *Breakdown*, of his three-volume study *Main Currents of Marxism*, downplayed Marcuse's significance as a Marxist political philosopher. In chapter 11 of *Breakdown*, "Herbert Marcuse: Marxism as a Totalitarian Utopia of the New Left," Kołakowski wrote:

> Marcuse did not become a well-known figure outside academic circles until the late 1960s, when he was acclaimed as an ideological leader by rebellious student movements in the U.S.A., Germany, and France. There is no reason to suppose that he sought the spiritual leadership of the "student revolution," but when the role devolved upon him he did not object. His Marxism, if that is the right name for it, is a curious ideological mixture.[896]

Kołakowski portrayed Marcuse's Marxism as confused. He attributed Marcuse's popularity with student radicals to his ability to articulate countercultural themes of the time:

> Originating in the interpretation of Hegel and Marx as prophets of a rationalist Utopia, it evolved into a popular ideology of "global revolution" in which sexual liberation played a prominent part, and in which the working class was rudely displaced from the center of attention to make way for students, racial minorities, and the lumpenproletariat. In the seventies Marcuse's importance has faded considerably, but his philosophy is still worth discussing, less on account of its intrinsic merits

than because it coincided with an important, though perhaps ephemeral, tendency in the ideological changes of our time. It also serves to illustrate the amazing variety of uses that can be made of Marxist doctrine.[897]

Kołakowski's conclusions about Marcuse gained significance from his mature rejection of Marx's revolutionary theory. In 1968, Poland expelled him from his teaching position at Warsaw University for his increasing criticism of Marxism. Kołakowski ultimately concluded that totalitarianism was not an aberration in Stalin's Soviet Union but a logically necessary consequence of Marxism.[898]

In 1978, in an interview broadcast on the BBC, Bryan Magee, the BBC broadcaster who featured interviews with prominent philosophers, asked Marcuse to evaluate his impact on the protest movement:

Magee: Why should it have been to your writings that the revolutionary and student movements of the 1960s and early 1970s turned?

Marcuse: Well, I was not the mentor of the student activities of the sixties and early seventies. What I did was formulate and articulate some ideas and goals that were in the air at the time. That's about it.[899]

Expanding on this answer, Marcuse explained that among the themes he articulated, the one that resonated with the student protesters was the argument that while fascism "was militarily defeated," a potential "for its revival is still here."[900] He continued: "I could also mention racism, sexism, general insecurity, pollution of the environment, the degradation of education, the degradation of work, and so on and so on."[901] Marcuse failed to acknowledge the theme he developed that most resonated with the student protesters in the 1960s and 1970s: sex. The 1961 Vintage Press first softcover edition of *Eros and Civilization*, ubiquitous on college campuses, bore a purple cubist–stylized design showing naked men and women walking trance-like across abstract space.[902] By emphasizing eros as a revolutionary theme, the paperback edition communicated that Marxist liberation means the end of sexual restraint. That was a popular theme with the sex, drugs, and rock and roll generation that emerged after the JFK assassination. Had a paperback edition of *Eros and Civilization* with a cover resonating the theme of joyous sex never been published, Marcuse may have remained in the same obscurity he enjoyed in 1955, when the leftist Beacon Press in Boston first published the hardcover edition of the book. Beacon Press chose a hackneyed green cover with two white boxes, one displaying the book's title and the second reprinting an advanced publication blurb from the *New York Times Book Review* that touted the book's treatment of Freud.[903]

While Marcuse, throughout his life, failed to produce a successful Marxist revolution, his sexual redefinition of Marxism has never really gone away. In his introduction to his Marcuse interview, Magee commented insightfully: "And although the revolution has not materialized, in the years since then [1968, the high point of student violence all over Europe and the United States] the ideas of Marcuse and the Frankfurt School have come to dominate some Social Science Departments in various universities in Europe, and through them to have a continued and important influence on some of the most intelligent young people in the West."[904]

Marcuse Embraces the 1960s Youth Counterculture

Douglas Kellner, a professor in the philosophy of education at the Graduate School of Education and Information Studies at the University of California, Los Angeles (UCLA), commented that in 1968, Marcuse, then seventy years old, found a way to reinvent himself with the New Left. Kellner, who has edited six volumes of Marcuse's collected papers, commented that Marcuse was encouraged by the student and anti-war movements that became known in the 1960s as the counterculture. "Marcuse sought in these forces the instruments of radical social change that classical Marxism found in the proletariat," Kellner wrote.[905] He noted that in the 1950s, Marcuse had turned pessimistic, thinking negatively about the revolutionary potential of the working class in an advanced industrial society that could produce goods and services in abundance while producing "conformist needs that integrated individuals into the existing system of production and consumption."[906] Marcuse found in the New Left a counterculture enthusiasm that demonstrated the power of Gramsci's shift from hoping for a working-class revolution to realizing the need to attack the culture of capitalism. Kellner wrote:

> Hence, a younger generation of political activists looked up to a white-haired German refugee in his mid-1960s for theoretical and political guidance. Disgusted by the excessive affluence of the advanced industrial societies and the violence of neo-imperialist interventions against developing societies in what was then called the "Third World," the generation that would produce a New Left found theoretical and political inspiration and support in Marcuse's writings. Marcuse in turn tirelessly

> criticized "advanced industrial society," U.S. imperialism, racism, sexism, environmental destruction, and the forms of oppression and domination that he perceived as growing in intensity and scope.[907]

Kellner made the point that since the working class was, in Marcuse's view, integrated into advanced capitalism, Marcuse "sought new radical political agency, successively, in non-integrated outsiders and minorities, in students and intellectuals, in a 'new sensibility,' and in 'catalyst groups.'"[908] Kellner elaborated on the point, noting that in contrast with the working-class focus of orthodox Marxism, "Marcuse championed non-integrated forces of minorities, outsiders, and radical intelligentsia and attempted to nourish oppositional thought and behavior while promoting radical thinking and opposition."[909]

Kellner was right that Marcuse in the 1960s began moving away from traditional Marxism. In a speech entitled "Liberation from the Affluent Society" that Marcuse gave to the Dialectics of Liberation conference held in the Roundhouse at Chalk Farm, London, from July 15 to July 30, 1967, Marcuse succinctly explained the problem with orthodox Marxism:

> Now as to today and our own situation, I think we are faced with a novel situation in history, because today we have to be liberated from a relatively well-functioning, rich, powerful society. I am speaking here about liberation from the affluent society, that is to say, the advanced industrial societies. The problem we are facing is the need for liberation not from a poor society, not from a disintegrating society, not even in most cases from a terroristic society, but from a society which develops to a great extent the material and even cultural needs of man—a society which, to use a slogan, delivers the goods to an ever larger part of the population. And that implies, we are facing liberation from a society where liberation is apparently without a mass basis.[910]

Earlier in his career, when Marcuse studied with Heidegger in Germany, he was a knowledgeable orthodox Marxist. Kellner commented that the dissertation that Marcuse wrote for his habilitation, *Hegel's Ontology and the Theory of Historicity* (1932), "contributed to the Hegel renaissance that was taking place in Europe by stressing the importance of Hegel's ontology of life and history, as well as his idealist theory of spirit and his dialectics."[911] Kellner noted that Marcuse's first significant work in English, his book *Reason and Revolution* (1941),[912] "traced the genesis of the ideas of Hegel, Marx, and modern social theory," demonstrating "the similarities between Hegel and Marx." Kellner also noted that *Reason and Revolution* "introduced many English-speaking readers to the Hegelian-Marxist tradition of dialectical thinking and social analysis."[913] He stressed that *Reason and Revolution* "continues to be one of the best introductions to Hegel and Marx and one of the best analyses of the categories and methods of dialectical thinking."[914] Marcuse dedicated *Reason and Revolution* to Max Horkheimer and the Institute of Social Research. The 1960s students constituting the base of the New Left had not studied orthodox Marxism profoundly. Marcuse acknowledged that his New Left followers were not deeply versed in his writings.

In a 1968 interview on the French Riviera in late summer 1968, Marcuse acknowledged, "Oh, there are very few students who have really read me, I think…"[915] Responding to that statement, the interviewer pressed Marcuse, suggesting that Marcuse was the theorist who had inspired the French students protesting throughout France in 1968. Marcuse politely explained that his influence on students in the 1960s was more a result of his political activism with the New Left movement than students reading his books. Marcuse explained as follows:

> If that is true [i.e., whether French students reading his books held Marcuse as a political theorist], I am very happy to hear it. But it's more a case of encounter than of direct influence.… In my books, I have tried to make a critique of society—and not only of capitalist society—in terms that avoid all ideology. Even the socialist ideology, even the Marxist ideology, I have tried to show that contemporary society is a repressive society in all its aspects, that even the comfort, the prosperity, the alleged political and moral freedom are utilized for oppressive ends.[916]

Marcuse continued:

> I have tried to show that any change would require a total rejection or, to speak the language of the students, a perpetual confrontation with this society. And that it is not merely a question of changing the institutions but rather, and this is more important, of totally changing human beings in their attitudes, their instincts, their goals, and their values.[917]

Marcuse ended this explanation by saying: "This, I think, is the point of contact between my books and the worldwide student movement."[918] Possibly the questioner had not read Marcuse's books either. But, with this response, Marcuse clearly appreciated that the New Left students worldwide had not read his early, dense writings on orthodox

Marxism. Truthfully, he was opportunistic in that he realized the New Left students worldwide were not profoundly read in traditional Marxism or the writings the Frankfurt School scholars had produced through the end of World War II. But he realized that theoretical grounding in Marxism was not helpful in the 1960s. He understood that the worldwide student unrest was indeed a revolution against capitalist culture, not one driven by orthodox Marxist economic theories anticipating a proletarian working-class revolt that was genuinely Communist. Marcuse's 1968 interview also suggested he had begun contemplating that achieving the Marxist utopia might involve the transformation of the human being into a more enlightened species.

In the French Riviera interview, Marcuse pointed out that the worldwide student rebellion contained a strong element of anarchy. Marcuse's comments reflected that he appreciated the destabilizing effect anarchy has on society—a fact he undoubtedly learned from the street fighting between Hitler's brown-shirt SAs with the Communist Antifa street thugs during the 1920s that Hitler leveraged to accelerate his rise to power. Consider the following exchange:

> **Interviewer**: Do you believe in the existence of a revolutionary impulse in the industrial societies?
>
> **Marcuse**: You know quite well that the student movement contains a strong element of anarchy. Very strong. And this is really new.
>
> **Interviewer**: Anarchy—new?
>
> **Marcuse**: In the revolutionary movement of the twentieth century, I believe it is new. At least on this scale, it is new. This means that the students have perceived the rigidity of the traditional political organizations, their petrification, and the fact that they have stifled any revolutionary impulse. So it is outside of these organizations that the revolt spontaneously occurs.
>
> But spontaneity is not enough. It is also necessary to have an organization. But a new, very flexible kind of organization, one that does not impose rigorous principles, one that allows for movement and initiative. An organization without the "bosses" of the old parties or political groups. This point is very important. The leaders of today are the products of publicity. In the actual movement there are no leaders as there were in the Bolshevik Revolution, for example.

Interviewer: In other words, it is anti-Leninist?

Marcuse: Yes. In fact, Daniel Cohn-Bendit [a student leader of the uprising of May 1968 in France] has severely criticized Leninism-Marxism on this ground.

Interviewer: Does this mean that you can rely on anarchism to bring about the revolution you desire?

Marcuse: No. But I believe that the anarchist element is a very powerful and very progressive force, and that it is necessary to preserve this element as one of the factors in a larger and more structured process.[919]

In July 1967, Marcuse gave a lecture in West Berlin. He acknowledged the New Left was a neo-Marxist political movement that included elements of cultural Maoism combined with anarchist tactics. Marcuse said the following:

> I must begin by sketching briefly the principal difference between the New Left and the Old Left. The New Left is, with some exceptions, neo-Marxist rather than Marxist in the orthodox sense; it is strongly influenced by what is called Maoism, and by the revolutionary movements in the Third World. Moreover, the New Left includes neo-anarchist tendencies, and it is characterized by a deep mistrust of the old leftist parties and their ideology. And the New Left is, again with exceptions, not bound to the old working class as the sole revolutionary agent. The New Left itself cannot be defined in terms of class, consisting as it does of intellectuals, of groups from the civil rights movement, and of youth groups, especially the most radical elements of youth, including those who at first glance do not appear political at all, namely the hippies, to whom I shall return later. It is very interesting that this movement has as spokesmen not traditional politicians but rather such suspect figures as poets, writers, and intellectuals. If you reflect on this short sketch, you will admit that this circumstance is a real nightmare for the "old Marxists."[920]

When Marcuse returned later in the lecture to discuss the hippies, he said the following: "I never said that the student opposition today is by itself a revolutionary force, nor have I ever seen in the hippies the 'heir of the proletariat'! Only the national liberation fronts of the developing countries are today in a revolutionary struggle."[921] In his many speeches, rally appearances, and interviews, Marcuse was always careful to avoid calling for a violent, revolutionary overthrow of the U.S. government. He preferred to characterize the New Left as a counterculture movement, understanding the lessons Gramsci had taught about culture and following German student radical Rudi Dutschke's advice in the 1960s to negate the culture by taking a "long march through the institutions."

By 1969, Marcuse went so far as to attack socialism, Marxism, and Soviet Russia. On February 25, 1969, Marcuse was interviewed on San Diego television. The interview came on the heels of a controversy raging over the retention of Marcuse as a university philosophy professor. The Board of Regents of the University of California, San Diego, had just voted to uphold Chancellor William McGill's decision to give Marcuse another one-year contract until June 1970. Harold Keen conducted the interview. Keen was a television and print journalist who carefully followed Marcuse's controversial involvement with the New Left. In this interview, Marcuse resisted any characterization that he was a Marxist theorist.

Mr. Keen: First of all, Dr. Marcuse, you've been described as a Marxist philosopher. Is this a correct designation?

Dr. Marcuse: Stalin described himself as a Marxist. The Communist rulers who engineered the invasion of Czechoslovakia described themselves as Marxists. If they are Marxists, I am certainly not.

Mr. Keen: Well then, I take it that you were opposed to the invasion of Czechoslovakia, opposed to Stalinism, and opposed to the government of Russia as it stands today.

Dr. Marcuse answered affirmatively to all three questions.

Mr. Keen: What is your definition of Marxism, then?

Dr. Marcuse: Well, Marxism as a theory is an analysis—political, social and economic—of capitalism, which comes to the conclusion that the capitalist system can preserve itself and develop only through increasing conflicts, waste of resources, destruction of resources, wars, and so on, and that the transition to socialism is the only solution in this philosophy.

Mr. Keen: Isn't Russia a socialist or communist state now? What objection do you have to the way it is operating?

> **Dr. Marcuse**: The objection I have, or let me put it this way, the way in which socialism in the Soviet Union deviates decisively from the Marxist concept is in the authoritarian and bureaucratic construction of Soviet society in which the regime is imposed upon the people instead of the people actually determining the development of their own society.[922]

Marcuse faced several obstacles in rising from obscurity as a Marxist theorist to becoming a significant figure of the New Left in the 1960s and 1970s. He was seventy years old in a youth movement where the widely repeated slogan was "Don't trust anybody over 30."[923] Marcuse had a thick German accent. He had worked for the OSS, the predecessor to the CIA, and for the State Department. These agencies are two of the pillars of the government war establishment that the anti-war movement has always opposed. Marcuse realized that orthodox Marxist revolutionary theories would never produce a revolution in an advanced industrial society like the United States. After World War II, capitalism in the United States absorbed the working class through the labor union movement. In the 1950s, workers began enjoying a middle-class lifestyle. To those who fought in World War II, a middle-class lifestyle meant creating families, moving to the suburbs, buying homes, and purchasing an automobile in the postwar era.

What Marcuse saw in the New Left was the emergence of a new revolutionary spirit that was sexually liberated and opposed to authority, but not easily identified by race or class. While his political philosophy had shifted to neo-Marxism, his desire to negate the culture was as strong as when he was a young man seeking to join the Institute of Social Research in Frankfurt. In 1937, he published an article entitled "The Affirmative Character of Culture" in a German journal. Marcuse understood that what Horkheimer and Adorno called the "culture industry" could make the proletariat feel comfortable. "This is the real miracle of affirmative culture," he wrote. "Men can feel themselves happy without being so at all. The effect of illusion renders incorrect even one's own assertion that one is happy."[924] Later in the article, Marcuse explained that the affirmative experience of culture had to be negated if the culture was going to be abolished. He wrote: "Insofar as in Western thought culture has meant affirmative culture, the abolition of its affirmative character will appear as the abolition of culture as such."[925] *Aufheben der Kultur* (in English, "negate the culture") is the one goal Marcuse held unwavering from the 1930s when he sought to join Horkheimer in Frankfurt to the 1960s when he championed the New Left as a father figure. But as his career progressed,

Marcuse began imagining that a truly liberated personality could only be realized in a society only the self-actualized could create. That Marcuse was thinking about reengineering human beings fundamentally was perhaps first evident in a close reading of *Eros and Civilization*.

Eros and Civilization (1955)

In the first sentence of the introduction, Marcuse formulated the Sigmund Freud proposition he wrote the book to refute: "Sigmund Freud's proposition that civilization is based on the permanent subjugation of the human instincts has been taken for granted."[926] Marcuse's book emerged from his lectures at the Washington School of Psychiatry in 1950–51.[927] Freud most comprehensibly articulated his conclusions in a short 127-page book published in Germany in 1930 as *Das Unbehagen in der Kultur* (in English, *The Discontent in Culture*). In English language publications, Freud's book is more commonly known as *Civilization and Its Discontents*—a translation that makes clear discussions in German about culture are discussions about the organizing principles of civilization. In the introduction to *Eros and Civilization*, Marcuse clarified that "civilization" is used interchangeably with "culture" as in Freud's *Civilization and Its Discontents*.[928]

In the introduction to *Eros and Civilization*, Marcuse correctly summarized that Freud assumes that civilization necessarily restricts sexual freedom. He explained as follows:

> Free gratification of man's instinctual needs is incompatible with civilized society: renunciation and delay in satisfaction are prerequisites of progress. "Happiness," said Freud, "is no cultural value." Happiness must be subordinated to the discipline of work as full-time occupation, to the discipline of monogamic reproduction, to the established system of law and order. The methodical sacrifice of libido, its rigidly enforced deflection to socially useful activities and expressions, is culture.[929]

Marcuse even acknowledged that the trade-off between unrestricted freedom and the limitations on personal license imposed by civilization has "paid off" in material advancement. He continued:

> The sacrifice has paid off well: in technically advanced areas of civilization, the conquest of nature is practically complete, and more needs of a greater number of people are fulfilled than ever before. Neither the mechanization and standardization of life, nor the mental impoverishment, nor the growing destructiveness of present-day progress provides

> sufficient ground for questioning the "principle" which has governed the progress of Western civilization. The continual increase of productivity makes constantly more realistic the promise of an even better life for all.[930]

What could be wrong with progress and greater material wealth for a more significant number of people? Marcuse explained the problem: "Throughout the world of industrial civilization, the domination of man by man is growing in scope and efficiency." He saw this increased domination as accelerating dangerously:

> Concentration camps, mass exterminations, world wars, and atom bombs are no "relapse into barbarism," but the unrepressed implementation of the achievements of modern science, technology, and domination. And the most effective subjugation and destruction of man by man takes place at the height of civilization, when the material and intellectual achievements of mankind seem to allow the creation of a truly free world.[931]

Marcuse challenged Freud, arguing that Freud's principles permit the possibility of non-repressive civilization. He elaborated the idea:

> In Freudian terms, is the conflict between the pleasure principle and reality principle irreconcilable to such a degree that it necessitates the repressive transformation of man's instinctual structure? Or does it allow the concept of a non-repressive civilization, based on a fundamentally different experience of being, a fundamentally different relation between man and nature, and fundamentally different existential relations?[932]

This is the starting point for Marcuse's inquiry into the possibility that exploring eros (i.e., human sex) is the key to unlocking the riddle of how to create an authentic human being capable of living in a non-repressive civilization. Freud clearly maintained that the requirements of civilization require inhibiting the human sex drive. In chapter 4 of *Civilization and Its Discontents*, Freud wrote the following about pedophilia:

> A high-water mark in such a development [i.e., civilization restricting sexual expression as a precaution taken out of fear of a revolt by suppressed elements] has been reached in our Western European civilization. A cultural community is perfectly justified, psychologically, in starting by proscribing manifestations of the sexual life of children, for

> there would be no prospect of curbing the sexual lusts of adults if the ground had not been prepared for it in childhood.[933]

Freud continued, explaining the limits civilization must place on mature adults:

> As regards the sexually mature individual, the choice of an object is restricted to the opposite sex, and most extra-genital satisfactions are forbidden as perversions. The requirement, demonstrated in these prohibitions, that there shall be a single kind of sexual life for everyone, disregards the dissimilarities, whether innate or acquired, in the sexual constitution of human beings; it cuts off a fair number of them from sexual enjoyment, and so becomes the source of serious injustice. The result of such restrictive measures might be that in people who are normal—who are not prevented by their constitution—the whole of their sexual interests would flow without loss into the channels that are left open. But hetero-sexual genital love, which has remained exempt from outlawry, is itself restricted by further limitations, in the shape of insistence upon legitimacy and monogamy. Present-day civilization makes it plain that it will permit sexual relationships on the basis of a solitary, indissoluble bond between one man and one woman, and that it does not like sexuality as a source of pleasure in its own right and is only prepared to tolerate it because there is so far no substitute for it as a means of propagating the human race.[934]

Marcuse dismissed Freud's argument. "This conception is as old as civilization and has always provided the most effective rationalization for repression."[935] He ridiculed Freud for assuming "the 'primordial struggle for existence' as 'eternal'" and for concluding that "the pleasure principle and the reality principle are 'eternally' antagonistic."[936] Marcuse charged that Freud's metapsychology is a lie designed to hide the "terrible necessity of the inner connection between civilization and barbarism, progress and suffering, freedom and unhappiness."[937] He concluded that the psychology of advanced capitalist society ultimately reduces to a conflict between *eros* (in English, "love") and *thanatos* (in English, "death"), in which thanatos has the upper hand. Marcuse's indictment of Freud revolved around the charge that Freud is captive to a capitalist culture that demands unfreedom and constraint as the prices we must pay to escape the primordial struggle for existence successfully.

Consider, for instance, Marcuse's discussion of the primal father, killed by a son covetous of sex with the primal mother:

> The primal father, as the archetype of domination, initiates the chain reaction of enslavement, rebellion, and reinforced domination which marks the history of civilization. But ever since the first, prehistoric restoration of domination following the first rebellion, repression from without has been supported by repression from within: the unfree individual introjects his masters and their commandments into his own mental apparatus. The struggle against freedom reproduces itself in the psyche of man, as the self-repression of the repressed individual, and his self-representation in turn sustains his masters and their institutions. It is this mental dynamic which Freud unfolds as the dynamic of civilization.[938]

Thus, according to Marcuse, capitalist culture is born at the cost of repressing sexual instincts to create a subservient worker taught to believe their unfree, alienated existential being is required for survival. He charged that Freud sides with thanatos, the death instinct, to protect life at the cost of enslaving eros, which Marcuse calls "the life instinct,"[939] as well as characterizing eros as sex or love. Refusing to accept that we must be repressed to live in society, Marcuse proclaimed the need for a Marx-Bakunin-Alinsky rebellion to reclaim the kingdom:

> Culture demands continuous sublimation; it thereby weakens Eros, the builder of culture. And desexualization, by weakening Eros, unbinds the destructive impulses. Civilization is thus threatened by an instinctual de-fusion, in which the death instinct strives to gain ascendency over the life instincts. Originating in renunciation and developing under progressive renunciation, civilization tends toward self-destruction.[940]

As the internal contradictions build over time, social cohesion and administrative power "are sufficiently strong to protect the whole from direct aggression, but not strong enough to eliminate the accumulated aggressiveness."[941] To protect civilization, thanatos turns against those not among the compliant. Thanatos, the death instinct, takes over, and eros, the foe, "appears as the archenemy and Antichrist himself: he is everywhere at all times; he represents hidden and sinister forces, and his omnipresence requires total mobilization."[942] The destructiveness of civilization's final phase of total domination demands the destructive action of eros to break free:

> In a world of alienation, the liberation of Eros would necessarily operate as a destructive, fatal force—as the total negation of the principle which governs the repressive reality.[943]

Thus, Marcuse unleashed eros to negate the repressive culture, *aufheben der Kultur*, freeing us from Freudian psychology's justification for death-dominance enslavement of civilization. In Christianity, we are reborn through Christ. In Marcuse's neo-Marxism, we are reborn through unbridled sexuality. He rejected Freud's repressed civilization as being capable only of producing inauthentic living:

> The high standard of living in the domain of the great corporations is *restrictive* in a concrete sociological sense: the goods and services that the individuals buy control their needs and petrify their facilities. In exchange for the commodities that enrich their life, the individuals sell not only their labor but also their free time. The better living is offset by the all-pervasive control over living. People dwell in apartment concentrations—and have private automobiles with which they can no longer escape into a different world. They have huge refrigerators filled with frozen foods. They have dozens of newspapers and magazines that espouse the same ideals. They have innumerable choices, innumerable gadgets which are all of the same sort and keep them occupied and divert their attention from the real issue—which is the awareness that they could both work less and determine their own needs and satisfactions.[944]

He argued that at the height of civilization's progressive achievements, "domination not only undermines its own foundations, but also corrupts and liquidates the opposition against domination."[945] In advanced industrial societies, the "alienation of labor is almost complete" with the "mechanics of the assembly line, the routine of the office, the ritual of buying and selling" that are "freed from any connection with human potentialities."[946] Individuality is lost as humans are conceptualized as "types," such as "vamp, housewife, Ondine [the water nymph in love with a man, but destined to die if the man is unfaithful], he-man, career woman, struggling young couple," and so on.[947] Our human existence is reduced to "mere stuff, matter, material," as "the interactions between ego, superego, and id congeal into automatic reactions."[948]

In rejecting Freud's psychological justification that the creation of a neo-Marxist utopia demands the creation of a sexually liberated human being, Marcuse embraced Rosseau's argument that civilization puts us in chains. Marcuse did not mention the Marquis de Sade by name in *Eros and Civilization*, other than references to "sadism"[949] or masochism.[950] Yet, the sexual rebellion of Sade's writings remains the subtext of *Eros and Civilization*, especially after the attention that Horkheimer and Adorno gave Sade in the *Dialectic of Enlightenment.* In *Eros and Civilization*, Marcuse described the sexual instinct as having "no extraneous temporal and spatial limitations on its subject and object," such that "sexuality is by nature 'polymorphous-perverse.'"[951] He attributed the segmentation of sexual acts as "perversions" to the repression of sexual instincts required by civilization. "The societal organization of the sex instinct taboos as *perversions* practically all its manifestations which do not serve or prepare for the procreative function," he wrote.[952] By eliminating the "surplus-repression" of extra goods and services, the "performance" principle would be reduced, lessening the taboos on bodily pleasure.[953] He explained the liberating consequences as follows:

> No longer used as a full-time instrument of labor, the body would be resexualized. The regression involved in this spread of libido would first manifest itself in a reactivation of all erotogenic zones, and consequently, in a resurgence of pregenital polymorphous sexuality and in a decline of genital supremacy.[954]

As a result, we would free ourselves from the restraints of procreation and monogamy to explore and enjoy sexuality for pleasure. Marcuse elaborated:

> The body in its entirety would become an object of cathexis, a thing to be enjoyed—an instrument of pleasure. This change in the value and scope of libidinal relations would lead to a disintegration of the institutions in which the private interpersonal relations have been organized, particularly the monogamic and patriarchal family.[955]

Marcuse realized the unrestrained polymorphous sexuality he advocated will include perverse behaviors. John Phillips, the emeritus professor of French literature and culture at London Metropolitan University we cited in the previous chapter, explored this point in his 2005 book *The Marquis de Sade: A Very Short Introduction.*[956] Phillips noted that sadism is "the perversion for which Sade is famous."[957] He also pointed out that the sex Sade described in books like *Juliette* can involve violent, even criminal sexual behavior. "All Sadean sex is based on the principle of transgression, and any perversion is itself, by definition, a transgressive activity since it exceeds the bounds of 'normal' sexuality, which for Freud has procreation as its sole or primary object."[958] He continued to observe that within Sade's writings "the erotic charge depends crucially on the libertines' awareness that they are crossing recognized bounds of behavior, by infringing moral laws (rape, murder), religious taboos (such as those on sodomy or blasphemy), conventional mores (which prohibit sex with the very old or the very young, for example), 'natural' or socially conditioned reflexes of repulsion (urophilia, coprophilia), gender or species boundaries (passive sodomy, transvestism, zoophilia)."[959] He stressed that typically "it is the very contrast—for instance between age and youth, between piety and blasphemy, or between beauty and ugliness—that libertines find erotic."[960]

Marcuse argued that in suppressed sexuality, "the libido continues to bear the mark of suppression and manifests itself in the hideous forms so well known in the history of civilization; in the sadistic and masochistic orgies of desperate masses, of 'society elites,' of starved bands of mercenaries, of prison and concentration-camp guards."[961] He strongly suggested that in the cultural revolution he advocated, "the free development of transformed libido within transformed institutions, while eroticizing previously tabooed zones, time, and relations, would *minimize* the manifestations of *mere* sexuality by integrating them into a far larger order, including the order of work."[962] Marcuse reasoned that once the alienation of a repressed society is eliminated, "sexuality tends to its own sublimation: the libido would not simply reactivate precivilized and infantile stages, but would also transform the perverted content of these stages."[963]

Marcuse also argued that sexual behavior that is considered perverse, given repressive civilization's emphasis on "monogamic genital supremacy,"[964] will not manifest as perverse in a non-repressive society. He pointed out that "within the historical dynamic of the [sexual] instinct," coprophilia and homosexuality "have a very different place and function."[965] He also suggested that "the function of sadism is not the same in a free libidinal relation and in the activities of SS Troops."[966] He insisted the "inhuman, compulsive, coercive, and destructive forms of these perversions seem to be linked with the general perversion of the human existence in a repressive culture." But he argued the same sexual activity may be "compatible with normality in high civilization."[967] He envisioned that sex will transform into eros in the non-repressive civilization:

> The organism in its entirety becomes the substratum of sexuality, while at the same time the instinct's objective is no longer absorbed by a specialized function—namely, that of bringing "one's own genitals into

> contact with those of someone of the opposite sex." Thus enlarged, the field and objective of the instinct becomes the life of the organism itself. This process almost naturally, by its inner logic, suggests the conceptual transformation of sexuality into Eros.[968]

Marcuse even considered "the idea of an erotic tendency toward work" in a non-repressive libidinous culture.[969] To argue that every human activity can be eroticized ignores that survival may still require us to do some work we would prefer not to do. To say that every human sexual perversion is a result of a repressive society assumes that in a non-repressive society, there will be no more pathologically psychological behavior that expresses itself in sexual perversion. Are all horrific sexual perversions the result of repressive civilization? Or will there always be sexually pathological individuals who engage in sexually perverse acts? How do we explain those among us who torture and murder in snuff films where victims are killed on camera? Marcuse refused to accept the ancient Latin principle: *Homo homini lupus* (in English, "man is the wolf of men"). Throughout human history, we have never eliminated sin or crime. As we saw in previous chapters, Communist utopias like Lenin's Soviet Russia and Mao's Red China have created murderous hellholes instead of the promised unalienated advanced level of human existence. Would Marcuse's unrestrained libido result in just another murderous Communist nightmare?

Tyrus Miller, a professor of art history and English at the University of California, Irvine, suggested that Marcuse neglects to mention the Marquis de Sade by name because he realized the threat to his utopian argument raised by the abundant sexual perversion in Sade's writings. In his 2018 paper "Perversion and Utopia: Sade, Fourier, and Critical Theory," Miller put his attention on how various authors, including Marcuse, focus on the "utopian potential of Sade's perverse texts" by sublimating or otherwise redeeming perversion "from the destructive implications of Sade's vision."[970] He commented that he considers it "notable that Marcuse simply elides Sade from consideration, given the attention to Sade paid by his colleagues Adorno and Horkheimer in *Dialectic of Enlightenment*."[971] He wrote the following:

> In their "excursus" to *Dialectic of Enlightenment* entitled "Juliette or Enlightenment and Morality," Horkheimer and Adorno treat Sade as the dark shadow of Kant, the negative side of Kant's *Aufklärung* [in English, "Enlightenment"], whose work betrays the self-consuming, destructive dynamic of Enlightenment rationality.[972]

Miller commented that Adorno and Horkheimer "present Juliette as an authentic *perversion* of Enlightenment: inseparable from the intellectual methods, themes, and concerns of Enlightenment thought, she turns them toward deviant ends of cruelty and pleasure."[973] Marcuse embraces the revolutionary potential of the sexual perversions Sade describes but neglects to mention Sade to downplay the bizarre conclusion that sexual perversion is the path to utopia and a higher human state.

In his history of the Frankfurt School, Rolf Wiggershaus acknowledged that *Eros and Civilization* was Marcuse's *Dialectic of Enlightenment*.[974] Wiggershaus also said Marcuse's *Eros and Civilization* was Marcuse's "major theoretical work."[975] Yet, as Erich Fromm found out, the Marxist embrace of Freud was not well received by the Frankfurt School. Wiggershaus reported that Horkheimer saw Marcuse's manuscript in the early stages, and Marcuse kept Horkheimer informed on his progress in writing. Still, in a letter Horkheimer wrote to Adorno, Horkheimer commented, "By the way, Herbert's work seems to me to be quite decent. Although the psychological approach does not really appeal to us, there are so many splendid things in the book that we should accept it completely."[976] Wiggershaus made clear that Adorno never really accepted Marcuse's book. In August 1955, Adorno wrote to Horkheimer and suggested the institute should do "absolutely nothing" to support Marcuse's book.[977] In 1957, a plan for the institute to publish *Eros and Civilization* fell through.[978]

In the summer of 1957, Adorno wrote Marcuse a letter suggesting that Marcuse should produce a German-language version of the book. "You only need to formulate your ideas in German to notice the sort of thing that was disturbing me and you'll change them in such a way that all of us will be able to stand behind them fully."[979] The contrast between the two books is readily detectible. Marcuse never mentioned the Marquis de Sade by name in *Eros and Civilization*. Horkheimer and Adorno mention Freud only five times in *Dialectic of Enlightenment*, with all five references relegated to footnotes. Yet both books embrace sexual liberation as the revolutionary lever capable of negating capitalism.

While Freud had a significant influence on the Frankfurt School, the institute resented Freud for substituting sex as the basis of repression. In contrast, orthodox Marxism demanded conceptualizing repression in terms of economics. For his part, Freud made his rejection of Marxism clear. In *Civilization and Its Discontent*, Freud explained that the "communists believe that they have found a path to deliverance from our evils. According to them [the Communists], man is wholly good and is well-disposed to his neighbor; but the institution of private property has corrupted his nature."[980] Freud continued:

> If we do away with personal rights over material wealth, there still remains prerogative in the field of sexual relationships, which is bound to become the source of the strongest dislike and the most violent hostility among men who in other respects are on equal footing. If we were to remove this factor, too, by allowing complete freedom of sexual life and thus abolishing the family, the germ-cell of civilization, we cannot, it is true, easily foresee what new paths the development of civilization could take; but one thing we can expect, and that is that this indestructible feature of human nature [the inclination to aggression], will follow it there.[981]

But in *Civilization and Its Discontents*, Freud held firm to his belief that human civilization would always involve repression of sexual instincts.

Polish philosopher Leszek Kołakowski found Marcuse's treatment of Freud particularly disappointing. He wrote:

> This 'Freudian' aspect of Marcuse's Utopia presents obscurities at all its vital points. Freud's theory was that the repression of instincts was necessary not only to liberate the energy needed for production but also to make possible the existence of any social life at all in the specifically human sense. Instincts are directed toward the satisfaction of purely individual desires; the death-instinct, according to Freud, can either work towards self-destruction or be transformed into external aggression; man ceases to be an enemy to himself, only in so far as he becomes an enemy to others.[982]

Freud concluded that society required inhibitions to function. Kołakowski continued as follows:

> The only way to prevent the death-instinct becoming a permanent source of enmity between each human being and all his fellow humans is to force its energies into other channels. The libido is likewise asocial, as it treats other human beings only as possible objects of sexual satisfaction. In short, the instincts not only have no power, left to themselves, to create human society or form the basis of a community, but their natural effect is to make such a community impossible. Leaving aside the difficult question how, in that case, societies can ever have come into existence, the situation is, in Freud's view, that the society which

> does exist can only maintain itself by numerous taboos, commands, and prohibitions, which keep the instincts under control at the price of unavoidable suffering.[983]

Kołakowski said outright that Marcuse does not address himself to the question. "He seems to agree with Freud that the suppression of instincts has been necessary 'up to now,' but holds that it has been an anachronism since the abolition of scarcity," he explained. "But while disputing Freud's theory of the eternal conflict between instincts and civilization, he accepts the view that instincts are essentially devoted to satisfying the individual's 'pleasure principle.'"[984] Kołakowski argued that it is not clear how the libidinous civilization can maintain itself and what forces will keep human society in being. This conundrum is especially problematic since Marcuse bases his theory of liberation on unleashing eros. Kołakowski ridiculed Marcuse, asking if Marcuse held, in opposition to Freud, that humans are naturally good and inclined to live in harmony with others. He puzzled whether Marcuse believed aggression was an accidental aberration of history that would disappear along with the disappearance of unalienated labor. Kołakowski expressed his biting dismissal of Marcuse's theories as follows:

> Marcuse seems to be unconcerned with these problems, as he is interested in society chiefly in so far as it constitutes a barrier to instinct, i.e., to individual satisfaction. He seems to believe that as all questions of material existence have been solved, moral commands and prohibitions are no longer relevant. Thus when Jerry Rubin, the American hippie ideologist, says in his book that machines will henceforth do all the work and leave people free to copulate whenever and wherever they like, he is expressing, albeit in a primitive and juvenile way, the true essence of Marcuse's Utopia.[985]

Kołakowski was not convinced Marcuse had a cogent argument. "As to Marcuse's qualifications of the notion of eroticism, they are too vague to convey any tangible meaning."[986] Or again: "Marcuse's whole inversion of Freud's theory seems to have no intelligible purpose other than a return to pre-social existence."[987] He stressed that at this point, Marcuse's reliance on Marx "is extremely dubious."[988] He noted that Marx thought that "the perfect society of the future would be so constituted that each individual would treat his own powers and abilities as direct social forces, thus removing the conflict between individual and communal needs."[989]

He stressed that Marx did not share Freud's view regarding the nature of instincts. But, for Kołakowski, the fatal flaw in Marcuse's Freudian argument was this:

> One cannot without contradiction maintain that men are instinctively and inevitably enemies of one another, and yet that their instincts must be liberated so that they can live together in peace and harmony.[990]

When it came to imagining liberation, Kołakowski also concluded that Marcuse is woefully short. What exactly does a liberated utopia, according to Marcuse, look like? "There is and can be no answer to these questions: we are at the mercy of arbitrary decisions by Marcuse and his followers," Kołakowski wrote. "In the same way, we do not know what the liberated world is going to look like, and Marcuse expressly says that it cannot be described in advance."[991] "All we are told," he pointed out, "is that we must completely 'transcend' existing society and civilization, carry out a 'global revolution,' create 'qualitatively new' social conditions, and so on." He understood the extent to which Marcuse is motivated primarily, if not exclusively, by the principle of *aufheben der Kultur*:

> The only positive conclusion to be drawn is that whatever tends to destroy existing civilization is praiseworthy: there is no reason to suppose, for instance, that the burning of books, which happened in various university centers in the U.S.A., was not a good way to start the revolutionary process of "transcending" the corrupt world of capitalism in the name of a higher reason *à la* Plato or Hegel.[992]

In his 2015 book *The Devil's Pleasure Palace*, Michael Walsh, a noted novelist and screenwriter with an astute appreciation of the impact of the Frankfurt School on American culture, explained how Marcuse's advocacy of polymorphous sexuality was the key to his goal to negate American culture. Walsh wrote:

> Herbert Marcuse, the author of *Eros and Civilization*, celebrated "polymorphous perversity," advocating the liberating power of sex, but only in the narrowest sense: liberation from (in his view) arbitrary and capricious structures laid down by culture and civilization. By following the directive to "make love, not war," the gullible individual might well have felt he was striking a blow at the hierarchy; in reality, though, perhaps he was simply expanding his creative, sexual energy in useless and unproductive ways. But Marcuse knew that a populace engaged in pointless

sexual intercourse was a populace uninterested in much of anything else; thus "polymorphous perversity" weakens the foundations of the society he sought to undermine.[993]

Walsh continued:

> Again, we must use the word "satanic," which, rightly defined, means the desire to tear down a longstanding, even elemental, order and replace it with...nothing. Critical Theory very effectively harnesses resentment, transmuting it into rage; it excuses solipsistic indolence, presenting it as "self-realization."[994]

Also largely absent from direct reference in *Eros and Civilization* is Martin Heidegger (relegated to one footnote mention), Marcuse's mentor when pursuing his postgraduate studies. Marcuse's estrangement from Heidegger is understandable, given Heidegger's decision to join the Nazi Party in 1933. Still, his influence is another subtext to *Eros and Civilization*. Marcuse's discussion of alienation owes less to Marx's emphasis on economic oppression and more to Heidegger's argument in *Being and Time* that alienation results from a failure of *Dasein* (in English, "being there") as *In-der-Welt-sein* (in English, "being-in-the-world") as a fully self-reflective experience. Still, *Eros and Civilization* is woefully deficient in explaining how a non-repressive society would produce the material necessities needed to sustain the billions of people living today in advanced industrial societies. What Marcuse drew from Heidegger was a pessimism centered on appreciating nihilism's emptiness. Heidegger, for instance, was explicit that when we die, we experience nothing but the void. Marcuse shared Heidegger's atheistic view that beyond our experience here, there is nothing more. Yet, the best Marcuse could offer was that we will live longer in a liberated society.

Specifically, Marcuse suggested that under "conditions of a truly human existence, the difference between succumbing to disease at the age of ten, thirty, fifty, or seventy, and dying a 'natural death' after a fulfilled life, may be a difference worth fighting for with all instinctual energy."[995] Without a belief in God, Marcuse envisioned the best a full-actualized human can hope to experience is a long and healthy life. To live a long and healthy life is a noble goal but not one that rises to the bliss of the Buddha in Hinduism. As the book concludes, Marcuse demeans religion, charging (much as does Freud in his book *The Future of an Illusion*[996]) that religion is another repressive system of domination. Marcuse wrote the following:

> Whether death is feared as a constant threat, or glorified as supreme sacrifice, or accepted as fate, the education for consent to death introduces an element of surrender into life from the beginning—surrender and submission. It stifles "utopian" efforts. The powers that be have a deep affinity to death; death is a token of unfreedom, of defeat. Theology and philosophy today compete with each other in celebrating death as an existential category: perverting a biological fact into an ontological essence, they bestow transcendental blessing on the guilt of mankind which they help to perpetuate—they betray the promise of utopia.[997]

Marcuse explained he deals with the religious concept of death through what he calls the "Great Refusal." He defined the "Great Refusal" as "the protest against unnecessary repression, the struggle for the ultimate form of freedom."[998] That death could be a final liberation is an ironic suggestion for neo-Marxists seeking to create utopia within the experience of life. But Marcuse suggested we could make death "rational" by making it painless. He added that "men can die without anxiety if they know that what they love is protected from misery and oblivion"—that is, the dying person is leaving behind a non-repressive society to loved ones. "After a fulfilled life, they may take it upon themselves to die—at a moment of their own choosing."[999] But for Marcuse, assisted suicide was nothing more than an exit strategy into Heidegger's black void.

Marcuse ended the book with sentences that give a hat tip to the Holocaust victims:

> But even the ultimate advent of freedom cannot redeem those who died in pain. It is the remembrance of them, and the accumulated guilt of mankind against its victims, that darken the prospect of a civilization without repression.

For Horkheimer, Adorno, and Marcuse, Hitler and the Holocaust are the ever present, ultimate subtext in all their various writings. In *The Devil's Pleasure Palace*, Walsh described the Frankfurt School as "a group of tiresome, quarrelsome, pedantic, mostly German- or Austrian-born intellectuals endlessly rehashing the theories and merits of an earlier generation of tiresome, pedantic, mostly German- or Austrian-born intellectuals, with the added layer of their largely shared (or rejected) Jewishness in common."[1000] What Walsh could have added was that while Jewish by ethnicity, the Frankfurt School intellectuals were atheists, or like Marx, theists who hated God.

One-Dimensional Man (1964)

Marcuse's next book, *One-Dimensional Man*, elaborated theoretically on the arguments he presented initially in *Eros and Civilization*. The book's primary purpose was to explain how the culture of technology in an advanced industrial society had increased alienation and intensified domination in the United States despite the operation of a capitalist economy that provided material abundance across class distinctions. As noted by London-based journalist Stuart Jeffries in his book on the Frankfurt School, *Grand Hyatt Abyss: The Lives of the Frankfurt School*,[1001] Marcuse "self-consciously recognized" his 1964 book *One-Dimensional Man* as "the western counterpoint" to his 1958 book *Soviet Marxism*.[1002] Jeffries explained:

> He [Marcuse] held that the capitalist west had consolidated itself in opposition to its foe, Soviet society. But he also held that the "totally administered" advanced industrial society, with its consumerism, militarism and sexual repression masqueraded as erotic-free-for-all, was a response, and a parallel, to the proverbial grimness of life under Stalin and his henchmen.[1003]

Jeffries commented that Marcuse "adhered to the Frankfurt School orthodoxy that monopoly capitalism was as much a form of totalitarianism as National Socialism or Soviet Marxism."[1004] In the post–World War II era, Marxists like Marcuse had soured on the Soviet Union, given the failure of Stalin to support the German Communist Party in the 1930s and the increasing disclosures about Stalin following Khrushchev's secret speech in 1956. In 1964, when *One-Dimensional Man* was published, the 1930s Walter Duranty–like enthusiasm for Stalin's Soviet Russia was dead for socialists in the United States and Frankfurt School thinkers like Marcuse.

In the introduction to the book, Marcuse acknowledged that *One-Dimensional Man* would vacillate between "two contradictory hypotheses: (1) that advanced industrial society is capable of containing qualitative change for the foreseeable future; (2) that forces and tendencies exist which may break this containment and explode the society."[1005] He acknowledged the material advantages of technologically driven capitalism in an advanced industrial society. But he also explained that "under the rule of a repressive whole, liberty can be made into a powerful instrument of domination."[1006] He wrote:

> The distinguishing feature of advanced industrial society is its effective suffocation of those needs which demand liberation—liberation also from that which is tolerable and rewarding and comfortable—while it sustains and absolves the destructive power and repressive function of the affluent society. Here, the social controls exact the overwhelming need for the production and consumption of waste...the need for modes of relaxation which soothe and prolong this stupefaction; the need for maintaining such deceptive liberties as free competition at administered prices, a free press which censors itself, free choice between brands and gadgets.[1007]

These ideas directly confront the presumption that free enterprise or personal freedoms can exist as defined by the Constitution. One of the critical points Marcuse worked to establish in *One-Dimensional Man* is that totalitarianism does not just exist in fascist or Communist societies under a terroristic dictatorship with a one-party system that holds power by eliminating all opposition. He saw the presumption that only terroristic dictatorships could be totalitarian was itself ideological. He perceived a different reality. He believed the culture of advanced industrial societies had introduced totalitarian tendencies into democratic states, including those democracies with the economic and political freedoms enjoyed in the United States. Marcuse conceptualized that totalitarian societies are those in which the private and public existence of the individual is controlled, exposed to standardized rules of behavior, imposed values, and manufactured needs.[1008] Thus, Marcuse argued that even freedom could be enslaving:

> Under the rule of a repressive whole, liberty can be made into a powerful instrument of domination. The range of choice open to the individual is not the decisive factor in determining the degree of human freedom, but *what* can be chosen and what *is* chosen by the individual. The criterion for free choice can never be an absolute one, but neither is it entirely relative.[1009]

He continued this paragraph with a specific example:

> Free election of masters does not abolish the masters or the slaves. Free choice among a wide variety of goods and services does not signify freedom if these goods and services sustain social controls over a life of toil and fear—that is, if they sustain alienation. And the spontaneous

> reproduction of superimposed needs by the individual does not establish autonomy; it only testifies to the efficacy of the controls.[1010]

Because advanced industrial societies "flatten out" the contrast between satisfied and unsatisfied needs, class distinctions become equalized:

> If the worker and his boss enjoy the same television program and visit the same resort places, if the typist is as attractively made up as the daughter of her employer, if the Negro owns a Cadillac, if they all read the same newspaper, then this assimilation indicates not the disappearances of classes, but the extent to which the needs and satisfactions that serve the preservation of the Establishment are shared by the underlying population.[1011]

He explained that in contemporary society, social needs intrude upon personal needs so extensively that the difference between social and personal needs becomes indistinguishable:

> Indeed, in the most highly developed areas of contemporary society, the transplantation of social into individual needs is so effective that the difference between them seems to be purely theoretical. Can one really distinguish between the mass media as instruments of information and entertainment, and as agents of manipulation and indoctrination? Between the automobile as nuisance and as convenience? Between the horrors and the comforts of functional architecture? Between the work for national defense and the work for corporate gain? Between the private pleasure and the commercial and political utility involved in increasing the birth rate?[1012]

The technological culture of advanced industrial states even erases the sense of alienation as the society enjoys the abundance of goods and services the advanced industrial state produces. But in the process, Marcuse argues the rational (i.e., Enlightenment) thinking at the heart of the advanced industrial society creates irrationality as its consequences:

> We are again confronted with one of the most vexing aspects of advanced industrial civilization: the rational character of its irrationality. Its productivity and efficiency, its capacity to increase and spread comforts, to turn waste into need, and destruction into construction, the extent to which this civilization transforms the object world into an extension of man's mind and body makes the very notion of alienation question-

able. The people recognize themselves in their commodities; they find their soul in their automobile, hi-fi set, split-level home, kitchen equipment. The very mechanism which ties the individual to his society has changed, and social control is anchored in the new needs which it has produced.[1013]

Technological progress in advanced industrial societies implies mass production and mass distribution that require a considerable degree of standardization and submission of the individual to pre-given and superimposed values, aspirations, and goals. The technological reality of the advanced industrial society so invades the self, the ego, and the inner, private sense of who we are that our individual consciousness becomes inseparable from public opinion and behavior:

> Today this private space has been invaded and whittled down by technological reality. Mass production and mass distribution claim the *entire* individual, and industrial psychology has long since ceased to be confined to the factory. The manifold processes of introjection seem to be ossified in almost mechanical reactions. The result is, not adjustment but *mimesis* [the representation of the real world or the self in art and literature]: an immediate identification of the individual with *his* society and, through it, with the society as a whole.[1014]

Immersion in the technological reality of the advanced industrial society so subsumes a person's individual identity that reason submits and internalizes the repressive elements of the advanced capitalist culture without realizing this is happening:

> The impact of progress turns Reason into submission to the facts of life, and to the dynamic capability of producing more and bigger facts of the same sort of life. The efficiency of the system blunts the individuals' recognition that it contains no facts which do not communicate the repressive power of the whole. If the individuals find themselves in the things which shape their life, they do so, not by giving, but by accepting the law of things—not the law of physics but the law of their society.[1015]

As individuals integrate their self-identity and faculties of reason into the advanced industrial state, we become one-dimensional entities reflecting the advanced industrial culture, not distinct self-actualizing human beings. The prevailing technological reality becomes an operational reality dictated by behaviorism in social scientists. How many units can a worker produce on an assembly line per hour? How many assembly line hours can a worker endure in each work shift? In this one-dimensional world, reason and social behaviorism meet on common ground. An advanced industrial society "makes scientific and technical progress into an instrument of domination."[1016]

Marcuse returned to reconsider Freudian psychology in *One-Dimensional Man* briefly. He introduced the term "repressive desublimation" to explain yet another way in which technologically advanced culture represses sexual urges. In classical Freudian psychology, sublimation is the process whereby an individual diverts an unacceptable unconscious sexual desire into a socially acceptable channel. Thus, instead of being acted out, impulses to commit incest or adultery can be sublimated into other activities, such as painting, writing poetry, etc. In both *Eros and Civilization* and *One-Dimensional Man*, Marcuse argued that the aesthetic experience of art or literature allowed an individual in a repressed society to gain "an intimation of freedom from the kind of repression that is attributable to the institutions of the totalized society."[1017] But technological society reduces the need for sublimation since advanced industrial civilization diminishes the erotic (i.e., romantic love) to intensify sexual energy.[1018] Thus, Marcuse argued, advanced industrial civilization engages in "repressive desublimation" by allowing sex to be more openly displayed in the culture. Marcuse explained:

> It has often been noted that advanced industrial civilization operates with a greater degree of sexual freedom—"operates" in the sense that the latter becomes a market value and a factor of social mores. Without ceasing to be an instrument of labor, the body is allowed to exhibit its sexual features in the everyday work world and in work relations. This is one of the unique achievements of industrial society—rendered possible by the reduction of dirty and heavy physical labor; by the availability of cheap, attractive clothing, beauty culture, and physical hygiene; by the requirements of the advertising industry, etc. The sexy office and sales girls, the handsome, virile junior executive and floor walker are highly marketable commodities, and the possession of suitable mistresses—once the prerogative of kings, princes, and lords—facilitates the career of even the less exalted ranks in the business community.[1019]

Marcuse continued:

> Functionalism, going artistic, promotes this trend. Shops and offices open themselves through huge glass windows and expose their personnel; inside, high counters and non-transparent partitions are coming down. The corrosion of privacy in massive apartment houses and suburban homes breaks the barrier which formerly separated the individual from the public existence and exposes more easily the attractive qualities of other wives and other husbands.[1020]

Marcuse argued that integrating sex into work and community creates controlled satisfaction (i.e., scientific libido management). Thus, repressive desublimation functions in the totalitarian advanced technological society as a means for social control. "The mobilization and administration of libido may account for much of the voluntary compliance, the absence of terror, the pre-established harmony between individual needs and socially-required desires, goals, and aspirations," he wrote. "The technological and political conquest of the transcending factors in human existence, so characteristic of the transcending factors in human existence, so characteristic of advanced industrial civilization, here asserts itself in the instinctual sphere: satisfaction in a way which generates submission and weakens the rationality of protest." Through the techniques of repressive desublimation, the pleasure principle gets increased expression, with the understanding that pleasure, thus adjusted by repressive desublimation, "generates submission."[1021]

Like *Eros and Civilization*, *One-Dimensional Man* is woefully short on describing Marcuse's utopia. In both books, Marcuse suggested that the best he can envision is that we might shorten the workday in advanced industrial societies after negating surplus repression. In *Eros and Civilization*, Marcuse wrote the following:

> Since the length of the working day is itself one of the principal repressive factors imposed upon the pleasure principle by the reality principle, the reduction of the working day to a point where the mere quantum of labor time no longer arrests human development is the first prerequisite for freedom.[1022]

Yet, even here, Marcuse noted that there is a trade-off:

> Such reduction [in the hours working] by itself would almost certainly mean a considerable decrease in the standard of living prevalent today in the most advanced industrial countries. But the regression to a lower

> standard of living, which the collapse of the performance principle would bring about, does not militate against progress in freedom.[1023]

Marcuse envisioned that reducing labor to necessary labor would result in the collapse of repressive constraints. He predicted this: "Eros, the life instincts, would be released to an unprecedented degree."[1024]

Researcher Barry M. Katz pointed out yet another Frankfurt School irony. In his 1979 article "Praxis and Poiesis: Toward an Intellectual Biography of Herbert Marcuse [1898–1979]," Katz pointed out how Marcuse and other Frankfurt School luminaries all came from privileged backgrounds. Katz wrote:

> The affluent, assimilated Jewish bourgeoisie of pre–World War I central Europe has proved to be an almost predictable source of some of the century's most radical political ideas: the elder Lukács managed the biggest bank in Szeged, Walter Benjamin's father was a wealthy Berlin art dealer, Horkheimer's was a prosperous member of the Stuttgart textile trade, and the list goes on. From rather modest beginnings, Carl Marcuse (the name, incidentally, is genealogically identical to that of Karl Marx) also established himself in the flourishing German textile industry, but prudently transferred his holdings to real estate before the war. The Marcuse family moved from Berlin to the fashionable suburb of Charlottenburg, and Herbert Marcuse, like so many of his future colleagues, grew up in circumstances which enabled him to take for granted the material achievements of industrial capitalism and set his sights elsewhere. [1025]

In the final analysis, capitalism afforded Marcuse the luxury of a comfortable life where he could appreciate art, literature, and sex. At the same time, he trashed the economic system that afforded him privileges. Having failed in Germany to block Hitler, the United States offered Marcuse, an atheistic Jew, the opportunity for refuge. Ungrateful, he set out to accomplish here what he failed to do in his home country: namely, to abolish capitalism by abolishing capitalism culture, even if that meant trashing the United States, whose good graces had allowed him to escape Hitler's death camps. In his book *The Devil's Pleasure Palace*, Michael Walsh observed the following:

> The problem with the Frankfurt School scholars was that they arrived with ideological blinders—men of the Left fighting other men of the Left back in the old *Heimat* [in English, "hometown"]—and were

> unable to see that there was another, different world welcoming them in the United States if only they would open their eyes. (How, for example, could they hate California?) They appear not so much scholarly as simple, viewing American capitalism as a vast, deliberate, conspiracy against their own socialist ideas, when, in fact, their ideas were simply wrong, their analysis flawed, and their animus ineradicable. They were creatures of their own time and place, with no more claim to absolute truth than the man on a soapbox in Speakers' Corner in Hyde Park or the lunatic staggering down Market Street in San Francisco talking to himself. Everybody's got a beef. [1026]

Walsh explained that in the aftermath of World War II, "a burgeoning transnational elite in New York City and Washington, DC, embraced not only the war's refugees but also many of their resolutely nineteenth-century 'modern' ideas."[1027] He argued that among the most pernicious of these European refugees were those of the Frankfurt School and its reactionary philosophy of critical theory.[1028] He observed that Frankfurt School authors like Marcuse brought their "fashionable Central European nihilism" to college campuses across the United States. "Seizing the high ground of academe and the arts, the new nihilists set about dissolving the bedrock of the country, from patriotism to marriage to the family to military service," Walsh wrote.[1029]

An Essay on Liberation (1969)

In his 1969 *Essay on Liberation*, Marcuse attempted to address liberation would require a fundamental change in the "nature of man."[1030] He characterized his envisioned reengineering of the human being as the development of "a new sensibility."[1031] Marcuse argued that the technological advances of capitalism had now made possible the termination of poverty and scarcity on a global scale. He posited that "the question is no longer: how can the individual satisfy his own needs without hurting others, but rather: how can he satisfy his needs without hurting himself, without reproducing, through his aspirations and satisfactions, his dependence on an exploitative apparatus which, in satisfying his needs, perpetuates his servitude?"[1032] Marcuse explained that the realization of this dream required a reconstruction of human nature:

> But the construction of such a society presupposes a type of man with a different sensitivity as well as consciousness: men who would speak a different language, have different gestures, follow different impulses;

> men who have developed an instinctual barrier against cruelty, brutality, ugliness.[1033]

Marcuse tried to give more definition to his idea of the superior human being by quoting Nietzsche, whose idea was that the *Übermensch* (in English, the "superman") would fill the void created by the death of God with his own will to power. In Zarathustra's prologue to Nietzsche's book *Thus Spoke Zarathustra*, Zarathustra proclaims: "Behold, I teach you the [*Übermensch*]. The [*Übermensch*] is the meaning of the earth. Let your will say: the [*Übermensch*] *shall be* the meaning of the earth! I beseech you, my brothers, *remain faithful to the earth*, and do not believe those who speak to you of otherworldly hopes!"[1034] Marcuse, another atheist like Nietzsche, thus predicates his idea of the "sensitive" human plea to transcend God by perfecting human nature. Marcuse continued:

> Such an instinctual transformation is conceivable as a factor of social change only if it enters the social division of labor, the production relations themselves. They would be shaped by men and women who have the good conscience of being human, tender, sensuous, who are no longer ashamed of themselves—for "the token of freedom attained, that is, no longer ashamed of themselves" (Nietzsche, *Die Fröhliche Wissenschaft* [In English, *The Gay Science*], Book III, 275).[1035]

Here Marcuse suggested God is the ultimate agent of repression. His idea of liberation involves human beings "self-actualizing" themselves as *Übermenschen*, capable of replacing God to create their own, unchained moral code.

> The imagination of such men and women would fashion their reason and tend to make the process of production a process of creation. This is the utopian concept of socialism which envisions the ingression of freedom into the realm of necessity, and the union between causality by necessity and causality by freedom.[1036]

Marcuse imagined that we will attain knowledge of good and evil once we expel God from the Garden of Eden that we create with our new sensibility as self-actualized *Übermenschen*. He engaged in a Thucydides-like redefinition of words, as he constructed his version of a Pieper pseudoreality:

> Obscenity is a moral concept in the verbal arsenal of the Establishment, which abuses the term by applying it, not to the expressions of its own morality but to those of another. Obscene is not the picture of a naked woman who exposes her pubic hair but that of a fully clad general who exposes his medals rewarded in a war of aggression; obscene is not the ritual of the Hippies but the declaration of a high dignitary of the Church that war is necessary for peace. Linguistic therapy—that is, the effort to free words (and thereby concepts) from...the Establishment—demands the transfer of moral standards (and of their validation) from the Establishment to the revolt against it.[1037]

Even when contemplating utopia, Marcuse never strayed far from the theme of negation:

> Dialectics of democracy: if democracy means self-government of free people, with justice for all, then the realization of democracy would presuppose abolition of the existing pseudo-democracy. In the dynamic of corporate capitalism, the fight for democracy thus tends to assume anti-democratic forms, and to the extent to which the democratic decisions are made in "parliaments" on all levels, the opposition will tend to become extra-parliamentary.[1038]

Marcuse expected that the extra-parliamentary action will arise from "the Commies and the Hippies and their like with the long hair and the beards and the dirty pants."[1039] He commented that never since the Middle Ages has "accumulated repression erupted on such global scale in organized aggression against those outside the representative system—'outsiders' within and without."[1040] He believed the breeding ground of dissent would be the universities, and he justified the disruption and the violence of student protests as being precisely the type of "extra-parliamentary" action needed to give birth to his envisioned *Übermenschen* utopia:

> If legitimate violence includes, in the daily routine of "pacification" and "liberation," wholesale burning, poisoning, bombing, the actions of the radical opposition, no matter how illegitimate, can hardly be called by the same name: violence. Can there be any meaningful comparison, in magnitude and criminality, between the unlawful acts committed by the rebels in the ghettos, on the campuses, on the city streets on the one side and the deeds perpetrated by the forces of order in Vietnam, in Bolivia, in Indonesia, in Guatemala, on the other?[1041]

Mahatma Gandhi and Martin Luther King Jr. advocated civil disobedience, not violence. Gandhi and Reverend King understood that violent action contradicts the higher moral principles of social justice they sought to achieve, in that violence breeds only more violence. In these passages, Marcuse completely embraced violent negation, assuming he can only create a higher-order civil society by destroying the existing civilization. To justify his embrace of dark forces, Marcuse again resorted to language perversion techniques:

> Can one meaningfully call it an offense when demonstrators disrupt the business of the university, the draft board, the supermarket, the flow of traffic, to protest against far more efficient disruption of the business of life of untold numbers of human beings by the armed forces of law and order? Here too, the brute reality requires a redefinition of terms: the established vocabulary discriminates a priori against the opposition—it protects the Establishment.[1042]

In his *Essay on Liberation*, Marcuse saw students as his neo-Marxist vanguard. He noted the student radicals displayed "a strong element of spontaneity, even anarchism, in this rebellion," that he saw as the "expression of the new sensibility, sensitivity against domination: the feeling, the awareness that the joy of freedom and the need to be free must precede liberation."[1043] As we have noted repeatedly, Marcuse's primary goal was negation. When it came to describing his utopia, he fell back on daring to "imagine" the future—a common theme in today's critical theory that wants to "reimagine gender," "reimagine race," "reimagine police," and so on. His vagueness on utopia prefigured the Beatles' John Lennon's song, "Imagine," in which Lennon invited us to imagine a world in which there was no heaven or hell.[1044] Lennon envisioned that getting rid of God, religion, and nation-states would allow us to live in peace. His lyrics suggested that if we got rid of possessions and personal property, humanity could live in harmony. Lennon's lyrics convey a typically vague neo-Marxist utopian future. We could enjoy material abundance and free sex if only we could get rid of capitalism, nationalism, and God.

Marcuse's idea of utopia suggested that his life in a comfortable home in beautiful Southern California was "alienated" because he still needed to teach at the university, his time for art and literature was limited, and his sex opportunities were restricted to his current spouse and his students. Stuart Jeffries in his book, *Grand Hotel Abyss*, described Marcuse's sex life as follows:

> Following the death of his first wife Sophie in 1951, Marcuse, who could neither drive nor cook, moved in with his friend [socialist political scientist] Franz Neumann and Neumann's wife Inge. This was one feature of the Grand Hotel Abyss [i.e., the Frankfurt School] that Lukács didn't pick up on—if the service was excellent at the Grand Hotel while its residents comfortably contemplated the abyss, that service was provided by women. After Franz Neumann died in a car crash in 1954, Herbert went on to marry Inge. Later, he had an affair with a graduate student and when Inge found out she banned the student from the house, though that didn't end the affair.[1045]

After Inge Marcuse died in 1972, Marcuse married one of his students, Erica "Ricky" Sherover, forty years younger than Marcuse, born in 1938.

Wilhelm Reich and the Sexual Revolution

Rolf Wiggershaus, in his history of the Frankfurt School, credits Wilhelm Reich (1897–1957), along with Erich Fromm, as being one of the "left Freudians who made an intriguing attempt to combine the Freudian theory of instinctual drives with Marx's class theory."[1046] Although Reich was never officially a member of the Frankfurt Institute for Social Research, he worked with Karl Landauer and Heinrich Meng. They were directors of the Frankfurt Institute of Psychoanalysis, which shared premises with the Institute of Social Research. Martin Jay, the Sidney Hellman Ehrman Professor of History at the University of California, Berkeley, and a specialist in the Franklin School, called the Institute of Social Research's "attempt to introduce psychological analysis into its neo-Marxist Critical Theory was…a bold and unconventional step."[1047] Jay added that the institute's desire to introduce Freud into Marxism was "a mark of the Institute's desire to leave the traditional Marxist straitjacket behind."[1048] Marcuse took objection to Reich's approach. In the epilogue to *Eros and Civilization* entitled "Critique of Neo-Freudian Revisionism," Marcuse commented dismissively that "sexual liberation per se becomes for Reich a panacea for individual and social ills."[1049] Marcuse's complaint about Reich was that Reich oversimplified Marxism by arguing that repressed sexual instincts were the cause of all individual psychological neuroses and psychoses and the cause of all repressive societal structures, including Nazism, the patriarchal family, and capitalism.

On March 24, 1894, Reich was born to Jewish parents, Leon and Cecilia Reich. He was born in a part of Galicia that then belonged to the

Austro-Hungarian Empire and is today part of southwestern Poland and western Ukraine. Although born to Jewish parents, Reich was not raised in a religious family, and his parents dissuaded him from speaking the Yiddish of his neighbors in favor of German. Soon after Reich's birth, the family moved to the town of Jujinetz in northern Bukovina, another province of the Austro-Hungarian Empire that is today divided between Romania and Ukraine. There, his father became a partner of his wife's uncle, Josef Blum, who owned a cattle farm on an estate of two thousand acres. Reich ran the cattle farm after his mother committed suicide and his father died of tuberculosis. Then in 1915, Russia invaded Bukovina and devastated the family estate. Reich lost everything—no parents, no farm, no money. He went to Vienna to stay with his maternal grandmother. But he was quickly inducted into the Austro-Hungarian army. During World War I, he served on the Italian front, where he commanded a group of some forty men. After the war, he headed to Vienna, where he studied medicine at the University of Vienna. Then in 1919, he met Sigmund Freud and decided to pursue a career in psychoanalysis.[1050]

The most impactful part of Reich's biography is his sexual history, which he detailed in his diaries published in 1988.[1051] His first incident involved the live-in housemaid and the live-in nurse to his younger brother Robert when Reich was four years old. As Reich told the story, the housemaid had an affair with the young, good-looking boy who served as the family's coachman. He secretly watched the housemaid and the coachman have sex. Then, one afternoon, he climbed into bed with the nurse taking a nap with his brother. He decided to try what he had seen the housemaid and coachman do, and the nurse allowed him to proceed. "I climbed on top of her, lifted her dress, and reached feverishly for her genitals (to her apparent enjoyment)," Reich wrote. "Her hair excited me particularly (I always slept with the maid, and several times before this I had made believe I was asleep and touched her genitals, plucking at her hair)."[1052]

He related another similar incident in which he lay down on top of his tutoress as she was taking a nap. He fantasized about having intercourse with her. "Even now, I cannot understand why she [the tutoress] allowed this," he wrote. "Was it 'fun' for her too, or was she not aware of what I had in mind? (Probably the former)."[1053] Reich watched the son of a farmhand lying in the sun in front of his house, wearing only a shirt, masturbating. "I enjoyed watching him play with himself and, through this, experienced highly pleasurable sensations," he wrote. "I cannot say whether or not my later intense pleasure in masturbating, which lasted for so many years, is rooted here. It is quite probable, however, due to the intensity of my sensations while watching the idiot and his performance."[1054]

He described another incident in which he grew excited looking at the animals on the farm. "I took a whip with a smooth grip, turned it around, and thrust the handle into the vagina of the mare," he described. "The animal was surprised at first but then seemed to enjoy it. She spread her legs wide and began to urinate while I had an orgasm (without ejaculation). From then on, I did this every day and extended my activities to other mares as well."[1055] At approximately eleven and a half years old, he had his first experience of intercourse. "She was the first to teach me the thrusting motion necessary for ejaculation and at that time it occurred so quickly and unexpectedly that I was frightened and thought it had been an accident," he explained. "From then on, I had intercourse almost every day for years—it was always in the afternoon, when my parents were napping."[1056]

Reich described perhaps the most dramatic event in his childhood when he spied on his mother having an affair with a live-in tutor. "I heard them kissing, whispering, and the horrible creaking of the bed in which my mother lay," he wrote. "Ten feet away stood her own child, a witness to her disgrace."[1057] He retold the story of his mother's death, adding an important detail—his desire to have sex with his mother:

> And so it happened night after night. I followed her to his door and waited there until morning. Gradually I became accustomed to it! My horror gave way to erotic feelings. Once I even considered breaking in on them and demanding that she have intercourse with me too (shame!), threatening that otherwise I would tell Father.[1058]

In his autobiography, Reich admitted to having told his father of his mother's affair with the tutor. "I trembled as I said that I knew nothing about our present tutor but that I had been a witness to Mother's relationship with S. from the beginning," he related. "He pressured me to tell him everything, and I did—unfortunately, too late. Haltingly, in broken sentences, I related how I had listened behind the door but had not dared to do anything, for fear of being killed."[1059] His father, whom Reich described as an authoritarian and violent man, having beat both him and his mother repeatedly, flew into a rage. Learning that her husband knew of the affair, his mother took poison but lived after her husband "poured an emetic into her, which helped."[1060] He described how his father began treating his mother even more brutally after learning of her infidelity. "His sudden temper and his anguish repeatedly gained the upper hand," Reich wrote. "In attacks of senseless rage which occurred almost daily, he would beat Mother mercilessly."[1061] Finally, his mother took such a lethal dose of poison that the physicians could not bring her back. After relating the drama of his mother's death, he told us that the first time he went to a brothel was at age fifteen.[1062] Reich admitted that he "succumbed to excessive masturbation."[1063]

There is some controversy over a Reich quotation that was taken from a 1975 publication of *The Function of an Orgasm* that was translated by Vincent R. Carfagno and originally published by Farrar, Straus and Giroux in 1973.[1064] The controversy involves a 2011 book highly critical of Reich that London journalist Christopher Turner published under the title *Adventures in the Orgasmatron: How the Sexual Revolution Came to America*.[1065] In that book, Turner cited the quotation as it appeared in the Carfagno translation.[1066] The Carfagno translation of the quotation was shorter and differently worded than the quotation that had appeared in Theodore P. Wolfe's version, first published in 1942 by Reich's Orgone Institute Press.[1067] The shorter quotation cited by Turner read as follows: "I maintain that every person who has succeeded in preserving a certain amount of naturalness knows this: those who are psychologically ill need but one thing—complete and repeated genital gratification."[1068] The longer quotation in the 1942 publication read as follows: "My contention is that every individual who has managed to preserve a bit of naturalness knows that there is only one thing wrong with neurotic patients: *the lack of full and repeated sexual satisfaction*."[1069] The longer version has a slightly different emphasis. The original 1942 quotation said neurosis results from sexual satisfaction, while the truncated version cited by Turner emphasized genital satisfaction.

Reich scholar Dr. Philip W. Bennett chided Turner for careless scholarship. In a published response piece, Bennett appeared to have assumed that Turner had truncated the quote, rewriting it from the 1927 edition of the book. Bennett charged that Turner "shortened" the quotation "with no indication in his text that he is doing so."[1070] Bennett evidently was unaware of the Carfagno translation. He can be excused for not recognizing Turner was using the Carfagno translation because Turner never footnoted either the 1973 or 1975 edition. What Turner footnoted was Reich's *Selected Writings* published in 1973. Again, Bennett took Turner to task for claiming the quotation came from the 1973 edition, when the quotation appeared only in the 1960 edition of Reich's *Selected Writings*.[1071] As far as Bennett was concerned, Turner's sloppy scholarship disqualified his points about Reich from serious consideration. But quoting Reich accurately requires an unusual care for precision and detail. Reich had no hesitancy to reuse a book title he liked on a different book he wrote subsequently. He also had no hesitancy to give a reprinted edition a different title than the original. Then too, Reich's texts that were written initially in German often take on distorted subtleties of meaning depending on the acuity of the translator.

But while Bennett was correct in criticizing Turner's scholarship, Turner's conclusion about the quotation in question captures accurately the general impression Reich created. Turner had a point: since Reich's sexual satisfaction requires orgasms, his emphasis remains on genital organs. Turner summed up Reich's preoccupation with orgasms as follows: "The orgasm was the panacea to cure all ills, he [Wilhelm Reich] thought, including the [Nazi] fascism that had forced him to leave Europe."[1072] Turner's conclusion about Reich appeared fair, even if highly critical in tone. The complications over this particular Reich quotation are discussed here at length because the academic controversy illustrates several important points: Reich remains a highly polarizing thinker, rejected by orthodox Freudians and orthodox Marxists even today. While he retains loyalty from many associates who worked with him, like Sharaf, and from ideologically aligned supporters, like Bennett, he is soundly rejected by critics like Turner who view his emphasis on orgiastic sex as confused and intentionally aimed at destroying the established order.

Although Reich derived much from his work with Freud, he insisted that he added a dimension to Freud's psychoanalytic theory of sexuality and libido by "amplifying the concept of genital function with the concept of orgastic potency and defining it in terms of energy." He explained as follows:

1) If every psychic illness has a core of dammed-up sexual excitation, it can be caused only by the distribution of capacity for orgastic gratification. Hence, impotence and frigidity are key to the understanding of the economy of neuroses.

2) The energy source of the neurosis is created by the difference between the accumulation and discharge of sexual energy. The ungratified sexual excitation which is always present in the neurotic psychic apparatus distinguishes it from the healthy psychic apparatus. This holds true not only for the stasis neu-

> rosis (in Freudian terminology, actual neuroses) but for all psychic illnesses.[1073]

Reich's emphasis on accumulated sexual energy led to perhaps his most notorious invention, the orgone accumulator. The orgone accumulator was a metal and wood apparatus about the size of a 1950s telephone booth. His idea was that a patient sitting in the orgone box would accumulate sexual energy he believed was a form of Earth's life-force energy. At any rate, his psychoanalytic techniques centered on making the patient conscious of their repressed sexual impulses—a method he believed a guaranteed cure. "In other words, this kind of therapy brings about a cure when the consciousness of the instinctual demands also restores the capacity for full orgastic gratification."[1074] Turner stressed that by attempting to reconcile psychoanalysis and Marxism, Reich sought to give "Freudianism an optimistic gloss, arguing that repression, which Freud came to believe was an inherent part of the human condition, could be shed."[1075] Turner commented that Reich's insistence that society could function without the inhibition of sexual impulses that Freud felt were indispensable to civilization led critics to dismiss it as "genital utopia," mocking Reich as "the prophet of bigger and better orgasms."[1076]

In 1933, Reich was expelled from the Communist Party in Germany for being a "sexual determinist." [1077] Then, at the 1934 International Psycho-Analytical Congress in Lucerne, Switzerland, Reich was expelled from the professional psychiatric association partly because of his radical Marxist politics, and partly because he was a Jew and a Communist in Hitler's Germany, but primarily because his psychoanalytic theory regarding sex diverged from Freud.[1078] The underlying conflict that divided Reich from Freud involved psychoanalytic theory. Freud began the modern sexual revolution by theorizing that sexuality started in childhood, and he insisted that sexual instincts repressed in childhood could cause adult neuroses. But Freud did not believe sexual liberation was the answer. For him, the purpose of psychoanalysis was to sublimate sexual instincts in a socially productive direction. In sharp contrast, Reich pursued psychoanalysis to release sexual inhibitions. Freud rejected Reich's sexual hypothesis, with the result that Reich found himself a heretic among Freudian true believers.

From 1929 to 1934, Reich was quite involved in politics, making his first attempt to revolutionize society through sexual liberation.[1079] In his 1933 book, *The Mass Psychology of Fascism*, Reich argued that sexual repression was key to the Nazi ability to take over Germany.[1080] Psychoanalyst

Myron Sharaf points out in his 1963 book, *Fury on Earth: A Biography of Wilhelm Reich*, that Reich began his book on fascism with a question that had haunted him from virtually the first day he arrived in Berlin, a question the entire Frankfurt School was attempting to answer: "Why did the masses turn to the Nazis instead of the Communists?"[1081] Sharaf first met Reich in 1944 when Sharaf was eighteen years old. Ultimately deciding to become a psychoanalyst, Sharaf worked closely with Reich as a student, patient, and coworker. He based his highly sympathetic biography of Reich on detailed notes he took while working with Reich. His last meeting with Reich was on May 26, 1956, shortly before Reich was imprisoned.[1082] As Sharaf noted, "according to Marxist theory, the 'objective conditions' for a socialist economy were present: a large industrial proletariat; economic impoverishment of the working class; a strong Communist Party to provide the 'vanguard' of the proletariat."[1083] Yet, Germany sided with Hitler. Reich concluded that social psychology was necessary to explain why the German proletariat did not revolt against their economic oppression. Sharaf explained as follows:

> The worker-as-child had learned obedience to his parents in particular and to authority figures in general; moreover, he had been taught to suppress his sexual impulses. Hence in the adult, rebellious and sexual impulses were accompanied by anxiety, since both had been indiscriminately suppressed by the child's educators. Fear of revolt, as well as fear of sexuality, were thus "anchored" in the character structures of the masses.[1084]

Thus, in his "sexual-political" work, Reich sought to get people more in touch with their sexual desires. His goal was to create the social psychology needed to get the proletariat to arise in a Marxian revolution to reject fascism and overthrow capitalism. He realized he had to "begin with the personal to politicize the personal."[1085] Reich argued that the Nazis, well aware of this dynamic, "constantly used sex-political propaganda" of a negative kind. He explained that the Nazis "played on people's fear of their own impulses and their fear of chaos by calling upon the need for moralistic defenses, for 'law and order,' for protection against the 'Bolshevik menace' to the family."[1086] Reich wrote that the Catholic Church "was the most powerful sex-political organization in the world."[1087] He concluded that the destruction of the patriarchal family was essential to release the sexual impulses needed to release a Marxist revolution.

Reich turned to the work of Johann Jakob Bachofen (1815–1887), who was a Swiss professor of Roman law at the University of Basel from 1841 to 1845. In his 1861 book *Das Mutterrecht* (in English, *Mother Right*), Bachofen argued that primitive societies were matriarchies.[1088] He believed cultures are products of the divinities they worship. He also observed that paleolithic totems or figurines tended to be female and that children in primitive societies were generally named after their mothers. Bachofen argued that prominent female deities portrayed as "earth-mothers" or "mother-goddess" shaped these primitive societies. Mother lineage was favored in societies where the concept of fatherhood did not exist since the connection between sex and conception was not fully understood. Reich listed Bachofen's first three postulates, derived from Greek and Roman mythology, of the original mother-right: (1) "unlimited sexual intercourse in prehistoric times"; (2) "indeterminate paternity, with, as a result, a maternal line of succession"; and (3) "the primacy of women."[1089]

A second influence on Reich was Bronisław Malinowski (1884–1942), a Polish British anthropologist, and his 1929 book *The Sexual Life of Savages in North-Western Melanesia*.[1090] The centerpiece of Malinowski's ethnographic work was his study of the Trobriand people who live on the Kiriwina island chain northeast of New Guinea. Reich discussed Malinowski's work extensively in his 1931 book *The Invasion of Compulsory Sex Morality*.[1091] What drew Reich's attention was not only Malinowski's description of the open sex practices of the Trobriand, but even more importantly, Reich embraced Malinowski's discussion of the Trobriand as a sexually open matriarchal society that practiced a form of "primitive communism."[1092]

Malinowski, in his *The Sexual Life of Savages in North-Western Melanesia*, made clear that the natives of the Trobriand Islands live in a matriarchal society. "Their views [i.e., the views of the natives] on the process of procreation, coupled with certain mythological and animistic beliefs, affirm, without doubt or reserve, that the child is of the same substance as its mother and that between the father and the child there is no bond of physical union whatsoever."[1093] He continued: "These natives have a well-established institution of marriage, and yet are quite ignorant of the man's share in the begetting of children. At the same time, the term 'father' has, for the Trobriander, a clear, though exclusively social, definition: it signifies the man married to the mother, who lives in the same house with her, and forms part of the household."[1094]

Malinowski stressed that native children indulge in sex play long before puberty. "They [Trobriand children] indulge in plays and pastimes in which they satisfy their curiosity concerning the appearance and function of the organs of generation, and incidentally receive, it would seem, a certain amount of positive pleasure," he wrote. "Genital manipulation and such minor perversions as oral stimulation of the organs are typical forms of this amusement. Small boys and girls are said to be frequently initiated by their somewhat older companions, who allow them to witness their own amorous dalliance."[1095] He described in detail orgiastic festivals: "Sexual acts would be carried out in public on the central place; married people would participate in the orgy, man or wife behaving without restraint, even though within hail of each other."[1096] In communal sex orgies, primitive societies cannot confirm paternity. Thus, according to Malinowski, men treat all children like their children, leading to the communal ownership of land and huts—a phenomenon Reich interpreted as primitive communism.[1097]

Reich argued that Malinowski's research confirmed an 1884 book Engels authored entitled *The Origin of the Family, Private Property and the State: In the Light of the Researches of Lewis H. Morgan.*[1098] American anthropologist Lewis H. Morgan (1818–1881) wrote a book in 1877 called *Ancient Society: Or Researches in the Lines of Human Progress from Savagery, Through Barbarism to Civilization* that combined his ethnographic studies of American Indian tribes with Darwin's evolutionary theories.[1099] Engels endorsed Morgan's conclusions about the impact of the family on the development of civilization from ancient times. Engels determined the following: "This rediscovery of the primitive matriarchal gens as the earlier stage of the patriarchal gens of civilized peoples has the same importance for anthropology as Darwin's theory of evolution has for biology and Marx's theory of surplus value for political economy."[1100]

Reich concluded that Malinowski's research of the Trobriand islanders established that patriarchal society grew out of matriarchal society. He wrote:

> We must now undertake a thorough investigation of the theory of Morgan and Engels, since not only are their discoveries and conceptions of the relations between mother-right, the patriarchate, and the development of the family and private property splendidly confirmed by Malinowski's researches (except for a few necessary corrections), but more than that, when supplemented by the discovery of the marriage dowry in the Trobriands and its socially transforming economic func-

> tion as described here, their theory becomes a complete conception of primitive history, against which the usual contradictory theories have even less chance of prevailing than at the time when Morgan's and Engels' theses were first established.[1101]

For Reich, Malinowski's research with the Trobriand islanders refuted Freud's argument that sexual inhibition was essential to creating a functioning and productive society. Reich stressed that in a matriarchically organized society such as that maintained by the Trobriand islanders, the dowry was the wife's property. In contrast, in a patriarchal society, a dowry becomes the husband's property as the price the wife's family paid to buy the woman into the marriage. Reich agreed with Engels that the origin of private property could be traced to the evolution of patriarchal families from mother-right primitive families. He contended that sexual repression began playing an inhibiting role in society when the father supplanted the mother as the head of the family. Before the advent of DNA testing, the only way a father could know a child was his child was to demand his wife's fidelity. Because the father no longer sees the community as an extended family, patriarchy leads to the rise of private property, which the father passes to his male heir.[1102]

Reich also saw that Malinowski's research and Engels's reflections on Morgan's theory of the evolution of the family through history affirmed his theory that sexual liberation was necessary to produce a cultural revolution. This conclusion allowed Reich to confirm the neo-Marxist revision of orthodox Marxism, which postulated that the proletariat would rise against sexual repression, not against economic oppression, to overthrow capitalism. Malinowski's research with the Trobriand islanders and Engels's conclusions from Morgan's research affirmed for Reich the importance of the political-sexual efforts Reich was making to inform people of their sexual needs. Sharaf explained as follows: "In this period of his work [i.e., his "sex-pol," sexual-political, efforts] Reich dealt with sexual need in a way similar to the Marxists' handling of economic want. That is, one heightened awareness, one "raised consciousness" about the problem. It could only be out of a concern with the problem that solutions would follow."[1103] Thus, Malinowski's research and Engels's 1884 book gave Reich the ideological ammunition to refute both Freud and Marx with his substitute ideological certainty that a sexual revolution rising against sexual repression was necessary to abolish the patriarchal family as the precondition to overthrowing capitalism.

English physician and eugenicist Henry Havelock Ellis (1859–1939) wrote the preface to Malinowski's *The Sexual Life of Savages in North-Western Melanesia*. Ellis wrote extensively on sex, venturing into examinations of homosexuality, transgenderism, and masturbation. Ellis placed Malinowski's study of the Trobriand islanders into the genre that traces back to the ancient Roman historian Tacitus and *De origine et Situ Germanorum* (in English, *On the Origin and Situation of the Germans*) written around AD 98. When observing German tribes living in primeval German forests, Tacitus was the first to discuss the "noble savage" living in "a state of nature."[1104] Ellis correctly observed the "noble savage" became a literary genre that fascinated European intellectuals in the eighteenth century. Ellis noted that Rousseau "had really been a careful student of the narratives of explorers in his time," though Ellis dismissed "Rousseau's superficial and imaginative vision of the natural man."[1105] Rousseau's view, which the formation of society was destructive of our authentic "born-free" resonates in Frankfurt School ideology, reaches its full expression in Reich's sexual liberation ideology.

Ellis understood that Malinowski's explorations of sex in primitive societies had a titillating impact for twentieth-century Victorian-era readers in Great Britain. Thus, Ellis took pains to present Malinowski as a legitimate scientist, a nonjudgmental anthropologist whose study of savages in primitive societies may inform us "that in some respects the savage has here reached a finer degree of civilization than the civilized man."[1106] While "savage" and "primitive society" are terms out of vogue today, Ellis's preface subtly supported Reich's argument that releasing sexual inhibitions by following the example of the Trobriand islanders may "reform"[1107] (i.e., revolutionize) advanced industrial societies. Nor should we assume that the social and sexual dynamics of relatively small, largely undeveloped, and comparatively isolated societies living in temperate climates are transferable to large industrial societies that have developed in traditionally colder Northern Hemisphere climates.

As ingenious as Reich's arguments reading Freud into Marx may be, the crucial point is that Reich understood sexual liberation was first and foremost a force that would destroy capitalist culture. Like Marcuse and the other Frankfurt School neo-Marxists, Reich is woefully deficient in providing proof that modern advanced industrial societies will thrive once traditional family structures are abandoned.

Reich created both the terms "culture war" and "sexual revolution" with a book he initially published in 1936 and republished in 1945 with a new title and substantial revisions. The 1936 book was written in German and published as *Die Sexualität im Kulturkampf: Zur Sozialistischen Umstrukturierung des Menschen* (in English, *Sexuality in the Culture War: On the Socialist Restructuring of Man*).[1108] The 1945 book was published in English as *The Sexual Revolution: Toward a Self-Governing Character Structure*.[1109] Both books were self-published, with Reich's Sex-Pol publishing company issuing the 1936 book and his Orgone Institute Press issuing the 1945 book.

As should be apparent in reviewing the change in the subtitle of the two editions, the 1945 revision of the book went to great lengths to edit out Reich's affinity for socialism or his reliance on Marxist revolutionary ideology.[1110] In the original 1936 German edition, *Kulturkampf* is more precisely translated into English as "culture struggle," not "culture war." In German, the precise word for "war" is *Krieg*. The word *Kampf* in German derives from the Latin word *campus*, meaning a "field." In High German, the word then took on the significance of a "battlefield," or "fight." *Kampf* is the word Hitler used in titling his 1925 autobiographical Nazi ideological manifesto, *Mein Kampf* (in English, *My Struggle*). American author Garry Wills conveyed a similar idea in titling his 1970 book on Richard Nixon, *Nixon Agonistes: The Crisis of the Self-Made Man*.[1111] An "agonist" is a person involved in a struggle. "Agonistes" comes from the ancient Greek ἀγών (*agṓn*), a word that signifies the field for an athletic contest, thus conveying the meaning of a struggle, from which we get ἄγωνῐστής (agōnistḗs), a contestant in an athletic contest. Another word in English from the same ancient Greek root is "agony." In a literary use, John Milton attached his poem "Samson Agonistes" to the 1671 publication of his *Paradise Regained*. The poem celebrated the biblical story of Samson collapsing the Philistine temple by bringing down the columns.[1112]

That Reich switched *Die Sexualität im Kulturkampf* as the 1936 title to *The Sexual Revolution* in 1945 reflects an evolution of his thinking, moving from a term that was not in the U.S. vocabulary in 1945 (i.e., "culture struggle") to a more understandable and direct term: "sexual revolution." The shift reflects a significant change in post–World War II neo-Marxism. Marcuse, Horkheimer, and Adorno understood just how adaptable capitalism has been resisting Marxist revolutionary impulses from the working-class proletariat. Marcuse stressed that capitalism is difficult to negate because capitalism produces material abundance for the middle class. Adorno and Horkheimer understood how capitalism is also adaptive at co-opting revolutionary themes to culture industry normalcy through marketing and Madison Avenue messaging. When capitalism proved capable of institutionalizing a union movement (that also has Communist roots in U.S. history), Marcuse, Horkheimer, and Adorno both understood that capitalism would never collapse to a working-class revolt.[1113]

As we saw earlier, which U.S. Communists like William Z. Foster came to understand, race and slavery are powerful social conflict issues capable of stirring revolutionary impulses. But race and slavery alone have also been co-opted by capitalism through the passage and enforcement of constitutional amendments and civil rights legislation from the post–Civil War era to the 1960s, continuing through to today. Reich captured ground zero for cultural neo-Marxism by understanding and championing the need to destroy capitalism through a cultural war whose major theme was sexual revolution. Even after the 1960s New Left dissipated once the Vietnam War was over and the military draft ended, the hippies and yippies left a legacy that propelled their sexual counterculture into today's critical gender theory that is increasingly accepting of premarital and extramarital sex, homosexuality and lesbianism, and transgenderism.

Again, we turn to Christopher Turner's book, *Adventures of the Orgasmatron*. As Bennett pointed out, Turner's book suffers from negligent scholarship that Bennett correctly observed could be found "by carefully reading the text and checking some of its citations."[1114] As noted earlier, what Turner lacks in scholarly skills, he counterbalances with the acute observation of a professional journalist. He accurately noted: "Reich could be said to have instigated 'the sexual revolution'; a Marxist analyst, he coined the phrase in the 1930s in order to illustrate his belief that a true political revolution would only be possible once sexual repression was overthrown, the one obstacle Reich felt had scuppered the efforts of the Bolsheviks."[1115] Even though *Kultur Kampf* is not *Kultur Kreig*, Reich prefigured the term "cultural wars" with his 1936 title. Reich's full proclamation of a "sexual revolution" awaited the 1945 reprinting and retitling of the revised 1936 book. Yet, Turner's analysis remains acute: orthodox Marxist revolutionary theory failed. Working-class revolutions did not succeed across Europe in 1848. The Bolsheviks never exported the 1919 revolution from Russia. Reich intended to solve that problem by insisting that a successful revolutionary force could only be released by unleashing the sexual energy of the orgasm. Marcuse, Horkheimer, and Adorno had hinted that a culture war promoting sexual revolution was the missing ingredient in orthodox Marxism, and Reich proclaimed that theme with abandon.

On November 3, 1957, Reich was discovered dead in his bed, fully clothed but for his shoes, in his cell at the federal penitentiary in Lewisburg, Pennsylvania. He had been sentenced to two years for violating a federal court's permanent injunction sought by the Food and Drug Administration (FDA) under various sections of the Federal Food, Drug, and Cosmetic Act. It had forbade him from transporting his orgone accumulator across state lines and banned him from distributing promotional literature.[1116] He had been under the investigation of the FBI as a suspected Communist virtually since his arrival in the United States in 1939.[1117] From his childhood, he demonstrated an obsession with sex. His childhood experiences of spying on his mother's sexual encounters with the live-in tutor appear a classic case of the Oedipus complex, complete with his desire to have sex with his mother, his betrayal of his mother to his father, and his resentment at his father for his cruel treatment and beatings of both him and his mother.[1118] In addition to the orgone accumulator, Reich invented the "cloud-buster," a pipe apparatus he claimed could draw on the orgone energy of the atmosphere to "influence the atmospheric potential [of orgone energy] either in the direction of concentration of energy (cloud formation) or in the direction of dispersal of energy (cloud dissipation)."[1119]

Reich abandoned Freud's strict rigor of maintaining distance between himself as the psychoanalyst and the patient lying on the couch. He sat where the patients on the couch could see him. He required patients on the couch to be naked or semi-nude, and he frequently touched his patients, manipulating muscles and balancing energies.[1120] Reich met his first wife, Annie Pink, as a patient—a taboo for orthodox Freudians trained to be aware of the hazards of the phenomenon of transference, wherein the patient identifies positively with the analyst, transferring to the analyst the patient's own feelings and desires. "For Reich, who had had such bad luck with women in the student dance halls, psychoanalysis provided a free pass to—and increasingly a rationale for—promiscuity," Turner wrote. "The sort of young, well-educated, and neurotic women who had previously ignored him were now patients in thrall to him."[1121] While married to Annie Pink, Reich had multiple affairs.

In September 1930, Reich moved from Vienna to Berlin.[1122] The increasing discomfort with Freud and the intensifying problems with his marriage may have been factors that led Reich to move.[1123] In May 1932, Reich met Elsa Lindenberg in the streets of Berlin at a Communist rally, when Elsa was looking for "sympathetic-looking men" who could serve as her "protector."[1124] Lindenberg was a free spirit who studied dance with Hertha Feist of the *Frei Körper Kultur* (in English, "free body culture"). Turner described Feist as "famous for her choreography of naked performances and her belief in the therapeutic powers of nude dance."[1125] He also commented that "for Lindenberg, the Dionysian aesthetic of modern dance was intimately linked to sexual freedom."[1126] The Berlin cabaret night scene was notorious for sexual excesses of nude theater and dance performances, open prostitution, and lesbian and homosexual night clubs, as well as clubs featuring encounters for "society gentlemen" with androgynous female-looking transvestite "third-sexers."[1127]

Feminists Separate Sex from Procreation

Since recorded civilization, hundreds of generations in the East and West have considered marriage a sacred institution between one man and one woman, sanctioned by God for procreating and raising children. Postmodernism and Marxism intersect in considering traditional marriage just another language construct that defines and limits reality. Horkheimer, Adorno, and Marcuse all realized that the promise of sexual liberation was a more powerful motivator to trigger a revolution than focusing on the economic oppression of workers in a capitalist society.[1128] The baby boomers in the 1960s gravitated in part to Marcuse's *Eros and Civilization* because the book justified sexual freedom. What has been lost in the pursuit of orgasms as an end in itself is the perception humans have had throughout recorded history that the primary biological purpose of sex is procreation, not simply pleasure.

Archaeological work on ancient Roman cities has provided a unique insight into sex and procreation in marriage. Ray Laurence, a professor of ancient history and the chair of the Department of History and Archaeology at Macquarie University in Sydney, Australia, in his 1994 book *Roman Pompeii: Space and Society*, discussed the location of brothels in ancient Pompeii. Laurence noted that the prostitute in ancient Roman society "should not be seen as the antithesis or enemy of the family and family values but, instead, as a preserver of those values."[1129] Laurence pointed out that ancient Roman society was based on monogamous marriage, and "the purpose of marriage was reproduction rather than sexual love."[1130] He stressed that "sexual love between husband and wife was a disaster for the woman, because she would die from repeated child bearing."[1131] He observed it was "equally disastrous for the husband not to find a sexual partner outside of marriage, because again the wife would die from repeated child bearing."[1132] Thus, prostitutes in ancient Rome were needed because the norms of society limited the availability of sexual partners outside marriage. For husbands, adultery with a married woman, if discovered, would bring harsh penalties under the Augustan legislation against adultery. An alternative would be for a husband to have a sexual relationship with a female slave in the household. However, a husband having sex with a household slave risked disrupting "the structure of power relations in that household."[1133]

> One alternative, for the husband, was to visit a prostitute. The recognition of this need was reflected in Roman law: the husband's sexual activity with a prostitute was not recognized as a form of adultery. The adultery law was promulgated to promote the stability of marriage and the family. For that family to be stable, it would have been necessary to ensure the possibility of the wife/mother surviving. In any case, sex with a prostitute did not endanger the marriage or family structure of inheritance. In fact, prostitution promoted the stability of the family in Rome's patriarchal society.[1134]

Aline Rousselle, an assistant professor of history at the University of Perpignan in France, in her 1992 article "Body Politics in Ancient Rome," pointed out that in the Roman Empire, the life expectancy of a woman at birth was twenty to thirty years. "One-fifth to one-quarter (perhaps more) of all girls died before reaching the age of five. Those who survived usually married by age twelve and certainly before age eighteen," she wrote. "If they lived that long they might hope to go on living until forty or so, but they knew perfectly well that childbirth could easily prove fatal."[1135]

Rousselle noted that men in the ancient Roman Empire were not raised to believe it was virtuous to refrain from sexual intercourse. "Boys learned to lust after the household's female slaves, always available for their pleasure," she explained. "For variety youths also visited prostitutes."[1136] Physicians counseled adult men that they should not suppress sexual desires. Slaves and the "disreputable" met the sexual needs of adult men. The disreputable, Rousselle detailed, were those "involved in theater, circus, and prostitution."[1137] She emphasized that for adult men in the Roman Empire, brief sexual encounters were not uncommon. But "male citizens generally entered into more permanent relations with concubines."[1138] She noted that "the practice of continence by upper-class women became a mark of distinction."[1139] Curiously, she added: "But not all women were lucky enough to have husbands who could amuse themselves with a slave or concubine. Some had to bear the burden—and it was a real burden—of multiple pregnancies. An amorous husband was a catastrophe."[1140] In ancient Rome, reduced life expectancy led to the acceptance of pedophile-age, prepubescent women being married without disgrace. Today, with life expectancy in the United States approaching eighty years, we lose sight of the degree to which the risk of multiple pregnancies induced reputable mothers and their daughters in ancient Rome to be fearful of sex.

The availability of reliable birth control pills in the 1960s was a historical development that set the ground for separating sex from procreation. Work on the birth control pill began in 1950, when eugenicist Margaret Sanger, the founder of Planned Parenthood, approached a scientist named Gregory Pincus to begin work on a reliable, hormone-based, easy-to-use contraceptive. At that time, Pincus worked at an independent laboratory in Massachusetts, the Worcester Foundation for Experimental Biology.[1141] In 1952, Sanger recruited Katharine McCormick, an advocate for women's suffrage who was heiress to the Cyrus McCormick International Harvester Company fortune, to assist her in funding Pincus's work. In 1960, their work resulted in the first hormonal birth control pill, Enovid, marketed by G. D. Searle and Company.[1142]

In 1965, Planned Parenthood of Connecticut won the U.S. Supreme Court case, *Griswold v. Connecticut*, 381 U.S. 479 (1965),[1143] which according to Planned Parenthood, "finally and completely rolled back state and local laws that had outlined the use of contraception by married couples."[1144] With the birth control pill, men and women engaging in sex could prevent pregnancy. Then in 1973, the U.S. Supreme Court decided *Roe v. Wade*, 410 U.S. 113, that inherent in the due process clause of the Fourteenth Amendment is an implied "right to privacy" that protects a pregnant woman's right to have an abortion.[1145] *Roe v. Wade* fueled the sexual revolution that began in the 1960s with the invention of the birth control pill. After *Roe v. Wade*, a woman could decide on her own to terminate the pregnancy.

For centuries, mothers had warned their daughters not to have sex before marriage. But after these two Supreme Court decisions, a woman could have sex without the risk of becoming pregnant or, if becoming pregnant, with the option to abort birth to the baby. Once sex no longer risked having a baby, women no longer considered marriage necessary to have sex. The pill and these two Supreme Court decisions propelled the women's movement for equal rights into a new dimension: the push for women's sexual liberation.

In 1957, on the fifteenth anniversary of her graduation from Smith College, Betty Friedan began interviewing Smith graduates for her planned book. Friedan's book *The Feminine Mystique*,[1146] published in February 1963, began the second wave of feminism. The first wave in the nineteenth and early twentieth centuries had focused on women's suffrage. The second wave expanded the idea of equal rights for women into the "women's liberation movement" that included an agenda for sexual liberation from the confines of childbearing and child-rearing. As per her biography in the National Women's History Museum documents, "Bettye Naomi Goldstein was born on February 4, 1921, in Peoria, Illinois, the oldest of three children of Harry Goldstein, a Russian immigrant and jeweler, and Miriam Horowitz Goldstein, a Hungarian immigrant who worked as a journalist until Bettye was born."[1147] Entering Smith College in 1938, Friedan edited the school's newspaper, the *Smith College Weekly*, espousing a Marxist, anti-war view opposing World War II.[1148] Graduating in 1942, she spent one year on a graduate fellowship to train as a psychologist at the University of California, Berkeley. At UC Berkeley, she dropped the "e" from her first name. In 1947, she married Carl Friedan, an advertising executive who sought to become a theater producer. Friedan had three children in 1948, 1952, and 1956 while she continued to work as a reporter. In 1956, the couple moved from Queens, New York, to suburban Rockland County, and Betty became a housewife, supplementing the family income with freelance writing for women's magazines.[1149]

Friedan's bestselling book launched a full-scale attack on "the vapidity of well-to-do housewives' existence."[1150] In her book, Friedan defined the "feminine mystique" as follows: "The feminine mystique says that the highest value and the only commitment for women is the fulfillment of their own femininity. It says that the great mistake of Western culture, through most of its history, has been the undervaluation of this femininity."[1151] The mistake, Friedan argued, was that "women envied men, women tried to be like men, instead of accepting their own nature, which can find fulfillment only in sexual passivity, male domination, and nurturing maternal love."[1152] She insisted the image this mystique gave to American women was: "Occupation: housewife."[1153] She gave what became her iconic characterization of the fate of women in post–World War II America:

> The new mystique makes the housewife-mothers, who never had a chance to be anything else, the model for all women; it presupposes that history has reached a final and glorious end in the here and now, as far as women are concerned. Beneath the sophisticated trappings, it simply

> makes certain concrete, finite, domestic aspects of feminine existence—as it was lived by women whose lives were confined, by necessity, to cooking, cleaning, washing, bearing children—into a religion, a pattern by which all women must now live or deny their femininity.[1154]

Friedan's point was that "fulfillment as a woman had only one definition for American women after 1949—the housewife-mother."[1155] *The Feminine Mystique* sold three million books "and convinced many women that they were not alone in their suburban homes with a 'growing sense of dissatisfaction.'"[1156]

While the book signaled a new chapter in the feminist movement, Friedan was soundly criticized by the political Left. Black feminist Gloria Jean Watkins (pen name: bell hooks) in her 1984 book *Feminist Theory: From Margin to Center* charged Friedan for being classist and racist. "She [Friedan] did not discuss who would be called in to take care of the children and maintain the home if more women like herself were freed from their house labor and given equal access with white men to the professions," hooks wrote. "She did not speak of the needs of women without men, without children, without homes. She ignored the existence of all non-white women and poor white women. She did not tell readers whether it was more fulfilling to be a maid, a babysitter, a factory worker, a clerk, or a prostitute than to be a leisure-class housewife."[1157]

In 1998, Daniel Horowitz, then the director of the American Studies program at Smith College, wrote a book entitled *Betty Friedan and the Making of* The Feminine Mystique*: The American Left, the Cold War, and Modern Feminism.*[1158] In that book, Horowitz exposed that Friedan had hidden her Old Left radical past. "Though most women's historians have argued that 1960s feminism emerged in response to the suburban captivity of white middle-class women during the 1950s, the material in Friedan's papers suggested additional origins—anti-fascism, radicalism, and labor union activism of the late 1940s," Horowitz wrote.[1159] His extensive research into Friedan's hidden past revealed that her radicalism began even in Peoria. He stressed that Friedan worked extensively writing pamphlets for the United Electrical, Radio and Machine Workers of America, commonly known as the UE—a union Horowitz characterized as "one of the most radical American unions in the postwar period."[1160] In an article published in *American Quarterly* in 1996, Horowitz quoted Wesleyan University U.S. history professor Ronald W. Schatz describing the UE in the 1940s as "the largest communist-led institution of any kind in the United States."[1161] In his *American Quarterly* article, he explained:

"However, if Rosa Parks refused to take a seat at the back of a segregated bus not simply because her feet hurt, then Friedan did not write *The Feminine Mystique* simply because she was an unhappy housewife."[1162]

In 1966, Friedan cofounded the National Organization of Women (NOW), with herself as president. NOW fought for women's equal employment rights by demanding that the Equal Employment Opportunity Commission enforce the provisions of Title VII of the Civil Rights Act of 1964, guaranteeing equality in employment.[1163] In 1971, Friedan was a significant supporter of adding the Equal Rights Amendment (ERA) to the U.S. Constitution. The conservative who challenged and ultimately defeated Friedan on the ERA was Phyllis Schlafly. In her 2011 book *The Flipside of Feminism*, coauthored with conservative author Suzanne Venker,[1164] Schlafly expanded on Horowitz's theme arguing that Friedan understood the Marxist principle that revolutionary activity aimed at overthrowing capitalism demands the identification of an oppressed group. Schlafly argued that Friedan's book *The Feminine Mystique* portrayed women as the victim because her goal, like Karl Marx's goal, was to destroy the family. Venker and Schlafly explained as follows:

> Knowing she couldn't appeal to women by defending Marxism, Friedan took advantage of something to which she knew women could relate: the mental and physical drain of raising young children. In *The Feminine Mystique*, she argued that a woman's devotion to her husband and children is a sacrifice of such magnitude that it inevitably stunts her growth as an individual. Raising children, Friedan argued, is a thankless pursuit that doesn't allow women to use their intelligence in a manner that benefits society. She had no appreciation for the economic advantage to any society when mothers, out of sheer duty and love, perform the awesome task of raising babies to become mature adults.[1165]

Schlafly recognized that Friedan was echoing Wilhelm Reich, alleging that capitalism required a patriarchy. Venker and Schlafly continued:

> Rather than get the personal help she needed, Friedan concluded that American women live in a patriarchy. Women aren't men's equals, she said. Men get to go out and lead independent lives while women are stuck at home with the kids. That men's lives can be just as unfulfilling or stressful (though in a different way) was never entertained. According to Friedan, there's only one reason for "the problem that has no name": women are oppressed. The way to remedy this injustice, she said, is

for women to forgo taking care of their children altogether and pursue fulfilling careers. In short, *The Feminine Mystique* offered American women an out—out of their maternal responsibilities.[1166]

Venker and Schlafly also picked up on the theme that the Left's promised land utopia is morally vacuous. "For forty years, women on the left have argued for the same tired notion of female independence—that women should be self-supporting, sexually uninhibited, and liberated from the sacrifices and demands of marriage and motherhood," they wrote.[1167] While this message has become firmly established in mainstream American culture, Venker and Schlafly argued that the result is a generation of young women who are chronically dissatisfied. "They're [young women are] bored with their sexual freedom (despite their insistence that one-night stands are liberating) and despondent from a life devoid of commitment."[1168] They insisted the source of this discontent is that "feminists have taught women to abandon the old standards but haven't provided them with any new rules that work!"[1169]

Radical feminists did not welcome Friedan with open arms because when she founded NOW, she rejected lesbianism and homosexuality.[1170] At a NOW meeting in 1969, Betty Friedan coined the phrase "lavender menace" to describe lesbians she felt were a threat to the NOW message of gaining economic and social equality for women. "Many lesbians had found a comfortable activism home within the rising feminist movement, and this exclusion [from NOW] stung," wrote Linda Napikoski. "If 'the personal is political'[1171] how could sexual identity, women identifying with women and not with men, *not* be part of feminism?"[1172] Napikoski explained that many feminists, not just Friedan, felt that "lesbian issues were irrelevant to the majority of women and would hinder the feminist cause, and that identifying the movement with lesbians and their rights would make it harder to win feminist victories."[1173]

In May 1970, at the National Organization for Women's Second Congress to Unite Women, a political action entitled "Lavender Menace" met in New York City to protest the rejection of lesbians by feminists in the second-wave women's liberation movement. The Lavender Menace political action was led by Radicalesbians, with women from the Gay Liberation Front and several other feminist organizations. The political action shifted into the conference just before the start of the Congress's plenary session to conduct planned anarchy. "The lights went out, people heard running, laughter, a rebel yell here and there, and when the lights were turned back on, those same 300 women found themselves in the hands of the LAVENDER MENACE," a description of the action explained.[1174] Finally, at the National Women's Conference in Houston, Texas, in 1977, Friedan apologized for her opposition to lesbians in NOW and agreed to support actively a resolution against sexual preference discrimination. In 1991, the newly elected NOW president, Patricia Ireland, announced her intention to live with a female partner. Ireland remained the NOW president for ten years, with NOW sponsoring a lesbian rights summit in 1999.[1175]

Gloria Steinem was born on March 25, 1934, in Toledo, Ohio. Her mother was Ruth Nuneviller, a Scotch Presbyterian raised in Theosophy, an esoteric religion with occult roots. Her father was Leo Steinem, a Jew with a family history from Germany and Poland.[1176] Steinem's paternal grandmother, Pauline Perlmutter Steinem, born in Germany, was a well-known women's rights activist who chaired the educational committee of the National Woman Suffrage Association and was a delegate to the 1908 International Council of Women, an organization cofounded in 1888 by noted woman's suffrage activist Susan B. Anthony who had Communist ties in the 1930s.[1177] Leo Steinem was an itinerant antique dealer who traveled with his family. Gloria did not spend a full year in school until she was twelve years old. In her 1983 book *Outrageous Acts and Everyday Rebellions*, Steinem described how her mother, at age thirty-four, before Gloria was born, had a serious mental illness diagnosed as "an anxiety neurosis" that kept her in and out of sanitoriums for the rest of her life. In 1944, when Steinem was ten years old, her parents divorced. In her 1983 book, Steinem related how she loved to send her mother gifts of clothes, jewelry, exotic soaps, and additions to her collection of tarot cards.[1178]

In their book, *The Flipside of Feminism*, Venker and Schlafly described the disturbed personal background of many leading feminists including Friedan, who "spent years in psychoanalysis 'talking endlessly about how I hated my mother and how she had killed my father.' 'All mothers should be drowned at birth,' she used to say."[1179] Here is what Venker and Schlafly wrote about Steinem:

> Gloria Steinem is yet another example. Her mother spent long periods in and out of sanitoriums for the mentally disturbed. She had a nervous breakdown that left her an invalid, trapped in delusional fantasies that occasionally turned violent. Steinem was only ten years old when her parents finally divorced in 1944, and Steinem spent six years living with her mother in a rundown home in Toledo, Ohio, before leaving for college. When asked about her feelings toward marriage and mother-

hood, she told *People* magazine, "I'd already been the very small parent of a very big child—my mother. I don't want to end up taking care of someone else."[1180]

Steinem first came to national prominence in 1963, when she got an assignment from *Show* magazine for which she dressed up as a "Bunny" at the Playboy Club and wrote an exposé "of the unglamorous working conditions of the club's glorified waitresses—sex objects in rabbit ears and cotton tails."[1181] On April 4, 1969, *New York* magazine published an article by Gloria Steinem entitled "After Black Power, Women's Liberation." Following Friedan's attack on the life of the American housewife, Steinem attacked the notion that sex was only for men. The first paragraph of the article read:

> Once upon a time—say, ten or even five years ago—a Liberated Woman was somebody who had sex before marriage and a job afterward. Once upon the same time, a Liberated Zone was any foreign place lucky enough to have an American army in it. Both ideas seem antiquated now, and for pretty much the same reason: Liberation isn't exposure to the American values of Mom-and-apple-pie anymore (not even if Mom is allowed to work in an office and vote once in a while); it's the escape from them.[1182]

The article propelled Steinem to national fame, positioning her to become the cofounder of *Ms.* magazine.[1183] She also attended Smith College, graduating in 1956. Upon graduation, she went to India for two years. In India, she joined in nonviolent protests against government policies that she considered strongly prejudiced against certain social classes (i.e., castes) of Indian society. In the 1970s and 1980s, she rivaled Friedan as a women's liberation movement leader.[1184] In recent years, Steinem has argued that feminism and advocacy for LGBT (lesbian, gay, bisexual, and transgender) rights are linked.[1185] Yet in her 1983 book *Outrageous Acts and Everyday Rebellions* Steinem republished a 1977 article in which she had expressed hesitation over sex change operations. "The point is to transform society so that a female *can* 'go out for basketball' and a male doesn't *have* to be 'the strong one,'" she wrote. "Better to turn anger outward toward changing the world than inward toward transforming and mutilating bodies."[1186]

In her 2014 book *Who Killed the American Family?* Phyllis Schlafly assessed the impact Friedan and Steinem had on the traditional American family:

> The feminist movement started its attack on traditional marriage with Betty Friedan's 1963 book *The Feminine Mystique*, which urged wives to leave their homes (called a "comfortable concentration camp"), join the workforce, and become independent of men. *The Adventures of Ozzie and Harriet*, a traditional-couple sitcom of the 1950s, became an epithet. After Gloria Steinem persuaded President Jimmy Carter to change the name of his White House Conference on "the Family" to "Families," it became de rigueur to speak of different kinds of "families" instead of "*the* family."[1187]

In his book, *The Devil's Pleasure Palace: The Cult of Critical Theory and the Subversion of the West*, Michael Walsh commented that Herbert Marcuse and Wilhelm Reich were the two figures associated with the Frankfurt School that had the most negative impact on culture.[1188] "What after all, did 'sexual liberation' accomplish?" Walsh asked. "The newfound 'liberation' led to a rapid increase in abortion, HIV and AIDS, and illegitimate children."[1189] Walsh asked another question: "Who knew that the slogan 'Every man a stud, every woman a slut?' could be a winner?"[1190] We might also ask what cultural low we have achieved when the LGBT-dominated feminist movement proclaims another slogan: namely that "a woman needs a man like a fish needs a bicycle."[1191]

The Lure of Androgyny[1192]

Philosophy professor Glenn Alexander Magee in his book *Hegel and the Hermetic Tradition* noted the Hegelian dialectic is "a magical power that converts [the negative] into being."[1193] Magee argued that Hegel bears a resemblance to alchemy: "Like the alchemists, Hegel's philosophical project is to free Spirit from nature. Just as alchemists believe that God is slumbering in matter and must be released by man, Hegel holds that nature is 'petrified intelligence' but that 'God does not remain petrified and moribund however, the stones cry out and lift themselves to spirit.'"[1194]

Thus, Magee concluded, "all things are in actuality by being contained within it; it is 'androgyne,' a unity of opposites."[1195] What results from the Hegelian dialectic then is a synthesis of thesis and antithesis that involves uniting opposites. "When Frankfurt [School] scholars contrive along psycho-Marxist lines, one notices a recurring theme that places

Western man in a fallen state in need of critical negation to restore him to a recovered pristine state," note Coughlin and Higgins in their book in *Re-Remembering the Mis-Remembered Left*.[1196] They continue:

> The strange comes into play when considering the cosmological—even theological—nature of such thinking among avowed atheist Marxists. However, it is through reference to Freud that the Hermetic pattern—the *prisca theologia*, the *philosophia perennis*, the time when race, gender and nationality were contained in a primitive state of nature if not an androgyne unity of opposites—is imported into Marxist critical theory while remaining silent on the archetype form. If the process of moving to the perfected end of history—the Marxist march of history—concerns the actualization of the perfected recollected form, then the process demands a convergence to that form, often expressed in terms of a restoration or return. Yet, never far from the pre-reflective thoughts of the Frankfurt cadre, "Eros" and sex linger in a peculiar—and peculiarly linked way.[1197]

The *prisca theologia* (in English, "ancient theology"), a term used interchangeably with *philosophia perennis* (in English, "perennial philosophy"), was first used by Florentine Renaissance Neoplatonic philosopher Marsilio Ficino (1433–1499) in the fifteenth century. The traditional interpretation of the *prisca theologica* argued that that there is a lineage of ancient philosophers tracing back to the Egyptian Hermes Trismegistus through Moses, Plato, and Aristotle that prefigures and complements biblical Hebrew theology and Christian revelations. In other words, the orthodox view of *prisca theologica* is the view that "ancient theology combined Neoplatonism with Hermeticism to assert the belief "in the existence of an accordance and continuity between classical philosophy, the Jewish tradition and Christianity."[1198] But the occult understanding of the *prisca theologica* is that Ficino gave a name to "a movement by para-pagan Renaissance philosophers and magicians to attempt to legitimize and Christianize a series of pagan books that they believed contained authentic philosophical and magical wisdom."[1199]

In his book *Hegel and the Hermetic Tradition*, Glenn Alexander Magee noted the "major event in the history of Hermeticism was the rediscovery by Europeans of the Jewish Kabbalah after the expulsion of the Jews from Spain in 1492."[1200] Frances Yates, a British historian of Renaissance esoteric history and philosophy, observed the following: "For the Renaissance mind, which loved symmetrical arrangements, there was a certain parallelism between the writings of Hermes Trismegistus, the Egyptian Moses, and Cabala which was a Jewish mystical tradition supposed to have been handed down orally from Moses himself."[1201] Magee also noted that Heinrich Cornelius Agrippa von Nettesheim (1486–1535) in his massive work *Three Books of Occult Philosophy* published in 1533 argued for the "Kabbalah, as a *prisca theologica* and for the power of magic based on Kabbalah."[1202] As a result of this work, Agrippa developed a reputation as a "black magician."[1203] Yates suggested that Ficino was "awe-struck" viewing the *Hermetica* (a series of ancient Egyptian Hermetic writings brought to Florence through Macedonia by a monk Cosimo de' Medici had employed to locate manuscripts for him) as "the pristine fount of illumination flowing from the Divine *Mens* [i.e., the mind of God], which would lead him to the original core of Platonism as a gnosis derived from Egyptian wisdom."[1204]

Freud derived his concepts of the subconscious, the conscious, and the superconscious from the teachings of the *Hermetica* via the Jewish Kabbalah. In his last book *Moses and Monotheism*, Freud argued that Moses was born an Egyptian noble who transmitted to the Jews the monotheistic religion of the sun god Aton that the young pharaoh Amenhotep IV (who changed his name to Akhenaton), who ascended the throne around 1375 BC.[1205] Thus, Coughlin and Higgins's point in the quotation above was that Freud was an atheistic Jew who agreed with Ficino's *prisca theologica* in that Freud believed the origin of Jewish theology was Egyptian mysticism. In *Moses and Monotheism*, Freud concluded: "I do not believe that one supreme great God 'exists' today, but I believe that in primeval times there was one person who must needs appear gigantic and who, raised to the status of a deity, returned to the memory of men."[1206] Freud continued, giving a psychoanalytic interpretation of his concept of a primeval God: "When Moses gave to his people the conception of an Only God it was not an altogether new idea, for it meant the reanimation of primeval experience in the human family that had long ago faded from the conscious memory of mankind. The experience was such an important one, however, and produced, or at least prepared, such far-reaching changes in the life of man, that, I cannot help thinking, it must have left some permanent trace in the human soul—something comparable to tradition."[1207]

In his 2016 paper "Moses: Freud's Ultimate Project," Old Testament scholar Risto Olavi Nurmela cited a letter Freud wrote to Max Eitingon, the cofounder and president of the Berlin Psychoanalytic Polyclinic from 1920 to 1933. In that letter, Freud wrote that *Moses and Monotheism* differed from his earlier book on religion, *The Future of an Illusion*, in admitting that religion was not merely illusion but also had "an historical kernel of truth, which explains its great effectiveness."[1208] The primeval deity Freud was referring to may have been the sun god Re, given Freud's statement that the origin of Egyptian monotheism was the school of the priests in the sun temple at Heliopolis.[1209] Curiously, Freud makes no mention of Hermes Trismegistus in *Moses and Monotheism*.

Art historian Agata Anna Chrzanowska argued that Florentine artist Domenico Ghirlandaio (1448–1494) in his painting the *Preaching of St. John the Baptist* (1485–1490), found in the Tornabuoni Chapel in Santa Maria Novella, contained figures from Ficino's *prisca theologica*. She identified the four men listening to St. John in the margin of the painting as Moses talking with Hermes Trismegistus (seated) and Aristotle and Plato standing behind them. In the painting's opposite margin, we see Jesus also listening. She explained as follows:

> St. John the Baptist, represented talking to Moses, Hermes Trismegistus, Aristotle and Plato, is shown here as the last of the prophets and a continuator of the great tradition of thinkers who gave voice to Divine Revelation. The Holy Spirit, who descends from heaven, blesses the preacher and confirms the divine nature of his revelations. The time represented in the fresco does not correspond to the earthly dimension of the story but reveals the fulfilment of messianic prophecies in the figure of Christ. In fact, Jesus himself stands behind the Baptist. Next to him, we can see a small hill with a tree growing on top—a clear reference to Golgotha and the Crucifixion. The completion of Jesus' sacrifice—his death and resurrection—are represented by the tomb placed directly behind him. Christ is therefore represented as the completion of the history of divine revelation, which unites Jewish and Christian theology with the pagan mystical tradition expressed in the figure of Hermes. The universal value of Christ's sacrifice and the mystical dimension of divine time, which encloses and penetrates human history, are represented by the inclusion of a contemporary city, possibly Florence, in the background. Salvation does not therefore belong to history but rather embraces the past and the present and gives sense to all past revelations.[1210]

Here we can turn to Italian philosopher and Hermetic occultist Giordano Bruno (1548–1600), a master of the *prisca theologia* tradition, whose "influence in Germany was significant enough for Hegel to devote a section of his *Lectures on the History of Philosophy* to him."[1211] In *Hegel and the Hermetic Tradition*, Magee wrote that Giordano Bruno Christianized the magic of the Kabbalah and developed it into the basis for a new Hermetic religion. Writing of Giordano Bruno, Magee explained: "His aim, in fact, was to return Renaissance occultism to its Pagan roots. Bruno conceived himself as the messiah of this new religion."[1212] In her 1964 book *Giordano Bruno and the Hermetic Tradition*, Frances Yates explained that Giordano Bruno maintained "that the magical Egyptian religion of the world was not only the most ancient but also the only true religion, which both Judaism and Christianity had obscured and corrupted."[1213]

Giordano Bruno maintained: "The true aim in life should be illumination, the true morality, the practice of justice, the true redemption should be the liberation of the soul from error, and its union with God through consciousness."[1214] Imprisoned and called before the Inquisition, Giordano Bruno defended himself: "Serenely he spoke of the universe, how there were infinite worlds in infinite space, how all things in all forms and species were divine. He tried to explain the unity of all things, the dependence and interdependence of all things, yet the existence of God in all."[1215] He insisted: "The body is in the soul, the soul in the mind, and the mind is in God"; therefore, "the life of the soul is the true life of man." From this, Giordano Bruno concluded: "So of all the facilities of man that which exalts his nature is Thought, for by it we can contemplate and comprehend the universe, and thus in turn become Creators."[1216] Bruno contemplated that opposites can be united but only in the mind of God. He also considered we could achieve the consciousness of opposites combined, but only through thought. Yet the idea that we might become "Creators" by achieving this thought level has a hermetic feel indicating that we humans can transform ourselves mystically to a higher level. On February 17, 1600, in the Campo de' Fiori in Rome, Giordano Bruno was hung upside down naked and burned at the stake after Pope Clement VII declared him a heretic and the Inquisition issued a death sentence.[1217]

In Giordano Bruno's mystical formulation of the *prisca theologia*, his central vision involved comprehending that all opposites, including male/female and good/evil, are combined but only in the entity of God. But the Hegelian dialectic demands the union of opposites in the here and now. The perfection of human beings involves a transcendence of the Hegelian Subjective Spirit into the universality of Absolute Spirit—an advancement to a utopian state that he maintained could only be achieved through the dialectic converting negation into being. The *prisca theologia* incorporated the Hermetic principle of polarity, a proposition concerning duality that argues all opposites, including male/female and good/evil, are combined, but only in the entity of God. The Kabbalistic teaching derived from the *Hermetica* was that all material existence occurs in the mind of God. Thus, by elevating human consciousness to a level of "superconscious" identification with God, we derive magical powers that allow us to participate with God as cocreators.

Thus, the fifteenth-century *prisca theologia* translated into twentieth- and twenty-first-century neo-Marxist critical theory involves a vision of future perfection where male/female become hermaphrodite, black/white/yellow races blend into a universal non-white uni-race, and distinctions of nations, states, and boundaries erase in a "citizen of the world" universality. In new age terms, the Hegelian dialectic that affects these changes involves transforming eros and sex to a higher level. Instead of normalizing monogamous heterosexual relations to promote procreation of offspring, eros and sex transform into a free-love concept where all combinations of partners and sex acts are presumed positive and productive. This androgynous *prisca theologia* future is Marcuse's utopia achieved through his formula of "polymorphous sexuality and in a decline of genital supremacy."[1218] But instead of producing the final stage of human self-actualization, Reich's sexual revolution "was, in reality, sexual devolution and 'free sex' resulted in slavery to sex."[1219]

Between 1943 and 1946, Wilhelm Reich composed a series of notes that he intended to be stored in the Archives of the Orgone Institute, not published. Then in 1948, as Reich's orgone research was coming under increasing denunciation, he decided to allow the Orgone Institute to publish these notes as a talk to the common person under the title *Listen, Little Man!* Reich had always portrayed the person typically dominated by authoritarian fascist regimes as the "man in the street," the "Little Man."[1220] In this book, Reich expressed his atheism as follows, addressing the Little Man: "I know that what you call 'God' actually exists, but in a different way from what you think: as the primal cosmic energy in the universe, as your love in your body, as your honesty and your feeling of nature in you and around you."[1221] Reich displayed resentment, hatred, and disdain, unlike Giordano Bruno, whose writings expressed love for himself and humanity. Reich's self-hatred is evident in his discussion of himself as a Jew: "I am moved by no feeling for the Jewish language, Jewish religion, or Jewish culture. I believe in the Jewish God no more than in the Christian or Indian God, but I know where you get your

God. I don't believe that the Jews are God's 'chosen people.' I believe that someday the Jewish animals on this planet will lose themselves among the masses of human animals on this planet and that this will be a good thing for them and their descendants."[1222] Railing against God, the negation of established culture, and hatred of everyone and everything (including themselves) are malignant characteristics that repeatedly appear endemic to the radical neo-Marxist Left.

In the occult Hermetic teachings of the Kabbalah known as "black magic," Lucifer is portrayed as a grotesque androgynous combination, as suggested by the tarot card number fifteen, "The Devil." Éliphas Lévi (born as Alphonse Louis Constant) described Baphomet and transcendental magic in his 1854 book *Dogme et Rituel de la Haute Magie* (in English, *Dogma and Ritual of High Magic*)[1223] and his 1860 book *Histoire de la Magie* (in English, *History of Magic*).[1224] Lévi portrayed the Kabbalistic Satan as Baphomet, the androgynous "Goat of Mendes." In Kabbalistic lore, Baphomet is a grotesquely androgynous figure, represented as a male humanoid with a goat's head, the wings of a bat, and a woman's breasts. In both books, Lévi explained that the doctrine of transcendental magic involved an initiation into Satanism that confers on humans the occult knowledge of good and evil. The result is that the initiated receive superhuman powers.

Occult transcendental black magic is at the heart of Lucifer's promise to Adam and Eve in the Garden of Eden that eating the apple would convey the secret of good and evil. The twisted subtheme of the serpent in the garden is that the God of the Bible is an "oppressive God" who wanted to keep humanity in obedient ignorance.[1225] The serpent claims to be the true savior of humanity, offering enlightenment if only Adam and Eve will disobey God. Unlocking the secret knowledge of good and evil in occult transcendental magic produces the androgynous utopian union of opposites. For Hermetic Kabbalists and Frankfurt School atheists, we can only accomplish this feat of transcendental magic by venturing into the secret of good and evil that demands the dialectical negation of all dualities. But how do we unlock that secret?

The key that unlocks the occult secret for Marcuse is polymorphous-perverse sexuality, or for Reich, the peak experience of orgasmic ecstasy. Through the Marquis de Sade's perverse sex, as Horkheimer and Adorno suggested, we unlock the door to good and evil, giving birth to homosexuality and lesbianism, transgenderism, and ultimately to Postgenderism (i.e., the state where gender is self-determined and infinitely variable). The postmodern abandon to libertine sexuality eschews the end goal of progenerating. Instead, the goal is to give rebirth to ourselves as transcendent, self-actualized Nietzschean *Übermensch* beyond good and evil. In the Frankfurt School's occult neo-Marxism, Horkheimer, Adorno, Marcuse, and Reich stand united that God plays no role in transforming human beings into Nietzschean *Übermensch*. Polymorphic-perverse sex is the transformative secret sauce required to bring forth in history Kant and Hegel's triumph of spirit in which transhuman Nietzschean *Übermensch* actualize God.

The Inquisition, one of the great episodes in human history of extraordinary popular delusions and the madness of crowds,[1226] burned Giordano Bruno to death at the stake. Pope Clement VII declared Bruno a heretic because he believed human consciousness could resolve the duality of good and evil through the union in thought with God. Unfortunately for Bruno, his beliefs were dangerously close to the gnostic heresy of Manichaeism, a religion that knowing oneself demanded "seeing one's soul as sharing in the very nature of God and as coming from a transcendent world."[1227] The neo-Marxists of the Frankfurt School embraced Lucifer's agenda "to corrupt and debauch God's children through the merging of opposites so that at Christ's second advent, none of them are found fit for God's eternal family household."[1228] Lucifer, the "Bearer of Light," is worshiped as the Divine Androgyne on the principle that we can perfect human nature in the here and now once we resolve to transcend good and evil to embrace the transhuman, transgender, transracial, transnational new world order.

The Frankfurt School blended Gramsci and Freud into Marxism, giving birth to Lukács's *aufheben der Kultur* admonition to destroy the culture. But what critical theory has brought forth is not utopia but a confused, nightmarish world where the "lure of androgyny"[1229] is the operating principle. Neo-Marxist critical theory produces a world of ambiguous sexuality in which God is discarded, capitalism dismantled, and the monogamous nuclear family abandoned. The Hegelian dialectic is an ingenious algorithmic formula for destruction, but the algorithm has no similarly effective formula for creation.

Conclusion: The Logic and Grammar of Atheism

In syllogistic logic, the union of opposites is problematic. Like syllogisms, logical opposition derives from the analytics of set theoretics. In simplest terms, logical opposition begins with negation. For example, "black" is not opposite of the color "white." The opposite of the color "white" is simply "not white." Each color can constitute its own separate set in set theoretics. Since there are many colors and infinite shades of colors, one particular color that is "not white" does not imply it must be "black." So too, "bitter" is not the logical opposite of "sweet." The logical opposite of "sweet" is "not sweet." The point is that in set theory, not all opposites are polar opposites.

Polar opposites in set-theoretic terms involve two and only two sets where not to be a member of one set, the item in question must be a member of the other set.[1230] "Being" and "Not-Being," terms central to understanding philosophers ranging from Kant through Heidegger, are polar opposites. If "Being" is true, "Not-Being" is false. In terms of set theoretics, if an entity belongs to the set "Being," that entity cannot also belong to the set "Not-Being." In Wittgenstein's terms of language games, Wittgenstein would insist the grammar of a concept like "Being" implies the concept of "Not-Being." We cannot understand what is being said unless we first accept that to posit, or say, "Being" implies that "Not-Being" must also exist, at least as a logical alternative. Set theory traces back to Aristotle's writing on logic. The Hegelian dialectic traces back to Plato's dialogues as refined by Aristotle's treatment of logical and polar opposites.

Wittgenstein appreciated that the grammar of language games adds another dimension to the rules of Aristotelian logic. For Aristotle to say that "Not-Being" exists would be a contradiction; for Wittgenstein to say "Not-Being" exists is a necessary language game consequence. In *Philosophical Investigations*, part 1, number 50, Wittgenstein puzzled the problem:

> What does it mean to say that we can attribute neither being nor non-being to elements?—One might say: if everything that we call "being" and "non-being" consists in the existence and non-existence of connections between elements, it makes no sense to speak of an element's being (non-being); just as when everything that we call "destruction" lies in the separation of elements, it makes no sense to speak of the destruction of an element.[1231]

Wittgenstein concluded number 50 by commenting that "non-being" must "be" but only in the sense that it is "a paradigm in our language-game"[1232] that is required for us to speak about existence.

Yet, even in Wittgenstein's philosophical system, not all language game conventions carry the same weight. For instance, the concept "unicorn" does not prove unicorns exist. So, the positing of "unicorn" does not imply "horse," or anything else for that matter, because the concept "unicorn" is fabricated. The opposite of the concept "unicorn" is not "not-unicorn" as the opposite of *τηεοσ* [theos] is *ατηεοσ* [atheos] (in ancient Greek, "God" or "non-God"). To say you do not believe in unicorns does not imply that unicorns exist. An obvious dismissal that the concept "unicorn" has a duality is the obvious retort: "Of course, you don't believe in unicorns. They don't exist." In *Philosophical Investigations*, part 1, number 370, Wittgenstein contemplated imagination, as when one person describes to another the contents of a room the listener has never seen. In the following number 371, Wittgenstein wrote only this: "*Essence* is expressed in grammar."[1233] In Wittgenstein's terms, describing a unicorn involves the language game of imagination. The grammar rule of the imagination language game does not demand unicorns exist. But when it comes to "being" and "not-being," both must exist for "being" to be comprehended.

At the core of the debate over neo-Marxism, the Frankfurt School, and the Hegelian dialectic is the denial that the concept of "good" demands the implication of "evil." For the Hegelian dialectic to operate logically, "good" and "evil" are polar opposites. Perhaps the point is made more evident by a brief consideration of the logical structure of Kant's antinomies. An antinomy in logic involves a contradiction between two beliefs or conclusions that are both reasonable such that both parts of the contradiction could be true. Logical dualities involving polar opposites are the inverse of antinomies. A true polar-opposite duality only exists when the positing of one term demands the implication of an opposing contradictory second term. If you say, "I don't believe in dark," the obvious next question would be: "Well, then do you believe in light?" If you say, "I believe I exist," as in the "*cogito, ergo sum*" that Descartes posited, we might retort: "So, you are refuting that you don't exist, because even if you are imagining you exist, you will have to exist to do the imagining."

Thus, atheists face an insurmountable logical problem in the positing of the concept of "atheism" (i.e., saying, "I don't believe in God). Saying you don't believe in God cannot be understood to have meaning without implying the concept of "God." Otherwise, what is it that an atheist is rejecting? Central to the assertion that a person is an atheist is the implication that the person does not believe in God. But how can you not believe in something that does not exist? The etymology of the word "atheism" in ancient Greek derives from ἄθεος [atheos], which means "not-God."

Thus, in the conventions of language, to say you do not believe in God demands positing the idea of God to reject God as existing.

Still, rejecting "atheism" does not demand we conceptualize God as monotheistic. Nature could be a "god," or we could imply polytheistic deities. Atheists, like Marx, Bakunin, or Alinsky, have no choice but to posit God's existence because they cannot hate or envy something that does not exist. Others, like Nietzsche, assume they (or at least the *Übermensch*) become God, replacing the "God" who has died.

In 1948, philosophy professors V. J. McGill and W. T. Parry published a paper in *Science & Society* entitled "The Unity of Opposites: A Dialectical Principle." In that paper, McGill and Parry noted that Lenin considered the unity of opposites the most important of the dialectical principles. They commented that Lenin's point was that "a thing is determined by its internal oppositions."[1234] They pointed out that "change involves a unity of opposites, of being and non-being."[1235] They explained how Lenin imagined "being" and "not-being" as uniting by reference to Heraclitus, who posited that it "is not true to say that the world is (being) or that it is not (non-being), but that it is becoming." But the paper demonstrates the philosophical difficulties of formulating consistent logical principles that would explain how polar opposites can be joined. McGill and Parry noted the following: "1. (a) *The conception (or perception) of anything involves the conception (or perception) of its opposite*;" and "1. (b) *The existence of a thing involves the existence of an opposite*."[1236]

McGill and Parry thus concluded that in symbolic logic, the unity of opposites demands a situation in which the existence of something (e.g., being) depends on the coexistence of at least two conditions that are polar opposites (e.g., being and not-being, or God and not-God) that are opposite each other, yet dependent on each other and presupposing each other, "within a field of tension."[1237] Yet, in an important footnote, they observed that in Hegelian and Marxist literature, the term "contradiction" is "used in a very broad sense, to include conflicts and opposing forces," but not necessarily to involve the polar opposites as conceptualized by rules of logic.[1238]

Again, today's Marxist literature utilizes the logic of the dialectic very loosely, in that the established order (thesis) contains contradictions that oppress human actualization (antithesis) such that the old order is destroyed and a new order is created (synthesis). Technically, the old order is not a union of opposites (i.e., in that a union of the established order with the forces of oppression is no longer a union of opposites), but the emergence of a new, higher utopian order blooms forth out of the contradiction between this old order and some idealized future utopia of "fully realized," socially just transcendent human beings, and the old order is destroyed. But when neo-Marxists like Marcuse and Reich derive critical theory from the Hegelian dialectic, their critical theory dialectical synthesis demands a future in which polar opposites are intentionally combined to produce a transracial, transnational, transsexual, and transhuman *Übermensch* who will rule the new world order utopia by repressing, banning, marginalizing, or otherwise eliminating the "repressive" nonpersons who refuse to sign on to the agenda that we humans can replace God to create for ourselves a heaven on earth.

Neo-Marxists like Marcuse and Reich, as well as Horkheimer and Adorno, go one step further and join Nietzsche in positing that we human beings in our ultimate "full realization" transcend human nature through the Hegelian dialectic. So in the neo-Marxist utopia, Lucifer becomes the *Ubër Götter* (in English, "Over-Gods"), transcending the powerless, now dead God of the Old Testament, and replacing the presumed equally dead Son of God, Jesus Christ, of the New Testament. Thus, the final magical spell cast by the Hegelian dialectic in history results in an earthly utopia in which the fallen human beings God abandoned in the Garden of Eden return to rule. Those "truly saved" in the neo-Marxist utopia are invited to partake of the true knowledge of good and evil that Satan as Lucifer (in Latin, the "Bearer of Light") will be expected to proclaim from the throne of God where Marx, Bakunin, and Alinsky assume he rightfully belongs.

CHAPTER 6

Woke Schizophrenic Totalitarianism

Marcuse's dilemma was that he wanted at the same time to remain a Marxist, be loyal to the project of critical theory developed by the Institute for Social Research, be an independent thinker, and be committed to the struggles of the New Left. In view of his writings and activity both before and after the publication of One-Dimensional Man, *it is clear that he fervently desired* total revolution, *described as a radical upheaval and overthrow of the previously existing order, bringing about wide-ranging changes that would eliminate capitalism and establish a new liberated society and way of life.*

—**Douglas Kellner**, introduction, *Herbert Marcuse: The New Left and the 1960s*, 2005[1239]

It [Communism] is not new. It is, in fact, man's second oldest faith. Its promise was whispered in the first days of Creation under the Tree of the Knowledge of Good and Evil: "Ye shall be as gods." It is the great alternative faith of mankind. Like all great faiths, its force derives from a simple vision. Other ages have had great visions. They have always been different versions of the same vision: the vision of God and man's relationship to God. The Communist vision is the vision of Man without God."

—**Whittaker Chambers**, "Foreword in the Form of a Letter to My Children," *Witness*, 1952[1240]

In a sense, it is strange that atheistic communists felt so mortally threatened by people believing in something they insisted did not exist. Yet, communists not only cared about that worship but became utterly obsessed with stopping it. Belief in God stood in the way of the totalitarian desire to transform human nature. God was a competitor to communist control of the body, mind, and spirit of man that Marx and Lenin wanted to redefine in their own image. In other words, the communists rightly recognized that belief in God was the chief impediment to the imposition of their atheistic creed.

—**Paul Kengor**, *The Devil and Karl Marx*, 2020[1241]

Herbert Marcuse: "Grandfather of the New Left"

Ronald Radosh was born in 1937 to a Communist family in New York City. He grew up in the Communist movement. In his 2001 book *Commies*, Radosh recalled that the most dramatic moment of his high school years was the execution of Julius and Ethel Rosenberg, two Communist spies found guilty of stealing U.S. military and atomic secrets for Stalin's Russia.[1242] On the night the Rosenbergs were executed, Radosh stood amidst thousands of New Yorkers gathered on East Seventeenth Street (the police had forbidden the demonstrators to use Union Square) for a protest and vigil. He described how to him, at that moment, "it was simply a given truth that the Rosenbergs were innocent progressives who were murdered because of their dedication to peace."[1243] Through the 1960s, he joined the New York City branch of the Students for a Democratic Society (SDS) to oppose the Vietnam War.[1244] The turning point in his life was the research he did for his 1983 book, *The Rosenberg File: A Search for the Truth*.[1245] After studying FBI declassified documents, Radosh began moving in a conservative direction, and it convinced him that Julius and Ethel Rosenberg were KGB spies seeking to pass U.S. atomic secrets to Stalin's Russia after World War II. Subsequently, he began reevaluating his life and moved away from Communism, taking a job ultimately with the Hudson Institute, a conservative think tank based in Washington, DC.

In *Commies*, Radosh told two stories that made it clear that Marcuse's neo-Marxism was never wholly in sync with the New Left. The first incident involved the second annual Socialist Scholars Conference held in New York City in September 1967:

> The now well-attended conference [the third Socialist Scholars Conference] shifted to the New York Hilton on Sixth Avenue, with speakers including a Who's Who in the academic Left. A packed session heard Herbert Marcuse expound on "Radicals and Hippies: Youth Responses to the Industrial Society." The presentation was considered phony by one of the audience, a relatively unknown young man who said he was a Yippie and despised academics, socialist or otherwise.

> It was Abbie Hoffman, who appeared in a cowboy suit with two toy guns, shooting caps as he rushed onstage. Lighting up a joint, Hoffman demanded that Marcuse stop talking and start smoking. Marcuse, who postured as an advocate of the counterculture, looked on aghast as Hoffman continued to rant and rave, causing the session to end in pandemonium—which was no doubt his purpose. [1246]

Radosh also recalled a second encounter with Marcuse in 1972, during the presidential campaign of Democratic "anti-war" presidential candidate George McGovern:

> In 1972, Allis [Rosenberg, granddaughter of Julius and Ethel, whom Radosh married in 1975] and I became involved in the McGovern campaign, although she did so reluctantly (considering McGovern too right-wing). I recall attending a debate between Herbert Marcuse and Stanley Aronowitz [professor of sociology at CUNY known for his "Old Left" labor union advocacy] at the Brooklyn College law school annex, where Marcuse condemned all those opposed to voting for McGovern as people "lurking in their sectarian tents." Perhaps for that reason, Marcuse was losing his cachet with the New Left.[1247]

Marcuse's reception with the McGovern campaign reminded Radosh of an incident in San Francisco in the early 1970s where the radical core of the New Left again rejected Marcuse:

> Hearing Marcuse endorse McGovern reminded me of the last time I had heard him speak, in 1970 or 1971 at the Fillmore East, the rock and roll palace run by promoter Bill Graham, who often handed over the facility to radical groups. The hall was filled to capacity as Movement leaders including Carl Oglesby, one of the top SDS leaders, and Bernadine [sic] Dohrn, later of the Weather Underground, held their own rally and concert to carry on the struggle. The place almost erupted when Dohrn introduced Marcuse as "*Time* magazine's most favored radical," saying the words with a sneer on her face and scorn in her voice—to which Marcuse feebly responded, "I am not responsible for *Time*'s characterization of me."[1248]

Not surprisingly, given the intellectual nature of his Marxist writings, Marcuse found his first acceptance by the radicals in Europe in the 1968 student uprisings. At the height of his popularity, he spoke to packed auditoriums of students in both the United States and Europe. In 2014, fifty years after the publication of *One-Dimensional Man*, Stephen Whitfield, then a professor of American civilization at Brandeis, wrote an article in *Dissent* magazine contemplating Marcuse's demise. "In the decades following the New Left's collapse, has the stature of any intellectual fallen more dramatically than that of Herbert Marcuse?" Whitfield asked.[1249]

Decades earlier, Marcuse objected when the news media began tagging him as the "Father of the New Left." In a 1979 interview with *Change* magazine, Marcuse brushed the hyperbole away. "It would have been better to call me not the father, but the grandfather, of the New Left," Marcuse quipped.[1250]

Ironically, at the end of his life, Marcuse found himself too old-fashioned. Marcuse was bookish and too polite for the yippies, who had replaced the hippies as neo-Marxism swept through the anti-war movement of the 1970s. Abbie Hoffman and Jerry Rubin were the intellectual heirs of Marcuse's revolution, willing to borrow Marcuse's intolerance of the United States fighting a "fascist" race war in opposing the Vietnamese liberation movement. But nihilistic extremism was rapidly moving to the center of a revolutionary movement that aimed to destroy the structures of liberty and freedom as articulated by the nation's Declaration of Independence, Constitution, and Bill of Rights. The subjective reality of Marcuse's utopian vision communicated a "higher morality" to a Nuremberg trial–standard of justice that demanded the destruction of the existing order.

Along with the godless nihilism at the center of the New Left's negation motives was intolerance of any idea, person, or view that asserted the existence of a God-centered natural law or natural right consciousness. What replaced God was the insistence that each person's self-actualization demanded a near schizophrenic assertion of "social justice," insisting that what is true of each self-actualized person must be accepted as valid by all. We, not God, became the reason we existed as we rushed headlong into the perfect abyss Satan's lies had finally crafted to triumph. Yet, as the grandfather of the New Left, Marcuse's intolerance of tolerance left a lasting mark.

The Birth of Woke Intolerance

In 1965, Marcuse published an essay entitled "Repressive Tolerance" that carried the theories he developed in *One-Dimensional Man* to another level. In "Repressive Tolerance," he concluded that "the realization of the objective of tolerance would call for intolerance toward prevailing policies, attitudes, opinions, and the extension of tolerance to policies, attitudes, and opinions which are outlawed or suppressed."[1251] Marcuse argued for "liberating tolerance," a redefinition of tolerance that requires the censoring of policies, attitudes, opinions, and so forth that are designed to reinforce the dominant repressive and alienating nature of advanced industrial societies like the United States. He left no doubt that his argument for liberating tolerance was central to his goal of negating advanced capitalist industrial society by transforming human beings into liberated, self-actualized beings. He wrote:

> The author is fully aware that, at present, no power, no authority, no government exists which would translate liberating tolerance into practice, but he believes that it is the task and duty of the intellectual to recall and preserve historical possibilities which seem to have become utopian possibilities—that it is his task to break the concreteness of oppression in order to open the mental space in which this society can be recognized as what it is and does.[1252]

Coughlin and Higgins in their book, *Re-Remembering the Mis-Remembered Left: The Left's Strategy and Tactics to Transform America*, explained the hidden meaning in this quotation:

> In the dialectical paradigm, when "such a society does not exist anywhere," it is the same as saying that the current society must be negated for one that will. Living in America at that time, this means Marcuse believed that America must be negated. This is academically concealed sedition. While a different Imaginer of a second reality, Marcuse's "Workers' Paradise" is Hegel's realized *Philosophia Perennis* [in English, "Perennial Philosophy," i.e., mystical unconscious wisdom]. Apparently, Herbert Marcuse had the reputation among fellow Frankfurt cadre for taking a nihilistic hardline. Since no society exists today that can provide Marcuse's "liberating tolerance," they must all be "*aufgehoben*" [in English, "be negated," past tense of the verb *aufhaben*, "to negate"].[1253]

Consistent with what he argued in *One-Dimensional Man*, Marcuse maintained in "Repressive Tolerance" that the dominant society utilizes First Amendment free speech and free press clauses to serve a repressing role. As desublimation allows sexuality to go public to repress eros, so too, Marcuse argued, even progressive movements threaten to become repressive to the degree to which the progressive movements accept the rules of the game:

> To take a most controversial case: the exercise of political rights (such as voting, letter-writing to the press, to Senators, etc., protest-demonstrations with a priori renunciation of counterviolence) in a society of total administration serves to strengthen this administration by testifying to the existence of democratic liberties which, in reality, have changed their content and lost their effectiveness. In such a case, freedom (of opinion, of assembly, of speech) becomes an instrument for absolving servitude.[1254]

For Marcuse, as a condition for creating a humane society, liberating tolerance allows only policies, attitudes, and opinions that seek the "elimination of violence, and the reduction of suppression to the extent required for protecting man and animal from cruelty and aggression."[1255] He quickly added that a humane society "does not yet exist."[1256] Instead, Marcuse warned, violence and suppression on a global scale reinforce dominant society messages of repression:

> As deterrents against nuclear war, as police action against subversion, as technical aid in the fight against imperialism and communism, as methods of pacification in neo-colonial massacres, violence and suppression are promulgated, practiced, and defended by democratic and authoritarian governments alike, and the people subjected to these governments are educated to sustain such practices as necessary for the preservation of the status quo. Tolerance is extended to policies, conditions, and modes of behavior which should not be tolerated because they are impeding, if not destroying, the chances of creating an existence without fear and misery.[1257]

Marcuse continued to list repressive messages that must not be tolerated:

> The toleration of the systematic moronization of children and adults alike by publicity and propaganda, the release of destructiveness in aggressive driving, the recruitment for and training of special forces, the impotent and benevolent tolerance toward outright deception in merchandising, waste, and planned obsolescence are not distortions and aberrations, they are the essence of a system which fosters tolerance as a means for perpetuating the struggle for existence and suppressing the alternatives. The authorities in education, morals, and psychology are vociferous against the increase in juvenile delinquency; they are less vociferous against the proud presentation, in word and deed and

> pictures, of ever more powerful missiles, rockets, bombs—the mature delinquency of a whole civilization.[1258]

Marcuse insisted that nowhere on earth does a society exist "in which 'the people' have become autonomous individuals, freed from the repressive requirements of a struggle for existence in the interest of domination, and as such human beings choosing their government and determining their life."[1259] Thus, he concluded that John Stuart Mill's call for all sides of a debate to be heard would only serve the repressive interests of the dominant advanced capitalist society.[1260] Marcuse insisted that it is possible to know policies, attitudes, and opinions that oppose war, support racial justice, advocate minority rights, and so on.[1261] Thus, he concluded that liberating tolerance "would mean intolerance against movements from the Right and tolerance of movements from the Left."[1262] Again, Marcuse based his thinking on Hitler:

> In past and different circumstances, the speeches of the Fascist and Nazi leaders were the immediate prologue to massacre. The distance between the propaganda and the action, between the organization and its release on the people had become too short. But the spreading of the word could have been stopped before it was too late: if democratic tolerance had been withdrawn when the future leaders started their campaign, mankind would have had a chance of avoiding Auschwitz and a World War.[1263]

Insisting that the "whole post-fascist period is one of clear and present danger," Marcuse demanded that "true pacification requires the withdrawal of tolerance before the deed stage, at the stage of communication in word, print, and picture."[1264] He expanded this theme:

> It should be evident by now that the exercise of civil rights by those who don't have them presupposes the withdrawal of civil rights from those who prevent their exercise, and that liberation of the Damned of the Earth presupposes suppression not only of their old but also of their new masters.[1265]

He transitioned from denying Nazis the right to speak to denying speech rights to those on the political Right in the United States:

> Withdrawal of tolerance from regressive elements *before* they can become active; intolerance even toward thought, opinion, and word,

> and finally, intolerance in the opposite direction, that is, toward the self-styled conservatives, to the political Right—these anti-democratic notions respond to the actual development of the democratic society which has destroyed the basis for universal tolerance.[1266]

Marcuse repeated that liberating tolerance begins with censoring words and ideas, not actions:

> When tolerance mainly serves the protection and the preservation of a repressive society, when it serves to neutralize opposition and to render men immune against other and better forms of life, then tolerance has been perverted. And when this perversion starts in the mind of the individual, in his consciousness, his needs, when heteronomous interests occupy him before he can experience his servitude, then the efforts to counteract his dehumanization must begin at the place of entrance, there where the false consciousness takes form (or rather: is systematically formed)—it must begin with stopping the words and images which feed this consciousness.[1267]

Marcuse acknowledged that outlawing words and ideas is more than just censorship:

> To be sure, this is censorship, even precensorship, but openly directed against the more or less hidden censorship that permeates the free media. Where the false consciousness has become prevalent in national and popular behavior, it translates itself almost immediately into practice: the safe distance between ideology and reality, repressive thought and repressive action, between the word of destruction and the deed of destruction is dangerously shortened. Thus, the break through the false consciousness may provide the Archimedean point for a larger emancipation—at an infinitesimally small spot, to be sure, but it is on the enlargement of such small spots that the chance of change depends.[1268]

Marcuse took the next leap, jumping right into the subject of thought control:

> More than ever, the proposition holds true that progress in freedom demands progress in the *consciousness* of freedom. Where the mind has been made into a subject-object of politics and policies, intellectual autonomy, the realm of "pure" thought has become a matter of *political education* (or rather: counter-education).[1269]

Coughlin and Higgins concluded that Marcuse's "Repressive Tolerance" weaponized neo-Marxist critical theory for use against America and the West. They wrote: "For Marcuse, the repressive tolerance of America was, and still is, in need of negation by a liberating tolerance—*Die Amerikanische Kultur muss aufgehoben werden* [in English, "American culture must be abolished"]."[1270] Coughlin and Higgins explained that for Marcuse, "America, along with its Western Judeo-Christian culture, was repressive and, hence, rightfully the object of negation precisely because it was Western and Judeo-Christian."[1271] They argued that with this full explanation of how the Hegelian dialectic is ever present in Marcuse's writings, the following passage makes clear the dialectical intent of *Aufheben* (negation):

> The ironical question: who educates the educators (i.e., the political leaders) also applies to democracy. The only authentic alternative and negation of dictatorship (with respect to this question) would be a society in which "the people" have become autonomous individuals, freed from the repressive requirements of a struggle for existence in the interest of domination, and as such human beings choosing their government and determining their life. Such a society does not yet exist anywhere.[1272]

Coughlin and Higgins noted that "Marcuse calls for subversion, undemocratic means, and the suspension of the First Amendment in furtherance of implementing a postmodern campaign of 'otherisms' based on racism, discrimination, etc."[1273] They stressed that when reading Franklin School materials, the "political right" and "fascism" should be understood to mean anything "that is either not from the left or is something about which 'the Left' disagrees."[1274] They pointed to the following passage from "Repressive Tolerance" to substantiate their argument:

> Surely, no government can be expected to foster its own subversion, but in a democracy such a right is vested in the people (i.e., in the majority of the people). This means that the ways should not be blocked on which a submissive majority could develop, and if they are blocked by organized repression and indoctrination, their reopening may require apparently undemocratic means. They would include the withdrawal of toleration of speech and assembly from groups and movements which promote aggressive policies, armament, chauvinism, discrimination on the grounds of race and religion, or which oppose the extension of pub-

> lic services, social security, medical care, etc. Moreover, the restoration of freedom of thought may necessitate new and rigid restrictions on teachings and practices in the educational institutions which, by their very methods and concepts, serve to enclose the mind within the established universe of discourse and behavior—thereby precluding a priori a rational evaluation of the alternatives.[1275]

Coughlin and Higgins pointed[1276] to a quotation by Mao cited in psychiatrist Robert Jay Lifton's 1961 book *Thought Reform and the Psychology of Totalism: A Study of "Brainwashing" in China.*[1277] The quotation from Mao was from a speech entitled "On the People's Democratic Dictatorship" that Mao gave on July 1, 1949, in commemoration of the twenty-eighth anniversary of the Chinese Communist Party:

> Under the leadership of the working class and the CP [Communist Party], these classes [the people] unite together to form their own state and elect their own government (so as to) carry out a dictatorship over the lackeys of imperialism—the landlord class, the bureaucratic capitalist class, and the KMT [the Kuomintang, the Chinese Nationalist Party under Chiang Kai-shek in mainland China] reactionaries and their henchmen representing these classes—to suppress them, allowing them only to behave properly and not to talk and act wildly. If they talk and act wildly their (action) will be prohibited and punished immediately. The democratic system is to be carried out within the ranks of the people, giving them freedom of speech, assembly, and association. The right to vote is given only to the people and not to the reactionaries. These two aspects, namely democracy among the people and dictatorship over the reactionaries, combine to form the people's democratic dictatorship.[1278]
>
> Mao added:
>
> Our benevolence applies only to the people, and not to the reactionary acts of the reactionaries and the reactionary classes outside the people.[1279]

Lifton commented in his book on Chinese brainwashing that the "totalist environment draws a sharp line between those whose right to existence can be recognized, and those who possess no such right."[1280] He commented on Mao's 1949 speech dealing with thought reform. Lifton wrote:

> In thought reform, as in the Chinese Communist practice generally, the world is divided into the "people: (defined as "the working class, the peasant class, the petite bourgeoisie, and the national bourgeoisie"), and the "reactionaries" or "lackeys of imperialism" (defined as "the landlord class, the bureaucratic capitalist class, and the KMT reactionaries and their henchmen").[1281]

Lifton observed that in Communist China in 1949, this division of the world was an "existential distinction."[1282] He explained the consequences of being a nonperson that prefigured Marcuse's division of the world into repressive forces (the political Right) and non-repressive forces (the political Left). Lifton wrote:

> Being "outside the people," the reactionaries are presumably nonpeople. Under the conditions of ideological totalism, in China and elsewhere, nonpeople have often been put to death, their executioners then becoming guilty (in [Albert] Camus' phrase) of "crimes of logic." But the thought reform process is one means by which nonpeople are permitted, through a change in attitude and personal character, to make themselves over into people. The most literal example of such dispensing of existence and nonexistence is to be found in the sentence given to certain political criminals: execution in two years' time, unless during that two-year period they have demonstrated genuine progress in their reform.[1283]

Coughlin and Higgins explained, "as with Mao, for Marcuse, the Frankfurt School, Marxists, and the Neo-Marxist Left, **all people and organizations who associated with repressive tolerance are to be designated as not being of the people and hence they should not be afforded the rights of a person as if they were. They are non-persons.**"[1284]

Coughlin and Higgins continued:

> The facially neutral manner in which the American left expresses its otherwise hardcore Marxist intent must be accounted for precisely because it is so disarming. When speaking of **building a "subversive majority,"** it should not be lost on the reader that Marcuse was **calling for a current minority to subvert the will of the majority.** Hence, the statement that "political correctness is the enforcement mechanism of postmodern narratives that implement cultural Marxism," speaks directly to the negation engine Marcuse's "Repressive Tolerance" put in motion that today culminates in hate speech narratives. **Political correctness is a Neo-Marxist line of effort.** It is an existential threat.[1285]

Coughlin and Higgins cautioned us to realize that the narratives of "Repressive Tolerance," embedded in the current Left's embrace of critical social justice theory, are hostile and alien to American understandings of the rule of law and Constitutional principles. They emphasized that the disarming statement of Marcuse's narratives hides that his arguments are carefully crafted dialectical constructs that he structured to negate American culture. After Marcuse, the neo-Marxist revolution in the United States transformed into a psychotically charged culture war. Coughlin and Higgins urged us not to underestimate the importance of Marcuse's essay "Repressive Tolerance." They explained as follows:

> Today, Marx's philosophical criticism manifests as the Frankfurt School's critical theory. Herbert Marcuse's repressive tolerance is one of the more prominent instances of it in America today. Seeking to fully integrate into the Left's larger effort, Marcuse put his critical theory construct at the service of the global Marxist movement. It adopted Mao's Long March strategy as the execution formula of choice. The latter is the mass-line counter-state political warfare strategy.[1286]

In rejecting free speech as "repressive tolerance," Marcuse justified transforming woke intolerance into politically correct censorship of all opposing views.

Jean Baudrillard, the High Priest of Nihilist Postmodernism

In 1981, French sociologist Jean Baudrillard (1929–2007) published an influential book entitled *Simulacra and Simulation*.[1287] In that book, Baudrillard proposed the radical concept that there is no objective reality behind our subjective perception of reality. Going one step further, he argued reality itself is nothing more than the images we create such that the images become the reality. The term "simulacrum" (the noun, singular person) derives from the Latin verb *simulare*, which means "to make like, imitate, copy, represent," from the stem of the adjective *similis*, which means "like, resembling, of the same kind."[1288] A simulation imitates a real-life operation, process, or experience that permits the viewer or participant to engage in the experience as if it were real. Baudrillard opened the book with a fictionalized "quotation" from Ecclesiastes. With this quotation, he signaled that he intends to question whether there is any "reality" other than simulacra and simulations.

Baudrillard's fictional quotation from Ecclesiastes reads as follows:

> The simulacrum is never what hides the truth—it
> is truth that hides the fact that there is none.
> The simulacrum is true.
> Ecclesiastes

The only attachment this fabricated quote has to King Solomon is that Baudrillard's fictitious rendering sounds like a proclamation of wisdom King Solomon might have articulated in Ecclesiastes. King Solomon laments that a life lived to pursue wisdom involves much grief and sorrow, contemplating human madness and folly (Ecclesiastes 1:17). Perhaps this is the conclusion we derive from reading Baudrillard. Namely, the madness and folly of his writing have propelled neo-Marxism and cultural Maoism to a new level of value relativity that has produced much subsequent grief and sorrow on earth. Baudrillard's point in his rendering of King Solomon is that simulacra and simulations are the only reality. His nihilistic denial of objective reality elevates every subjective human perception of reality, including the subjective perception of schizophrenics, to the level of a natural law that all must accept as universally accurate and true.

Baudrillard followed this opening "quotation" with a discussion of a one-paragraph short story Argentinian author Jorge Luis Borges wrote in 1946 entitled "On Exactitude in Science."[1289] Borges typically presented this short story as a quotation from Suárez Miranda's book *Viajes de varones prudentes* (in English: *Journeys of Wise Men*), a nonexistent book that Borges described as book IV, chapter XLV, published in 1658. The passage Borges "cited" describes an unspecified empire that cartographers had so precisely mapped that the map became the empire. As the empire disappeared from the face of the earth, the only remnant of the empire was a tattered ruin of the map still inhabited by animals and beggars. Baudrillard's takeaway was to use Borges's story as an allegory to mean that simulacra and simulations are the only "true" reality that we humans can experience. Thus, Baudrillard implies that rather than experience reality, we experience reality as "hyperreal"—that is, an experience "above" or "beyond" reality. He explained this concept as follows:

> Today abstraction is no longer that of the map, the double, the mirror, or the concept. Simulation is no longer of a territory, a referential being, or a substance. It is the generation by models of a real without origin or reality: a hyperreal.[1290]

Baudrillard explained what he means by the "hyperreal" by dissecting the Borges map story as follows:

> The territory no longer precedes the map, nor does it survive it. It is nevertheless the map that precedes the territory—*precession of simulacra*—that engenders the territory, and if one must return to the fable, today it is the territory whose shreds slowly rot across the extent of the map. It is the real, and not the map, whose vestiges persist here and there in deserts that are no longer those of the Empire, but ours. *The desert of the real itself.*[1291]

For Baudrillard, the cartographer's exactitude was so precise that the cartographer created a "coextensivity of map and territory." The map became the empire. Thus, we live amongst simulacra (e.g., the map as a picture of the empire is the empire), not realizing we are living in the simulation of the empire, not the empire itself.

Baudrillard laid out four "successive phases" of the image (i.e., the simulacrum), suggesting a progression in time, much like the Hegelian dialectic. The four phases are:

1) The image is the reflection of a profound reality.

2) The image masks and denatures profound reality.

3) The image masks the absence of a profound reality.

4) The image has no relation to any reality whatsoever: it is its own pure simulacrum.[1292]

At times, Baudrillard wrote like our ability to live within a world of simulacra and simulations is a recent development. He argued that we live in a world of pure simulacra and simulations made possible by technological advances that have gone from motion pictures to feature films, television, the internet, video game technology, and finally, to the "meta-reality" companies like Facebook aspire to create. The word "meta" derives from the Greek μετά (meta) that means "after" or "beyond." Thus, the word "metaphysics" refers to a philosophical understanding that transcends physics. So, the "metaverse" is a universe that transcends the objective reality to create a fictional reality. Yet, for Baudrillard to attribute historicity of this nature to his concept would not be revolutionary. In the 1950s, authors like Marshall McLuhan informed us that "the medium is the message."[1293]

Baudrillard's point seems to be that humans have always lived in a world of simulacra and simulations. Advancements in technology are finally permitting us to realize that an objective world has always been an illusion. That simulacra and simulations are the only accurate perception of "reality" appears to be the full meaning of Baudrillard's invented quotation that he attributed to Ecclesiastes. When discussing the transition in how people perceive images in history, Baudrillard explained that the view of images as accurate reflections of a profound external reality led to the mistaken beliefs in God, theology, and natural law. Now that technology allows us to appreciate that there is no objective reality to perceive, we can finally perceive that there never was God. We also understand that theology implying the necessity of a Last Judgment to impose natural law rulings on the morality of human lives was, as Freud maintained, an illusion we created for social control purposes. Baudrillard elaborated as follows:

> The transition from signs that dissimulate something to signs that dissimulate that there is nothing marks a decisive turning point. The first reflects a theology of truth and secrecy (to which the notion of ideology still belongs). The second inaugurates the era of simulacra and simulation, in which there is no longer a God to recognize his own, no longer a Last Judgment to separate the false from the true, the real from its artificial resurrection, as everything is already dead and resurrected in advance.[1294]

In the following sentence, Baudrillard asserted that "when the real is no longer what it was, nostalgia assumes its full meaning."[1295] For him, the harsh reality is that "myths of origin" and "signs of reality" were always false. However, we poor humans still regret losing these wrongly conceived but comfortable illusions, refusing to accept that our reality is a reality of nothingness.

Proudly, in the concluding chapter of his book, entitled "On Nihilism," Baudrillard declares: "I am a nihilist."[1296] Again, he explained, as Shakespeare had posited, that life is "full of sound and fury, signifying nothing."[1297]

> I observe, I accept, I assume the immense process of the destruction of appearances (and the seduction of appearances) in the service of meaning (representation, history, criticism, etc.) that is the fundamental fact of the nineteenth century. The true revolution of the nineteenth century, of modernity, is the radical destruction of appearances, the disen-

chantment of the world and its abandonment to the violence of interpretation and of history.[1298]

Baudrillard rejected Kant and Hegel because they presumed an advancement of the human spirit through the workings of the historical dialectic. Disagreeing, Baudrillard concluded the only "working out" we humans can do in history is to realize how deluded we were to assume objective reality, natural laws of right and wrong, and a creator, an all-knowing, benevolent God who ruled heaven and earth. Instead, Baudrillard reveled in the celebration that the twentieth century was the dawning of human consciousness to appreciate that our existence amounted to nothing. He continued:

> I observe, I accept, I assume, I analyze the second revolution, that of the twentieth century, that of postmodernity, which is the immense process of the destruction of meaning, equal to the earlier destruction of appearances. He who strikes with meaning is killed by meaning.[1299]

Baudrillard made sure that we do not confuse him with Kant or Hegel, or with the Frankfurt School's critical theory:

> The dialectic stage, the critical stage is empty. There is no more stage. There is no therapy of meaning or therapy through meaning: therapy itself is part of the generalized process of indifferentiation.[1300]

In a sentence or two, Baudrillard dismissed the neo-Marxist critical theory of Frankfurt School thinkers as notable as Theodor Adorno and Walter Benjamin, dismissing them for suffering "a melancholy attached to the system itself, one that is incurable and beyond any dialectic."[1301]

With Baudrillard, the departure from Descartes is final and complete. In his second meditation, Descartes transformed his famous "*cogito, ergo sum*" into "I am, I exist."[1302] From there, Descartes proclaimed his certainty that God exists, writing: "And when I consider the fact that I have doubts, or that I am a thing that is incomplete and dependent, then there arises in me a clear and distinct idea of a being who is independent and complete, that is, an idea of God. And from the mere fact that there is such an idea within me, or that I who possess this idea exist, I clearly infer God also exists, and that every single moment of my entire existence depends on him."[1303] When Baudrillard looked inward, he saw nothing. He proclaimed himself to be "obsessed by the mode of disappearance."[1304]

In the end, for Baudrillard, there was nothing, no finality or transition with death, just a disappearance into nothingness.[1305]

From Baudrillard, subsequent thinkers have surmised that life is a simulation, perhaps best conceptualized by the hypothesis that we live in a computer simulation.[1306] Larry Wachowski and Andy Wachowski, the writers of the screenplay for *The Matrix*, claimed Baudrillard was their inspiration for the movie, going so far as to feature *Simulacra and Simulation* as a prop in one of the movie's opening scenes. Yet, when the Wachowskis reached out to Baudrillard to get him involved in the subsequent *Matrix* movies, he refused. Goodwin College English professor Randy Laist explained Baudrillard's refusal as differences over how "reality is structured." Laist explained Baudrillard's objection to the *Matrix* movies as follows:

> The clear philosophical debt in the Wachowski brothers' film is to Plato and the condition he describes in the Allegory of the Cave, in which prisoners of a false reality are freed to discover that there is a true reality the existence of which they had not suspected. The foundational insight of Baudrillard's theory in *Simulacra and Simulation*, however, is that the Platonic duality between reality and representation has imploded in the modern world, resulting in a hyperreal condition to which criteria of truth or falsity no longer apply. As Baudrillard himself explains in an interview, "the real nuisance in this movie is that the brand-new problem of simulation is mistaken with the very classic problem of the illusion already mentioned by Plato. Here lies the mistake.[1307]

Laist took the Baudrillard quotation from an interview Baudrillard gave to *Le Nouvel Observateur* in 2003. As we already observed, a common interpretation of Baudrillard is that he was saying technological advances have transformed our experience of reality from an objective experience of an external world into a subjective experience of reality as a simulacrum or a simulation. In other words, Laist's understanding of Baudrillard is consistent with a less revolutionary understanding of Baudrillard's meaning. Laist suggested that modern media has blurred reality with illusion such that today "people have been robbed of their ability to decipher between fact and fiction."[1308] What Baudrillard told *Le Nouvel Observateur*, however, was somewhat different.

***Le Nouvel Observateur* interviewer Aude Lanceli**: Your reflections on reality and the virtual are some of the key references used by the makers

> of *The Matrix*. The first episode explicitly referred to you as the viewer saw the cover of *Simulacra and Simulation*. Were you surprised by this?
>
> **Jean Baudrillard**: Certainly there have been misinterpretations, which is why I have been hesitant until now to speak about *The Matrix*. The staff of the Wachowski brothers contacted me at various times following the release of the first episode in order to get me involved with the following ones, but this wasn't really conceivable. (laughter). Basically, a misunderstanding occurred in the 1980s when New York–based Simulationist artists contacted me. They took the hypothesis of the virtual for an irrefutable fact and transformed it into a visible phantasm. But it is precisely why we can no longer employ categories of the real in order to discuss the characteristics of the virtual.[1309]

Later in the interview, Baudrillard expanded his comments about the *Matrix* movies to say the following:

> The actors are in the matrix, that is, in the digitized system of things; or, they are radically outside it, such as Zion, the city of resistors. But what would be interesting is to show when the two worlds collide. The most embarrassing part of the film is that the new problem posed by simulation is confused with its classical, Platonic treatment. This is a serious flaw. The radical illusion of the world is a problem faced by all great cultures, which they have solved through art and symbolization. What we have invented, in order to support this suffering, is a simulated real, which henceforth supplants the real and is its final solution, a virtual universe from which everything dangerous and negative has been expelled. And *The Matrix* is undeniably part of that. Everything belonging to the order of dream, utopia and phantasm is given expression, "realized." We are in uncut transparency. *The Matrix* is surely the kind of film about the matrix that the matrix would have been able to produce.[1310]

Baudrillard's problem with both Plato's cave allegory and the Wachowskis' movie is that both suggest there is a world of simulacra and simulation that is "unreal"—that is, not objective reality, but that we experienced as real. Plato's cave analogy and the Wachowskis' *Matrix* movies also suggest there is a correct dimension of objective reality that the cave prisoners perceive when freed to escape the cave, similar to the actual dimension of objective experience that the *Matrix* rebels can only enjoy when they flee into Zion. Baudrillard objected to this distinction because this duality implies the existence of objective external reality.

Baudrillard's point is that modern simulacra and simulation technology finally allow us to appreciate that there never was anything other than subjective reality. We now understand this because the technology of simulacra and simulations has caught up with the truth. We can only share our subjective experiences of reality because we live in the "fictional narrative" of reality that simulacra and simulation have always weaved. For human beings, Baudrillard believes there is no objectively true experience of objective reality because objective reality does not exist. Outside of our misperception of reality, outside of the reality within simulacra and simulations, there is nothing. Baudrillard could not be a nihilist if he believed otherwise.

Perhaps Baudrillard's most outrageous book was his 1995 *The Gulf War Did Not Happen*, a collection of essays he wrote during the first Gulf War of 1991. [1311] In his introduction to his English translation of the book, Paul Patton, Scientia Professor of Philosophy in the School of History and Philosophy at the University of New South Wales, Sydney, Australia, pointed out that "the central thesis of Baudrillard's essays appears to be directly contradicted by the facts."[1312] Patton posed the central question: "So why did he [Baudrillard] pursue this line of argument which appears to deny the reality of the Gulf War?"[1313] He explained that Baudrillard's argument "is not that nothing took place, but rather that what took place was not a war."[1314] For Baudrillard, the 1991 Gulf War was a staged media event whose reality was the virtual experience of the technological battlefield and the electronic media experience that was our experience of the "war."

Fundamentally, Baudrillard is challenging not simply the virtual reality in which we fight technologically advanced wars but the construction of "false narratives" that convey a "purpose" to the war. Baudrillard explained:

> Brecht: "This beer isn't a beer, but that is compensated for by the fact that this cigar isn't a cigar either. If this beer wasn't a beer and this cigar was really a cigar, then there would be a problem." In the same manner, this war is not a war, but this is compensated for by the fact that information is not information either. Thus everything is in order. If this war had not been a war and the images had been real images, there would have been a problem. For in that case, the non-war would have appeared for what it is: a scandal. Similarly, if the war had been a real war and

> the information had not been information, this non-information would have appeared for what it is: a scandal. In both cases, there would have been a problem.[1315]

Baudrillard suggested that everything we experience is "fake news" (i.e., narratives fabricated to explain events "happening" in invented reality). He continued that thought:

> There is one further problem for those who believe that this war took place: how is it that a real war did not generate real images? Same problem for those who believe in the Americans' "victory": how is it that Saddam is still there as though nothing had happened?[1316]

For Baudrillard, the only "reality" to the Gulf War, or to any war for that matter, has always involved the ability to construct and impose a "fake news" false reality to disguise what is nothing more than the liquidation of radical challenges. He summed this up with examples, starting with the purpose he perceived as driving the Gulf War false narrative:

> The crucial stake, the decisive stake in this whole affair is the consensual reduction of Islam to the global order. Not to destroy but to domesticate it, by whatever means: modernization, even military, politicization, nationalism, democracy, the Rights of Man, anything at all to electrocute the resistances and the symbolic challenge that Islam represents for the entire West. There is no miracle, the confrontation will last as long as this process has not reached its term: by contrast, it will stop as though of its own accord the day when this form of radical challenge has been liquidated.[1317]

He continued:

> This was how it happened in the Vietnam war: the day when China was neutralized, when the "wild" Vietnam with its forces of liberation and revolt was replaced by a truly bureaucratic and military organization capable of ensuring the continuation of Order, the Vietnam war stopped immediately—but ten years were necessary for this political domestication to take place (whether it took place under communism or democracy is of no importance). Same thing with the Algerian war: its end, which was believed to be impossible, took place of its own accord, not by virtue of De Gaulle's sagacity, but from the moment the maquis with their revolutionary potential were finally liquidated and an Algerian

> army and a bureaucracy, which had been set up in Tunisia without ever engaging in combat, were in a position to ensure the continuation of power and the exercise of order.[1318]

Baudrillard's postmodernist lesson implies that all narratives are fake news and all realities virtual (i.e., subjective). Next we encounter Jürgen Habermas, who posits the question: If reality is a simulacrum, then why shouldn't neo-Marxists, cultural Maoists, and anarchists use discourse ethics to realize the self-actualizing identity-affirming values that Marcuse's utopia presupposes?

Jürgen Habermas: The Theories of Communicative Action and Discourse Ethics

Born in 1929, Jürgen Habermas as a teenager experienced Hitler's rise to power by becoming a member of the Hitler Youth. In an analysis of his work published in the *Stanford Encyclopedia of Philosophy*, James Bohman and William Rehg observed that "the Nuremberg Trials were a key formative movement that brought home to him [Habermas] the depth of Germany's moral and political failure under National Socialism."[1319] In his definitive study of the Frankfurt School, Rolf Wiggershaus noted that Habermas was Adorno's research assistant at the Institute of Social Research in the 1950s.[1320] As a graduate student, Habermas immersed himself in Heidegger's existentialism. In 1953, when Habermas publicly called for an explanation of Heidegger's affiliation with the Nazi Party, Heidegger's "silence confirmed Habermas's conviction that the German philosophical tradition had failed in its moment of reckoning, providing intellectuals with the resources neither to understand nor to criticize National Socialism."[1321]

Habermas's philosophical writings are voluminous. We shall narrow our focus here to his theories of communicative action and discourse ethics, the two Habermas theories that bear most significantly on the development of critical theory regarding morals and politics. Habermas shared the Frankfurt School's preoccupation with understanding why Germany had fallen into the grips of Hitlerian totalitarianism to prevent it from recurring. Like Adorno, Horkheimer, and Marcuse, Habermas was also a neo-Marxist who wanted to craft a critical social science capable of destroying capitalism to create a future socialist utopia.

Habermas's mature work explored the influence of language on ethics. Fundamental to his theory of communication was that humans needed a language of shared meanings to conduct a meaningful dialogue. In *The Theory of Communicative Action*, Habermas tackled a problem central to Kant. In doing so, Habermas reframed Kant's phenomenological distinction between objective versus subjective experience. He agreed with Kant that all human knowledge is subjective in that our primary encounter with the material world is through our senses. But he distinguished that for communication to be possible, people needed to reach an intersubjective interpretation of words and meanings derived from their shared culture, society, history, and traditions. Habermas's word for this intersubjectively shared world was "lifeworld." He explained as follows:

> The abstract concept of the world is a necessary condition if communicatively acting subjects are to reach understanding among themselves about what takes place in the world or is to be effected in it. Through this *communicative practice* they assure themselves at the same time of their common life-relations, of an intersubjectively shared *lifeworld*. This lifeworld is bounded by the totality of interpretations presupposed by the members as background knowledge.[1322]

In his book *Moral Consciousness and Communicative Action*, Habermas applied this concept of a shared subjective experience to ethics. For him, value judgments remain subjective because each person has individual experiences. But elevating value opinions to societal norms remains a shared experience. Values become objectified only when all participants in society engage in argumentation, with the "valid norms" being those that meet the approval of all. He wrote:

> Argumentation as an intersubjective procedure is necessary only because in establishing a collective mode of action, we have to coordinate our individual intentions and come to a joint decision. Only when this decision emerges from argumentation, only when it comes about in accordance with pragmatic rules of discourse do we consider the resulting norm justified. One has to make sure everyone concerned has had a chance to freely give his consent. Argumentation is designed to prevent some from simply suggesting or prescribing to others what is good for them. On this view, then, argumentation is designed to make possible not impartiality of judgment but freedom from influence or autonomy in will formulation. To that extent the rules of discourse themselves have a normative quality, for they neutralize imbalances of power and provide for equal opportunities to realize one's interests.[1323]

Later in the book, Habermas expressed the point even more succinctly. He wrote: "For a norm to be valid, the consequences and the side effects of its general observance for the satisfaction of each person's particular interests must be acceptable to all."[1324]

Steve Hoenisch, the editor of Criticism.com, explained that Habermas's formulation of discourse ethics depends on his theory of communicative action. As a result, Habermas's universality principle differs significantly from Kant's categorical imperative. "Jürgen Habermas's theory of discourse ethics contains two distinctive characteristics: (i) It puts forth as a fundamental tenet a prerequisite in argumentation for testing the validity of a norm, and (ii) it transforms the individual nature of Kant's categorical imperative into a collective imperative by reformulating it to ensure the expression of a general will and by elevating it to a rule of argumentation," Hoenisch wrote. "As the practical discourse on a norm unfolds, Habermas's universalization principle, adapted from Kant's categorical imperative, guides the argumentation of the participants while guarding its rationality." But Hoenisch correctly observed that Habermas's formalization of the universality principle demands universal agreement, while "Kant's categorical imperative permits an individual to ascribe as valid for everyone any maxim that he would will to be a universal law."[1325]

Habermas's discourse ethics abandon Kant's perception that transcendental knowledge acts as synthetic a priori judgments at a higher level of idealized understanding that allows us to formulate necessary statements as natural laws. To Kant, Habermas's argumentation methodology would establish "universal norms" simply because the individuals involved in a given society wanted those rules to be valid. Kant understood that God created two genders: male and female. Habermas could imagine that sex differs from gender such that a given society could perceive multiple gender identities as consistent with their higher-level self-fulfillment and utopian self-actualization goals. Unlike Kant, Habermas excluded God from his philosophic equations. Without God, the philosophical system is grounded only on a human agreement, without a transcendental standard of natural law or rights.

What in Habermas's theory of communicative action would prevent a society of psychologically disturbed or mentally ill citizens from being in control of the discourse? What if the world embraces Satanism and agrees to make pagan depravity and sexual perversion the norm that discourse ethics articulates as that society's sexual or gender standards? Granted, Habermas wanted normative standards to be in accord with everyone's perception of self-interest. But if we apply Marcuse's logic of repressive tolerance, would a society of Satanists feel compunction about insisting a group of Christians should have a right to speak? If the Satanists exclude traditionally moral, God-fearing citizens from communicative action, what norms will the discourse ethics produce?

Habermas insisted that his discourse ethics require "each person's particular interests must be acceptable to all."[1326] Under such an all-inclusive requirement, how would Habermas prevent destructive, dangerous, pathological schizophrenics from asserting their values in communicative action? His logic elevates Rousseau's general will to be in control. Like the other Frankfurt School philosophers, Habermas joins Adorno, Horkheimer, and Marcuse in assuming capitalism is inherently evil. Marcuse would insist that anti-capitalists should use discourse ethics to self-actualize uninhibited sexual expression. Neo-Marxists, cultural Maoists, and anarchists would welcome the opportunity to utilize discourse ethics to destroy capitalism by eliminating the hydrocarbon fuels that an increasingly advanced global industrial civilization requires to maintain populations currently expanding on this productive planet. The bottom line is that Habermas's theories of communicative action and discourse ethics again provide a postmodern justification for negating and destroying the culture of capitalism with a tactical strategy promoting value relativity achieved through linguistic construction of language rules regarding ethics and morality.

When we add Baudrillard into the mix, the postmodernist twist is that all political narratives are subjective constructions. Applying this perception to Habermas's theory of discourse ethics gives neo-Marxists, cultural Maoists, and anarchists the green light to postulate their utopian lifeworld values to be whatever they want in discourse ethics. Why not create a metaverse utopia with bizarre language conventions regarding human behavior that can be universalized for everyone to believe?

Let's tie the phenomenological and philosophical arguments of this Volume 2 of the Great Awakening Trilogy into the climate science themes of Volume 1 on energy, global warming, and climate change. What do true believers mean by claiming there is a "scientific consensus" that anthropogenic global warming will create climate disasters? The United Nations' Intergovernmental Panel on Climate Change (IPCC) knows thousands of scientists disagree that burning hydrocarbon fuels since the Industrial Revolution has emitted enough carbon dioxide to cause catastrophic climate change. If we combine Baudrillard's simulacra theory with Habermas's communicative action theory, what woke global warmers mean by "scientific consensus" is that in their utopian view of how climate science should operate, burning hydrocarbon fuels ought to be bad for the planet. In 2018, the IPCC issued a policy statement requiring governments to limit or discontinue the burning of hydrocarbon fuels to reduce the emission of carbon dioxide (CO2) with the goal of limiting the impact on global warming to keep the planet from exceeding 1.5°C above preindustrial levels.[1327] The United Nations understands this policy statement is not a statement of what actual climate scientists today believe, just as Baudrillard understood that Operation Desert Storm happened. The international organization's "scientific consensus" is a statement of what global warming anti-capitalists believe climate scientists must agree to believe. Why? Because the IPCC assumes all who love Earth must think we have no choice but to abandon hydrocarbon fuels. The global warming consensus is a statement resulting from discourse ethics that insist we can only achieve climate sustainability if we shift to renewable energies. The "scientific consensus" is operative then on a normative level, not as a statement of fact. In Baudrillard's world, all facts are nothing more than statements of fact. Baudrillard insists the simulacra are true. Habermas provides a methodology for transforming the norms of a neo-Marxist utopian simulacrum into lifeworld categorical-imperative values.

John Rawls and Justice as Fairness

In his *A Theory of Justice*, John Rawls defines justice in terms of fairness.[1328] For our discussion, the essential part of Rawls's theory involved his reconstruction of the "original state of nature" that led to the creation of a "social contract" in which humans agreed to form a government. In his famous 1651 book *Leviathan*, British political philosopher Thomas Hobbes characterized the state of nature as a "war of every man against man."[1329] Hobbes lamented that human life was "solitary, poor, nasty, brutish, and short."[1330] To escape this condition, Hobbes imagined humans had formed a social contract, agreeing to limit their absolute rights of nature to live in civil society. For Hobbes, humans create governments not to protect inalienable, God-given rights or to provide fair treatment to all citizens. We form governments to escape the chaos of living in a stateless condition in the hope that a government would make life a bit less solitary, poor, nasty, brutish, and short. The most well-known social-contract political philosophers include John Locke, Jean-Jacques Rousseau, and Thomas Hobbes. The central idea of social contract theory is that we enter into a social contract that creates government out of necessity. Without the overarching authority of the state created by the social contract there is no protection from foreign enemies or criminals within.

Rawls fundamentally redefined social contract theory. He invented the concept of a veil of ignorance to explain that the founders of the social contract would not know their position within the government and society the social contract formed. Thus, the guiding principles of Rawls's social contract rule formation were to conceptualize that achieving justice was the primary reason for creating the state, and that for the state to be legitimate, justice must fair. Redefining justice as fairness was the fundamental contribution Rawls made to political philosophy. Since no one would know where they would land in the society they formed, the founders would have to ensure the elimination of all forms of discrimination from the definition of rights and obligations in the community they created. In his 1971 book *A Theory of Justice*, Rawls explained as follows:

> In justice as fairness the original position of equality corresponds to the state of nature in the traditional theory of the social contract. This original position is not, of course, thought of as an actual historical state of affairs, much less as a primitive condition of culture. It is understood as a purely hypothetical situation characterized so as to lead to a certain conception of justice. Among the essential features of this situation is that no one knows his place in society, his class position or social status, nor does any one know his fortune in the distribution of natural assets and abilities, his intelligence, strength, and the like. I shall even assume that the parties do not know their conceptions of the good or their special psychological propensities. The principles of justice are chosen behind a veil of ignorance. This ensures that no one is advantaged or disadvantaged in the choice of principles by the outcome of natural chance or the contingency of social circumstances. Since all are similarly situated and no one is able to design principles to favor his particular condition, the principles of justice are the result of a fair agreement or bargain.[1331]

Rawls argued that since the founders of his imagined state would not know if they would be white, privileged, wealthy, and an inheritor of a fortune or a minority born into slavery, those formulating the social contract would have to set the rules of justice to be fair to everyone. Again, he explained:

> No society can, of course, be a scheme of cooperation which men enter voluntarily in a literal sense; each person finds himself placed at birth in some particular position in some particular society, and the nature of this position materially affects his life prospects. Yet a society satisfying the principles of justice as fairness comes as close as a society can to being a voluntary scheme, for it means the principles which free and equal persons would assent to under circumstances that are fair. In this sense its members are autonomous and the obligations they recognize self-imposed.[1332]

In contrast to Habermas, Rawls anticipates that the veil of ignorance inherent to his social contract model will produce fair rules because the veil of ignorance will force everyone out of self-interest to take a moral view of equality issues. Thus, Rawls can anticipate that his social contract will result in racial equality, gender equality, and all other forms of equality that social justice activists demand. The mechanics of Habermas's discourse ethics do not require that the norms set through argumentation have an outcome consistent with traditional moral principles, including fairness. Rawls acknowledged that his formulation of justice as fairness is compatible with Kant's categorical imperatives in that both methodologies result in objectively justified morals. He wrote:

> Kant held, I believe, that a person is acting autonomously when the principles of his action are chosen by him as the most adequate possible expression of his nature as a free and equal rational being. The principles he acts upon are not adopted because of his social position or natural endowments, or in view of the particular kind of society in which he lives or the specific things that he happens to want. To act on such principles is to act heteronomously. Now the veil of ignorance deprives the persons in the original position of the knowledge that would enable them to choose heteronomous principles. The parties arrive at their choice together as free and equal rational persons knowing only that those circumstances obtain which give rise to the need for principles of justice.[1333]

Rawls went so far as to claim his principles of justice were morally equivalent to Kant's categorical imperatives, even though differently formulated:

> The principles of justice are also categorical imperatives in Kant's sense. For a categorical imperative Kant understands a principle of conduct

> that applies to a person in virtue of his nature as a free and equal rational being. The validity of the principle does not presuppose that one has a particular desire or aim.[1334]

In his acceptance of absolute moral principles, Rawls's theory agrees with Kant that rational thinking articulates objectively determined values not set by the subjective cultural experiences inherent to Habermas's lifeworld concept. In this sense, Rawls is a natural law and natural rights political philosopher. He differs from Kant in that he does not appear to believe ideal transcendental values can be discerned through pure reason, as does Kant. Instead, he argues his veil of ignorance demands a decision standard under which rational actors have no choice but to perceive justice as fairness. Habermas assumes a neo-Marxist society would create norms demanding social justice. He also believes neo-Marxist values formulated as discourse ethics would allow late-term abortions, acceptance of LGBT sexual agendas, and the teaching of gender identity theories to kindergarten children. In his concern to eliminate all forms of economic and social inequality in forming his ideal society, Rawls does not discuss the controversial sexual issues raised by today's social justice identity politics.

In political philosophy, justice and fairness are not equivalent terms. While many philosophers, including Aristotle, have argued that justice must be fair, we would not need two distinct (i.e., not synonymous) words. The concept of justice includes legal issues such that justice involves making sure a criminal gets the punishment that is appropriately severe for the crime. While we might also say appropriate criminal standards must be fair, is capital punishment a just or fair sentence for murder because a murder must compensate for the life the crime extinguished? The point relevant here, however, is not to debate whether justice as fairness is or is not a legitimate philosophical equivalence. The point relevant to this discussion is that Rawl's theory of justice as fairness has had a profound impact on how critical theory has come to view social justice issues.

After the 1971 publication of Rawl's *A Theory of Justice*, woke critical theory embraced fairness as the primary determinant of social justice. As we have discussed earlier, Communists since the Russian Revolution have recognized the power of focusing on racial discrimination to deconstruct American society. Social justice thinkers consider racism unjust mainly because the social and economic treatment majority communities give minorities is unfair. Thus, social and economic disadvantages based on skin color imposed by the majority of citizens are the heart of the argument against racial discrimination. All right-thinking persons would undoubtedly agree that skin color is not a characteristic justifying the exclusion of minority races from the equal opportunity to live freely, compete, and benefit economically from their full participation in society. But under the rubric of neo-Marxism, social justice ideologues demand more than equal opportunity. As we will see in the next chapter, social justice idealogues require negating majority white privilege. These ideologues also insist upon the redistribution of economic and social benefits to advantage minorities preferentially as partial reparation for the harm done to them by their history of slavery and racial discrimination.

French economist Thomas Piketty, a self-avowed socialist, in his 2021 book *A Brief History of Equality* displays a subtle Hegelian bias. He wrote: "Between 1780 and 2020, we see developments tending toward greater equality of status, property, income, genders, and races within most regions and societies on the planet, and to a certain extent when we compare these societies on the global scale."[1335] Again, all right-thinking persons would embrace the concept of sharing the wealth. But when establishing equality requires government-forced redistribution of income measures, we begin to appreciate the destructive aspects inherent to equating justice with fairness. The book's last chapter, "Toward a Democratic, Ecological, and Multicultural Socialism," warned Western powers that by persisting "in defending an obsolete, hypercapitalist model,"[1336] they will never attain the utopia of social equality Piketty envisions. Piketty insisted the best political model to achieve equality among social classes is "democratic socialism," a code word masking the neo-Marxist principles that underlie Piketty's analysis.[1337]

Applying principles of justice as fairness, two Columbia University sociologists developed an income-redistribution system aimed at destroying capitalism as a precondition to establishing equality. On May 2, 1966, professor of social work Richard A. Cloward and his then-research associate Frances Fox Piven wrote a pivotal article in *The Nation*, articulating "a strategy to end poverty."[1338] In what became known as the Cloward–Piven strategy, the paper argued a revolutionary approach to mobilizing the poor through class warfare against capitalist forces viewed as exploiting labor and oppressing the poor. David Horowitz, a long-time student of leftist political movements in the United States, characterized the Cloward–Piven strategy as seeking "to hasten the fall of capitalism by overloading the government bureaucracy with a flood of impossible demands, thus pushing society into crisis and economic collapse."[1339]

Truthfully, nothing is fair about life. Each of the billions of humans on this planet arrives at a particular time, in a specific place, to a particular set of economic and social realities. Each person at birth has a specific set of intellectual and physical capabilities. Each human who has ever lived on this planet is unique, endowed with time, circumstances, and gifts no other human has ever shared identically. The only equality we have at birth involves God-bestowed rights to life, liberty, and the pursuit of happiness. Our equality rests in equal opportunity while our material circumstances vary dramatically. The majesty of God's creation is that all persons are valued and needed. Jean-Paul Sartre sipping his espresso and smoking his cigarette in a Paris outdoor café required someone to grow, harvest, and process the coffee beans and tobacco plants on which his momentary pleasures depended. By human nature, we are not equal except by spiritual qualities. Rawls's concept of "justice as fairness" is seductive in that no right-thinking person wants to force inequality on their neighbors. But his conception functions primarily to advance Hegelian negation in that a capitalist society advances materially because a capitalist society rewards achievement. When people have no personal incentive to achieve, or when the benefits of achievement are distributed to those who do not achieve, the motivation required for economic and social progress is diminished.

In his 1944 book *The Road to Serfdom*, Austrian economist Friedrich Hayek quoted Alexis de Tocqueville on the distinction between democracy and equality. "Democracy and socialism have nothing in common but one word: equality," de Tocqueville wrote. "But notice the difference: while democracy seeks equality in liberty, socialism seeks equality in restraint and servitude."[1340] In his book, Hayek explained how viewing justice as fairness is nothing but an ideological narrative crafted to have us walk willingly into serfdom:

> A confusion largely responsible for the way in which we are drifting into things which nobody wants must be cleared up. This confusion concerns nothing less than the concept of socialism itself. It may mean, and is often used to describe, merely the ideals of social justice, greater equality, and security, which are the ultimate aims of socialism. But it means also the particular method by which most socialists hope to attain these ends and which many competent people regard as the only methods which they can be fully and quickly attained. In this sense socialism means the abolition of private enterprise, of private ownership of the means of production, and the creation of a system of "planned

economy" in which the entrepreneur working for profit is replaced by a central planning body.[1341]

Hayek again quoted Alexis de Tocqueville, pointing out that "democratic socialism" is an oxymoron in that democracy has nothing to do with socialism. He introduced this point by noting: "Only under the influence of the strong democratic currents preceding the revolution of 1848 did socialism begin to ally itself with the forces of freedom. But it took the new 'democratic socialism' a long time to live down the suspicions aroused by its antecedents. Nobody saw more clearly than De Tocqueville that democracy as an essentially individualistic institution stood in irreconcilable conflict with socialism."[1342] After this introduction, Hayek quoted de Tocqueville saying: "Democracy extends the sphere of individual freedom, socialism restricts it. Democracy attaches all positive value to each man; socialism makes each man a mere agent, a mere number."[1343]

Hayek correctly argued that the legitimate principle of "equality before law" is incompatible "with any activity of the government deliberately aiming at material or substantive equality of different people, and that any policy aiming directly at a substantive ideal of distributive justice must lead to the destruction of the Rule of Law."[1344] Hayek's logic is sound. "To produce the same result for different people, it is necessary to treat them differently," he explained. "It cannot be denied that the Rule of Law produces economic inequality—all that can be claimed for it is that this inequality is not designed to affect particular people in a particular way."[1345] He argued against the principle of "privilege" that would give particular people particular advantages, such in the past deemed that "landed property were reserved to members of the nobility."[1346] But to have the state rectify this injustice by "interfering" to punish the nobility by seizing their land for the poor is a step toward serfdom, not an advancement of justice or fairness. Hayek also correctly observed that Marxists achieve power by appealing to aggrieved minorities by promising to establish a more plentiful economy for all "to justify the privileges they promised to their supporters."[1347] The result of achieving totalitarian control is not utopia. As we have seen in previous chapters regarding both Stalin's Leninist Russia and Mao's Communist China, the result is an oppressive restriction of freedoms that ended in famine, killing millions of supporters the Marxists had promised to save.

Today's woke social justice warriors have expanded the war on inequality beyond racial discrimination to apply equally to all self-actualized identities, regardless of how bizarre many self-identified identities appear to those with traditional Judeo-Christian values. Rawls was concerned that we eliminate primarily economic and social discrimination. But the Frankfurt School established self-actualization as the standard of utopian liberalization. Thus, even microaggressions involving pronoun use are punishable. Why? Insensitive speech is discriminatory because microaggression mistreats the offended person. Suppose Rawls were required to expand his understanding of unequal treatment beyond economic and social discrimination to include microaggressions. In that case, it is hard to see how his veil of ignorance would function any differently than Habermas's discourse ethics.

Critical Race Theory

The scholarly and popular literature on critical race theory (CRT) is massive, tracing back to the work of Derrick Bell and the origin of critical legal theory at Harvard. CRT theorists have compiled a nearly five-hundred-page compilation of *The Key Writings That Formed the Movement*,[1348] starting with two articles Derrick Bell published in law journals, one in 1976[1349] and the other in 1980.[1350] As James Lindsay pointed out in his 2022 book *Race Marxism*, CRT is an ideological belief system formed by scholars and activists who aim to fundamentally negate the historical understanding of race, racism, and power in America. Lindsay explained CRT is "Race Marxism."[1351] CRT's goal is revolutionary, based on a "deep dissatisfaction with traditional civil rights discourse" that distinguishes CRT from "conventional liberal and conservative legal scholarship about race and inequality."[1352] CRT conducts an ideological offensive against civil rights reform, seeking instead to consolidate a Gramsci-like, power-based "common sense" understanding of race and racism in America that "defies both reason and contemporary reality" regarding race and racism in the United States.[1353] Lindsay further explained how "white supremacy" has replaced Marx's emphasis on class warfare as the grievance moving the neo-Marxist CRT dialectic:

> In other words, Critical Race Theory regards "white supremacy" as generative of a neo-Marxist superstructure called "structural racism" that it intends to analyze in essentially the same way classical Marxism analyzes economic class with a view to the "capitalist superstructure" that's upheld by "bourgeois values" (i.e., a vast conspiracy theory). For those unfamiliar with Marxist-speak, this means that, in fact, Critical Race Theorists hold a belief that racism is *systemic* and a *fundamental organizing prin-*

> *ciple of society* changeable *only by sociocultural revolution*. Not only that, this understanding of the relationship between race, racism, and power at the heart of Critical Race Theory is fundamentally a Marxist analysis utilizing "whiteness" as a scapegoat concept that runs in parallel to that of private property or capital in classical ("vulgar") Marxism.[1354]

The best way to comprehend CRT is to jump into the middle of CRT insanity. Kimberlé Williams Crenshaw, the Isidor and Seville Sulzbacher Professor of Law at Columbia Law School and a Distinguished Professor of Law at the University of California, Los Angeles, published a 1991 article in the *Stanford Law Review* entitled "Mapping the Margins: Intersectionality, Identity Politics, and Violence against Women of Color."[1355] In 1989, Crenshaw invented the term "intersectionality," one of the most critical CRT concepts. In set theory, intersectionality involves overlapping sets. For instance, in set theory, if the set of race grievances overlaps with the set of gender grievances, the black woman experiences intersectionality with more severe and complex discrimination grievances than a black person who is not a woman. Additional overlapping grievance sets increase the grievance quotient in the area of the Venn diagram where three or more grievance sets overlap. Thus, a black woman who has emigrated from a colonial country has an intersectionality quotient above that of a black woman who was not born in a colonial country and is not an immigrant to the United States. In her 1991 article, Crenshaw identified her purpose as redefining the examination of rape and battering to view male violence against minority women not simply in feminist or antiracist terms. Her goal was to consider male violence against women of color as an intersectional identity. She wrote:

> Focusing on two dimensions of male violence against women—battering and rape—I consider how the experiences of women of color are frequently the product of intersecting patterns of racism and sexism, and how these experiences tend not to be represented within the discourses of either feminism or antiracism. Because of their intersectional identity as both women *and* of color within discourses shaped to respond to one *or* the other, women of color are marginalized in both.[1356]

Earlier in the article, she stressed that the purpose of identity politics was not simply to identify discrimination grievances but to serve as "a source of strength, community, and intellectual development."[1357]

In postmodern terms, Crenshaw sought to create a "woman of color" identity as a separate and unique social construct. The examination of intraracial male violence against the "women of color" intersectional identity thus becomes a "resistance strategy" for the "disempowered" group "women of color" to occupy and assert a "positive discourse of self-identification."[1358] But as Lindsay asked, what racial synthesis does CRT exist to achieve? He answered his question: "Like all Marxists, they don't know. They call it 'racial justice,' which is the race-centered equivalent of Communism, and lacking any description, it exists with an awful lot of 'imagining.'"[1359] Lindsay noted CRT "advocates ruthlessly criticizing the aspects of society it wants to change while leveraging the political space opened up by all that negativity to push itself into power."[1360] He continued, arguing that CRT theorists "want to seize power to establish and enforce a racial-equity variant of Socialism, the managed state in which the racially critically conscious will guide society to a stateless, (racially) classless society by virtue of its awakened (Woke) consciousness."[1361] He concluded that all CRT needs to succeed is "Hegelian statist totalitarian control" to put their vague, unspecified utopia in place.[1362]

The 1619 Project

> In the meantime, for example, the Left uses America's history of slavery to delegitimatize the founding fathers. This targeting of the Founders is used to delegitimatize the nation they fought to create and the Constitution they formed to run it. As the narratives are structured to suggest, how can institutions created by such evil and fundamentally flawed white men be given respect today?
>
> Stephen Coughlin and Richard Higgins, *Re-Remembering the Mis-Remembered Left*, 2019[1363]

> The 1619 history serves as a tool to alter reality, to get students to disbelieve their lying eyes and "see" that this is a racist nation, one requiring an overhaul, an overhaul that begins with their psyches.
>
> Mary Grabar, *Debunking the 1619 Project: Exposing the Plan to Divide America, 2021*[1364]

In August 2019, Nikole Hannah-Jones, a former *New York Times* staff writer, launched the 1619 Project with an entire issue of the *New York Times Magazine*. That issue involved a compilation of writings commemorating the four hundredth anniversary of the British ship *White Lion* dropping anchor in Jamestown, bringing the first African slaves to arrive in colonial Virginia. In 2020, the Pulitzer Board announced they were awarding the Pulitzer Prize for Commentary to Hannah-Jones for creating the 1619 project.[1365] In 2021, Hanna-Jones edited a hardcover book, *The 1619 Project: A New Origin Story*, containing a series of essays and poems aimed at redefining the American history of the nation's founding in terms of slavery, with an emphasis on the continuing impact of slavery on the nation's racial relations.[1366] That same year, Hannah-Jones coauthored a children's book, *The 1619 Project: Born on the Water*.[1367] Hannah-Jones currently holds the Knight Chair in Race and Journalism at the Howard University Cathy Hughes School of Communications, where she founded the Center for Journalism and Democracy with funding provided by a $5 million grant from the MacArthur Foundation and a $5 million grant from the Ford Foundation.[1368]

As Hannah-Jones explained in the preface to the hardcover book, her goal with the 1619 project was to "reframe our understanding of U.S. history by considering 1619 as our country's origin point, the birth of our defining contradictions."[1369] Hannah-Jones's revisionist theory of the nation's founding stressed that left out of our nation's "founding mythology" is "the fact that one of the primary reasons the colonists decided to declare their independence from Britain was because they wanted to protect the institution of slavery." She continued: "The linking of slavery and the American Revolution directly challenged the cornerstone of national identity embedded in our public history, the narratives taught to us in elementary schools, museums and memorials, Hollywood movies, and in many scholarly works as well."[1370] Reframing the nation's birth from 1776 to 1619 was a radical idea, placing the preservation and perpetuation of enslaving black people at the center of our nation's raison d'être. By establishing slavery as the nation's founding purpose, Hannah-Jones negated the founding importance of the Declaration of Independence and Thomas Jefferson's bold statement on the birth of liberty that our rights are inalienable, bestowed by God, and not granted by the state.

The 1619 Project does not attempt to hide its neo-Marxist orientation. Matthew Desmond, a sociology professor at Princeton University, authored chapter 6, "Capitalism," in *The 1619 Project: A New Origin Story*. In this article, Desmond argued that America's unique brand of aggressive, discriminatory capitalism is a legacy of our founding principle, the protection of slavery. He writes:

> As a source of the fledgling nation's financial might, slavery shaped our political institutions and our founding documents, our laws governing private property and financial regulation, our management techniques, and accounting systems, and our economic systems and labor unions. By the eve of the Civil War, the Mississippi Valley was home to more millionaires per capita than anywhere else in the United States. Cotton grown and picked by enslaved workers was the nation's most valuable export. The combined value of enslaved people exceeded that of all the railroads and factories in the nation. In the mid-1830s, New Orleans boasted a denser concentration of banking capital than New York City. Small wonder, then, that "American slavery is necessarily imprinted on the DNA of American capitalism," as the historians Sven Beckert and Seth Rockman have written. The task now, they argue, is "cataloging the dominant and recessive traits" that have been passed down to us, tracing the unsettling and often unrecognized lines of descent by which America's national sin is even now being visited upon the third and fourth generations.[1371]

In chapter 18, "Justice," the concluding chapter to *The 1619 Project: A New Origin Story*, Hannah-Jones embraced CRT, arguing reparations are the only way to right the numerous injustices, including still existing economic and social inequality, that the institution of slavery has inflicted on black people. Her argument reduced to the insistence that America is a systematically racist nation that maintains a mythology of racial equality of rights that has never been reflected in material conditions. "The inclination to bandage over and move on is a definitive American feature when it comes to anti-Black racism and its social and material effects," she insisted.[1372] Hannah-Jones accused white America of a "remarkable imperviousness to facts when it comes to white advantage and architected Black disadvantage."[1373]

In response to the 1691 Project, President Trump established the President's Advisory 1776 Commission that, in January 2021, issued its own *1776 Report*.[1374] The goal of the 1776 Commission was to articulate the facts of our nation's founding. The *1776 Report* stressed:

> The principles of the American founding can be learned by studying the abundant documents contained in the record. Read fully and carefully, they show the American people have ever pursued freedom and justice, which are the political conditions for living well. To learn this history is

> to become a better person, a better citizen, and a better partner in the American experiment of self-government.[1375]

The *1776 Report* argues that "neither America nor any other nation has perfectly lived up to the universal truths of equality, liberty, justice, and government by consent. But no nation before America ever dared state those truths as the formal basis for its politics, and none has strived harder, or done more, to achieve them."[1376] In 2021, Mary Grabar, a resident fellow at the Alexander Hamilton Institute for the Study of Western Civilization, wrote *Debunking the 1619 Project: Exposing the Plan to Divide America*. In that book, Grabar documented that the origins of the 1619 Project trace back to the neo-Marxist history of America written by Howard Zinn, as discussed in chapter 1.[1377] Grabar argued in her previous book, *Debunking Howard Zinn: Exposing the Fake History That Turned a Generation against America*, "Howard Zinn's presentation of American history follows the old-style Marxist line." She noted that Zinn's rhetoric is drawn directly from William Z. Foster, the Stalin-era CPUSA official we discussed thoroughly in chapter 1.[1378] Grabar correctly asserted that Hannah-Jones intended to utilize her 1619 Project to indoctrinate history students in neo-Marxist lies about race in America to tear down America. We return to what we discussed in chapter 1: Bella Dodd, in her 1953 testimony before the House Un-American Activities Committee, Communists in the United States have long appreciated the divisive power of race in America and the need to begin anti-American indoctrination in the schools. It may have taken the radical Left seventy years, but in 2023, schools across the nation will be teaching students the fundamentals of the 1619 Project as if they were preaching from the Bible.

Peter W. Wood, the president of the National Association of Scholars, published a 2020 book, *1620: A Critical Response to the 1619 Project*. Wood explained his choice of book title as follows:

> I chose the title *1620* mainly as a riposte to the claim that the arrival of slaves in Virginia was the real founding of America. In November 1620, the passengers on the Mayflower drew up an agreement on how they would conduct their public affairs when they disembarked. That document, the Mayflower Compact, I argue—as have many others—pointed the way toward America's self-government. It is the beginning of ordered liberty in the New World. That is the vantage point from which I survey the 1619 Project. America never was a "slavocracy." It

> was and is humanity's great attempt to create a society based on principles of freedom and equality.[1379]

Wood also recognized that the aim of the 1619 Project was not to uncover the truth about slavery in America's founding but to accomplish the revolutionary goal of rubbing the tensions in America's racial past abrasively to promote replacing the Constitution with the doctrines of woke CRT Marxism. He wrote:

> The larger aim of the 1619 Project is to change America's understanding of itself. Whether it will ultimately succeed in doing so remains to be seen, but it certainly has already succeeded in shaping how Americans now argue about key aspects of our history. The 1619 Project aligns with the views on the progressive left who hate America and would like to transform it radically into a different kind of nation. Such a transformation would be a terrible mistake: it would endanger our hard-won liberty, our self-government, and our virtues as a people. Little is to be gained, however, by progressives and conservatives lobbing boulder-sized principles back and forth across the lines that divide them.[1380]

Wood objected to Hannah-Jones's lack of scholarship in presenting her arguments.

> The usual way for disputes about history to be resolved is for historians to present their best arguments, and their sources, in journal articles; each side can then examine the evidence for themselves and hammer out the truth. The 1619 Project evades this kind of transparency. The lead author, Nikole Hannah-Jones, who makes some of the most audacious claims, cites no sources at all: the project as presented in the [*New York Times*] magazine contains no footnotes, no bibliography, or other scholarly footholds.[1381]

Noting that the 1619 Project is not an ordinary piece of newspaper journalism, Wood charges the 1619 Project "is an attempt to wrest control of the grand narrative of American history."[1382] He objected that polemics are not the proper role of a newspaper. "The *Times* stumbled badly by presenting unsourced and unsupported assertions as the writing of history," Wood argued. "Much of the controversy that followed consisted of historians' challenging the claims and the *Times*' scrambling to find some plausible substantiating evidence."[1383]

However, criticism of the 1619 Project's many factual errors and undocumented claims largely misses the mark. Hannah-Jones's work has to be viewed from the perspective of Jean Baudrillard, as discussed in the previous chapter. As noted, in denying that the 1991 Gulf War had occurred, Baudrillard was not disputing that President George H. W. Bush assembled a thirty-five-country military coalition of nations to invade Iraq over the country's invasion of Kuwait. From Baudrillard's postmodernist perspective, all narratives about current or historical events are social constructs. Social constructs are subjectively fabricated stories about what is happening. Thus, Baudrillard viewed all the mainstream media reporting on the 1991 Gulf War to be nothing more than official propaganda, the view of reality governments involved in conducting the war advance to reframe the event for public consumption. As discussed in the previous chapter, Baudrillard stressed that at the end of the 1991 Gulf War, nothing much had changed. President Bush ordered General Norman Schwarzkopf from advancing on Bagdad, and Saddam Hussein remained in power. From this perspective, the 1619 Project is a neo-Marxist narrative constructed to reflect the values of a higher CRT truth, namely that slavery was and still is the fundamental organizing principle of America's founding document, as well as all subsequent Supreme Court decisions. The economic and social inequality between blacks and whites in America is an intended consequence of a society that proclaims liberty and equality for all, knowing this is a hollow promise for American citizens of color. Insisting America is a "systematically racist" country, CRT radicals see the white privilege of slaveholders as the operative principle in a nation dedicated to ensuring "justice as fairness" does not apply to minorities. Factual refutation does not jar 1619 Project true believers. Why? Because postmodern neo-Marxists and cultural Maoists view factual refutation as a product of a racist consciousness that should not be allowed. Please recall that Gramsci and Marcuse both argued that the culture of capitalism produces a capitalist "common sense" that shapes the narrative framing of all so-called facts.

The 1619 Project exists in an ideological dimension of CRT reality. For postmodern neo-Marxists and cultural Maoists, "reality" has nothing to do with Enlightenment assumptions that "documented facts" are testable by empirical verification. The interpretation of history in the 1619 Project has a meaning established only within the value judgments consistent with the higher understanding of a neo-Marxist, cultural Maoist utopia. As discussed in chapter 1, neo-Marxism and cultural Maoism involve a perversion of language in which utopian terms no longer translate into traditional Enlightenment era meanings. Thus, conservative historians seeking to refute the 1619 Project narrative find a disconnect when their arguments about facts and values fail to resonate or dissuade neo-Marxist and cultural Maoist true believers.

Woke values are meaningful only in a simulacra reality that postmodernists like Baudrillard would understand. "America First" MAGA ("Make America Great Again") supporters of Donald Trump have no clue how to navigate the bizarre phenomenological reality that is at the heart of wokism. Wokism exclusively operates within its particular language constructs. Through the university system, a generation of young Americans have been indoctrinated into wokism, educated not from traditional textbooks consistent with the Judeo-Christian tradition but from the hundreds of thousands of books and academic articles published by woke scholars and educators.

Queer Theory

> For example, while my partner has a female-ish body, she tends toward Banana Republic menswear (but recently bought her first skirt in two decades) and is often mistaken for a young boy. Her relationship with me doesn't exactly qualify her as either a lesbian or a heterosexual. Romantically, she is comfortable as butch or femme, top or bottom, or all the things in between. We have no name for this type of gender. Whatever she is, it is assumed not to exist. It is silenced. She, in fact, is often silenced when she tries to explain herself to others. She is denied the words with which to tell her story, to communicate something as basic and fundamental as *this is who I am, how I see myself, how I want you to see me.*
>
> Riki Wilchins, *Queer Theory, Gender Theory: An Instant Primer*, 2004.[1384]

One of the most influential authors in critical gender studies is Judith Butler. She was born in 1956 in Cleveland, Ohio. Her Wikipedia page reads: "In 1993, Butler began teaching at the University of California, Berkeley, where they have served, beginning in 1998, as the Maxine Eliot Professor in the Department of Comparative Literature and the Program of Critical Theory. They are also the Hanna Arendt Chair at the European Graduate School." A note on the Wikipedia page explains that Butler uses "she/her" and "they/them" as pronouns. But in 2020,

Butler explained the preference of "they/them" for consistency. The use of non-sex-identifying pronouns is a central demand of queer theory. Thus, when Wikipedia explains that "they" began teaching at Berkeley in 1993, the sentence means that Butler started working at Berkeley in 1993. The pronoun "they" is plural, but the reference is singular—that is, to Butler and no one else.

In her seminal 1990 book, *Gender Trouble: Feminism and the Subversion of Identity*,[1385] Butler distinguished that gender and sex were not equivalent terms. Butler defined sex as a person's biological makeup, consisting of male or female sex organs and internal sex organs. She distinguished that gender was a cultural construct identifying a person's sexual inclinations. Thus, Butler insisted gender was not binary (i.e., male or female) but involved a spectrum of possible orientations. Butler insisted her worldview was more post-structural than postmodern. But for this discussion, the distinction between "postmodern" and "post-structural" is highly technical. Both "postmodern" and "post-structural" are nearly synonymous terms. Each term emphasizes viewing reality as a linguistically formed construct. Structuralism is a social sciences theory and methodology that understands elements of culture and society through the network of relationships that define how the particular cultural or societal element interacts with other elements. Butler's influential conclusion was that gender is understood not by examining how sexual elements in culture or society network and interact but through performative acts over time. Butler insisted the only valid methodology to comprehend gender involved internalizing her understanding of how performative acts define gender. This insistence leads to a convoluted discussion of transgender performative acts. In *Gender Trouble*, Butler wrote:

> The performance of drag plays upon the distinction between the anatomy of the performer and the gender that is being performed. But we are actually in the presence of three contingent dimensions of significant corporeality: anatomical sex, gender identity, and gender performance. If the anatomy of the performer is already distinct from the gender of the performer, and both of those are distinct from the gender of the performance, then the performance suggests a dissonance not only between sex and performance, but sex and gender, and gender and performance. As much as drag creates a unified picture of "woman" (which its critics often oppose), it also reveals the distinctness of those aspects of gendered experience which are falsely naturalized as a unity through the regulatory fiction of heterosexual coherence. In imitating gender, drag implic-

> itly reveals the imitative structure of gender itself—as well as its contingency. Indeed, part of the pleasure, the giddiness of the performance is in the recognition of a radical contingency in the relation between sex and gender in the face of cultural configurations of casual unities that are regularly assumed to be natural and necessary. In the place of the law of heterosexual coherence, we see sex and gender denaturalized by means of a performance which avows their distinctness and dramatizes the cultural mechanism of their fabricated unity.[1386]

The quoted paragraph is typical of the convoluted writing that generally characterizes critical theory. The takeaway for our purposes is that, according to Butler, gender is a behavioral characteristic, such that sexual identity manifests through the culturally understood sexual behaviors that identify the particular nature of a person's sexual inclinations. As the above-quoted paragraph indicates, transgender males in drag are challenging because their gender performance is a staged performance that acts out or imitates female sexuality as a parody. For Butler, sex at birth is not determinative of gender. A person born male may define their gender as female, and a person born female may define their gender as male. In Butler's term, sex is a physical term that refers primarily to genital organs, while gender is a mental (or identity) term that refers to the acts in which a person engages that display their sexual orientation.

Critical gender theory (CGT) has embraced the common parlance of "Queer Theory." Although initially an offensive term, "queer" has come to mean anyone whose sexual identification does not fall neatly into binary distinctions of male or female. The initials LGBT identify the initial grouping of queer categories that emerged after the publication of Butler's book *Gender Trouble*. The LGBT initials stand for lesbian, gay, bisexual, and transgender. Now, more than three decades after the publication of *Gender Trouble*, the initial list has expanded to a longer string of initials: LGBTQI. In this expanded version, the initial "Q" stands for "queer," and "I" stands for "intersex."[1387] Intersex is a term that applies to those born with sex markers (i.e., genitals, hormones, or chromosomes) that are neither male nor female. Written "LGBTQI+" the acronym opens to additional, perhaps yet to be defined, genders.

The University of California, Riverside, has published a long list of terms in an extensive list of CGT terminology. The UC Riverside eleven-page list notes that intersex people are "sometimes defined as having 'ambiguous' genitalia."[1388] The list does not define the term hermaphrodite. The UC Riverside staff compiling the CGT terminology list consider intersex a more inclusive set of sexual identities that would include hermaphrodite as a subset. Chapter 5 discussed hermaphrodites as a sexual term with occult implications identifying those born with both male and female sex organs. Evidently, in modern CGT terminology, the highest state of Marcuse's "polymorphic sexuality" moves beyond transforming eros into a hermaphrodite unisex. In a world where the list of imaginable gender identities may be unlimited, the postgenderism transformation of eros involves all possible multivariate sexual identities evolved into a universal intersex of "ambiguous genitalia."

In 2018, Marieta Pehlivanova published an article in the *International Journal of Sexual Health*, coauthored by colleagues in the Division of Perceptual Studies, Department of Psychiatry and Neurobehavioral Sciences at the University of Virginia, School of Medicine in Charlottesville, Virginia. The article was titled "Childhood Gender Nonconformity and Children's Past-Life Memories." The article described a study of childhood gender nonconformity (GNC) involving 469 children reporting past-life memories. The study concluded that children "who remembered a life involving a different natal sex were much more likely to exhibit GNC than children who remembered a same-sex life."[1389] In 2008, Kathleen C. Gerbasi, an assistant professor in the Social Science Division, Psychology at the Niagara County Community College in Sanborn, New York, and a group of colleagues published a paper in *Society and Animals*. The article, entitled "Furries from A to Z (Anthropomorphism to Zoomorphism)," identified a psychological condition the authors termed "species identity disorder," in which humans develop an identity "other than human."[1390] In 2016, Pê Fiejó, a graduate student in rhetoric at the University of California, Berkeley, published an article on Academia.edu entitled "Doctors Herding Cats: The Misadventures of Modern Medicine and Psychology with NonHuman Identities."[1391] Fiejó traced through popular and psychological literature the history of human beings feeling as if they were a nonhuman species trapped in a human body. In 1997, Patrick Califia, a bisexual, transgender man known for writing gay erotic literature, wrote: "I'm never sure if I have gender dysphoria or species dysphoria. I often try to explain that I'm really a starfish trapped in a human body and I'm very new to your planet."[1392]

Neither CRT nor CGT aim to make race or sexual orientation disappear as an issue in America. On the contrary, CRT and CGT emphasize racial and sexual tensions to destroy traditional American culture. In attacking "white privilege," CRT's value system elevates people of color to the first rank. By saying people of color deserve reparation payments to erase the horrific crime of slavery, CRT gives racial preference to people of color, elevating non-white minorities above whites as more deserving of the right to social and economic advancement. Similarly, by insisting that an infinite variety of sexual orientations must be considered normal, CGT elevates the LGBT community to a preferred social position. Today, as the CGT ideology has become firmly entrenched in universities and government bureaucracies across the land, transgender activists are pushing for the right to introduce a CGT agenda into elementary schools, starting at the kindergarten level. We have reached a point where gender is a purely subjective self-defined identity, and the CGT agenda has advanced to the point where there is no objective reality to gender.

Dr. Michelle Forcier is a medical doctor with a master of public health degree, an associate professor of pediatrics, and assistant dean of admissions at the Warren Alpert Medical School of Brown University. She also serves as faculty to the National LGBTQIA+ (Lesbian, Gay, Bisexual, Transexual, Queer, Intersex, Asexual) and Health Education Center.[1393] Appearing in filmmaker and author Matt Walsh's documentary *What Is a Woman?*, Dr. Forcier said prepubescent children are ready for transgender hormone therapy "whenever they ask for it." In the documentary, Dr. Forcier explained: "That [the prepubescent child asking for transgender hormone therapy] could be a kiddo who is just starting puberty and panicking because they're just getting breast buds, or their penis is getting bigger and busier, and they're worried about all kinds of masculine changes." She claimed that physicians can prescribe puberty blockers safely, claiming puberty blockers are "completely reversible" and "don't have permanent effects."[1394] Among pharmaceutical drugs prescribed to block premature puberty is the prescription medicine Lupron Depot (leuprolide acetate), which also treats endometriosis and prostate cancer and chemically castrates sex offenders.

Gender theorist and political activist Riki Wilchins, in her 2004 book *Queer Theory, Gender Theory: An Instant Primer*, noted that women and gay rights advocates "made phenomenal mainstream progress in the 1970s and the 1980s." But she correctly observed the subsequent importance of the transgender movement. "But in the 1990s, gender advocacy received an incredible infusion of energy from two sources: the unexpected rise of an energetic transgender rights movement, and the amazing conquest of academia by postmodernism, particularly queer theory."[1395] She stressed that the term "transgender" has expanded beyond defining merely cross-dressers to "include anyone who is gender variant or gender non-conforming."[1396] Thus, "transgender" today has created a "reverse-hierarchy," forming "around who is *most transgressive* and therefore *least privileged*. As one friend put it, 'Transsexuals should come first because they are the most oppressed.'"[1397]

Reading *Queer Theory, Gender Theory* makes clear the turmoil coming with consistent, generally agreed concepts as fundamental as answering the question: What is a woman? Wilchins criticized assertions that "biology is not destiny" or that "one is not born a woman but becomes one." She charged that these statements "require women to assume maternity and femininity" such that "essence of selfhood, in effect reducing women to another stereotype, even if this time it is an entirely positive—or even 'superior'—one."[1398] Instead, Wilchins grappled with "transgender male, boy-identified dyke, or intersectional female" [1399] as genders "on the margins of identity."[1400] She insisted queer theory and gender theory have adapted to accept these subjectively identified gender identities so as "to make the offending messy realities disappear."[1401]

But to further examine the "messy realities" of postmodern gender identities, let's take the case of a serial killer who derives sexual pleasure from murdering women and cannibalizing their corpses. If contemporary queer and gender theories demand acceptance of "This is who I am, how I see myself, how I want *you* to see *me*,"[1402] are there limits? Sexually motivated serial killers are the type of psychopathic murderers that author Thomas Harris wrote about in his two fictitious books *Red Dragon*[1403] and *The Silence of the Lambs*.[1404] Richard Chase, nicknamed the "Vampire of Sacramento," was a well-known serial killer, cannibal, and necrophile.[1405] Minimizing the focus on transgender serial killers is a current movement in critical psychology. Students of the subject examine "psychiatry's construction of gender diversity and sexual violence" including that involving transgender persons, to question "whether it is violence that the profession finds so intriguing, or the gender nonconformity it represents."[1406] This normalization of gender-based sexual violence resonates with the tendency of critical theory to see perpetrators of sexual violence not as criminals but as victims of society's abnormal binary gender concepts.

Queer totalitarian ideologues are determined to turn the transgender agenda into a state-protected right. On September 26, 2022, the *New York Times* reported that an increasing number of teenage women born with female genitalia are choosing to have breast-removal surgery. The newspaper described the story of Michael, seventeen years old, who had breast removal surgery performed by a plastic surgeon in Miami. The moment arrived for Michael to remove the bandages from his newly flattened chest. "After years of squeezing into compression undershirts to conceal his breasts, the teenager was overcome with relief that morning last December," the *New York Times* noted. "Wearing an unbuttoned shirt, he posed for photos with his mother and the surgeon, Dr. [redacted by author], happy to share his bare chest with the doctor's large following on social media."[1407] The *New York Times* reporter, Azeen Ghorayshi, explained: "Michael is part of a very small but growing group of transgender adolescents who have had top surgery, or breast removal, to better align their bodies with their experience of gender. Most of these teenagers have also taken testosterone and changed their name, pronouns or clothing style."[1408]

On April 6, 2021, the Arkansas legislature overrode Republican Governor Asa Hutchinson's veto of legislation prohibiting "'sex reassignment' surgery" or hormone-blocker treatments for minors. The bill expressly prohibited physicians from performing or rendering "'gender transition procedures' on residents under age 18" and banned the expenditure of taxpayer dollars on sex change medical procedures performed on minors.[1409] Once enacted, gender activists challenged Arkansas's Save Adolescents from Experimentation (SAFE) Act in federal district court. The following month, on May 25, 2021, the ACLU (American Civil Liberties Union) filed a suit in federal district court challenging the "ban on health care for transgender youth" to access "medically necessary health care."[1410] On July 13, 2021, a coalition of seventeen state attorneys general led by Alabama Attorney General Steve Marshall filed an amicus brief in the U.S. District Court for the Eastern District of Arkansas. The amicus brief argued that "Arkansas was well within its rights" to prohibit experimental, life-threatening medical procedures for children and adolescents.[1411] The seventeen-state amicus brief began by stating: "Like Arkansas, amici are concerned about the surge in recent years of children suffering from gender dysphoria and other forms of gender-related psychological distress. And like Arkansas—and like Plaintiffs—amici are concerned because these vulnerable are suffering greatly and need help."[1412] The amicus brief continued:

> Spend just a little time with the scientific literature in this field and a few things become abundantly clear: the science in this area is largely unsettled; nearly everyone agrees that far more research is needed; and the currently popular approach to care in the United States is not supported

> by well-researched, evidence-based studies. What is known, however, is that most cases of gender dysphoria in children resolve naturally with time, and it's impossible to know ahead of time whose dysphoria will persist into adulthood and whose won't."[1413]

The amicus brief continued:

> Yet the evidence also shows that nearly all children whose gender dysphoria is treated with puberty blockers to "buy time" will proceed to take cross-sex hormones and seek other medical interventions with irreversible, lifelong consequences—complications such as infertility, loss of sexual function, increased risk of heart attack and stroke, bone-density problems, risk of altered brain development, social harms from delayed puberty, and mental health concerns. Sadly, but for the "gender-affirming" "care" they received, most of these children would neither suffer from gender dysphoria nor from lifelong medical harm as adults.[1414]

As this manuscript is being written, *Brandt v. Rutledge* is still being litigated in the Arkansas U.S. District Court.

On October 23, 2022, President Biden gave an interview to Now This News in which he said it was "wrong" for states to ban surgeries and hormone treatment for children who say they want to change their sex.[1415] On October 24, 2022, an appeals court in Indiana upheld a trial court's decision to remove from a family home a child because the parents refused to acknowledge their child's insistence on a transgender identity. The trial court found that as a consequence of the parents' unwillingness to accept their child's sexual uncertainty, the state had the right to remove the child from the care and protection of the child's parents. The court case involved a report that the Indiana Department of Child Services (DCS) received "alleging the mother was verbally and emotionally abusing [their] then-sixteen-year-old child by using rude and demeaning language toward [the] child regarding [the] child's transgender identity, and as a result, [the] child had thoughts of self-harm." If courts can remove a child from the parents' custody because the parents' refusal to "affirm" the child's gender identity is "abuse," we as a society are on a dangerous path of making state wards of all minor children who radical queer ideologues coach to question their sexual identity.[1416]

In her Senate confirmation hearings, Justice Ketanji Brown Jackson could not answer Senator Marsha Blackburn's (R-TN) simple question:

Senator Blackburn: Can you provide a definition of the word "woman"?

Justice Jackson: "No, I can't."

Senator Blackburn: "You can't?"

Justice Jackson: "I'm not a biologist."[1417]

In a statement following the exchange, Senator Blackburn said, "It's a simple question. What is a woman? It is telling when a nominee, supported by far-left advocacy groups, will not even answer the question."[1418] We now have a justice on the Supreme Court who is obviously an adherent to the ideology of queer critical theory.

Liberation Theology

Critical theory has also had a substantial impact on Christianity. In the Catholic Church, the "liberation theology" movement traces back to the second Latin American bishops' conference held in Medellín, Colombia, in 1968. At that conference, the attending bishops authored a document that explained that Jesus Christ had aimed his teachings to affirm the rights of the poor while criticizing industrial nations who enriched themselves at the expense of developing countries.[1419] The liberation theology movement views Jesus Christ as a socialist concerned about social injustice. Thus, liberation theology shifts the traditional understanding that the mission of Jesus Christ on earth was to redeem the human race from original sin, opening the gates of Heaven to those who had led moral lives devoted to the service of God.

Peruvian Gustavo Gutiérrez, a Dominican priest, published the seminal text of Catholic liberation theology, a book entitled *Teología de la liberación* (*A Theology of Liberation*) in 1971. In his book, Gutiérrez explained how liberation theology views the role of Jesus Christ:

> Christ is presented as the one who brings us to liberation. Christ the Savior liberates from sin, which is the ultimate root of all disruption of friendship and all injustice and oppression. Christ makes humankind truly free, that is to say, he enables us to live in communion with him; and this is the basis for all human fellowship.[1420]

Gutiérrez argued that Hispanic-speaking countries in the Western Hemisphere, including the United States, are demanding the Catholic Church to take an active role in the social justice movement. He wrote:

> Further, in the face of the immense misery and injustice, ought not the Church especially in those areas such as Latin America where it has great social influence—intervene more directly and abandon the field of lyrical pronouncements? In fact, the Church has done so at times, but always clarifying that this was a merely supplementary role. The scope and omnipresence of the problem would seem to render this argument inadequate in our day. More recent options, such as that offered at Medellín, have transcended these limitations and now require another theological foundation.[1421]

Gutiérrez concluded:

> In short, political options have become radicalized, and the specific commitments which Christians are assuming demonstrate the inadequacies of the theological-pastoral model of the distinction of planes.

Rather than separate church and state, Gutiérrez argued for a politically active Catholic Church that would seek to fight social injustice along neo-Marxist lines.

Gutiérrez ends up reinterpreting the New Testament as a call to the Catholic faithful and clergy to become political activists. Here is how he reinterpreted the Beatitudes (Luke 6:20):

> "Blessed are you poor for yours is the Kingdom of God" does not mean, it seems to us: "Accept your poverty because later this injustice will be compensated for in the Kingdom of God." If we believe that the Kingdom of God is a gift which is received in history, and if we believe as the eschatological promises—so charged with human and historical content—indicate to us, that the Kingdom of God necessarily implies the reestablishment of justice in this world, then we must believe that Christ says that the poor are blessed because the Kingdom of God has begun: "The time has come; the Kingdom of God is upon you" (Mark 1:15). In other words, the elimination of the exploitation and poverty that prevent the poor from being fully human has begun; a Kingdom of justice which goes even beyond what they could have hoped for has begun. They are blessed because the coming of the Kingdom will put an end to their poverty by creating a world of brotherhood. They are blessed because the Messiah will open the eyes of the blind and will give bread to the hungry. Situated in a prophetic perspective, the text in Luke uses the term *poor* in the tradition of the first major line of thought we have studied: poverty is an evil and therefore incompatible

> with the Kingdom of God, which has come in its fullness into history and embraces the totality of human experience.[1422]

Gutiérrez thus succeeded in writing the teachings of Jesus Christ into the Hegelian dialectic. He transforms the redemption and salvation message Christ taught into a neo-Marxist utopian call to crush economic and social oppression in a revolutionary movement aimed at abolishing all forms of social injustice, including poverty, in the here and now.

On August 26, 2022, Cardinal Vincenzo Paglia, president of the Pontifical Academy for Life, announced on an Italian news television program that the Catholic Church had no interest in opposing Italy's Law 194. That law, enacted in 1978, legalized abortions in the first trimester and allowed them afterward if the pregnancy endangered the mother's life or if doctors found "serious abnormalities or malformations" in the unborn child. "I believe that at this point Law 194 is a pillar of our social life," Paglia said. "In my opinion, I have written as much, I would like to see more emphasis on the part that is hardly spoken of, namely, the right to motherhood, to see our country grow, in the face of the drama of a generational imbalance that is quite dramatic." When the interviewer pressed if Law 194 was up for debate, Cardinal Paglia responded, "No, absolutely not."[1423]

On September 6, 2022, Canadian politician Christopher Skeet wrote an article in *American Thinker* entitled "The Next Pope Should at Least Be Catholic."[1424] Skeet wrote:

> Pope Francis doesn't like America. Pope Francis doesn't like capitalism. It is unclear whether Pope Francis even likes Catholicism. Whatever the case may be, he seems to be doing everything he can to dissuade Catholics from remaining in the Church, and to keep prospective Catholics from joining.[1425]

He pointed out the following:

- "[Pope Francis] blamed[1426] capitalism for much of the world's 'pain, death, and destruction,' and referred to it as the 'dung of the devil.' He called for 'structural change' and a 'just distribution' of land, lodging, and labor."
- "[Pope Francis] sneered[1427] that market capitalism and neoliberalism are 'magic theories,' and blamed them not only for the spread of coronavirus, but also for inequality in general."

- "[Pope Francis] blamed[1428] the ghastly murders of Europeans by Muslim immigrants, as well as the creation of ISIS, on the world's alleged worship of the 'god of money,' and referred to capitalism as the 'terrorism against all of humanity.'"[1429]

Skeet summarized his conclusion about Pope Francis's politics: "Pope Francis has a rigid, inflexible worldview, born of the putrid liberation theology upon which he was weaned in Peronist Argentina. This worldview holds that capitalism is evil, and the United States is its most sinful devotee."[1430]

Social justice critical theory ideology has also penetrated the Protestant religions. In 2019, a resolution was introduced at the annual Southern Baptist Convention affirming critical race theory and intersectionality.[1431] In the wake of the George Floyd protests, several U.S. Protestant churches active in the era of slavery embraced the social justice movement, pledging millions of dollars to race-related reparations. Among these Protestant churches are "the Episcopal Diocese of Texas, which acknowledges that its first bishop in 1859 was a slaveholder, and a New York Episcopal Church, which erected a plaque noting the building's creation in 1820 was made possible by the wealth resulting from slavery."[1432]

Another essential root of liberation theology is black liberation theology. A core belief of black liberation theology is that the historical Jesus Christ was black and, as such, the ancient Romans oppressed Christ when the Romans, the white imperialists of their day, colonized Israel. Black liberation theologians see the biblical teachings of Jesus Christ as radical revolutionary teachings, delivering a social and political message that black people need to overthrow white imperial oppression to achieve liberation. Today, black liberation theology advocates the overthrow of America as a nation with a history of enslaving and colonizing black people in modern ghettoes of urban poverty. Thus, black liberation theology reinterprets the biblical teachings of Jesus Christ to advance a revolutionary racial message.

Conclusion: "White Privilege," the Ultimate Villain

The concept of "white privilege" originated not with today's critical race theory or Black Lives Matter but with Theodore ("Ted") William Allen. Born in 1919, Allen became radicalized during the Great Depression. He joined the CPUSA in the 1930s and spent three years as a coal miner in West Virginia until a back injury forced him to leave. Allen arrived in New York in 1948, where he taught classes in economics at the CPUSA-founded Jefferson School of Social Science. In 1958, when Allen left the CPUSA, a revolution was no longer viable in the postwar prosperity. He spent his last forty years researching the role of white supremacy in U.S. history, resulting in his two-volume publication titled *The Invention of the White Race*.[1433]

Ted Allen and Noel Ignatiev were both members of the radical Students for a Democratic Society (SDS) movement in the 1960s. Allen and Ignatiev were prime movers of the Radical Youth Movement (RYM) that broke with the SDS in 1969, declaring itself the "real SDS." Following Allen and Ignatiev's lead, the RYM announced the race issue focusing on "white privilege" was the key to producing the desired Communist revolution.

With political philosophers like Rawls advancing a radical redefinition of the liberal social contract tradition to insist justice is fairness, we have come full circle. Although Rawls wanted to modernize Kant's categorical imperative, he ended up powering Habermas's discourse requiring us to accept as normal all personally defined identities, regardless of how idiosyncratic, bizarre, and shifting those subjective realities may be. The reality of identity politics is anarchy, pure and simple. Identity politics is perhaps the most effective psycho-reality narrative designed to destroy the existing order. Identity politics, however, cannot create the promised neo-Marxist, cultural Maoist utopia. Living in an identity politics utopia amounts to living in a reality in which the inmates have taken over the management of the asylum.

CONCLUSION

Quo Vadimus? (Where Are We Going?)

Communism restores man to his sovereignty by the simple method of denying God.

—**Whittaker Chambers**, "Foreword in the Form of a Letter to My Children," *Witness*, 1952[1434]

Pope Leo XIII (papacy 1878–1903) had a vision of Satan's devastation on earth in our times. Monsignor Carl Vogl (1874–1941) related the legend of Leo XIII's vision and the prayer to St. Michael the Archangel as follows:

> May Christians learn to treasure the Prayer of St. Michael more than ever before. A rather peculiar circumstance induced Pope Leo XIII to compose this powerful prayer. After celebrating Mass one day he was in conference with the Cardinals. Suddenly he sank to the floor. Several doctors were summoned at once but found no sign of a pulse—the very life seemed to have ebbed away from the fragile and aging body. Suddenly he recovered and said: "What a horrible vision I have been shown!" He saw the ages to come, the seductive powers and ravings of the devils against the Church in every land. But St. Michael appeared in the moment of greatest distress and cast Satan and his cohorts back into the abyss of hell. Such was the occasion that caused Pope Leo XIII to prescribe this prayer for the universal Church.[1435]

Leo XIII's prayer to St. Michael reads as follows:

> Saint Michael, the Archangel, defend us in battle; be our protection against the wickedness and snares of the devil. May God rebuke him, we humbly pray, and do thou, O prince of the heavenly host, by the power of God, thrust into Hell, Satan and all the other evil spirits who prowl throughout the world, seeking the ruin of souls. Amen.[1436]

In 1886, Pope Leo XIII decreed that this prayer to St. Michael should be said at the end of every Mass throughout the universal Catholic Church. Pope Pius VI removed the prayer to St. Michael from Mass with the proclamation of Vatican II in 1963. Traditional Catholics see Pope Pius VI's ecumenical movement as an attempt to delude traditional Catholic theology and liturgy by Freemasons who had infiltrated the Catholic hierarchy. Saint Padre Pio once quipped about Pope Paul VI: "Courage, courage, courage! For the Church is already invaded by Freemasonry."[1437]

Father Domenico Pechenino was an Italian priest ordained in 1896. He rose to the position of major rector for the Oblates of the Virgin Mary, a position he held through World War II. In 1947, Father Pechenino submitted an article for the Italian newspaper *La Settimana del Clero* (*The Week of the Clergy*). The article was entitled "La Tragedia dei Tempi Nostri e l'Opera di Satana" ("The Tragedy of Our Times and the Work of Satan"). The article was written in two parts and published in two separate issues. Father Pechenino claimed to have special knowledge of Leo XIII's vision in the second part. He described the vision as follows:

> Permit me here to mention more than a little known fact which throws a vivid beam of light on the order of ideas that I mentioned. I have drawn the fact to a trusted source (and I am willing to reveal it, if required): and let each one weigh the consequence! I don't remember the precise year. It was a little after 1890. One morning, the great Pontiff, Leo XIII—who had already gained admiration of the entire civil world and the wrath of international freemasons—had celebrated Holy Mass, and was assisting at another Mass (for his thanksgiving) as usual. At a certain point, he seemed to straighten vigorously his head, fixing his gaze intensely on something that was above the head of the celebrant. He looked at it intently, without batting an eyelid, but with a sense of dread and wonder, becoming pale and fearful. Something strange, something significant was happening to him...

Father Pechenino continued:

> Finally, as if keeping it to himself, giving a light but energetic touch of his hand, he got up. He started heading toward his favorite study. His closest friends and assistants (*i familiari*) [*the familiar*] hastily and anxiously followed him. "Holy Father!" they solemnly cried out. "Do you not feel well? Do you need anything?" He responded: "No, nothing!" And he closed himself in his study. After a half hour, he called to the Secretary of the Sacred Congregation of Rites, and gave him a piece of paper, ordering him to make copies and to send it to all the Ordinaries of the world. What did it contain? The prayer which we recite at the end of the Mass (*cum popolo*) [*with the people*] imploring Mary and the fiery invocation to the Prince of heavenly powers, St Michael: "*Sancte Michaël, defend nos in proelio*" ["*Saint Michael, protect us in battle*"]... imploring God to drive him to hell, "*et in infernum detrude*!" ["*and cast him into hell*"].[1438]

Father Pechenino continued his description of Pope Leo XIII's vision, adding that in his vision, the pope witnessed a conversation between God and Satan:

> Then what happened? This is what happened. God had shown to the Vicar of his divine Son on earth, just like He did with Job. Satan was bragging that he had already devastated the Church on a large scale. In fact, there were tumultuous times for Italy, for many nations in Europe, and a bit around the world. The freemasons ruled, and governments hadn't become docile instruments. With the audacity of a boaster, Satan put a challenge to God—"And if you give me a little more freedom, you could see what I would do for your church!"—"What would you do?"—"I would destroy it."—"Oh, that would be something to see. How long would it take?"—"Fifty or sixty years."—"Have more freedom, and the time that you need. Then we'll see what happens."[1439]

The reference to the biblical book of Job puts Pope Leo XIII's vision into the context of God allowing Satan to reign free on earth to test the faith of believers like Job, a prosperous man of the times. Satan had taunted God that Job's faith was rooted in his prosperity. Satan wagered that if Job lost his possessions, family, children, and finally his health, Job would curse God. Pope Leo XIII's vision of God's discussion with Satan suggests we are now in a time when God has allowed Satan to reign on earth once again. Yesterday's Freemasons are today's godless "new world order" globalists. The suggestion is that today's neo-Marxist, cultural

Maoist social justice ideology is the great apostasy that will bring devastation to all nations of the world by negating Enlightenment's continuation of natural law philosophy.

Cardinal Carlo Viganò, the former apostolic nuncio from the Vatican to the United States, stated that supernatural powers are carrying out a globalist coup d'état aimed at destroying the traditional moral order. In an interview conducted by Dr. Armando Manocchia for Italian television on April 2, 2022, Cardinal Viganò said the following:

> We are facing a global coup that involves both civil society and the [Catholic] Church. Both are infiltrated and controlled by characters who use their power and the authority that derives from it, not for the purposes of the institutions they govern, but in order to destroy them. This crisis of authority must be denounced because the action of those who have reached the highest levels of leadership both of nations and of the Church is a subversive and criminal act.[1440]

In the interview, Viganò charged that the corrupt part of the Catholic Church, which he characterized as the "deep church," is "subservient to Satan, hates the Church as the Mystical Body of Christ, and intends to kill Her."[1441]

The point of the Garden of Eden story in Genesis is that Satan can seduce us to sin—that is, to commit evil. In biblical terms, we are a "fallen" species that must learn the distinction between "right" and "wrong." Equally important, we must make the moral decision to "do good" and "avoid evil." When Moses came down from Mount Sinai with the tablets on which God had written the Ten Commandments, he found the Jews worshiping a golden calf (Exodus 32:19). Moses smashed the tablets and destroyed the golden calf.

When Moses came down from the mountain for the second time, he carried the second set of stone tablets on which the finger of God had written the covenant in the form of the Ten Commandments (Exodus 20). The first commandment affirms monotheism, ruling out the possibility that different gods might have different moral rules. In the following two commandments, God instructs the Israelites to keep the Sabbath holy and to avoid taking the name of the Lord in vain. The following seven commandments instruct us to honor our fathers and mothers, not to steal, not to kill one another, not to commit adultery, not to lie, and not to covet each other's spouses or goods. These moral rules written on stone tablets by the finger of God did not require an advanced education or genius intelligence to comprehend. While technology advances with time, moral understanding does not pass from parent to child via genetics, nor does it advance in time. Moses's moral principles in Exodus are the same simple, commonsense rules of decent living a productive society follows even today.

The end days of the woke social justice utopia are dystopian. Governments and currencies collapse, mass numbers of people die through starvation and disease, and the world plunges into thermonuclear war. But the end of times need not be written this way. Getting the truth about neo-Marxism, cultural Maoism, and anarchy into print is an important first step. When enough people understand the critical theory lies that dominate this age of disinformation, we have a chance of becoming awake instead of woke. We today look upon the madness that descended over Europe as Hitler's Nazism battled with Stalin's Communism and we wonder how civilized people living in cultures considered advanced could possibly have descended into the horrors of World War II. The human species survived World War II, but it may not survive a thermonuclear World War III.

Pope Leo XIII would have envisioned today's postmodern woke culture as the best version of the Garden of Eden's "tree of knowledge" lie that Satan has ever constructed. Let us resolve to continue shining the light of truth to dispel the lies neo-Marxists, cultural Maoists, and anarchists would have us believe. Let us pray in the spirit of 2 Chronicles 7:14 that God hears our repentance for allowing America to descend into this madness. Let us move forward with certainty that this twenty-first century "woke" social justice popular delusion will soon pass from the face of the earth, never again to return. With God, all things are possible, and the hour is never too late for redemption.

ENDNOTES

INTRODUCTION

1 Charles Mackay, Extraordinary Popular Delusions and the Madness of Crowds (London: L. C. Page, 1932), preface to 1852 edition, xix–xx, at xix.

2 Stephen Coughlin and Richard Higgins, Re-Remembering the Mis-Remembered Left: The Left's Strategy and Tactics to Transform America, An Unconstrained Analytics Report (Washington, DC: Unconstrained Analytics, February 2019), version 1.2, updated July 2019, "Executive Summary," 156. Bold type in original.

3 The slogan "march through the institutions" is commonly attributed to Antonio Gramsci but was actually coined into a "succinct mission statement" by Marxist student activist Rudi Dutschke in the 1960s. See: Bobby Harrington, "The Long March through the Institutions of Society," Renew.org, n.d., *https://renew.org/the-long-march-through-the-institutions-of-society/*.

4 Jerome R. Corsi, The Truth about Energy, Global Warming, and Climate Change: Exposing Climate Lies in an Age of Disinformation (Nashville, TN: Post Hill Press, 2022).

CHAPTER 1

5 Coughlin and Higgins, Re-Remembering the Mis-Remembered Left, 2.

6 Thucydides, History of the Peloponnesian War, trans. Charles Foster Smith (Cambridge, MA: Harvard University Press, reprinted and revised, 1930), Book 3, 82, 4–5, pp. 144–145.

7 Josef Pieper, Abuse of Language—Abuse of Power (San Francisco: Ignatius Press, 1992), trans. Lothar Krauth (Kosel-Verlag, Munich, 1974), 32–33.

8 Trevor Loudon, "Communists and Race," Trevor Loudon Presents New Zeal, Shining the Torch for Freedom, blog, TrevorLoudon.com, March 25, 2019, *https://www.trevorloudon.com/2019/03/communists-and-race/*.

9 David Azerrad, PhD, "What the Constitution Really Says about Race and Slavery," Heritage.org, December 28, 2015, *https://www.heritage.org/the-constitution/commentary/what-the-constitution-really-says-about-race-and-slavery*.

10 Garry Wills, "The Words That Remade America: The Significance of the Gettysburg Address," The Atlantic, The Civil War Issue, November 23, 2011, *https://www.theatlantic.com/magazine/archive/2012/02/the-words-that-remade-america/308801/*. Wills expanded this article into the following book: Garry Wills, Lincoln at Gettysburg: The Words That Remade America (New York: Simon & Schuster, 1992).

11 Wills, Lincoln at Gettysburg, 90.

12 Ibid., 146–147.

13 Coughlin and Higgins, Re-Remembering the Mis-Remembered Left, 2. Bold type in original.

14 Abraham Lincoln, Second Annual Message to Congress, December 1, 1862, The American Presidency Project, Presidency.UCSB.edu, n.d., *https://www.presidency.ucsb.edu/documents/second-annual-message-9*.

15 "War Is the Health of the State: An Interview with Howard Zinn," Institute for Anarchist Studies, Perspectives on Anarchist Theory 7, no. 1, (Spring 2003): 1, 8–10, quotation at 10. Archived on the "Wayback Machine" by Paul Glavin and Chuck Morse at *http://www.cwmorse.org/archives/perspectives.on.anarchist.theory.vol7.no1-spring2003.pdf*.

16 Howard Zinn, A People's History of the United States, 1942–Present (New York: HarperCollins, 1980, 20th anniversary ed., 1999).

17 Ibid., chap. 2, "Drawing the Color Line," 23.

18 Ibid., 72.

19 Ibid., 73.

20 Ibid. Zinn explained that Jefferson's use of the phrase "all men are created equal" was "probably not a deliberate attempt to make a statement about women." But Zinn continued to insist that to Jefferson "women were beyond consideration as worthy for inclusion" because in 1776 women were "politically invisible." Quotations at 73.

21 Ibid., 89.

22 David Greenberg, "Agit-Prof: Howard Zinn's Influential Mutilations of American History," New Republic, March 18, 2013, *https://newrepublic.com/article/112574/howard-zinns-influential-mutilations-american-history*.

23 Jonathan M. Wiener, "Radical Historians and the Crisis in American History, 1959–1980," Journal of American History 76, no. 2 (September 1989): 399–436, *https://www.jstor.org/stable/1907976*.

24 Coughlin and Higgins, Re-Remembering the Mis-Remembered Left, 3.

25 Ibid.

26 Thucydides, History of the Peloponnesian War, 144–145.

27 Ibid.

28 John Wilson, "'The Customary Meanings of Words Were Changed'—Or Were They? A Note on Thucydides 3.82.4," Classical Quarterly 32, no. 1 (May 1982): 18–20, Cambridge University Press, *https://www.cambridge.org/core/journals/classical-quarterly/article/abs/customary-meanings-of-words-were-changed-or-were-they-a-note-on-thucydides-3824/D41C67034FFF652D6392E100B672AB4C*.

29 Ibid. Italics in original.

30 Ibid.

31 Ibid.

32 Coughlin and Higgins, Re-Remembering the Mis-Remembered Left, 2.

33 Hannah Knowles and Isaac Stanley-Becker, "Some Officers March and Kneel with Protesters, Creating Dissonant Images on Fraught Weekend of Uprisings," Washington Post, June 1, 2020, *https://www.washingtonpost.com/nation/2020/06/01/some-officers-march-kneel-with-protesters-creating-dissonant-images-fraught-weekend-uprisings/*.

34 Egan Millard, "Fire Causes Minor Damage to St. John's, the 'Church of the Presidents' in Washington, during Night of Riots," Episcopal News Service, June 1, 2020, *https://www.episcopalnewsservice.org/2020/06/01/fire-causes-minor-damage-to-st-johns-the-church-of-presidents-in-washington-during-night-of-riots/*. See also: Egan Millard, "St. John's Church in Washington Vandalized Again," Episcopal News Service, June 1, 2020, *https://www.episcopalnewsservice.org/2020/06/23/st-johns-church-in-washington-vandalized-again/*.

35 Karina Brown, "Portland DA Won't Pursue Charges against Most Protesters," Courthouse News Service, August 11, 2020, *https://www.courthousenews.com/portland-da-wont-pursue-charges-against-most-protesters/*.

36 Emma Colton, "District Attorney to Drop Charges against Hundreds of Portland Protesters," Washington Examiner, August 12, 2020, *https://www.washingtonexaminer.com/news/district-attorney-to-drop-charges-against-hundreds-of-portland-protesters*.

37 Coughlin and Higgins, Re-Remembering the Mis-Remembered Left, 4.

38 "Capitol Breach Cases," United States Attorney's Office, District of Columbia, Justice.gov, *https://www.justice.gov/usao-dc/capitol-breach-cases*.

39 Brian Naylor, "FACT CHECK: What Pence and Congress Can and Can't Do about the Election," National Public Radio, NPR.org, January 5, 2021, *https://www.npr.org/2020/12/22/949134479/congress-role-in-election-results-heres-what-happens-jan-6*.

40 Coughlin and Higgins, Re-Remembering the Mis-Remembered Left, 5. Bold type in original.

41 Ibid. Bold type in original.

42 Ibid. Bold type in original.

43 Pieper, Abuse of Language—Abuse of Power, 34–35. Italics in original.

44 Coughlin and Higgins, Re-Remembering the Mis-Remembered Left, 2.

45 Ibid. Bold type in original.

46 Ibid., 14. Bold type in original.

47 Ibid., 10. Bold type in original.

48 Ibid., 4. Bold type in original.

49 Helen Pluckrose and James Lindsay, Cynical Theories: How Activist Scholarship Made Everything about Race, Gender, and Identity—and Why This Harms Everybody (Durham, NC: Pitchstone Publishing, 2020), 32.

50 Ibid., 33.

51 Coughlin and Higgins, Re-Remembering the Mis-Remembered Left, 3.

52 Ibid. Bold type in original.

53 Ibid. Bold type in original.
54 Pluckrose and Lindsay, Cynical Theories, 40.
55 Ibid.
56 Ibid.
57 Ibid., 48.
58 Ibid., 61–61.
59 Coughlin and Higgins, Re-Remembering the Mis-Remembered Left, 96. Parentheses in original.
60 Ibid. Bold type in original.
61 Mao Tse-tung: "On the People's Democratic Dictatorship (July 1, 1949)," in Conrad Brandt, Benjamin Schwartz, and John K. Fairbank, A Documentary History of Chinese Communism (Cambridge, MA: Harvard University Press, 1952), 449–463, quotation at 450.
62 Ibid., 62. Italics in original.
63 Trevor Loudon, The Enemies Within: Communists, Socialists and Progressives in the U.S. Congress, 2013–2015 edition (Las Vegas, NV: Pacific Freedom Foundation, 2013).
64 Trevor Loudon, Barack Obama and the Enemies Within (Las Vegas, NV: Pacific Freedom Foundation, 2011).
65 Loudon, Barack Obama and the Enemies Within, 6.
66 Ibid., 11–12.
67 Ibid., 145.
68 Ibid., 82.
69 Coughlin and Higgins, Re-Remembering the Mis-Remembered Left, 10. Bold type in original.
70 Don McIntosh, "Talking Socialism/Catching Up with AOC," Democratic Left, dsausa.org, March 19, 2021, *https://www.dsausa.org/democratic-left/aoc/.*
71 Ibid.
72 Nisha Stickles and Barbara Corbellini Duarte, "Exclusive: Alexandria Ocasio-Cortez Explains What Democratic Socialism Means to Her," Business Insider, March 4, 2019, *https://www.businessinsider.com/alexandria-ocasio-cortez-explains-what-democratic-socialism-means-2019-3.*
73 Jennie Neufeld, "Alexandria Ocasio-Cortez Is a Democratic Socialists of America Member. Here's What That Means," Vox.com, June 27, 2018, *https://www.vox.com/policy-and-politics/2018/6/27/17509604/alexandria-ocasio-cortez-democratic-socialist-of-america.*
74 "Russian Social-Democratic Workers' Party," Britannica.com, n.d., *https://www.britannica.com/topic/Russian-Social-Democratic-Workers-Party.*
75 "Testimony of Bella V. Dodd, June 17, 1953," Investigation of Communist Activities in the Columbus, Ohio, Area, Hearings Before the Committee on Un-American Activities, House of Representatives, Eighty-Third Congress, First Session, June 17 and 18, 1953 (Washington, DC: Government Printing Office, 1953), 1741–1777.

76 Coughlin and Higgins, Re-Remembering the Mis-Remembered Left, 10.
77 "Testimony of Bella V. Dodd, June 17, 1953," Investigation of Communist Activities in the Columbus, Ohio, Area, 1748.
78 Ibid.
79 Ibid., 1757.
80 Ibid., 1758.
81 Ibid., 1760.
82 Ibid., 1761.
83 Ibid., 1747.
84 Ibid., 1768.
85 Ibid.
86 Ibid., 1769.
87 Ibid., 1770.
88 Ibid.
89 Ibid., 1771.
90 Ibid.
91 Ibid., 1768.
92 Ibid., 1769.
93 Ibid., 1769.
94 "Testimony of Bella V. Dodd, November 16, 1953," Investigation of Communist Activities in the Philadelphia Area—Part 1, Hearings Before the Committee on Un-American Activities, House of Representatives, Eighty-Third Congress, First Session, November 16, 1953 (Washington, DC: Government Printing Office, 1953), 2886–2910.
95 Ibid., 2898.
96 Ibid.
97 Ibid, 2900.
98 Bella V. Dodd, School of Darkness (Kettering, OH: Angelico Press, rep. ed., 2017), 150. Originally published in 1954 by P. J. Kenedy & Sons, New York.
99 Bella Dodd quoted Trachtenberg in a 1953 lecture at Fordham University. See: "Bella Dodd Explains Communism Ducks," YouTube.com, *https://www.youtube.com/watch?v=VLHNz2YMnRY.*
100 "Testimony of Bella V. Dodd, June 17, 1953," Investigation of Communist Activities in the Columbus, Ohio, Area, 1758.
101 Jacques Duclos, "On the Dissolution of the Communist Party of the United States," published in Cahiers du Communisme, April 1945. Reprinted in William Z. Foster et al., Marxism-Leninism vs. Revisionism (New York: New Century Publishers, 1946), 21–35, *https://www.marxists.org/history/usa/parties/cpusa/1945/04/0400-duclos-ondissolution.pdf.*
102 "Testimony of Bella V. Dodd, June 17, 1953," Investigation of Communist Activities in the Columbus, Ohio, Area, 1744–1745.
103 Ibid., 1747.
104 Ibid.

105 Sean McMeekin, Stalin's War: A New History of World War II (New York: Basic Books, 2021), 58.

106 Ibid., 163.

107 Henry Kissinger, A World Restored: Metternich, Castlereagh and the Problems of Peace 1812–22 (Boston: Houghton Mifflin, 1957).

108 "Testimony of Bella V. Dodd, November 16, 1953," Investigation of Communist Activities in the Philadelphia Area—Part 1, 2897.

109 "Testimony of Bella V. Dodd, June 17, 1953," Investigation of Communist Activities in the Columbus, Ohio, Area, 1752.

110 Ibid.

111 Ibid, 1744–1746.

112 Ibid.

113 Ibid., 1747.

114 "Testimony of Bella V. Dodd, November 16, 1953," Investigation of Communist Activities in the Philadelphia Area—Part 1, 2888.

115 Ibid., 2904–2905, quotation at 2904.

116 William Z. Foster, The Twilight of World Capitalism (New York: International Publishers, 1949), 150.

117 Ibid.

118 "Testimony of Bella V. Dodd, November 16, 1953," Investigation of Communist Activities in the Philadelphia Area—Part 1, 2904–2905, quotation at 2905.

119 William Z. Foster, Toward Soviet America (New York: International Publishers, 1932). See also: John Rossomando, "The ACLU's Untold Stalinist Heritage," Daily Caller, January 4, 2011, *https://dailycaller.com/2011/01/04/the-aclu%E2%80%99s-untold-stalinist-heritage/*.

120 "William Z. Foster Is Dead at 80; Ex-Head of Communists in U.S.," New York Times, September 2, 1961, *http://www.gompers.umd.edu/Foster%20obit.pdf*.

121 Dodd, School of Darkness, 199–200.

122 Joseph Stalin, Marxism and the National Question: Selected Writings and Speeches (New York: International Publishers, 1942), archived on Marxism.org, *https://www.marxists.org/reference/archive/stalin/works/1913/03a.htm#s1*.

123 Loudon, "Communists and Race."

124 Ibid.

125 Ibid.

126 J. V. Stalin, Marxism and the National Question: The Nation, initially published in Prosveshcheniye, nos. 3–5 (March–May 1913), archived on *Marxists.org*, *https://www.marxists.org/reference/archive/stalin/works/1913/03a.htm#s1*.

127 Trevor Loudon, "How Stalin's Plan from 100 Years Ago Is Influencing America Today," Counterpunch with Trevor Loudon, YouTube.com, premiered July 28, 2021, *https://www.youtube.com/watch?v=yqf5Q-MjyOE*.

128 "On the History of the CPUSA and the CI (Communist International, or Comintern) on the Right to Self-Determination," Workers' Advocate

Supplement 1, no. 9 (November 15, 1985), archived on Marxists. org, *https://www.marxists.org/history/erol/ncm-8/mlp-ci-bnq.htm.*

129 Hannah Foster, "Black Belt Republic (1928–1934)," BlackPast.org, March 9, 2014, *https://www.blackpast.org/african-american-history/black-belt-republic-1928-1934/.*

130 William Z. Foster, The Negro People in American History (New York: International Publishers, 1954).

131 Ibid., preface, 13.

132 Hannah Foster, "Black Belt Republic."

133 William Z. Foster, The Negro People in American History, 13–14, quotation at 14.

134 Loudon, "Communists and Race."

135 "Testimony of Bella V. Dodd, November 16, 1953," Investigation of Communist Activities in the Philadelphia Area—Part 1, 2906.

136 Ibid.

137 Ibid.

138 Coughlin and Higgins, Re-Remembering the Mis-Remembered Left, 11.

139 T. Michael Holmes, The Specter of Communism in Hawaii (Honolulu: University of Hawaii Press, 1994), 183–189, quotation at 183.

140 All quotations in this paragraph come from the following source: Investigation of Communist Activities in the Territory of Hawaii—Part 4, Testimony of Jack H. Kawano before the Committee on Un-American Activities, House of Representatives, Eighty-Second Congress, First Session, July 6, 1951 (Washington, DC: Government Printing Office, 1951), *https://archive.org/stream/hearingsregardinhaw1951unit/hearingsregardinhaw1951unit_djvu.txt.*

141 Paul Kengor, The Communist: Frank Marshall Davis—The Untold Story of Barack Obama's Mentor (New York: Threshold Editions/Mercury Ink, 2012), 144.

142 Ibid.

143 Ibid., 142.

144 Ibid., 167–168.

145 Investigation of Communist Activities in the Territory of Hawaii—Part 4, Testimony of Jack H. Kawano before the Committee on Un-American Activities.

146 Kengor, The Communist: Frank Marshall Davis, 218.

147 Ibid.

148 Ibid., 218–219.

149 Ibid., "Appendix: Frank Marshall Davis Documents," Figure 1, 306.

150 Barack Obama, Dreams from My Father: A Story of Race and Inheritance (New York: Crown Publishers, 1995, 2004), 76.

151 Ibid.

152 Mike Dorning, "Bill Clinton Grants Clemency, Frees Reynolds," Chicago Tribune, January 21, 2001, *https://www.chicagotribune.*

com/news/ct-xpm-2001-01-21-chi-january-2001-bill-clinton-grants-clemency-frees-reynolds-20140218-story.html.

153 "Life under Socialism: An Afro-American Journalist in the USSR," People's Daily World, June 19, 1986, 18-A. The author is indebted to researcher Max Friedman for finding this newspaper article.

154 For more on Alice Palmer's Communist associations see: "Alice Palmer," in David Horowitz website, Discover the Networks, DiscoverTheNetworks.com, n.d., *https://www.discoverthenetworks.org/individuals/alice-palmer*. See also: Trevor Loudon, "Obama File 90 Alice Palmer Re-Examined—Was Obama's First Political Boss a Soviet 'Agent of Influence?'" WWW Broadcast Network, WorldWideWeekend.com, November 26, 2009, *https://www.worldviewweekend.com/news/article/obama-file-90-alice-palmer-re-examined-was-obamas-first-political-boss-soviet-agent.*

155 "History: Weather Underground Bombings," FBI.gov, n.d., *https://www.fbi.gov/history/famous-cases/weather-underground-bombings.*

156 Charles P. Nemeth, Homeland Security: An Introduction to Principles and Practice (Boca Raton, FL: CRC Press, 2nd ed., 2013), 20.

157 "The Friends of Barack Obama, Part 1," PowerLineBlog.com, April 22, 2008, *http://www.powerlineblog.com/archives2/2008/04/020358.php.*

158 David Hines, "Days of Rage," Status451.com, January 20, 2017, *https://status451.com/2017/01/20/days-of-rage/*. Hines's piece is a review of the following book: Bryan Burrough, Days of Rage: America's Radical Underground, the FBI, and the Forgotten Age of Revolutionary Violence (New York: Penguin Press, 2015).

159 Ben Smith, "Obama Once Visited '60s Radicals," Politico.com, February 22, 2008, at *https://www.politico.com/story/2008/02/obama-once-visited-60s-radicals-008630.*

160 Mentioned in Joanna Weiss, "How Obama and the Radical Became News," Boston Globe, April 18, 2002, *http://archive.boston.com/news/nation/articles/2008/04/18/how_obama_and_the_radical_became_news/?page=2.*

161 Maria Warren, "Get to Know Barack Obama," posted on the blog Musings & Migraines, January 27, 2005, *https://web.archive.org/web/20050207020133/https://warrenpeacemuse.blogspot.com/*

162 David Jackson and Ray Long, "Showing His Bare Knuckles," Chicago Tribune, April 4, 2007, *https://www.chicagotribune.com/news/ct-xpm-2007-04-04-0704030881-story.html.*

163 Christi Parsons, "Once Obama's Mentor, Alice Palmer Now Campaigns for Clinton," Los Angeles Times, April 26, 2008, *http://latimesblogs.latimes.com/washington/2008/04/once-obamas-men.html.*

164 Ibid.

165 Stanley Kurtz, "Obama and Ayers Pushed Radicalism on Schools," Wall Street Journal, opinion piece, September 23, 2008, https://www.wsj.com/articles/SB122212856075765367.

166 Ibid.

167 Alexander Lane, "Not a Radical Group, and Ayers Didn't Run It," PolitiFact.com, October 10, 2008, *https://www.politifact.com/factchecks/2008/oct/10/john-mccain/not-a-radical-group-and-ayers-didnt-run-it/*.

168 Ibid.

169 Stanley Kurtz, Radical-in-Chief: Barack Obama and the Untold Story of American Socialism (New York: Threshold Editions, an imprint of Simon & Schuster, 2010).

170 Ibid., 17.

171 Ibid., 17–18.

172 Ibid., 18. Italics in original.

173 Ibid.

174 Bernie Quigley, "Obama and Bill Ayers: Together from the Beginning," The Hill, September 24, 2008, *https://thehill.com/blogs/pundits-blog/presidential-campaign/32072-obama-and-bill-ayers-together-from-the-beginning*.

175 Dinitia Smith, "No Regrets for a Love of Explosives; In a Memoir of Sorts, a War Protester Talks of Life with the Weathermen," New York Times, September 11, 2001, *https://www.nytimes.com/2001/09/11/books/no-regrets-for-love-explosives-memoir-sorts-war-protester-talks-life-with.html*.

176 Bill Ayers, Fugitive Days: Memoirs of an Antiwar Activist (Boston: Beacon Press, 2001; paperback ed., 2009), afterword, 307–316, quotation at 311.

177 Weather Underground, Prairie Fire Distributing Committee, Political Statement of the Weather Underground, Prairie Fire: The Politics of Revolutionary Anti-Imperialism (New York: Communications Co., July 1974).

178 "William Ayers' Forgotten Communist Manifesto: Prairie Fire," ZombieTime.com, posted October 22, 2008, *https://www.zombietime.com/prairie_fire/*.

179 Burrough, Days of Rage, 312.

180 Ibid., 312–313, quotation at 312.

181 Prairie Fire, unnumbered pages, printed before chap. 1.

182 Prairie Fire, 1–2. Quoted in: State Department Bombing by Weatherman Underground, Hearings before the Subcommittee to Investigate the Administration of the Internal Security Act and Other Internal Security Laws, Committee on the Judiciary, United States Senate, Ninety-Fourth Congress, First Session, January 31, 1975 (Washington, DC: Government Printing Office, 1975), 27.

183 "William Ayers' Forgotten Communist Manifesto."

184 Ibid.

185 Prairie Fire, 2.

186 Ibid.

187 Ibid, 6.

188 Ibid.

189 Ibid., 7. Underlining in original.

190 Ibid., 141.

191 Burrough, Days of Rage, 59.

192 Ibid.
193 Ibid.
194 Ibid., 68.
195 Ibid.
196 Ibid., 27.
197 Ibid.
198 Ibid.
199 Coughlin and Higgins, Re-Remembering the Mis-Remembered Left, 3. Bold type in original.
200 Ibid., 5. Bold type in original.

CHAPTER 2

201 Coughlin and Higgins, Re-Remembering the Mis-Remembered Left, 97.
202 Mao Tse-tung: "On the People's Democratic Dictatorship (July 1, 1949)," in Conrad Brandt, Benjamin Schwartz, and John K. Fairbank, A Documentary History of Chinese Communism (Cambridge, MA: Harvard University Press, 1952), 449–463, quotation at 449.
203 Frank Dikötter, Mao's Great Famine: The History of China's Most Devastating Catastrophe, 1958–1962 (New York: Bloomsbury Publishing, Inc., paperback ed., 2017; originally published in Great Britain 2010), preface, 3. This book, published in 2010, is the first book Dikötter published in his trilogy on the history of communism in China, but it is the second book in terms of the chronological history, covering the years from 1945 to 1976.
204 Ibid.
205 Anna M. Cienciala, chap. 9, "The Chinese Revolution and Chinese Communism to 1949," Lecture Notes, History 557, University of Kansas, 1999, *https://acienciala.ku.edu/communistnationssince1917/ch9.html*. The history of communism in China discussed in this chapter subsection is drawn largely from this source: Anna M. Cienciala, Communist Nations Since 1917, History 557, Lecture Notes, University of Kansas, 1999, *https://acienciala.ku.edu/hist557/*. See also: Encyclopedia Britannica, "Nationalist collapse and the establishment of the People's Republic of China (1949)," revised and updated by Amy McKenna, Britannica.com, n.d., *https://www.britannica.com/event/Chinese-Civil-War/Nationalist-collapse-and-the-establishment-of-the-Peoples-Republic-of-China-1949*.
206 Ibid.
207 "Chiang Kai-shek," History.com, November 9, 2009, updated on August 21, 2018, *https://www.history.com/topics/china/chiang-kai-shek*.
208 Dikötter, Mao's Great Famine, 3.
209 Ibid, 4.
210 Ibid, 6.
211 Frank Dikötter, The Tragedy of Liberation: A History of the Chinese Revolution, 1945–1976, preface, xii. This book, published in 2013,

is the second book Dikötter published in his trilogy on the history of communism in China, but it is the first book in terms of the chronological history, covering the years from 1945 to 1976.

212 Ibid., xii.
213 Ibid.
214 Ibid.
215 Ibid., xiii.
216 Ibid.
217 Ibid., xiv.
218 Ibid.
219 Yang Jisheng, Tombstone: The Great Chinese Famine 1958–1962 (New York: Farrar, Straus and Giroux, 2008), excerpts from 13, 14, and 17.
220 Dikötter, Mao's Great Famine, preface, xi.
221 Ibid.
222 Ibid., xii.
223 Jisheng, Tombstone, 19.
224 Ibid.
225 Ibid.
226 Ibid.
227 Ibid., 392.
228 Ibid., 393.
229 Ibid., 392.
230 Ibid., 22.
231 Ibid., 21.
232 Ibid., 249.
233 Anne Applebaum, "How Stalin Hid Ukraine's Famine from the World," The Atlantic, October 13, 2017, *https://www.theatlantic.com/international/archive/2017/10/red-famine-anne-applebaum-ukraine-soviet-union/542610/*.
234 S. J. Taylor, Stalin's Apologist: Walter Duranty: The New York Times's Man in Moscow (Oxford: Oxford University Press, 1990), 5.
235 Ibid., 113.
236 Ibid.
237 Ibid., 192.
238 Ibid.
239 Ibid.
240 Ibid.
241 Ibid., 6.
242 Applebaum, "How Stalin Hid Ukraine's Famine from the World."
243 Taylor, Stalin's Apologist, 206.
244 This paragraph is drawn with minor paraphrasing from the following source: S. J. Taylor, Stalin's Apologist, 200.
245 Ibid., 200–201.

246 Ibid., 204–205.
247 Ibid. Quotation at 205. The quotation is from a dispatch Muggeridge sent to the Manchester Guardian via the British Embassy in Moscow, dated March 22, 1933.
248 Taylor, Stalin's Apologist, 206. The quotation is from the following source: Ian Hunter, Malcolm Muggeridge: A Life (London: Collins, 1980), 84.
249 Taylor, Stalin's Apologist, 206.
250 Ibid., 207–208.
251 Ibid., 207.
252 Ibid., 208.
253 Ibid.
254 Ibid.
255 Ibid.
256 Ibid., 208–209. The quotation "throwing down Jones" is attributed to Eugene Lyons the United Press correspondent in Moscow in 1933, as reported in Marco Carynnyk, "The Famine the Times Couldn't Find," Commentary, November 1983, 33, *https://www.commentary.org/articles/marco-carynnyk/the-famine-the-times-couldnt-find/*.
257 Taylor, Stalin's Apologist, 28–38. The relationship between Duranty and Crowley is also covered in the following source: Paul Kengor, The Devil and Karl Marx: Communism's Long March of Death, Deception, and Infiltration (Gastonia, NC: TAN Books, 2020), 4.
258 Taylor, Stalin's Apologist, 30.
259 Ibid.
260 Ibid., 32.
261 Ibid., 29.
262 Kengor, The Devil and Karl Marx, 324.
263 Ibid.
264 Taylor, Stalin's Apologist, 36–37, quotation at 36. Kengor, The Devil and Karl Marx, 329–331.
265 Kengor, The Devil and Karl Marx, 331.
266 S. J. Taylor, "The British Playboy Who Was Stalin's Stooge: How War Reporter Walter Duranty Covered Up a Kremlin-Created Famine That Killed Millions and Allowed the Left to Continue Worshiping a Mass Murderer," Daily Mail, March 7, 2020, *https://www.dailymail.co.uk/news/article-8086905/How-war-reporter-Walter-Duranty-covered-Kremlin-created-famine-killed-millions.html*.
267 Ibid.
268 Ibid.
269 Ibid.
270 Jisheng, Tombstone, 14.
271 Ibid.
272 Ibid.
273 Ibid., 14–15.

274 Felix Greene, A Curtain of Ignorance: How the American Public Has Been Misinformed About China (Garden City: Doubleday & Company, 1964).

275 Edgar Snow, Red Star Over China (New York: Random House, The Modern Library, 1938, 1944), 117.

276 Mary Hui, "A US Journalist Who Dined with Mao Is Beijing's Ideal for Who Should Cover China," Quartz, April 15, 2021, *https://qz.com/1993229/us-reporter-edgar-snow-is-beijings-ideal-foreign-journalist/*. See also: Edgar Snow, Red Star Over China (London: Victor Gollancz, 1937). See, in addition: Edgar Snow, The Other Side of the River: Red China Today (New York: Random House, 1962).

277 Jisheng, Tombstone, 21.

278 Ibid., preface, xii.

279 Ibid.

280 Dikötter, The Tragedy of Liberation, 275–266. See also: John Rettie, "The Secret Speech That Changed World History," The Guardian, February 25, 2006, *https://www.theguardian.com/world/2006/feb/26/russia.theobserver*.

281 Frank Dikötter, The Cultural Revolution: A People's History, 1962–1976 (New York: Bloomsbury Publishing, 2016), preface, xii. This book, published in 2016 is the third book Dikötter published in his three-book series and the third book chronologically, covering the years 1962–1976.

282 Ibid., xiii.

283 Roderick MacFarquhar, The Origins of the Cultural Revolution: Volume 3, The Coming of the Cataclysm 1961–1966 (Oxford, UK: Oxford University Press, and New York: Columbia University Press, 1997; published for the Royal Institute of International Affairs, Studies of the East Asia Institute), 6.

284 Tom Phillips, "The Cultural Revolution: All You Need to Know about China's Political Convulsion," The Guardian, May 10, 2016, *https://www.theguardian.com/world/2016/may/11/the-cultural-revolution-50-years-on-all-you-need-to-know-about-chinas-political-convulsion*.

285 Ibid.

286 Roderick MacFarquhar, "The Once and Future Tragedy of the Cultural Revolution," published online by Cambridge University Press, October 26, 2016, originally published as a preface to "Red Shadows: Memories and Legacies of the Chinese Cultural Revolution," The China Quarterly 227 (September 2016), 599–603, *https://www.cambridge.org/core/journals/china-quarterly/article/once-and-future-tragedy-of-the-cultural-revolution/FA2DC2E9B3976DBE5DA26767DF58DDB0*.

287 Phillips, "The Cultural Revolution."

288 Edward Weisband, "Shame Disciplines in the Chinese Cultural Revolution: Lurid and Ludic," in Lene Auestad and Amal Treacher Kabesh, eds., Traces of Violence and Freedom of Thought—Studies in the Psychosocial series (London: Palgrave MacMillan, 2017), 123–148.

289 Phillips, "The Cultural Revolution."

290 Andrew G. Walder, Agents of Disorder: Inside China's Cultural Revolution (Cambridge, MA: Belknap Press of Harvard University Press, 2019), 1–2.

291 Yang Jisheng, The World Turned Upside Down: A History of the Chinese Cultural Revolution (New York: Farrar, Straus and Giroux, 2016), xxix.

292 Ibid., xxiv.

293 Dikötter, The Cultural Revolution, 84.

294 Ibid.

295 Ibid., 87.

296 Ibid., 89–90.

297 Ibid., 91.

298 Ibid.

299 Ibid., 85.

300 Doug Bandow, "The Chinese Cultural Revolution: Lessons for America's Cancel Culture," American Spectator, September 14, 2020, *https://spectator.org/the-chinese-cultural-revolution-lessons-for-americas-cancel-culture/*.

301 Ibid.

302 Ibid.

303 Dr. Tao Peng, PhD, "Can the BLM Movement Be Equated with China's Cultural Revolution?" Center for International Relations, International Affairs Forum, May 25, 2020, *https://www.ia-forum.org/Content/ViewInternal_Document.cfm?contenttype_id=1&ContentID=9030*.

304 Quoted in Edward P. Johanningsmeier, Forging American Communism: The Life of William Z. Foster (Princeton, NJ: Princeton University Press, 1994), 338.

305 Stéphane Courtois, Nicolas Werth, Jean-Louis Panné, Andrzej Paczkowski, Karel Bartošek, and Jean-Louis Margolin, The Black Book of Communism: Crimes, Terror, Repression, ed. Mark Kramer, trans. Jonathan Murphy and Mark Kramer (Cambridge, MA: Harvard University Press, 1999). Originally published in France as Le livre noir du Communisme: Crimes, terreur, repression (Paris: Editions Robert Laffont, S.A., 1997).

306 Ibid., 23.

307 Ibid.

308 Robert Gellately, Lenin, Stalin, and Hitler: The Age of Social Catastrophe (New York: Alfred A. Knopf, 2007), 7.

309 Ibid.

310 Ibid.

311 Ibid.

312 Ibid., 8.

313 Ibid., 10.

314 Ibid.

315 Ibid.

316 Jisheng, Tombstone, 21.

317 Ibid., 478.

318 Ibid., 482.

319 "Biography: Thomas A. Marks, Ph.D., Department Head and Professor, Department of War and Conflict Studies, College of International Security, National Defense University," n.d., CISA.NDU.edu, *https://cisa.ndu.edu/Portals/76/Documents/About/FacultyBios/TMarksBio.pdf.*

320 Thomas A. Marks, Maoist People's War in Post-Vietnam Asia (Bangkok: White Lotus Press, 2007), 7.

321 Ibid., 9.

322 Ibid.

323 Ibid.

324 Ibid., 9–10.

325 Ibid., 10.

326 Conrad Brandt, Benjamin Schwartz, and John K. Fairbank, A Documentary History of Chinese Communism (Cambridge, MA: Harvard University Press, 1952), 15.

327 Ibid.

328 Ibid., 19.

329 Marks, Maoist People's War in Post-Vietnam Asia, 10–11.

330 Ibid., 11.

331 Ibid.

332 Ibid.

333 Quotation from Mao, found in Thomas A. Marks, Maoist People's War in Post-Vietnam Asia, 11.

334 Ibid., 13.

335 Ibid.

336 Jisheng, Tombstone, 5.

337 Ibid.

338 Ibid., 11.

339 Ibid.

340 Ibid., 12.

341 Coughlin and Higgins, Re-Remembering the Mis-Remembered Left, 100.

342 Roxanne Dunbar-Ortiz, Not a Nation of Immigrants: Settler Colonialism, White Supremacy, and a History of Exclusion (Boston: Beacon Press, 2021).

343 Ibid., introduction, xiii.

344 Ibid., xii.

345 Ibid., xiii.

346 Ibid., xv.

347 William F. Jasper, "Dispelling Disinformation," part one of a three-part interview of Christopher Story, editor of the London-based Soviet Analysist, an intelligence commentary, and editor of The Perestroika Deception written by Soviet defector Anatoliy Golitsyn, conducted by William F. Jasper, senior editor, The New American, September 18, 1995, *https://thenewamerican.com/dispelling-disinformation/*. See: Anatoliy Golitsyn, The

Perestroika Deception: The World's Slide Toward the "Second October Revolution" (London: Edward Harle, 1995). Italics in original.

348 Jefferson Morley, The Ghost: The Secret Life of CIA Spymaster James Jesus Angleton (New York: St. Martin's Press, 2017), 108.

349 Michael Pillsbury, The Hundred-Year Marathon: China's Secret Strategy to Replace America as the Global Superstar (New York: Henry Holt, 2015), 21.

350 Ibid.

351 Morley, The Ghost, 107–109.

352 Anatoliy Golitsyn, New Lies for Old: An Ex-KGB Officer Warns How Communist Deception Threatens the Survival of the West (New York: Dodd, Mead, 1984), 38.

353 Ibid., 37.

354 Ibid., 43–44.

355 Ibid., 44.

356 Ibid., 160.

357 Ibid., 43.

358 Ibid., 45.

359 Ibid., 153–157, quotation at 157.

360 Ibid., 161–162, quotation at 162.

361 Ibid., 276.

362 The Contemplative Observer, "Anatoliy Golitsyn: The Key to Understanding Today's World Situation," TheContempletativeObserver.wordpress.com, February 14, 2013, *https://thecontemplativeobserver.wordpress.com/tag/the-perestroika-deception/*.

363 Golitsyn, New Lies for Old, 346.

364 Ibid., 232.

365 Ibid., 231.

366 Ibid.

367 Ibid., 346–347.

368 Golitsyn, The Perestroika Deception.

369 Jasper, "Dispelling Disinformation."

370 Anatoliy Golitsyn, "Danger for the West: An Assessment of the Rise of Mikhail Gorbachev, the Role of 'Liberalization' in Soviet Strategy, and Its Grave Implications for the West," Memorandum to the CIA, August 1985, in The Perestroika Deception: The World's Slide Towards the "Second October Revolution," 188–194, quotation at 188.

371 Ibid.

372 Anatoliy Golitsyn, "Western Counter-Strategy against 'Perestroika,'" Memo to the CIA, September 1988, in The Perestroika Deception: The World's Slide Towards the "Second October Revolution," 66–70, quotation at 69.

373 Mark Riebling, Wedge: The Secret War between the FBI and CIA (New York: Alfred A. Knopf, 1994), 407–408.

374 Ibid., 407. See also: Golitsyn, New Lies for Old, 327.

375 Riebling, Wedge, 407.
376 Golitsyn, New Lies for Old, 339.
377 Ibid.
378 Ibid., 340.
379 Riebling, Wedge, 407–408.
380 Ibid., 408.
381 Ibid., 409.
382 Ibid., 407.
383 Thomas D. Schuman [Yuri Bezmenov], Love Letter to America (Los Angeles: W.I.N. Almanac Panorama, 1984).
384 Yuri Bezmenov lectures and interviews can be found in the following sources: (1) "Yuri Bezmenov: Psychological Warfare & Control of Western Society (Complete)," video of a 1983 lecture in Los Angeles, California, YouTube.com, posted February 23, 2011, *https://www.youtube.com/watch?v=5gnpCqsXE8g&t=2s*; (2) "Full Interview with Yuri Bezmenov: The Four Stages of Ideological Subversion (1984)," YouTube.com, posted August 22, 2020, *https://www.youtube.com/watch?v=yErKTVdETpw*; (3) "Yuri Bezmenov: Deception Was My Job (Complete)," recording of G. Edward Griffin's interview with Yuri Bezmenov in 1984, interview entitled "Soviet Subversion of the Free World Press," YouTube.com, posted December 5, 2017, *https://www.youtube.com/watch?v=AhAzGLb1j40*. Bezmenov quotations in this chapter subsection are drawn from these sources. See also: Yuri Bezmenov: The Life and Legacy of the Influential KGB Informant Who Defected to the West (Ann Arbor: Charles River Editors, 2020). See also: "Four Stages of a Marxist Subversion of a Country: KGB Defector Yuri Bezmenov Warns America of Marxist Subversion," Unconstrained Analytics, October 2, 2020, *https://unconstrainedanalytics.org/kgb-defector-yuri-bezmenov-warns-america-of-marxist-subversion/*. See in particular a subsection of the Unconstrained Analytics page "Yuri Bezmenov Quotes." To find a digital copy of Bezmenov's book Love Letter to America, see: Yuri Bezmenov, Love Letter to America (Los Angeles: W.I.N. Almanac Panorama, 1984), archived on archive.org, *https://archive.org/details/BezmenovLoveLetterToAmerica/page/n1/mode/2up*. While Bezmenov's English is understandable, English was obviously not his native language. In these various sources, Bezmenov tended to repeat the same points in roughly the same order, but with variations in how he expressed his thoughts. The quotes in this chapter subsection include various combinations of his wordings drawn from these multiple sources. Thus, the Bezmenov quotations in this chapter subsection are not precise word-for-word quotations, but the quotations are accurate and faithful to what Bezmenov wrote and spoke.
385 Schuman [Yuri Bezmenov], Love Letter to America, 24.
386 Ibid.
387 Ibid., 23.

388 "Yuri Bezmenov Quotes," a subsection of "Four Stages of a Marxist Subversion of a Country: KGB Defector Yuri Bezmenov Warns America of Marxist Subversion," Unconstrained Analytics, October 2, 2020, *https://unconstrainedanalytics.org/kgb-defector-yuri-bezmenov-warns-america-of-marxist-subversion/*.

389 Ibid.

390 Ibid.

391 Ibid.

392 Ibid.

393 Ibid., 40.

394 Schuman [Yuri Bezmenov], Love Letter to America, 42. Italics in original.

395 Ibid.

396 Ibid., 43.

397 Ibid., 43–44.

398 Ibid., 44. Italics in original.

399 Ibid. Italics in original.

400 Ibid., 44 and 46.

401 "Yuri Bezmenov: Deception Was My Job (Complete)," recording of G. Edward Griffin's interview with Yuri Bezmenov in 1984 entitled "Soviet Subversion of the Free World Press," YouTube.com, posted December 5, 2017, *https://www.youtube.com/watch?v=AhAzGLb1j40*. For a transcription of this quotation, see: Coughlin and Higgins, Re-Remembering the Mis-Remembered Left, fn. 121, p. 48. Bracketed clarifications are from the original text.

402 Viktor Suvorov, The Chief Culprit: Stalin's Grand Design to Start World War II (Annapolis: Naval Institute Press, 2008), "Introduction," xv–xxii, quotation at xvi.

403 Viktor Suvorov, Icebreaker: Who Started the Second World War? (London: Hamish Hamilton, 1990; first published in France by Editions Olivier Organ in 1988).

404 Luke Harding, "'Will They Forgive Me? No': Ex-Soviet Spy Viktor Suvorov Speaks Out," The Guardian, December 29, 2018, *https://www.theguardian.com/world/2018/dec/29/ex-soviet-spy-viktor-suvorov*.

405 Viktor Suvorov, The Chief Culprit: Stalin's Grand Design to Start World War II, acknowledgments, xiii–xiv, quotation at xiii.

406 Ibid.

407 Ibid., preface, ix–xi, quotation at ix.

408 Lawrence K. Samuels, "The Socialist Economics of Italian Fascism," EconLib.com, July 6, 2015, *https://www.econlib.org/library/Columns/y2015/Samuelsfascism.html*. See also: Jonah Goldberg, Liberal Fascism: The Secret History of the American Left from Mussolini to the Politics of Meaning (New York: Doubleday, 2008). The radical Left in the United States consistently insists the Nazis, like Mussolini, were fascists on the political right. See: Ronald J. Granieri, "The Right Needs to Stop Falsely Claiming the Nazis Were Socialists," Washington Post, February 5, 2020, *https://www.washingtonpost.*

com/outlook/2020/02/05/right-needs-stop-falsely-claiming-that-nazis-were-socialists/. Granieri is a Templeton Education Fellow at the Foreign Policy Research Institute and a history professor at the U.S. Army War College.

409 Constitutional Rights Foundation, "Mussolini and the Rise of Fascism," Bill of Rights in Action 25, no. 4 (Summer 2010), *https://www.crf-usa.org/bill-of-rights-in-action/bria-25-4-mussolini-and-the-rise-of-fascism.html*.

410 "March 23, 1919: Mussolini Founds the Fascist Party," History.com, "This Day in History, March 23," originally published February 9, 2010, last updated July 28, 2019, *https://www.history.com/this-day-in-history/mussolini-founds-the-fascist-party*.

411 Joseph Goebbels, The Nazi-Sozi, a pamphlet that was one of Goebbels's earliest publications, archived at Research.Calvin.edu, *https://research.calvin.edu/german-propaganda-archive/nazi-sozi.htm*. The pamphlet is also archived in its original German-language print edition at Archive.org, *https://archive.org/details/Goebbels-Joseph-Der-Nazi-Sozi/page/n1/mode/2up*.

412 Laurence Berns, "Thomas Hobbes (1588–1679)," in Leo Strauss and Joseph Cropsey, History of Political Philosophy (Chicago: University of Chicago Press, 3rd ed., 1987), 396–420, quotation at 401. Robert A. Goldwin, "John Locke (1632–1704)," in Leo Strauss and Joseph Cropsey, History of Political Philosophy, 476–511.

413 Suvorov, The Chief Culprit, 29.

414 Ibid., 30.

415 Ibid.

416 Ibid.

417 Ibid., 32–33.

418 Ibid., 33.

419 Ibid.

420 Ibid.

421 Suvorov, Icebreaker, 2.

422 Ibid.

423 Ibid., 3.

424 Golitsyn, The Perestroika Deception, in foreword by the author, xvii–xxvi, quotation at xvii.

425 Ibid., xv. See: Sun Tzu, The Art of War.

426 William Z. Foster, The Twilight of World Capitalism, 17.

427 Ibid.

428 Ibid.

429 Ibid.

430 Ibid., 87.

431 Ibid.

CHAPTER 3

432 Eric Voegelin, "On Hegel—A Study in Sorcery," in J. T. Fraser, F. C. Haber, G. H. Müller (eds.), The Study of Time, Proceedings of the First Conference of the International Society for the Study of Time, Oberwolfach (Black Forest), West Germany (Berlin and Heidelberg, Germany: Springer-Verlag, 1972), 418–451, quotation at 424.

433 Michael Rohlf, "Immanuel Kant, Life and Works," Stanford Encyclopedia of Philosophy, Plato.Stanford.edu, first published May 20, 2010, substantive revision on July 28, 2020, *https://plato.stanford.edu/entries/kant/#LifWor*.

434 Immanuel Kant, Critique of Pure Reason (Riga: Johann Fredrich Hartnoch, 2nd ed., 1787). All quotations in the text and page references in the footnotes are to the following edition: Immanuel Kant, The Critique of Pure Reason, eds. and trans. Paul Guyer and Allen W. Wood (Cambridge: Cambridge University Press, first published 1998, sixth printing 2019), a volume in The Cambridge Edition of the Works of Immanuel Kant.

435 Ibid., A2, 127. References to the Critique of Pure Reason are given by the pagination of the first ("A") and/or second ("B") edition.

436 Ibid.

437 Ibid. Italics in original.

438 Plato, The Republic of Plato, trans. Allan Bloom (New York: Basic Books, originally published in 1968, 2016 ed.), Book VII, 514a, 193.

439 Ibid., book 7, 515a, 193. All page references to Plato's Republic are from the 2016 ed.

440 Kant, Critique of Pure Reason, A2, 128.

441 Ibid., A5, B9, 129.

442 Ibid., A6, B10, 130. Italics in original.

443 Ibid., A7, B11, 130.

444 Ibid.

445 Ibid., A9, B13, A10, 131–132.

446 Ibid., A10, B24, A11, 132.

447 Ibid. A11, B25, 132–133.

448 Ibid., A11, B25, 133.

449 Ibid, A568, B596, 551.

450 Ibid., A569, B596, 552. Bold type in original.

451 Ibid.

452 Ibid.

453 Ibid., A855, B883, 704.

454 This quotation is drawn from the following source: Christine M. Korsgaard, Harvard University, introduction, in Immanuel Kant, Groundwork of the Metaphysics of Morals, eds. and trans. Mary J. Gregor and Jens Timmermann, rev. ed. trans. Jens Timmermann (Cambridge: Cambridge University Press, rev. ed., 2012), a separate volume in The Cambridge History of Philosophy, ix–xxxvi, quotation at xix.

455 Ibid.

456 Ibid.

457 Immanuel Kant, Groundwork of the Metaphysics of Morals, "Section II: Transition from Popular Moral Philosophy to Metaphysics of Morals," p. 34, marginal pagination 4:421. For all Kant's works, except the Critique of Pure Reason, the marginal pagination notes are traditionally taken by academic convention from the Academy Edition of Kant's Collected Works. The first number in the marginal pagination refers to the volume in the collected works; the second number refers to the page in that volume. Thus, here the notation "4:421," the number "4" refers to volume 4 in Kant's Collected Works and the number "421" refers to the specific page number in volume 4 where the quotation can be found. "Wilhelm Dilthey (1833–1911) inaugurated the Academy Edition (the Akademie Ausgabe) of Kant's writings in 1894–95 and served as the first general editor. See: Kant's gesammelte Schriften (1900–) [Kant's Collected Works (1900–)], published under the auspices of the Königlich Preußischen Akademie der Wissenschaften [Royal Prussian Academy of Sciences]. The pagination in the Academy Edition has served subsequently as the page reference convention that standardizes all subsequent publications of Kant's many works. Source: Steve Naragon, Manchester University, North Manchester, Indiana, "Academy Edition," in "Kant in the Classroom," Users.Manchester.edu, last modified July 2021, *https://users.manchester.edu/facstaff/ssnaragon/kant/Helps/AcadEd.htm*. Thus, to Kant scholars, the marginal page reference in this footnote would be understood as: [AK] 4:421, meaning that the quoted passage could be found on p. 421, in vol. 4, of the Academy [AK] Edition.

458 Ibid., p. 34, 4:421. Italics and bold type in original.

459 See: Joseph Kranak, "Chapter 6: Kantian Deontology," in Christina Hendricks (series editor), Introduction to Philosophy: Ethics, Rebus Community, an Open Textbook in the "Introduction to Philosophy Series," with version 1.0 originally published online on December 9, 2019, *https://press.rebus.community/intro-to-phil-ethics/chapter/kantian-deontology/*.

460 Kant, Groundwork of the Metaphysics of Morals, p. 40, 4:428.

461 Allen W. Wood, "General Introduction," xiii–xxxiii, quotation at xix, in Immanuel Kant, Practical Philosophy, ed. and trans. Mary J. Gregor (Cambridge: Cambridge University Press, 1996, first paperback ed., 1999), a volume in The Cambridge Edition of the Works of Immanuel Kant.

462 Kant, Groundwork of the Metaphysics of Morals, p. 46, 4:434. Bold type in original.

463 Ibid.

464 Ibid., p. 56, 4:447.

465 Immanuel Kant, Toward Perpetual Peace, in Practical Philosophy, 311–351, quotation at 328, 8:357. Italics in original.

466 Ibid., p. 328, 8:357.

467 Ibid., p. 325, 8:354. Italics and Latin in original. Brackets not in original; brackets added for clarity.

468 Ibid., p. 327, 8:356. Italics and Latin in original.

469 Ibid., p. 327, 8:356.

470 Immanuel Kant, The Metaphysics of Morals, in Practical Philosophy, 65–603, quotation at 491, 6:355. The phrase "a priori" is not italicized in Mary J. Gregor (ed. and trans.) edition of The Metaphysics of Morals used here.

471 Paul Redding, "Georg Wilhelm Friedrich Hegel," Stanford Encyclopedia of Philosophy, Plato.Stanford.edu, first published on February 13, 1997, with a substantive revision on January 9, 2020, *https://plato.stanford.edu/entries/hegel/#LifWorInf.*

472 Georg Wilhelm Friedrich Hegel, The Phenomenology of Spirit (Bamberg and Würzburg, Germany: Joseph Astos Goebhardt, 1807). All quotations in the text and page references in the footnotes are to the following edition: George Wilhelm Friedrich Hegel, The Phenomenology of Spirit, ed. and trans. Terry Pinkard (Cambridge: Cambridge University Press, 2018). The marginal pagination is from Hegel's Collected Works. See: Georg Wilhelm Hegel, Gesammelte Werke, edited under the sponsorship of the Deutsche Forschungsgemeinschaft (Hamburg: Felix Meiner, 1968), p. 253, p. 238 in margin.

473 Ibid.

474 Ibid., 253–254, 238–239 in margin.

475 Glenn Alexander Magee, The Hegel Dictionary (New York: Continuum International Publishing Group, 2010).

476 Ibid., 226.

477 Ibid., 226–227. "Spirit" is capitalized in the original.

478 Antje Allroggen, "Hegel: The Philosopher Father of the 'Zeitgeist,'" DW.com, August 27, 2020, *https://www.dw.com/en/hegel-the-philosopher-who-viewed-history-as-inevitable-progress/a-54707032.*

479 Terry Pinkard, introduction, in George Wilhelm Friedrich Hegel, The Phenomenology of Spirit, xxix.

480 "Hegel and the Zeitgeist," posted by "Brady" on TheLycaeum.wordpress.com, May 25, 2015, *https://thelycaeum.wordpress.com/2014/05/25/hegel-and-the-zeitgeist/.*

481 Magee, The Hegel Dictionary, 260.

482 Coughlin and Higgins, Re-Remembering the Mis-Remembered Left, 16.

483 Ibid., 259.

484 Georg Wilhelm Friedrich Hegel, Lectures on the Philosophy of World History, trans. H. B. Nisbet (Cambridge: Cambridge University Press, 1975), a volume in The Cambridge Studies in the History and Theory of Politics, 82.

485 Ibid.

486 Judith N. Shklar, Freedom: A Study of the Political Ideas of Hegel's "Phenomenology of Mind" (Cambridge: Cambridge University Press, 1976), 13.

487 Terry Pinkard, introduction, in Georg Wilhelm Friedrich Hegel, The Phenomenology of Spirit, xxix–xxx.

488 Hegel, Lectures on the Philosophy of World History, 82–83.

489 Ibid., 83.

490 "Letter," Hegel to Niethammer, written October 13, 1806, in Hegel: The Letters, trans. Clark Butler and Christine Seller (Bloomington: Purdue Research Foundation, Indiana University Press, 1985), 114. This subsection closely follows the order of argument and the quotations cited by Stephen Coughlin and Richard Higgins, Re-Remembering the Mis-Remembered Left: The Left's Strategy and Tactics to Transform America, "All Roads Lead to Hegel," 16–25.

491 Arthur Schopenhauer, The World as Will and Idea, Volume 2 (of 3), trans. R. B. Haldane and J. Kemp (London: Kegan Paul, Trench, Trübner, 6th ed., 1909, from the original German written in 1859). Also see: Arthur Schopenhauer, The World as Will and Idea, Volume 2 (of 3), a Project Gutenberg eBook, Gutenberg.org, released June 27, 2012, as eBook #40097, p. 239, *https://www.gutenberg.org/files/40097/40097-pdf.pdf.*

492 Glenn Alexander Magee, Hegel and the Hermetic Tradition (Ithaca: Cornell University Press, 2001), 1.

493 Alan M. Olson, Hegel and the Spirit: Philosophy as Pneumatology (Princeton: Princeton University Press, 1992), 58. This quotation from Olson is cited by Coughlin and Higgins, Re-Remembering the Mis-Remembered Left, 16. The passage is also cited in Magee's Hegel and the Hermetic, 76.

494 Magee, Hegel and the Hermetic Tradition, 150–151.

495 Ibid., 150.

496 Ibid., 152. Capitalization and italics in original.

497 Ibid.

498 Ibid.

499 Ibid. Magee quotes Hegel here, p. 152. Italics in original.

500 Ibid., 153.

501 Ibid., introduction, 1.

502 Ibid.

503 Ibid.

504 Ibid., introduction, 9.

505 Ibid., 9–10. Capitalization and parentheses in original.

506 Coughlin and Higgins, Re-Remembering the Mis-Remembered Left, 16.

507 Georg Wilhelm Friedrich Hegel, The Philosophy of History, trans. J. Sibree (Kitchener, Ontario, Canada: Batoche Books, 2001), with prefaces by Charles Hegel and J. Sibree, p. 54. Capitalization and punctuation in original.

508 Ibid.

509 Georg Wilhelm Friedrich Hegel, Philosophy of Right, trans. S. W. Dyde (London: G. Bell, 1896), §258.

510 Hegel, The Philosophy of History, 457.

511 Ibid.

512 Coughlin and Higgins, Re-Remembering the Mis-Remembered Left, 17.

513 Benedict Thomas Viviano, "The Adoration of the Magi: Matthew 2:1–12 and Theological Aesthetics," in Catholic Hermeneutics Today: Critical Essays (Eugene, OR: Cascade Books, 2014), 131.

514 Bertrand Russell, "Hegel," in History of Western Philosophy and Its Connection with Political and Social Circumstances from the Earliest Times to the Present Day (New York: Simon & Schuster, 1945), chap. 22, 730–752, quotation at 730. See also the internet version of this article available as: "The Philosophy of Hegel (1946)," Internet Archive, Archive.org, *https://archive.org/details/RUSSELLHEGEL1946/page/n1/mode/2up*.

515 Ibid.

516 Ibid.

517 Ibid.

518 Ibid.

519 Ibid., 738.

520 Ibid.

521 Ibid., 739.

522 Ibid.

523 Ibid.

524 Ibid.

525 Ibid., 738.

526 Voegelin, "On Hegel—A Study in Sorcery," 420.

527 Coughlin and Higgins, Re-Remembering the Mis-Remembered Left, 17–18.

528 Ibid., 18. Emphasis in original.

529 Ibid.

530 Ibid.

531 Ibid.

532 Magee, The Hegel Dictionary, 213.

533 Ibid., 48. See also: Cecilia Muratori, "Hegel as Interpreter of Böhme," in The First German Philosopher: The Mysticism of Jacob Böhme as Interpreted by Hegel (Heidelberg, Germany: Springer-Verlag GmbH, 2016), part of the International Archives of the History of Ideas Archives (Internationales d'Histoire des Idées) book series (ARCH, vol. 2017), 201–288.

534 Magee, Hegel and the Hermetic Tradition, 48.

535 Magee, The Hegel Dictionary, 49.

536 Coughlin and Higgins, Re-Remembering the Mis-Remembered Left, 20. Here Coughlin and Higgins are referencing Eric Voegelin, "On Hegel—A Study in Sorcery."

537 Ibid., 20.

538 Bertrand Russell, "Philosophy and Politics," Unpopular Essays (London: George Allen & Unwin, 1950), 19–20.

539 Ibid., 20.

540 Ibid., 22.

541 Ibid., 23.

542 Ibid., 23–24.

543 Ibid. 24.

544 Ibid.

545 Ibid., 19.

546 Chris Hedges, "What Every Person Should Know about War," New York Times, July 6, 2003, *https://www.nytimes.com/2003/07/06/books/chapters/what-every-person-should-know-about-war.html*. Excerpted from: Chris Hedges, What Every Person Should Know about War (New York: Free Press, 2003).

547 Russell, "Philosophy and Politics," 61.

548 Bertrand Russell, Wisdom of the West (London: Rathbone Books, 1959). See also the oversized book edition published by Doubleday in 1959: Bertrand Russell, Wisdom of the West, ed. Paul Foulkes and designer Edward Wright (Garden City, NY: Doubleday, 1959), 249.

549 Ibid., 247.

550 Ibid., 248.

551 Ibid.

552 Ibid.

553 Ibid.

554 Ibid.

555 Coughlin and Higgins, Re-Remembering the Mis-Remembered Left, 3.

556 Ibid.

557 Ibid., 12.

558 Terry Pinkard, "Translator's Note," in Georg Wilhelm Friedrich Hegel, The Phenomenology of Spirit, xxxix–xl, quotation at xl.

559 Arthur Schopenhauer, On the Basis of Morality. The following is the translation used here: Arthur Schopenhauer, On the Basis of Morality, trans. E. F. J. Payne (Indianapolis: Hackett Publishing, 1995), preface to 1st ed., 15–16.

560 Ibid.

561 Richard Wurmbrand, Marx & Satan (Bartlesville, OK: Living Sacrifice Book Company, 1986), 29. Emphasis in original.

562 Franz Mehring, Karl Marx: The Story of His Life (New York: Covici, Friede Publishers, 1935), 552. See also: James Simpson, Who Was Karl Marx? The Men, the Motives, and the Menace Behind Today's Rampaging American Left (Baltimore: Simpson Publishing, 2021), 11;

563 Kengor, The Devil and Karl Marx, 67.

564 Ibid., 71–72.

565 Karl Marx, Critique of Hegel's "Philosophy of Right," trans. Annette Jolin and Joseph O'Malley (Cambridge: Cambridge University Press, 1970).

566 Hegel, Philosophy of Right, para. 273, p. 264. See also: Arend Theodoor van Leeuwen, associate professor of Christian ethics, Catholic University of Nijmegen, 1918 to 1993, "Critique of Hegel's Philosophy of Right," The Gifford Lectures, GiffordLectures.org, *https://www.giffordlectures.org/books/critique-earth/5-critique-hegels-philosophy-right*. From the book: Arend Theodoor Van Leeuwen, Critique of Earth: The Second Series of the Gilford Lectures Entitled "Critique of Heaven and Earth" (New York: Charles Scribner's Sons, 1947).

567 Ibid.

568 Ibid., para. 275, p. 288, and para. 276, pp. 288–289. See also: Pierre Hassner, "Georg W. F. Hegel," in Leo Strauss and Joseph Cropsey, History of Political Philosophy (Chicago: University of Chicago Press, 3rd ed., 1987), 732–760, quotation at 748.

569 Karl Marx, "A Contribution to the Critique of Hegel's Philosophy of Right: Introduction," in Karl Marx, Critique of Hegel's 'Philosophy of Right,'' trans. Annette Jolin and Joseph O'Malley (Cambridge, UK: Cambridge University Press, 1970), 129–142, quotation at 131.

570 Ibid.

571 Ibid.

572 Ibid., 142.

573 Ibid.

574 Kengor, The Devil and Karl Marx, 4. Kengor references Engles's letter to Marx dated November 23–24, 1847, p. 4, *https://www.marxists.org/archive/marx/works/1847/11/prin-com.htm.*

575 Kengor, The Devil and Karl Marx, 4.

576 Ibid., 5.

577 Ibid.

578 Russell, Wisdom of the West, 271.

579 Ibid., 272.

580 Ibid.

581 Ibid.

582 Ibid., 272–273.

583 Ibid., 273.

584 Ibid.

585 Stephen Bates, "Pastor Richard Wurmbrand," The Guardian, March 15, 2001, *https://www.theguardian.com/news/2001/mar/16/guardianobituaries.stephenbates.*

586 Wurmbrand, Marx & Satan, 9.

587 Ibid., 15.

588 Ibid., 25.

589 Franz Mehring, Karl Marx: The Story of His Life, 430.

590 Mikhail Bakunin, God and State (New York: Dover Publications, 1970), 10.

591 Ibid.

592 Ibid., 11–12.

593 Ibid., 12. Italics in original.

594 Friedrich Nietzsche, Beyond Good and Evil: Prelude to a Philosophy of Future, eds. Rolf-Peter Hortsmann and Judith Norman, trans. Judith Norman (Cambridge: Cambridge University Press, 2001), 66.

595 Bakunin, God and State, 24.

596 Voltaire, "Epître à l'auteur de livre des Trois imposteurs" ["Epistle to the author of the book of the The Three Impostors"], ed. Louis Moland, Oeuvres completes de Voltaire [Complete Works of Voltaire] (Paris: Garnier, 1877–1885), vol. 10, 402–405. See also: The Voltaire Society,

"If God did not exist, it would be necessary to invent him," Whitman.edu, n.d., *https://www.whitman.edu/VSA/trois.imposteurs.html.*

597 Bakunin, God and State, 28.

598 Coughlin and Higgins, Re-Remembering the Mis-Remembered Left, 80.

599 Ibid., 32.

600 Saul Alinsky, Rules for Radicals: A Pragmatic Primer for Realistic Radicals (New York: Vintage, 1971), ix.

601 Interview by Eric Norden, "Saul Alinsky: Playboy Interview," Playboy, March 1972, archived at ScraptsFromTheLoft.com, archive date, May 1, 2018, *https://scrapsfromtheloft.com/comedy/saul-alinsky-playboy-interview-1972/.*

602 Coughlin and Higgins, Re-Remembering the Mis-Remembered Left, 33.

603 Kengor, The Devil and Karl Marx, 52. Parentheses in original.

604 Ibid., preface, xvii.

605 Sergey Nechayev, Catechism of a Revolutionary (Pattern Books, 2020), https://ia903203.us.archive.org/16/items/coarev/COARingram111.pdf.

606 Ibid., 3.

607 Ibid., 7.

608 The biographical information on Sergey Nechayev's life is drawn from the "Russian Anarchism," Spunk Library, Sprunk.org, n.d., *http://www.spunk.org/texts/places/russia/*. See also: "Sergey Nechayev 1869: The Revolutionary Catechism," archived in the "Russian Archive," Marxist.org, n.d., *https://www.marxists.org/subject/anarchism/nechayev/catechism.htm.*

609 Sean McMeekin, The Russian Revolution: A New History (New York: Basic Books, 2017).

610 Ibid., introduction, xv.

611 Ibid.

612 Ibid.

613 Ibid., xii. McMeekin is referring to the following book: Richard Pipe, The Russian Revolution (New York: Alfred A. Knopf, 1990). In this and the next quotation, McMeekin quoted from Pipe's 1990 book.

614 Ibid.

615 Ibid., xv.

616 Ibid., xv–xvi.

617 Ibid., 350–351.

618 Ibid., 348.

619 Ibid., xiii.

620 Carl K. Y. Shaw, "Hegel's Theory of Modern Bureaucracy," American Political Science Review 86, no. 2 (June 1992): 381–389, *https://www.jstor.org/stable/1964227.*

621 Hegel, Philosophy of Right, §287–298, pp. 283–289.

622 Sean Peek, "The Management Theory of Max Weber," Business.com, April 27, 2020, *https://www.business.com/articles/management-theory-of-max-weber/.* See also: "Max Weber's Bureaucratic Theory: Characteristics and Principles,"

Harappa Education, May 13, 2021, updated February 21, 2023, *https://harappa.education/harappa-diaries/max-weber-theory-of-bureaucracy/*. See also: Stanislav Andreski, ed., Max Weber on Capitalism, Bureaucracy and Religion: A Selection of Texts (London: George Allen & Unwin, 1983).

623 M. W. Jackson, "Bureaucracy in Hegel's Political Theory," Administration & Society 18, no. 2 (August 1986): 139–157, *https://journals.sagepub.com/doi/abs/10.1177/009539978601800201*.

624 Fritz Sager and Christian Rosser. "Weber, Wilson, and Hegel: Theories of Modern Bureaucracy," Public Administration Review 69, no. 6 (2009): 1136–1147, *https://www.academia.edu/5970267/Weber_Wilson_and_Hegel_Theories_of_Modern_Bureaucracy?auto=citations&from=cover_page*.

625 Max Weber, Economy and Society, trans. Guenther Roth and Claus Wittich (Oakland: University of California Press, 1978).

626 Woodrow Wilson, "The Study of Administration," Political Science Quarterly 2, no. 2 (June 1887): 197–222, *https://www.jstor.org/stable/2139277?seq=1#metadata_info_tab_contents*.

627 Sager and Rosser, "Weber, Wilson, and Hegel.

628 "Woodrow Wilson: The Father of Public Administration," Kent State Online, OnLineDegrees.Kent.Edu, August 21, 2018, *https://onlinedegrees.kent.edu/political-science/master-of-public-administration/community/father-of-public-administration*.

629 Roland J. Pestritto, Woodrow Wilson: The Essential Political Writings (Lanham, MD: Lexington Books, 2005), 233.

630 Roland J. Pestritto, "The German Stamp on Wilson's Administrative Progressivism," American Mind, May 22, 2019, *https://americanmind.org/salvo/the-german-stamp-on-wilsons-administrative-progressivism/*.

631 Magee, Hegel and the Hermetic Tradition, 188.

632 Coughlin and Higgins, Re-Remembering the Mis-Remembered Left, 23.

633 Woodrow Wilson, The New Freedom: A Call for the Emancipation of the Generous Energies of a People (New York and Garden City: Doubleday, Page, 1913). The quotation is taken from the 2018 publication of this work. See: Woodrow Wilson, The New Freedom (Frankfurt am Main, Germany: Outlook Verlag GmbH, Deutschland, 2018, a reproduction of the original), 26.

634 "New Freedom," Britannica.com, n.d., article revised and updated by Michael Ray, *https://www.britannica.com/topic/New-Freedom*.

635 Ibid., 27.

636 Woodrow Wilson, Constitutional Government in the United States (New York: Columbia University Press, 1908), 57.

637 Coughlin and Higgins, Re-Remembering the Mis-Remembered Left, 23–24. Brackets, quotation marks, and bolding all in original.

638 Russell, "Hegel," in History of Western, 744. Italics in original.

639 Coughlin and Higgins, Re-Remembering the Mis-Remembered Left, 25.

640 Ibid.

641 C. S. Lewis, The Abolition of Man (New York: Macmillan, 1955), 87.

642 John G. West, "The Magician's Twin," in John G. West, ed., The Magician's Twin: C. S. Lewis on Science, Scientism, and Society (Seattle: Discovery Institute Press, 2012), 19–45, quotation at 19.

643 Ibid.

644 Ibid., 24. Italics in original.

645 Ibid., 29.

646 Leo Strauss, Natural Right and History (Chicago: University of Chicago Press, 1953), introduction, 1.

647 Ibid., 1–2.

648 Ibid., 2.

649 Ibid., 42.

650 Ibid., 43.

651 Ibid., 12.

652 Ibid., 28.

653 Ibid., 29.

654 Ibid.

655 Ibid., 6.

656 Ibid., 5.

657 Ibid.

658 Ibid., 16.

659 Ibid., 45.

CHAPTER 4

660 Arif Dirlik, "The Predicament of Marxist Revolutionary Thought: Mao Zedong, Antonio Gramsci, and the Reformulation of Marxist Revolutionary Theory," Modern China 9, no. 2 (April 1983): 182–211, quotation at 184, *https://journals.sagepub.com/doi/abs/10.1177/009770048300900202?journalCode=mcxa.*

661 Stephen R. C. Hicks, Explaining Postmodernism: Skepticism and Socialism from Rousseau to Foucault (Roscoe, IL: Ockham's Razor Publishing, 1st ed., 2004, exp. ed., 2011), 137.

662 George Hoare and Nathan Sperber, An Introduction to Antonio Gramsci: His Life, Thought, and Legacy (New York: Bloomsbury Academic, 2016), 19–20.

663 Ibid., 119. This paragraph is drawn largely from George Hoare and Nathan Sperber, An Introduction to Antonio Gramsci: His Life, Thought, and Legacy, chapter 5, 118–119.

664 Ibid.

665 "Eighth Notebook [1930–1932] §173," in Antonio Gramsci, Prison Notebooks, vol. 3, ed. and trans. Joseph A. Buttigieg (New York: Columbia University Press, 2007), 333–334.

666 "Eighth Notebook [1930–1932] §173," 334. All quotes from Gramsci in this paragraph come from this source at pp. 333–334.

667 "Eighth Notebook [1930–1932] §213," 360.

668 Ibid., 185.

669 Brian Duignan, "Postmodernism: Philosophy," Encyclopedia Britannica, Britannica.com, n.d., *https://www.britannica.com/topic/explanation.*

670 Rolf Wiggershaus, The Frankfurt School: Its History, Theories, and Political Significance, trans. Michael Robertson (Cambridge, MA: MIT Press, 1994), introduction, 1.

671 Ibid., 5.

672 Ibid.

673 Ibid.

674 Ibid. Wiggershaus referenced the young Marx and the 1844 Manuscripts as follows: Karl Marx, Ökonomisch-philosophische Manuskripte [in English, Economic-Philosophic Manuscript], 1844. Wiggershaus cited the source for Marx's 1844 manuscript as follows: Karl Marx, "Economic and Philosophic Manuscripts," in Early Writings, trans. Rodney Livingstone and Gregor Benton (London: Penguin Books, 1975), 279–400.

675 Ibid., 96.

676 Ibid., 5.

677 Antonio Gramsci, Selections from the Prison Notebooks of Antonio Gramsci, eds. and trans. Quinton Hoare and Geoffrey Nowell Smith (New York: International Publishers, 1971).

678 William S. Lind, "Who Stole Our Culture?" in Ted Baehr and Pat Boone, The Culture-Wise Family: Upholding Christian Values in a Mass Media World (Ventura, CA: Regal Books, 2007), 178–185, quotation at 179.

679 German Communist Rudi Dutschke, a Herbert Marcuse disciple, coined the phrase "long march through the institutions" in the 1960s. See: Mike Gonzalez, "The Long March through the Corporations," Heritage Foundation, Heritage.org, March 26, 2021, *https://www.heritage.org/progressivism/commentary/the-long-march-through-the-corporations.*

680 Hicks, Explaining Postmodernism, 39.

681 Ibid.

682 Ibid.

683 Jean-François Lyotard, The Postmodern Condition: A Report on Knowledge, trans. Geoff Bennington and Brian Massumi (Minneapolis: University of Minnesota Press, 1984). Originally published as: Jean-François Lyotard, La Condition postmoderne: rapport sur le savoir (Paris: Les Éditions de Minuit, 1979).

684 Ibid., introduction, xxiv.

685 Ibid.

686 Ibid.

687 Ibid.

688 Ludwig Wittgenstein, Philosophical Investigations, trans. G. E. M. Anscombe (Oxford, England: Basil Blackwell, 1968).

689 Ludwig Wittgenstein, Tractatus Logico-Philosophicus, trans. D. F. Pears and B. F. McGuinness (London: Routledge & Kegan Paul, 1922).

690 Matt McManus, "Ludwig Wittgenstein: A Post-Modern Philosopher?" MeronWest.cm, January 10, 2021, *https://merionwest.com/2021/01/10/ludwig-wittgenstein-a-post-modern-philosopher/*.

691 Wittgenstein, Philosophical Investigations, part 1 [the part Wittgenstein had completed by 1945], no. 275, p. 96e [96 English, the right-hand pages translating into English the German page 96 positioned in the left-hand page of the open book]. Punctuation, italics, British spelling all in original.

692 Walter Truett Anderson, "Introduction: What's Going On Here?" in The Fontana Postmodernism Reader, 4. Italics and parentheses in original.

693 Ibid.

694 Ibid.

695 Ibid., 5.

696 Ibid.

697 Ibid.

698 "Gender-Neutral Language in Writing," SkillsYouNeed.com, n.d., *https://www.skillsyouneed.com/write/gender-neutral-language.html.*

699 Helen Pluckrose and James Lindsay, Cynical Theories: How Activist Scholarship Made Everything about Race, Gender, and Identity—and Why This Harms Everybody (Durham, NC: Pitchstone Publishing, 2020), 31.

700 Jean Baudrillard, Simulacra and Simulation, trans. Sheila Faria Glaser (Ann Arbor: University of Michigan Press, 2017).

701 Fredric Jameson, Postmodernism: Or the Cultural Logic of Late Capitalism (New York: Verso Books, 2019).

702 Gilles Deleuze and Felix Guattari, Anti-Oedipus: Capitalism and Schizophrenia, trans. Robert Hurley, Mark Seem, and Helen R. Lane (New York: Penguin Books, 2009). Originally published in France: Gilles Deleuze and Felix Guattari, L'Anti-Oedipe (Paris: Les Éditions de Minuit, 1972).

703 Ibid., 39. This point and the following three points are drawn almost word for word from the original source, with minor paraphrasing.

704 Ibid., 39–40.

705 Ibid., 41.

706 Ibid., 42.

707 Ibid., 43.

708 Originally published as: Jean-Jacques Rousseau, Du Contract Social; ou, Principes du Droit Politique [In English, The Social Contract: Or Principles of Political Right] (Amsterdam, Holland: Marc Michel Rev., 1762). The quotation comes from book 1 of Rousseau's Social Contract.

709 Pluckrose and Lindsay, Cynical Theories, 37.

710 Ibid., 38. Italics in original.

711 Jacques Derrida, De la Grammatologie (Paris: Les Éditions de Minuit, 1967).

712 Jacques Derrida, L'Écriture et la Différence (Paris: Éditions du Seuil, 1967).

713 Jacques Derrida, La Voix et le Phénomène (Paris: Presses Universitaires de France, 1967).

714 Mark C. Taylor, "What Derrida Really Meant," University of Chicago Press, Press.UChicago.edu, n.d., *https://press.uchicago.edu/books/derrida/taylorderrida.html*. See also: Mark Lilla, "The Politics of Jacques Derrida," New York Review, June 25, 1998, *https://www.nybooks.com/articles/1998/06/25/the-politics-of-jacques-derrida/*.

715 Pluckrose and Lindsay, Cynical Theories, 40. See also: Nasrullah Mambrol, "Deconstruction," Literary Theory and Criticism, Literariness.org, March 22, 2016, *https://literariness.org/2016/03/22/deconstruction/*.

716 Catherine Prendergast, "The Unexceptional Schizophrenic: A Post-Postmodern Introduction," Journal of Literary & Cultural Disability Studies 2, no. 1 (2008): 55–62, *https://www.liverpooluniversitypress.co.uk/journals/article/48277*. The article was also published here: Catherine Prendergast, "The Unexceptional Schizophrenic: A Post-Postmodern Introduction," in Lennard J. Davis, ed., The Disability Studies Reader (New York: Routledge, 4th ed., 2013), 236–245. Quotations are identified by page numbers from the publication of Prendergast's paper in this book.

717 Ibid, 236.

718 "Schizophrenia: Overview," Mayo Clinic, MayoClinic.org, n.d., *https://www.mayoclinic.org/diseases-conditions/schizophrenia/symptoms-causes/syc-20354443*.

719 Gilles Deleuze and Felix Guattari, Anti-Oedipus: Capitalism and Schizophrenia, trans. Robert Hurley, Mark Seem, and Helen R. Lane (New York: Penguin Books, 2009), 87. Originally published in France: Gilles Deleuze and Felix Guattari, L'Anti-Oedipe (Paris: Les Éditions de Minuit, 1972).

720 Prendergast, "The Unexceptional Schizophrenic," 237.

721 Ibid., 236.

722 Ibid.

723 Ibid., 237.

724 René Descartes, Discourse on Method, 1637. Original publication: René Descartes, Discours de la Méthode Pour bien conduire sa raison, et chercher la vérité dan les sciences (Leyde, Netherlands: De l'Imprimerie de Ian Marie, 1637).

725 Wiggershaus, The Frankfurt School, 12.

726 Ibid., 12–13, quotation at 13.

727 Ibid., 9.

728 Ibid., 34.

729 Ibid., 37.

730 The German Bundestag website explains the November Revolution (1918) as follows:

The revolution of November 1918 was a consequence of the military defeat of the German Empire in the First World War and was triggered by the naval mutiny at the beginning of November 1918. Within only a few days this insurgency spread throughout the Empire with no appreciable resistance from the old order. It developed into a mass movement against the monarchical system as the working classes joined forces with the troops. Throughout the Empire, Workers' and Soldiers' Councils were formed and assumed political and military powers. The Social Democratic parties, which had been split since 1917 into the Majority Social Democratic Party of Germany (MSPD) and the Independent Social Democratic Party of Germany (USPD), put themselves at the head of the revolution; along with the Councils, they became the key political players in the November revolution. Most of the Councils were politically close to the MSPD. On 9 November 1918, the Imperial Chancellor, Prince Max of Baden (1867–1929), announced the abdication of Emperor [Kaiser Wilhelm II]. Prince Max handed over the office of Chancellor of the Reich to Friedrich Ebert (1871–1925), chairman of the MSPD. There was, however, no strong sense of commitment to parliamentary democracy and the republic among military officers, the police, the judiciary and the administration and civil service. This lack of republican spirit would be a heavy burden for the new Weimar Republic.

The German Bundestag website explains the Spartacist Revolt of January 1919 as follows:

On 28 December 1918, the alliance between the MSPD and the USPD in the provisional government collapsed when the USPD withdrew from the Council of People's Representatives because of differences over a military operation. The conflict over the future course of the revolution escalated into what became known as the Spartacist Revolt of January 1919, when troops of the MSPD government waged bloody battles with representatives of the USPD and the Communist KPD, the government troops being assisted by the right-wing Freikorps. On 15 and 16 January 1919, Freikorps troops murdered the KPD leaders Rosa Luxemburg (1871–1919) and Karl Liebknecht (1871–1919).

Finally, the German Bundestag website explains the formation of the Weimar Republic as follows:

On 6 February, the National Assembly constituted itself in Weimar and on 11 February elected Friedrich Ebert President of the Reich. The first government of the Reich to be accountable to Parliament, the Weimar Coalition of Majority SPD, the Centre Party and the German Democratic Party (DDP), under the premiership of Philipp Scheidemann (MSPD), took office on 12 February 1919. Most of the Workers' and Soldiers' Councils had dissolved themselves by the summer of 1919.

Source: Deutscher Bundestag, "The November Revolution, 1918/1919," Historical Exhibition Presented by the German Bundestag, Bundestag.de, March 1, 2006, *https://www.bundestag.de/resource/blob/189772/8b9e17bd8d64e64e8e3a95fc2305e132/november_revolution-data.pdf*.

731 Wiggershaus, The Frankfurt School, 47. Wiggershaus is the source of the biographical information in this paragraph on Max Horkheimer, 41–52.

732 Max Horkheimer, "Traditional and Critical Theory," in Critical Theory: Selected Essays, trans. Matthew J. O'Connell et al. (New York: Continuum Publishing, 1972), 188–243.
733 Ibid., 194.
734 Ibid., 199.
735 Wiggershaus, The Frankfurt School, 48.
736 Horkheimer, "Traditional and Critical Theory," 208.
737 Ibid.
738 Ibid., 212.
739 Ibid., 213.
740 Ibid.
741 Ibid.
742 Ibid.
743 Ibid., 213–214.
744 Ibid., 215.
745 Ibid., 241.
746 Wiggershaus, The Frankfurt School, 53. Again, Wiggershaus is the source for the biographical material on Erich Fromm included in this section, pp. 52–60.
747 Ibid., 53.
748 Ibid., 54.
749 Ibid.
750 Ibid.
751 Ibid.
752 Ibid, 54–55, quotation at 55.
753 Ibid., 55.
754 Ibid. The quotation is from the following source: Karl Marx and Friedrich Engels, The Holy Family, or Critique of Critical Criticism, trans. Richard Dixon and Clemens Dutt (Moscow, USSR: Progress Publishers, 1956), 116. The original book was published in 1845. Marx and Engels aimed the book against Bruno Bauer and Ludwig Feuerbach, two young Hegelians who defended religion against Marx's attacks. See: Roland Boer, "Contradiction: The Crucible of Historical Materialism," originally published in Cultural Commentary, April 26, 2016, archived on CultureMatters.org, *http://www.culturematters.org.uk/index.php/culture/theory/item/2276-contradiction-the-crucible-of-historical-materialism*.
755 Ibid.
756 Georg Lukács, History and Class Consciousness: Studies in Marxist Dialectics, trans. Rodney Livingstone (Cambridge, MA: MIT Press, 1971).
757 Georg Lukács, "Preface to the New Edition (1967)," in History and Class Consciousness, xvii, italics in original.
758 Titus Stahl, "Georg [György] Lukács," Stanford Encyclopedia of Philosophy, Plato.Stanford.edu, first published November 4, 2013, substantive revision January 18, 2018, *https://plato.stanford.edu/entries/lukacs/*.
759 Lukács, History and Class Consciousness, 87.

760 Ibid., 88.
761 Ibid., 91.
762 Ibid., 92.
763 Ibid.
764 Wiggershaus, The Frankfurt School, 55.
765 Ibid., 56.
766 Ibid., 58.
767 Ibid., 59.
768 Ibid.
769 Eric Fromm, The Dogma of Christ and Other Essays on Religion, Psychology and Culture (New York: Holt, Rinehart and Winston, 1963), 75. The essay, "The Dogma of Christ," first appeared in German in 1930.
770 Ibid., 48–49.
771 Ibid., 52.
772 Ibid.
773 Wiggershaus, The Frankfurt School, 58.
774 Ibid., 58–59.
775 Ibid., 60.
776 Dima Vorobiev, "Is Sigmund Freud a Communist?" Quora.com, May 21, 2020, *https://www.quora.com/Is-Sigmund-Freud-a-communist.*
777 Martin Heidegger, Being and Time, trans. John Macquarrie and Edward Robinson (Oxford, England: Blackwell Publishers, 1962).
778 Ibid., 78–79.
779 Georg Lukács, The Theory of the Novel: A Historico-Philosophical Essay on the Forms of Great Epic Literature, trans. Anna Bostock (Cambridge, MA: MIT Press, 1971), preface, 11.
780 Georg Lukács, "Preface to the New Edition (1967)," xiv.
781 Georg Lukács, "The Old Culture and the New Culture," Telos 1970, no. 5 (Spring 1971): 21–30, quotation at 26–27. *http://journal.telospress.com/content/1970/5/21.full.pdf+html.*
782 Ibid., 28. Italics in original.
783 Ibid., 29.
784 Ibid., 29.
785 Coughlin and Higgins, Re-Remembering the Mis-Remembered Left, 60.
786 Ibid., 61.
787 Ibid.
788 Wiggershaus, The Frankfurt School, 127–128, quotation at 128. Wiggershaus is the source for the historical material included in this section, pp. 127–148.
789 Ibid., 146.
790 Ibid., 148.
791 Ibid., 133–134.

792 Wiggershaus, The Frankfurt School, 290–291, quotation at 291. Wiggershaus is the source for the historical material on the relocation of the Frankfurt School to the United States included in this section, pp. 291–302.

793 Ibid., 149.

794 Wiggershaus, The Frankfurt School, 67. Wiggershaus is the source for the historical material on the relocation of the Frankfurt School to the United States included in this section, pp. 291–302.

795 Ibid., 81.

796 Ibid.

797 Original edition: Max Horkheimer and Theodor W. Adorno, Dialektid der Aufklärung (New York: Social Studies Association, 1944). See also: James Schmidt, "The Making and the Marketing of the Philosophische Fragmente: A Note on the Early History of the Dialectic of Enlightenment (Part I)," PersistentEnlightenment.com, January 9, 2017, *https://persistentenlightenment.com/2017/01/09/philfrag1/*.

798 Max Horkheimer and Theodor W. Adorno, Dialektid der Aufklärung (Amsterdam: Querido Verlag XV, 1947).

799 Max Horkheimer and Theodor W. Adorno, Dialectic of Enlightenment, trans. John Cumming (New York, Continuum Publishing, 1986), introduction, xi. Page numbers associated with quotations from the Dialectic of Enlightenment are referenced from this edition of the book.

800 Ibid., xiii.

801 Max Horkheimer and Theodor W. Adorno, "The Culture Industry: Enlightenment as Mass Deception," in Dialectical Enlightenment, 120–167, quotation at 121.

802 Ibid., 120.

803 Ibid.

804 Ibid., 121.

805 Ibid.

806 Ibid.

807 Ibid., 133.

808 Ibid., 165.

809 Ibid., 167.

810 Max Horkheimer and Theodor W. Adorno, "Juliette or Enlightenment and Morality," in Dialectical Enlightenment, 81–119. Italics in original.

811 Ibid., 84.

812 Ibid.

813 Ibid.

814 Ibid., 85.

815 Ibid.

816 Ibid. Parentheses in original.

817 Ibid., 85–86.

818 Ibid., 86.

819 Ibid., 147.
820 Ibid.
821 Ibid., 86.
822 Ibid., 87–88. Quotation is from the following source: Marquis de Sade, L'Histoire de Juliette (en Holland, 1797), vol. 5, 319f. The 1797 edition was illustrated with erotic engravings. See: Sixty Erotic Engravings from Juliette (New York: Grove Press, Inc., 1969).
823 Ibid., 88. Quotation is from the following source: Marquis de Sade, L'Histoire de Juliette, vol. 5, 322f.
824 Ibid. Quotation is from the following source: Marquis de Sade, L'Histoire de Juliette, vol. 5, 324.
825 John Phillips, The Marquis de Sade: A Very Short Introduction (Oxford: Oxford University Press, 2005), 92.
826 Ibid., 92 and 94 (93 is a full-page illustration). The reference to Pauvert is to the following source: Jean-Jacques Pauvert, "Notice Bibliographique," in Marquis de Sade, Oeuvres Complètes [Complete Works], éd. mise en place per Annie Le Brun et Jean-Jacque Pauvert (Paris: J.-J. Pauvert, 1996), vol. 8 (first vol. of Juliette), 18.
827 Horkheimer and Adorno, "Juliette or Enlightenment and Morality," 155.
828 Ibid.
829 Ibid., 155–156.
830 Coughlin and Higgins, Re-Remembering the Mis-Remembered Left, 82–85, quotation at 84.
831 Horkheimer and Adorno, "Juliette or Enlightenment and Morality," 119.
832 Ibid., 101. Latin quotation is taken from Spinosa, Pars. VI, Appendix, Cap. XVI.
833 Horkheimer and Adorno, "Juliette or Enlightenment and Morality," 119.
834 Ibid., 120.
835 Coughlin and Higgins, Re-Remembering the Mis-Remembered Left, 84.
836 Ibid., 84–85. Bold type in original.
837 T. W. Adorno, Else Frenkel-Brunswik, Daniel J. Levison, and R. Nevitt Sanford, in collaboration with Betty Anon, Maria Hertz Levinson, and William Morrow, The Authoritarian Personality (New York: Harper & Row, 1950). The edition used here is the 2019 edition published by Verso Books in New York. The pagination for quotations is taken from the 2019 Verso edition. The 2019 Verso edition included a new introduction by Peter E. Gordon, the Amabel B. James Professor of History at Harvard University, a scholar of Adorno and the Frankfurt School. In addition, the 2019 Verso edition published a previously unpublished "Remarks on The Authoritarian Personality" by T. W. Adorno. Subsequently, we will refer to the 2019 Verso edition as T. W. Adorno, et al., The Authoritarian Personality.
838 Ibid., 21.
839 Ibid., "Construction of the Anti-Semitism (A-S) Scale," 57–71.

840 Ibid., "Construction of the Ethnocentrism (E) Scale," 104–109.

841 Ibid., "Construction of the Politico-Economic Conservativism (PEC) Scale," 153–178.

842 Fabian Freyenhagen, "Adorno and Horkheimer on Anti-Semitism," in Peter E. Gordon, Espen Hammer, and Max Pensky, eds., A Companion to Adorno (Hoboken, NJ: John Wiley & Sons, 2020), 103–122.

843 Horkheimer and Adorno, Dialectic of Enlightenment, 187.

844 Ibid., 208.

845 Ibid., 187.

846 Adorno et al., The Authoritarian Personality, 976.

847 Wiggershaus, The Frankfurt School, 421.

848 Adorno et al., The Authoritarian Personality, 976.

849 Peter E. Gordon, "Introduction to The Authoritarian Personality," in Adorno et al., The Authoritarian Personality, xxiii–xl, at xxiii. Italics in original.

850 Ibid.

851 Ibid., xxiii–xxiv.

852 Ibid., xxv–xxvi.

853 William F. Stone and Laurence D. Smith, "Authoritarianism: Left and Right," in W. F. Stone et al., ed., Strength and Weakness (New York: Springer-Verlag New York, 1993), 144–156, quotation at 144.

854 Ibid.

855 Edward A. Shils, "Authoritarianism: 'Right' and 'Left,'" in Richard Christie and Marie Jahoda, eds., Studies in the Scope and Method of "The Authoritarian Personality" (Glencoe, IL: The Free Press, 1954), 24–49.

856 Stuart Jeffries, Grand Hyatt Abyss: The Lives of the Frankfurt School (London: Verso, 2016), 278.

857 Bob Altemeyer, Right-Wing Authoritarianism (Winnipeg, Canada: University of Manitoba Press, 1981). See also: Bob Altemeyer, Enemies of Freedom: Understanding Right-Wing Authoritarianism (San Francisco: Jossey-Bass, 1988). See also: John W. Dean and Bob Altemeyer, Authoritarian Nightmare: The Ongoing Threat of Trump's Followers (Brooklyn, NY: Melville House Publishing, 2020). See also: Benjamin A. Saunders and Josephine Ngo, "The Right-Wing Authoritarianism Scale," in Virgil Zeigler-Hills and Todd K. Shackelford, eds., Encyclopedia of Personality and Individual Differences (Cham, Switzerland: Springer International Publishing AG 2020), *https://www.researchgate.net/profile/Benjamin-Saunders-6/publication/318260321_The_Right-Wing_Authoritarianism_Scale/links/59c57cccaca272c71bb8ea4e/The-Right-Wing-Authoritarianism-Scale.pdf*.

858 "Strength through Joy," Erenow.com, n.d., *https://erenow.net/ww/hitlers-revolution-ideology-social-programs-foreign-affairs/14.php*.

859 Real Time with Bill Maher, HBO, September 9, 2005. Quoted in: Jonah Goldberg, Liberal Fascism: The Secret History of the American Left from Mussolini to the Politics of Meaning (New York: Doubleday, 2008), 1.

860 Richard J. Evans, The Coming of the Third Reich (New York: Penguin Press, 2003), 173.
861 Ibid.
862 Ibid.
863 Ibid.
864 Ibid., 173–174.
865 Ibid., 174.
866 Ibid.
867 Quoted by Walter Truett Anderson, "Introduction: What's Going On Here?" in The Fontana Postmodernism Reader, 3–4. Original source of the quotation: David Harvey, The Condition of Postmodernity: An Enquiry into the Origins of Cultural Change (Cambridge, England: Basil Blackwell, 1989), 27.
868 Charles H. Kahn, The Art and Thought of Heraclitus: An Edition of the Fragments with Translation and Commentary (Cambridge: Cambridge University Press, 1979).
869 Joshua J. Mark, "Gorgias' on Nature (On the Non-Existent)," World History Encyclopedia, March 1, 2022, *https://www.worldhistory.org/article/1952/gorgias-on-nature-on-the-non-existent/*.
870 Friedrich Nietzsche, Twilight of the Idols or How to Philosophize with a Hammer, in Alan D. Schrift, Duncan Large, and Adrian Del Caro, eds., Adrian Del Caro, Carol Diethe, Duncan Large, et al., trans., The Complete Works of Friedrich Nietzsche (Stanford: Stanford University Press, 2021), vol. 9, 41–132, at 58. Ellipses and quotation marks in original.
871 Ibid., fn. 5 to Twilight of the Idols, in the original at p. 472.
872 The reference (459c) is to the standard paragraph numbering scheme used in publishing various editions and translations of Plato's dialogues. C. Francis Higgins, University of Louisiana, Lafayette, "Gorgias (483–375 B.C.E.)," Internet Encyclopedia of Philosophy, IEEP.UTM.edu, n.d., *https://iep.utm.edu/gorgias/*.

CHAPTER 5

873 Daniel Bell, Marxian Socialism in the United States (Princeton: Princeton University Press, 1967) introduction, xvii. First published in Donald Drew Egbert and Stow Parsons, eds., Socialism and American Life (Princeton: Princeton University Press, 1952), Princeton Studies in American Civilization, no. 4, chap. 6.
874 Leszek Kołakowski, "Herbert Marcuse: Marxism as a Totalitarian Utopia of the New Left," in Main Currents of Marxism: Its Origins, Growth and Dissolution: Volume 3, The Breakdown, P. S. Falla, trans. (Oxford: Oxford University Press, 1978), Chapter 11, "Herbert Marcuse: Marxism as a Totalitarian Utopia of the New Left," 396–420, quotation at 415.
875 Olivia Laing, "Wilhelm Reich: The Strange, Prescient Sexologist Who Sought to Set Us Free," The Guardian, April 17, 2021, *https://www.theguardian.com/books/2021/apr/17/wilhelm-reich-the-strange-prescient-sexologist-who-sought-*

to-set-us-free. See: Michel Foucault, The History of Sexuality: Volume 1, An Introduction, trans. Robert Hurle (New York: Vintage Books, 1990), 131. For the original French edition, see: Michel Foucault, Histoire de la Sexualité, 1: La Volonté de Savoir (Paris: Éditions Gallimard, 1976), 173.

876 John M. Newman, JFK and Vietnam: Deception, Intrigue, and the Struggle for Power (New York: Time Warner, 1992), 442.

877 James DiEugenio, Destiny Betrayed: JFK, Cuba, and the Garrison Case (New York: Skyhorse Publishing, 1992), 370. The pagination is taken from the second edition of the book, published in 2012.

878 Kirkpatrick Sale, SDS: The Rise and Development of the Students for a Democratic Society, the Organization That Became the Major Expression of the American Left in the Sixties—Its Passage from Student Protest to Institutional Resistance, to Revolutionary Activism, and Its Ultimate Impact on American Politics and Life (New York: Random House, 1973).

879 Ibid., 204.

880 Ibid., 204–205.

881 "John Lewis—March from Selma to Montgomery, 'Bloody Sunday,' 1965," Confrontations for Justice, Eyewitness, National Archives, Archives.gov, n.d., *https://www.archives.gov/exhibits/eyewitness/html.php?section=2*.

882 "Selma to Montgomery March," History.com, originally posted on January 28, 2010, updated on January 11, 2022, *https://www.history.com/topics/black-history/selma-montgomery-march#edmund-pettus-bridge*.

883 The biographical information on Herbert Marcuse in this and the following four paragraphs is sourced from the following: (1) Arnold Farr, "Herbert Marcuse," Stanford Encyclopedia of Philosophy, Plato.Stanford.Edu, first published on December 18, 2013, substantive revision on April 10, 2019, *https://plato.stanford.edu/entries/marcuse/*; (2) Douglas Kellner, "Herbert Marcuse," archived at Professor Kellner's faculty page, "Illuminations folder," at the Graduate School of Arts and Sciences, University of California, Los Angeles (UCLA), gseis.UCLA.edu, n.d., *https://pages.gseis.ucla.edu/faculty/kellner/Illumina%20Folder/kell12.htm*; (3) Richard Wolin, "Herbert Marcuse, American Philosopher," Britannica.com, n.d., *https://www.britannica.com/biography/Herbert-Marcuse*; (4) Kenneth A. Briggs, "Marcuse, Radical Philosopher, Dies," New York Times, July 31, 1979, section A, p. 1, *https://www.nytimes.com/1979/07/31/archives/marcuse-radical-philosopher-dies-largely-unnoticed-before-60s.html*; and (5) "Herbert Marcuse," Wikipedia.org, n.d., *https://en.wikipedia.org/wiki/Herbert_Marcuse*.

884 John Goetz, "Berlin Offers Marcuse Respect and a Final Home," Los Angeles Times, July 18, 2003, *https://www.latimes.com/archives/la-xpm-2003-jul-18-et-goetz18-story.html*.

885 Information in this paragraph and the following paragraph regarding Marcuse's teaching career at Brandeis University is sourced from: Michael Horowitz, "Portrait of the Marxist as an Old Trouper," Playboy, September 1970, *https://www.marcuse.org/herbert/newsevents/1970/709PlayboyInt.htm*.

886 Ibid.

887 Savannah Munoz, "Who Is Angel Davis?" Triton Magazine, May 6, 2019, *https://tritonmag.com/who-was-angela-davis/*.

888 Ibid.

889 Judith Moore, "Marxist Professor Herbert Marcuse's Years at USCD," San Diego Reader, September 11, 1986, *https://www.sandiegoreader.com/news/1986/sep/11/angel-apocalypse/*.

890 George Katsiaficas, "Afterword: Marcuse as Activist: Reminiscences on His Theory and Practice," in Douglas Kellner, ed., Herbert Marcuse: The New Left and the 1960s—Volume 3, Collected Papers of Herbert Marcuse (London: Routledge, 2005), afterword, 192–203, quotation at 192.

891 Ibid., 194.

892 Ibid., 192.

893 Briggs, "Marcuse, Radical Philosopher, Dies."

894 "Bill Moyers: A Conversation with Herbert Marcuse," in Douglas Kellner, ed., Herbert Marcuse: The New Left and the 1960s—Volume 3, Collected Papers of Herbert Marcuse, 154–165, quotation at 154.

895 Ibid., 155–156.

896 Kołakowski, "Herbert Marcuse: Marxism as a Totalitarian Utopia of the New Left," 396.

897 Ibid.

898 Reuters Staff, "Polish Philosopher and Author Kołakowski Dead at 81," Reuters, July 17, 2009, *https://www.reuters.com/article/entertainmentNews/idUSTRE56G67Q20090717*.

899 Bryan Magee, "Marcuse and the Frankfurt School: Dialogue with Herbert Marcuse," in Talking Philosophy: Dialogues with Fifteen Leading Philosophers (Oxford: Oxford University Press, 1978), 43–55, quotation at 45. The Magee interview with Marcuse can also be seen here: Philosophy Overdose, "The Frankfurt School—Herbert Marcuse & Bryan Magee," YouTube.com, posted April 2, 2022, *https://www.youtube.com/watch?v=U23HoOm_SvO*.

900 Ibid., 45.

901 Ibid.

902 Herbert Marcuse, Eros and Civilization: A Philosophical Inquiry into Freud (New York: Vintage Books, 1961). First paperback edition of Eros and Civilization published in the United States.

903 Herbert Marcuse, Eros and Civilization: A Philosophical Inquiry into Freud (Boston: Beacon Press, 1955).

904 Magee, "Marcuse and the Frankfurt School," 44.

905 Douglas Kellner, "Introduction: Radical Politics, Marcuse, and the New Left," in Herbert Marcuse: The New Left and the 1960s—Volume 3, Collected Papers of Herbert Marcuse, 6.

906 Ibid., 5.

907 Ibid., 2.

908 Ibid., 11.

909 Ibid., 5.

910 Herbert Marcuse, "Liberation from the Affluent Society," in Douglas Kellner, ed., Herbert Marcuse: The New Left and the 1960s—Volume 3, Collected Papers of Herbert Marcuse, 76–86, quotation at 77.

911 Douglas Kellner, "Herbert Marcuse," archived at Professor Kellner's faculty page, "Illuminations folder," at the Graduate School of Arts and Sciences, University of California, Los Angeles (UCLA).

912 Herbert Marcuse, Reason and Revolution: Hegel and the Rise of Social Theory (New York: Oxford University Press, 1941).

913 Kellner, "Herbert Marcuse."

914 Ibid.

915 Herbert Marcuse, "Marcuse Defines His New Left Line," in Douglas Kellner, ed., Herbert Marcuse: The New Left and the 1960s—Volume 3, Collected Papers of Herbert Marcuse, 100–117, quotation at 100. In a footnote, Kellner explained that this interview was originally published in the French journal Express and was translated for the New York Times Magazine and published on October 27, 1968. Ellipsis in the original.

916 Ibid., 101.

917 Ibid.

918 Ibid.

919 Ibid.,102.

920 Herbert Marcuse, "The Problem of Violence and Radical Opposition," in Douglas Kellner, ed., Herbert Marcuse: The New Left and the 1960s—Volume 3, Collected Papers of Herbert Marcuse, 57–75, quotation at 57–58. In a footnote, Douglas Kellner explained that "The Problem of Violence and Radical Opposition" was a translation of a lecture that Marcuse gave at the Free University of West Perlin in July 1967, translated by Jeremy J. Shapiro and Shierry M. Weber and published in Herbert Marcuse, Five Lectures: Psychoanalysis, Politics and Utopia (Boston: Beacon Press, 1970). The questions and answers at the end of the lecture were translated for Das Ende der Utopie [in English, The End of Utopia] (Berlin: Verlag Peter von Maikowshi, 1967). The questions were abridged by the translators and the answers provided in full.

921 Ibid., 64.

922 "Mr. Harold Keen: Interview with Dr. Herbert Marcuse," in Douglas Kellner, ed., Herbert Marcuse: The New Left and the 1960s—Volume 3, Collected Papers of Herbert Marcuse, 128–136, quotation at 128–129. Douglas Kellner explained in a footnote that the interview was broadcast on San Diego KFMB-TV on February 25, 1969.

923 The statement is properly attributed to Jack Weinberg, the twenty-four-year-old leader of the Free Speech Movement at the University of California, Berkeley, with a San Francisco Chronicle reporter around 1965. Bartleby.com cites as a source for this the Washington Post, March 23, 1970, p.

Endnotes

1. See: "Respectfully Quoted: A Dictionary of Quotations," Bartleby.com, 1989, Number 1828, *https://www.bartleby.com/73/1828.html.*

924 Herbert Marcuse, "The Affirmative Character of Culture," originally published in German in Zeitschrift für Sozialforschung [in English, Journal of Social Research], vol. 7, 1937l. See: Herbert Marcuse, "The Affirmative Character of Culture," in Negations: Essays in Critical Theory, trans. Jeremy J. Shapiro (Boston: Beacon Press, 1968), 88–133, quotation at 122.

925 Ibid., Herbert Marcuse, "The Affirmative Character of Culture," in Negations: Essays in Critical Theory, 130.

926 Herbert Marcuse, Eros and Civilization: A Philosophical Inquiry into Freud (Boston: Beacon Press, 1955), introduction, 3.

927 Ibid., preface, xii.

928 Ibid., introduction, 8.

929 Ibid., 3.

930 Ibid., 3–4.

931 Ibid., 4.

932 Ibid., 5.

933 Sigmund Freud, Civilization and Its Discontents, trans. James Strachey (Scotts Valley, CA: CreateSpace Independent Publishing Platform, 2018), chapter 4, 34–35, quotation at 35. All page references for quotations from Freud's Civilization and Its Discontents are from this edition of the book.

934 Ibid., 34.

935 Ibid., 17.

936 Ibid.

937 Ibid.

938 Marcuse, Eros and Civilization, 16.

939 Ibid., 82.

940 Ibid., 83.

941 Ibid., 101.

942 Ibid.

943 Ibid., 95.

944 Ibid., 100. Italics in original.

945 Ibid., 102.

946 Ibid.

947 Ibid., 103.

948 Ibid.

949 Ibid., 203.

950 Ibid., 202.

951 Ibid., 49.

952 Ibid. Italics in original.

953 Ibid., 201.

954 Ibid.

955 Ibid.

956 John Phillips, The Marquis de Sade: A Very Short Introduction (Oxford: Oxford University Press, 2005).
957 Ibid., 107.
958 Ibid., 110.
959 Ibid.
960 Marcuse, Eros and Civilization, 202.
961 Ibid.
962 Ibid. Italics in original.
963 Ibid.
964 Ibid., 203.
965 Ibid.
966 Ibid.
967 Ibid.
968 Ibid., 205. The cited quotation is from the following source: Sigmund Freud, An Outline of Psychoanalysis (New York: W. W. Norton, 1949), 26.
969 Ibid., 212–213.
970 Tyrus Miller, "Perversion and Utopia: Sade, Fourier, and Critical Theory," College Literature 45, no. 2 (Spring 2018): 330–359, quotation at 332, *https://muse.jhu.edu/article/690410*.
971 Ibid., 341.
972 Ibid.
973 Ibid. Italics in original.
974 Wiggershaus, The Frankfurt School, 499.
975 Ibid., 498.
976 Ibid., 497.
977 Ibid.
978 Ibid., 498.
979 Ibid.
980 Freud, Civilization and Its Discontents, 40.
981 Ibid., 40–41.
982 Leszek Kołakowski, "Herbert Marcuse: Marxism as a Totalitarian Utopia of the New Left," in Main Currents of Marxism: Its Origins, Growth and Dissolution—Volume 3, The Breakdown, P. S. Falla, trans., 405.
983 Ibid.
984 Ibid.
985 Ibid., 406.
986 Ibid.
987 Ibid.
988 Ibid., 407.
989 Ibid.
990 Ibid.
991 Ibid., 416.
992 Ibid., 417.

993 Michael Walsh, The Devil's Pleasure Palace: The Cult of Critical Theory and the Subversion of the West (New York: Encounter Books, 2015), 83.
994 Ibid.
995 Marcuse, Eros and Civilization, 235.
996 Sigmund Freud, The Future of an Illusion (New York: W. W. Norton, 1927).
997 Marcuse, Eros and Civilization, 236.
998 Ibid., 149.
999 Ibid., 236–237.
1000 Walsh, The Devil's Pleasure Palace, 84.
1001 Stuart Jeffries, Grand Hyatt Abyss: The Lives of the Frankfurt School (London: Verso, 2016).
1002 Ibid., 303–304. Also: Herbert Marcuse, Soviet Marxism: A Critical Analysis (New York: Columbia University Press, 1958).
1003 Jeffries, Grand Hyatt Abyss, 304.
1004 Ibid., 303.
1005 Marcuse, One-Dimensional Man, introduction, xv.
1006 Ibid.
1007 Ibid., 7.
1008 Statements of Marcuse's views on totalitarianism are drawn from the following source: Biophily2, "Herbert Marcuse Interview about One-Dimensional Man (1964)," YouTube.com, October 2, 2016, *https://www.youtube.com/watch?v=9gyL5ie6-x0&t=2738s.*
1009 Marcuse, One-Dimensional Man, 7. Emphasis in original.
1010 Ibid., 7–8.
1011 Ibid., 8.
1012 Ibid., 8–9.
1013 Ibid., 9.
1014 Ibid., 10. Italics in original.
1015 Ibid., 11.
1016 Ibid., 16.
1017 Brian O'Connor, Marcuse and the Problem of Repression, in Peter E. Gordon, Espen Hammer, and Axel Honneth, eds., The Routledge Companion to the Frankfurt School (New York: Routledge, 2019), 311–322, quotation at 320.
1018 Marcuse, One-Dimensional Man, 75.
1019 Ibid., 74.
1020 Ibid., 74–75.
1021 Ibid., 75.
1022 Marcuse, Eros and Civilization, 152.
1023 Ibid., 152–153.
1024 Ibid., 153–154, quotation at 154.
1025 Barry M. Katz, "Praxis and Poiesis: Toward an Intellectual Biography of Herbert Marcuse [1898–1979]," New German Critique, no. 18,

(Autumn 1979): 12–18, *https://www.jstor.org/stable/487844?refreqid=excelsior%3A111730468c531c11b9c0063bfbe2ecea.*

1026 Walsh, The Devil's Pleasure Palace, 2.

1027 Ibid., 1.

1028 Ibid.

1029 Ibid.

1030 Ibid., 5

1031 Ibid., chap. 2, "The New Sensibility," 23–48.

1032 Herbert Marcuse, An Essay on Liberation (London: Allen Lane–Penguin Press, 1969), introduction, 4. The book was simultaneously published in the United States in 1969 by Beacon Press in Boston, Massachusetts. Pagination for quotations cited here is taken from the London edition.

1033 Ibid.

1034 Friedrich Nietzsche, Thus Spoke Zarathustra: A Book for All and None, trans. Walter Kaufmann (New York: The Modern Library, 1995), "Zarathustra's Prologue," part 3, p. 13. Here Übermensch is substituted for "overman" in the Kaufmann translation. Italics in original.

1035 Marcuse, An Essay on Liberation, 21. Marcuse quotes Nietzsche, The Gay Science, trans. Walter Kaufmann (New York: Vintage Books, 1974), book 3, no. 275, p. 220. Kaufmann translates this passage somewhat differently: "What is the seal of liberation?—No longer being ashamed in front of oneself." Italics in the original of Kaufmann's translation.

1036 Ibid., 21–22.

1037 Ibid., 8.

1038 Ibid., 65–66.

1039 Ibid., 76.

1040 Ibid.

1041 Ibid., 76–77.

1042 Ibid., 77.

1043 Ibid., 89.

1044 John Lennon lyrics, "Imagine," from Imagine: John Lennon soundtrack, 1970, AZLyrics.com, 1970, *https://www.azlyrics.com/lyrics/johnlennon/imagine.html.*

1045 Jeffries, Grand Hyatt Abyss, 312.

1046 Wiggershaus, The Frankfurt School, 54.

1047 Martin Jay, The Dialectical Imagination: A History of the Frankfurt School and the Institute of Social Research, 1923–1950 (Boston: Little, Brown, 1973), 87.

1048 Ibid.

1049 Marcuse, Eros and Civilization, "Epilogue: Critique of Neo-Freudian Revisionism," 238–274, quotation at 239.

1050 Myron Sharaf, Fury on Earth: A Biography of Wilhelm Reich (New York: St. Martin's Press, 1963), chap. 3, "Reich's Childhood and Youth: 1897–1917," 36–52, and chap. 4, "Becoming a Psychoanalyst: 1918–1920," 53–64.

1051 Wilhelm Reich, Passion of Youth: An Autobiography, 1897–1922, eds. Mary Bond Boyd Higgins and Chester M. Raphael, trans. Philip Schmitz and Jerri Tompkins (New York: Farrar, Straus and Giroux, 1988).

1052 Ibid., 5–6, quotation at 6.

1053 Ibid., 12.

1054 Ibid., 13.

1055 Ibid., 22

1056 Ibid., 25.

1057 Ibid., 29.

1058 Ibid., 29.

1059 Ibid., 31.

1060 Ibid.

1061 Ibid., 33.

1062 Ibid., 42–43.

1063 Ibid., 43.

1064 Wilhelm Reich, The Function of the Orgasm: Sex-Economic Problems of Biological Energy, vol. 1 of The Discovery of the Orgone series, trans. Vincent R. Carfagno (New York: Farrar, Straus and Giroux, 1973), 96. The Carfagno translation was reprinted in a 1975 paperback publication. See: Wilhelm Reich, The Function of the Orgasm: Sex-Economic Problems of Biological Energy, vol. 1 of The Discovery of the Orgone series, trans. Vincent R. Carfagno (New York: Penguin, Pocket Book Edition, 1975), 84–85, with the quotation also reprinted on the back cover.

1065 Christopher Turner, Adventures in the Orgasmatron: How the Sexual Revolution Came to America (New York: Farrar, Straus and Giroux, 2011). Note also the "Orgasmatron" in Turner's title was taken from the spoof in Woody Allen's 1973 movie Sleeper, ridiculing Reich's orgone accumulator. See: Rich Barlow, "Ever Tried an Orgasmatron?" BU [Boston University] Today, BU.edu, August 9, 2012, *https://www.bu.edu/articles/2012/ever-tried-an-orgasmatron/*.

1066 Turner, Adventures in the Orgasmatron, 5.

1067 Wilhelm Reich, The Function of the Orgasm: Sex-Economic Problems of Biological Energy, trans. Theodore P. Wolfe (New York: Orgone Institute Press, 1942).

1068 Wilhelm Reich, The Function of the Orgasm: Sex-Economic Problems of Biological Energy, vol. 1 of The Discovery of the Orgone series, trans. Vincent R. Carfagno (New York: Farrar, Straus and Giroux, 1973), 96. See also: Wilhelm Reich, The Function of the Orgasm: Sex-Economic Problems of Biological Energy, vol. 1 of The Discovery of the Orgone series, trans. Vincent R. Carfagno (New York: Penguin, Pocket Book Edition, 1975), 84–85, with the quotation in question also reprinted on the back cover.

1069 Wilhelm Reich, Selected Writings: An Introduction to Orgonomy (New York: Farrar, Straus and Cudahy, 1960), 37. Italics in original.

1070 Philip W. Bennett (Graduate School of Education, retired, Fairfield University, Fairfield, CT), "Rapid Response: Response to Quin's Positive Review of Turner's Adventures in the Orgasmatron," BMJ, October 7, 2011, *https://www.bmj.com/rapid-response/2011/11/03/response-quins-positive-review-turners-adventures-orgasmatron*

1071 Reich, Selected Writings.

1072 Turner, Adventures in the Orgasmatron, 5.

1073 Reich, Selected Writings, part 2, "The Orgasm Theory: The Development of the Orgasm Theory," 13–41, quotation at 37–38.

1074 Ibid., 38.

1075 Turner, Adventures in the Orgasmatron, p. 5.

1076 Ibid.

1077 Peter B. Thompson, "Return to Conception: Wilhelm Reich's Later Work as a Product of European Cultural Modernism" (master's thesis, University of Maine, 2014), published in Electronic Theses and Dissertations, *https://digitalcommons.library.umaine.edu/etd/2093/*.

1078 Sharaf, Fury on Earth, 186–188.

1079 Wilhelm Reich, Sex-Pol: Essays 1929–1934, ed. Lee Baxandall, trans. Anna Bostock, Tom DuBose, and Lee Baxandall (New York: Vintage Books, 1972). Reich originally published these essays in a 1934 book written and published in Germany. See: Wilhelm Reich, Sex-Pol, Band: 1, 1934: Zeitschrift für Politische Psychologie und Sexualokonomie [in English, Sex-Pol, Volume 1, 1934: Journal of Political Psychology and Sex Economics] (West Berlin, Germany: Bundolo, 1969). Wilhelm Reich founded the Journal of Political Psychology and Sex Economics in Copenhagen, Denmark, in May 1934. "Sex-Pol" is an abbreviation for "Sex-Politics."

1080 Originally published as: Wilhelm Reich, Die Massenpsychologie des Faschismus (Kopenhagen, Prag, Zürich: Verlag für Sexualpolitik, 1933). First reprinted in the United States in English as: Wilhelm Reich, The Mass Psychology of Fascism, trans. Theodore P. Wolfe (New York: Orgone Institute Press, 1946). The 1946 edition in English is a translation from the German manuscript "third, revised and enlarged edition."

1081 Sharaf, Fury on Earth, 163.

1082 Ibid., 456. Details on Sharaf's career with Reich are drawn from the 1963 book, chap. 2, "My Relationship with Reich," 15–33.

1083 Ibid.

1084 Ibid., 164,

1085 Ibid., 132.

1086 Ibid.

1087 Ibid., 132–133.

1088 Johann Jakob Bachofen, Das Mutterrecht: eine Untersuchung über die Gynaikokratie der alten Welt nach ihrer religiösen und rechtlichen Natur [in English, The Mother Right: An Inquiry into the Old

World Gynecocracy According to Its Religious and Legal Nature] (Stuttgart, Germany: Verlag von Krais und Hoffmann, 1861].

1089 Reich, Sex-Pol, "Imposition of Sexual Morality," 89–249, quotation at 184.

1090 Bronisław Malinowski, The Sexual Life of Savages in North-Western Melanesia: An Ethnographic Account of Courtship, Marriage and Family Life among the Natives of the Trobriand Islands, British New Guinea (New York: Readers League of America, distributed by Eugenics Publishing Company, 1929). The other two books in Malinowski's trilogy were (1) Bronisław Malinowski, Argonauts of the Western Pacific: An Account of Native Enterprise and Adventure in the Archipelagoes of Melanesian New Guinea (London: Routledge & Kegan Paul, 1922); and (2) Coral Gardens and Their Magic: A Study of the Methods of Tilling the Soil and of Agricultural Rites in the Trobriand Islands (New York: Readers League of America, distributed by Eugenics Publishing Company, 1929).

1091 Wilhelm Reich, Der Einbruch der Sexualmoral: zur Geschichte der sexuellen Ökonomie (in English, The Collapse of Sexual Morality: On the History of Sexual Economy] (Kopenhagen: Verlag für Sexualpolitik, 1935). Reich finished writing this book in September 1931. In 1932, Reich self-published this book. See: Philip Bennett and the Institute for Orgonomic Science, contributors, "Wilhelm Reich: Research & Publications," Wilhelm Reich Museum, WilhelmReichMuseum.org, n.d., *https://wilhelmreichmuseum.org/about/research-and-publications/*. The 1935 edition is the book included in Wilhelm Reich, Sex-Pol: Essays 1929–1934, under the title Imposition of Sexual Morality, a translation of the 1935 second edition printed with Reich's 1931 introduction, 89–249.

1092 Reich, Sex-Pol, 29.

1093 Malinowski, The Sexual Life of Savages in North-Western Melanesia, 3–4.

1094 Ibid., 5.

1095 Ibid., 55.

1096 Ibid., 258.

1097 Russell Walter, "Wilhelm Reich & the Sexual Revolution," YouTube.com, posted April 6, 2021, *https://www.youtube.com/watch?v=2NEMYeuTVC4*.

1098 Friedrich Engels, Der Ursprung der Familie, des Privateigenthums und des Staats: im Anschluss an Lewis H. Morgan's Forschungen [in English, The Origin of the Family, Private Property and the State: Following Lewis H. Morgan's Research] (Hottingen-Zürich, Germany: Verlag der Schweizerischen Volksbuchhandlung, 1884). The modern printing used here for footnotes is the following: Friedrich Engels, The Origin of the Family Private Property and the State (New York: Penguin Books, 2010).

1099 Lewis H. Morgan, Ancient Society: Or Researches in the Lines of Human Progress from Savagery, Through Barbarism to Civilization (New York: Henry Holt, 1877).

1100 Friedrich Engels, The Origin of the Family, Private Property and the State, preface to the 4th edition, 38–50, quotation at 48.

1101 Reich, Sex-Pol, 183.

1102 Walter, "Wilhelm Reich & the Sexual Revolution."

1103 Sharaf, Fury on Earth, 133.

1104 Havelock Ellis, preface in Bronisław Malinowski, The Sexual Life of Savages in North-Western Melanesia, vii-xiii, quotation at vii.

1105 Ibid., vii–viii.

1106 Ibid., xiii.

1107 Ibid.

1108 Wilhelm Reich, Die Sexualität im Kulturkampf: Zur Sozialistischen Umstrukturierung des Menschen (Kopenhagen, Dänemark: Sexpol-Verlag, 1936).

1109 Wilhelm Reich, The Sexual Revolution: Toward a Self-Governing Character Structure, trans. Theodore P. Wolfe (New York: Orgone Institute Press, 1945).

1110 See, for instance, Boris Fraenkel's introduction to the Italian publication of Die Sexualität im Kulturkampf: Zur Sozialistischen Umstrukturierung des Menschen. Here is the citation for the modern printing of Reich's book translated into Italian, with Fraenkel's introduction: Wilhelm Reich, La sessualità nella battaglia culturale: per la ristrutturazione socialista dell'uomo [in English, Sexuality in the Cultural Battle: For the Socialist Restructuring of Man], introduzione di Boris Fraenkel; trans. Enrica Albites-Coen and Roberto Massar (Roma, Italia: Massari Editore, 1992). Fraenkel's translation of Reich's 1936 book reverted to the original title. But prior to Fraenkel's translation, several editions of Reich's books appeared in Italian under the 1945 title. See, for instance: Wilhelm Reich, La rivoluzione sessual, trans. Vittorio Di Giuro (Milano: Feltrinelli, 1963). The Di Giuro 1963 translation can be found in the Biblioteca nationale centrale di Firenze [in English, the National Library, Central Florence, Italy]. Boris Fraenkel was a Trotsky Marxist who translated into French and Italian works by Marcuse and Reich. Fraenkel committed suicide in Paris at the age of eighty-five. See: Le Monde, "Suicide d'intellectuel Boris Fraenkel," May 1, 2006, *https://www.lemonde.fr/societe/article/2006/05/01/suicide-de-l-intellectuel-boris-fraenkel-l-homme-qui-a-revele-le-passe-trotskiste-de-lionel-jospin_767168_3224.html.*

1111 Garry Wills, Nixon Agonistes: The Crisis of the Self-Made Man (Boston: Houghton Mifflin, 1970).

1112 John Milton, Paradise Regained, a Poem in IV Books, to Which Is Added Sampson Agonistes (London: Printed by J. M. for John Starkey at the Mitre in Fleet Street, near Temple Bar, 1671).

1113 Randi Storch, "Communism and the Labor Movement," American History, Oxford Research Encyclopedias, OxfordRe.com, June 30, 2020, *https://oxfordre.com/americanhistory/view/10.1093/acrefore/9780199329175.001.0001/acrefore-9780199329175-e-784#:~:text=Under%20the%20auspices%20of%20the,and%20United%20Mine%20Workers'%20unions.*

1114 Bennett, "Rapid Response: Response to Quin's Positive Review of Turner's Adventures in the Orgasmatron."

1115 Turner, Adventures in the Orgasmatron, 4–5.

1116 For a detailed discussion of Reich's legal problems regarding the interstate distribution of his orgone accumulator, see: Sharaf, Fury on Earth, chap. 28, "The FDA Injunction and Reich's Responses: 1951–1956," 410–434; chap. 29, "Background to the Trial for Contempt of Injunction: 1955–1956," 435–445; and chap. 30, "The Trial," 446–456.

1117 Turner, Adventures in the Orgasmatron, 237–238. In 2000, the FBI released Reich's file. See: Federal Bureau of Investigation, Freedom of Information Act Release, Wilhelm Reich File, parts 1–6, 789 pages, *https://archive.org/details/WilhelmReichFBI/reich1/*.

1118 Sharaf, Fury on Earth, 46.

1119 Ibid., 378–382, quotation at 379.

1120 Ibid., 24, 234–235, 238–239, 241–242. Turner, Adventures in the Orgasmatron, 179. For a review of Sharaf's book that discusses Reich's unconventional psychoanalytic techniques, see: Webster Schott, "Wilhelm Reich: A Prisoner of Sex," Washington Post, February 6, 1983, *https://www.washingtonpost.com/archive/entertainment/books/1983/02/06/wilhelm-reich-a-prisoner-of-sex/10e319e7-fab3-4e69-9ce4-5b93b1e91f8c/*.

1121 Turner, Adventures in the Orgasmatron, 57. Turner made this comment in the context of discussing Reich's relationship to Annie Pink.

1122 Sharaf, Fury on Earth, 152.

1123 David Elkind, "Wilhelm Reich—The Psychoanalyst as Revolutionary," New York Times, April 18, 1971, *https://www.nytimes.com/1971/04/18/archives/wilhelm-reich-the-psychoanalyst-as-revolutionary-wilhelm-reich.html*.

1124 Sharaf, Fury on Earth, 194–195, quotation at 195.

1125 Turner, Adventures in the Orgasmatron, 157.

1126 Ibid.

1127 Mel Gordon, Voluptuous Panic: The Erotic World of Weimar Berlin (Los Angeles: Feral House, exp. ed., 2006), 90–91. See also: Matthew H. Birkhold, "A Lost Piece of Trans History," Paris Review, TheParisReview.org, January 15, 2019, *https://www.theparisreview.org/blog/2019/01/15/a-lost-piece-of-trans-history/*.

1128 For an interesting article on marriage and promiscuity, see: Jonathan Ang, "Are We Hoodwinked into Sexual Promiscuity? Understanding Where It All Came From," Vibrant Dot, n.d., *https://vibrantdot.co/are-we-hoodwinked-into-sexual-promiscuity/*.

1129 Ray Laurence, Roman Pompeii: Space and Society (London: Routledge, 1994), 71.

1130 Ibid.

1131 Ibid.

1132 Ibid.

1133 Ibid.

1134 Ibid.

1135 Aline Rousselle, "Body Politics in Ancient Rome," in Pauline Schmitt Pantel, ed., Arthur Goldhammer, trans., A History of Women in the West:

I. From Ancient Goddesses to Christian Saints (Cambridge, MA: Belknap Press of Harvard University Press, 1992), 296–337, quotation at 318.

1136 Ibid., 319.

1137 Ibid.

1138 Ibid.

1139 Ibid., 321.

1140 Ibid., 322.

1141 Sarah Kliff, "The Secret History of Birth Control Pills," Vox.com, October 23, 2014, *https://www.vox.com/2014/10/23/6994695/the-secret-history-of-birth-control-pills#:~:text=Development%20on%20the%20birth%20control,Worcester%20Foundation%20for%20Experimental%20Biology.*

1142 Aliya Buttar and Sheraden Seward, "Envoid: The First Hormonal Birth Control Pill," Embryo Project Encyclopedia, January 20, 2009, *https://embryo.asu.edu/pages/enovid-first-hormonal-birth-control-pill#:~:text=Enovid%20was%20the%20first%20hormonal,as%20a%20contraceptive%20in%201960.*

1143 Griswold v. Connecticut, 381 U.S. 479 (1965), Oyez.org, n.d., *https://www.oyez.org/cases/1964/496.*

1144 "The Birth Control Pill: A History," Planned Parenthood, Planned Parenthood.org, last updated June 2015, *https://www.plannedparenthood.org/files/1514/3518/7100/Pill_History_FactSheet.pdf.*

1145 Roe v. Wade, 410 U.S. 113 (1973)," Oyez.org, n.d., *https://www.oyez.org/cases/1971/70-18.* The Supreme Court 6–3 decision in Dobbs v. Jackson, 597 U.S. __ (2022), overruled Roe v. Wade, ruling there is no constitutional right to an abortion and remanding the issue of regulating abortion to the states.

1146 Betty Friedan, The Feminine Mystique (New York: W. W. Norton, 1963).

1147 Debra Michals, ed., "Betty Friedan (1921–2006)," National Women's History Museum, WomensHistory.org, n.d., *https://www.womenshistory.org/education-resources/biographies/betty-friedan.*

1148 Jason Pierce, Angelo State University, "Betty Friedan and the Women's Movement," Bill of Rights Institute, BillofRightsInstitute.org, n.d., *https://billofrightsinstitute.org/essays/betty-friedan-and-the-womens-movement.* See also: Betty Friedan, Life So Far: A Memoir (New York: Simon & Schuster, 2006). See also: Michals, "Betty Friedan (1921–2006)."

1149 Michals, "Betty Friedan (1921–2006)."

1150 Christopher Caldwell, The Age of Entitlement: America Since the Sixties (New York: Simon & Schuster, 2020), 4.

1151 Friedan, The Feminine Mystique, 39.

1152 Ibid., 39–40.

1153 Ibid., 40.

1154 Ibid.

1155 Ibid.

1156 Rachel Shteir, "Why We Can't Stop Talking about Betty Friedan," New York Times, February 3, 2021, *https://www.nytimes.com/2021/02/03/us/betty-friedan-feminism-legacy.html.*

1157 bell hooks, Feminist Theory: From Margin to Center (Boston: South End Press, 1984), 1–2.

1158 Daniel Horowitz, Betty Friedan and the Making of The Feminine Mystique: The American Left, the Cold War, and Modern Feminism (Amherst: University of Massachusetts Press, 1998).

1159 Ibid., 7.

1160 Ibid., 1.

1161 Daniel Horowitz, "Rethinking Betty Friedan and The Feminine Mystique: Labor Union Radicalism and Feminism in Cold War America," American Quarterly 48, no. 1 (March 1996): 1–42, quotation at 1, *https://www.jstor.org/stable/30041520*. Horowitz quoted Schatz from the following source: Ronald W. Schatz, The Electrical Workers: A History of Labor at General Electric and Westinghouse, 1923–60 (Urbana: University of Illinois Press, 1983), xiii.

1162 Horowitz, "Rethinking Betty Friedan and The Feminine Mystique," 30.

1163 Michals, "Betty Friedan (1921–2006)."

1164 Suzanne Venker and Phyllis Schlafly, The Flipside of Feminism: What Conservative Women Know—and Men Can't Say (Washington, DC: WND Books, 2011).

1165 Ibid., 29.

1166 Ibid.

1167 Ibid., 31.

1168 Ibid., 31–32.

1169 Ibid., 32.

1170 Nina Renata Aron, "Lesbians Battled for Their Place in 1960s Feminism," Timeline.com, January 19, 2017, *https://timeline.com/lesbians-battled-for-their-place-in-1960s-feminism-25082853be90.*

1171 Christopher J. Kelly, "The Personal Is Political," Britannica, Britannica.com, last updated on March 1, 2022, *https://www.britannica.com/topic/the-personal-is-political.*

1172 Linda Napikoski, "Lavender Menace: the Phrase, the Group, the Controversy," ThoughtCo.com, updated on February 28, 2019, *https://www.thoughtco.com/lavender-menace-feminism-definition-3528970.*

1173 Ibid.

1174 "Lavender Menace Action at the Second Congress to Unite Women," NYC LGBT Historic Sites Project, NYCLGBTSites.org, *https://www.nyclgbtsites.org/site/lavender-menace-action-at-second-congress-to-unite-women/*. The website attributed the quotation to the RAT Subterranean News, May 1970.

1175 Napikoski, "Lavender Menace."

1176 Debra Michals, ed., "Gloria Steinem (1934–)," National Women's History Museum, WomensHistory.org, n.d., *https://www.womenshistory.*

org/education-resources/biographies/gloria-steinem#:~:text=Steinem%20was%20born%20on%20March,mentally%20ill%20mother%20in%20Toledo. Also: Letty Cottin Pogrebin, "Gloria Steinem (1934–)," Jewish Women: A Comprehensive Historical Encyclopedia, JWA.org, March 20, 2009, archived at *http://jwa.org/encyclopedia/article/steinem-gloria*.

1177 "International Council of Women," Social Networks and Archival Context (SNAC), SNACCooperative.org., n.d., *https://snaccooperative.org/ark:/99166/w6zs739c*.

1178 Gloria Steinem, Outrageous Acts and Everyday Rebellions (New York: Holt, Rinehart and Winston, 1983), 140–141.

1179 Venker and Schlafly, The Flipside of Feminism, 36. The quotes from Betty Friedan were sourced from the following: Betty Friedan, Life So Far: A Memoir (New York: Simon & Schuster, 2006), 26, 121, and 131.

1180 Ibid., 36–37. The Steinem quotation was sourced from the following: "Gloria Steinem (1934–)," Biography, Biography.com, April 27, 2017, *https://www.biography.com/activist/gloria-steinem*.

1181 Letty Cottin Pogrebin, "Gloria Steinem (1934–)," Jewish Women: A Comprehensive Historical Encyclopedia. In her 1983 book Outrageous Acts and Everyday Rebellions, Steinem discussed the Show magazine assignment (p. 16) and reprinted the article with her commentary (pp. 29–69).

1182 Gloria Steinem, "After Black Power, Women's Liberation," New York magazine, NYMag.com, April 4, 1969, *https://nymag.com/news/politics/46802/*.

1183 "Gloria Steinem: Influential Political Activist and Feminist," The Connecticut Forum, Ctforum.org, n.d., *https://www.ctforum.org/panelist/gloria-steinem*.

1184 "Gloria Steinem," Encyclopedia.com, updated May 29, 2018, *https://www.encyclopedia.com/people/literature-and-arts/journalism-and-publishing-biographies/gloria-steinem*.

1185 Eve Kucharski, "Gloria Steinem Emphasizes That Feminism and LGBT Rights Linked," Pride Source, PrideSource.com, March 14, 2018, *https://pridesource.com/article/gloria-steinem-emphasizes-that-feminism-and-lgbt-rights-linked/*. See also, Gloria Steinem, "Op-ed: On Working Together Over Time," Advocate, Advocate.com, October 2, 2013, *https://www.advocate.com/commentary/2013/10/02/op-ed-working-together-over-time*.

1186 Steinem, Outrageous Acts and Everyday Rebellions, 206–210, quotation at 210. Italics in original.

1187 Phillis Schlafly, Who Killed the American Family? (Washington, DC: WND Books, 2014), 10. The quotation regarding the "comfortable concentration camp" can be found in Betty Friedan, The Feminine Mystique, chap. 12, "Progressive Dehumanization: The Comfortable Concentration Camp," 262–287, quotation at 262.

1188 Walsh, The Devil's Pleasure Palace, 145.

1189 Ibid., 148–149.

1190 Ibid., 149.

1191 Gary Martin, "The Meaning and Origin of the Expression: A Woman Needs a Man Like a Fish Needs a Bicycle," The Phrase Finder, Phrases.org.uk, n.d., *https://www.phrases.org.uk/meanings/a-woman-needs-a-man-like-a-fish-needs-a-bicycle.html.*

1192 Mary Eberstadt, "The Lure of Androgyny," Commentary, October 2019, *https://www.commentary.org/articles/mary-eberstadt/the-lure-of-androgyny/.*

1193 Glenn Alexander Magee, Hegel and the Hermetic Dialectic (Ithaca: Cornell University Press, 2001), 212. Brackets in original.

1194 Ibid.

1195 Ibid.

1196 Coughlin and Higgins, Re-Remembering the Mis-Remembered Left, 78.

1197 Ibid.

1198 Agata Anna Chrzanowska (Art History Institute in Florence—Max Plank Institute), "Ghirlandaio, Ficino and Hermes Trismegistus: The Prisca Theologica in the Tornabuoni Frescoes," Instituto per la Storia del Pensiero Philosofico e Scientifico Moderno [in English, Institute for the History of Modern Philosophic and Scientific Thought], Laboratorio dell'ISPF 13 (2016), *http://www.ispf-lab.cnr.it/2016_CHG.pdf.*

1199 William Hamblin, "What Is Prisca Theologica?" Patheos.com, March 10, 2013, *https://www.patheos.com/blogs/enigmaticmirror/2013/03/10/what-is-prisca-theologia/.*

1200 Magee, Hegel and the Hermetic Tradition, 28–29.

1201 Frances Yates, Giordano Bruno and the Hermetic Tradition (Chicago: University of Chicago Press, 1964), 84.

1202 Magee, Hegel and the Hermetic Tradition, 31.

1203 Ibid.

1204 Yates, Giordano Bruno and the Hermetic Tradition, 17.

1205 Sigmund Freud, Moses and Monotheism, trans. Katherine Jones (London: Hogarth Press and the Institute of Psycho-Analysis, 1939), 34–35.

1206 Freud, Moses and Monotheism, 204.

1207 Ibid., 204–205.

1208 Risto Olavi Nurmela, "Moses: Freud's Ultimate Project," Jewish Studies in the Nordic Countries Today, Scripta Instituti Donneriani Aboensis 27 (2016): 223–242.

1209 Freud, Moses and Monotheism, 35.

1210 Chrzanowska, "Ghirlandaio, Ficino and Hermes Trismegistus," 15–16.

1211 Magee, Hegel and the Hermetic Tradition, 33.

1212 Ibid.

1213 Yates, Giordano Bruno and the Hermetic Tradition, 11.

1214 Coulson Turnbull, Life and Teachings of Giordano Bruno, Philosopher, Martyr, Mystic (San Diego: Gnostic Press, 1913), 54.

1215 Ibid., 68.

1216 Ibid., 68–69.

1217 Angelo Mercati, "Il Sommario del Processo di Giordano Bruno, con appendice di Documenti sull'eresia e l'inquisizione a Modena nel secolo XVI," Miscellanea Archivistica Angelo Mercati, Studi e Testi, n. 165, Biblioteca Apostolica Vaticana, Roma, Italia. In English: Angelo Mercati, "The Summary of the Process by Giordano Bruno, with an Appendix of Documents on Heresy and the Inquisition in Modena in the 16th Century," Angelo Mercati Archival Miscellany, Studies and Texts, n. 165, Vatican Apostolic Library, Rome, Italy.

1218 Marcuse, Eros and Civilization, 201.

1219 Ken Ammi, The Occult Roots of Postgenderism: And a History of Changes to Psychiatry and Psychology (self-pub., CreateSpace Independent Publishing Platform, 2017), 3.

1220 Wilhelm Reich, Listen, Little Man!, trans. Theodore P. Wolfe (New York: Orgone Institute Press, 1948). Wilhelm Reich, Listen, Little Man! trans. Theodore P. Wolfe, "A Document from the Archives of the Orgone Institute" (New York: Noonday Press, a division of Farrar, Straus and Giroux, 2nd printing, 1966), introduction, 9.

1221 Ibid., Noonday Press edition, 25.

1222 Reich's tirade against Jews was edited out of the 1966 Noonday Press edition. But it can be found in the following source: Wilhelm Reich, Listen, Little Man! trans. Ralph Manheim (New York: Farrar, Straus and Giroux, 1974, paperback ed., 16th printing, 1999), 25.

1223 Éliphas Lévi, Transcendental Magic, Its Doctrine and Ritual: A Complete Translation of "Dogme et Ritual de la Haute Magie," with a Bibliographical Preface, trans. Arthur Edward Waite (London: George Redway, 1896).

1224 Éliphas Lévi, The History of Magic: Including a Clear and Precise Exposition of Its Rites and Mysteries, trans. Arthur Edward Waite (London: Rider & Co., 1913).

1225 Ammi, The Occult Roots of Postgenderism, 5.

1226 Charles Mackay, Extraordinary Delusions and the Madness of Crowds (New York: L. C. Page, 1932).

1227 "Manichaeism: Ancient Religious Movement," Encyclopedia Britannica, Britannica.com, last updated March 14, 2022, *https://www.britannica.com/topic/Manichaeism.*

1228 Steve Barwick, "Lucifer: The Divine Androgyne, Ancient God of the Modern Transgender Movement," Have Ye Not Read? an independent Christian Bible study ministry unaffiliated with any church or denomination, HaveYeNotRead.com, n.d., *https://haveyenotread.com/wp-content/uploads/2018/04/Lucifer-the-Divine-Androgyne-Ancient-God-of-the-Modern-Transgender-Movement.pdf.*

1229 Mary Eberstadt, "The Lure of Androgyny," Commentary, October 2019, *https://www.commentary.org/articles/mary-eberstadt/the-lure-of-androgyny/.*

1230 The logical complications of understanding logical opposites versus polar opposites is a challenge commonly found on the Law School Admission Test (LSAT). See, for instance: "Admission Knowledge: Logical Opposition," posted by "unknown" on AdmissionUpdateNews.blogspot.com, December 23, 2013, *https://admissionupdatenews.blogspot.com/2013/12/logical-opposition html.* See also: "What Is the Opposition of 'X' and Why Are 'Opposites' in the Same Category?" asked by Perik Onti on Philosophy. StackExchange.com, November 1, 2013, *https://philosophy.stackexchange.com/questions/8556/what-is-the-opposite-of-x-and-why-are-opposites-always-in-the-same-category.*

1231 Ludwig Wittgenstein, Philosophical Investigations, trans. G. E. M. Anscombe (Oxford: Blackwell Publishing, revised 50th anniversary commemorative ed., 2001), 21–22, quotation at 21.

1232 Ibid., 22.

1233 Ibid., 98. Italics in original.

1234 V. J. McGill and W. T. Parry, "The Unity of Opposites: A Dialectical Principle," Science & Society 12, no. 4 (Fall 1948): 418–444, quotation at 418, *http://thetempleofnature.org/_dox/unity-of-opposites-dialectic.pdf.* McGill quoted Lenin from the following source: V. I. Lenin, Collected Works: Volume 13 (New York: International Publishers 1927), 321.

1235 McGill and Parry, "The Unity of Opposites," 418–419.

1236 Ibid., 421. Italics in original.

1237 "Unity of Opposites," Wikipedia.com, *https://en.wikipedia.org/wiki/Unity_of_opposites.* The quotation is a lucid description of a key point McGill and Parry make in their 1948 article. The contents in the brackets are not in the original.

1238 McGill and Parry, "The Unity of Opposites," fn. 7, 421.

CHAPTER 6

1239 Douglas Kellner, "Introduction: Radical Politics, Marcuse, and the New Left," in Herbert Marcuse: The New Left and the 1960s—Volume 3, Collected Papers of Herbert Marcuse (London: Routledge, 2005), 1–37, quotation at 7. Italics in original.

1240 Whittaker Chambers, "Foreword in the Form of a Letter to My Children," in Witness (New York: Random House, 1952), 3–22, quotation at 9.

1241 Kengor, The Devil and Karl Marx, 107–108.

1242 Ronald Radosh, Commies: A Journey through the Old Left, the New Left and the Leftover Left (San Francisco: Encounter Books, 2001), 45.

1243 Ibid., 29.

1244 Ibid., 90.

1245 Ronald Radosh and Joyce Milton, The Rosenberg File: A Search for the Truth (New York: Holt, Rinehart and Winston, 1983).

1246 Radosh, Commies: A Journey Through the Old Left, the New Left and the Leftover Left, 99–100.

1247 Ibid., 119.

1248 Ibid.

1249 Stephen Whitfield, "Refusing Marcuse: 50 Years After One-Dimensional Man," Dissent magazine, Fall 2014, *https://www.dissentmagazine.org/article/refusing-marcuse-fifty-years-after-one-dimensional-man*.

1250 Tom Bourne, "Herbert Marcuse: Grandfather of the New Left," Change 11, no. 6 (September 1979): 36–37 and 64, quotation at 36, *https://www.jstor.org/stable/40163236*.

1251 Herbert Marcuse, "Repressive Tolerance," in Robert Paul Wolff, Barrington Moore Jr., and Herbert Marcuse, A Critique of Pure Tolerance (Boston: Beacon Press, 1965), 81–117, quotation at 81. Quotations here are drawn from the 1969 edition of the book that contained the "Postscript 1968" that Marcuse wrote to his essay "Repressive Tolerance." In the 1969 edition, Marcuse's "Postscript 1968" appears at pp. 117–123.

1252 Ibid., 81–82.

1253 Coughlin and Higgins, Re-Remembering the Mis-Remembered Left, 65.

1254 Marcuse, "Repressive Tolerance," 83–84.

1255 Ibid., 82.

1256 Ibid.

1257 Ibid.

1258 Ibid., 83.

1259 Ibid., 105.

1260 Ibid., 86–92, 106, and 121.

1261 Ibid., 105–108.

1262 Ibid., 109.

1263 Ibid., 109.

1264 Ibid.

1265 Ibid., 110.

1266 Ibid., 110–111. Italics in original.

1267 Ibid., 111.

1268 Ibid.

1269 Ibid., 112. Italics and quotation marks in original.

1270 Coughlin and Higgins, Re-Remembering the Mis-Remembered Left, 66.

1271 Ibid., 67.

1272 Marcuse, "Repressive Tolerance," 104–105.

1273 Coughlin and Higgins, Re-Remembering the Mis-Remembered Left, 69.

1274 Ibid.

1275 Marcuse, "Repressive Tolerance," 100–101.

1276 Coughlin and Higgins, Re-Remembering the Mis-Remembered Left, 70.

1277 Robert Jay Lifton, Thought Reform and the Psychology of Totalism: A Study of "Brainwashing" in China (New York: W. W. Norton, 1961). The pagination for quotations from this book is drawn from the 1963 paperback edition published in the Norton Library.

1278 Mao Tse-tung, "On the People's Democratic Dictatorship: In Commemoration of the Twenty-eighth Anniversary of the CCP [Chinese

Communist Party], July 1, 1949," in Conrad Brandt, Benjamin Schwartz, and John K. Fairbank, A Documentary History of Chinese Communism (Cambridge, MA: Harvard University Press, 1952), 449–463, quotation at 456.

1279 Ibid., 457.

1280 Lifton, Thought Reform and the Psychology of Totalism, 433.

1281 Ibid.

1282 Ibid.

1283 Ibid.

1284 Coughlin and Higgins, Re-Remembering the Mis-Remembered Left, 70. Bold type in original.

1285 Ibid., 70–71. Bold type in original.

1286 Ibid., 156.

1287 Jean Baudrillard, Simulacra and Simulation, trans. Sheila Faria Glaser (Ann Arbor: University of Michigan Press, 1994). Originally published in French as: Jean Baudrillard, Simulacres et Simulation (Paris: Éditions Galilée, 1981).

1288 "Simulacrum," Online Etymology Dictionary, updated September 4, 2018, *https://www.etymonline.com/word/simulacrum*.

1289 Jorge Luis Borges, "On Exactitude in Science," originally published in the March 1946 edition of Los Anales de Buenos Aires [in English, The Annals of Buenos Aires]. See: Jorge Luis Borges, "On Exactitude in Science," in Jorge Luis Borges Collected Fictions, trans. Andrew Hurley (New York: Penguin Books, 1998, 46th printing), 325.

1290 Baudrillard, Simulacra and Simulation, 1.

1291 Ibid. Emphasis in original.

1292 Ibid., 6.

1293 Marshall McLuhan, Understanding Media: The Extensions of Man (New York: McGraw-Hill, 1964), chap. 1, "The Medium Is the Message," 7–21.

1294 Baudrillard, Simulacra and Simulation, 6.

1295 Ibid.

1296 Ibid., "On Nihilism," 159–164, quotation at 160.

1297 William Shakespeare, Macbeth, act 5, scene 5, lines 16–27. Macbeth says:

Out, out brief candle
Life's but a walking shadow, a poor player
That struts and frets his hour upon the stage.
And then is heard no more. It is a tale
Told by an idiot, full of sound and fury,
Signifying Nothing.

1298 Baudrillard, Simulacra and Simulation, 160–161.

1299 Ibid., 161.

1300 Ibid.

1301 Ibid., 162.

1302 René Descartes, Meditations on First Philosophy, ed. and trans. John Cottingham (Cambridge: Cambridge University Press, 2nd ed., 2017), "Second Meditation," 21.

1303 Ibid., "Fourth Meditation," 42.

1304 Baudrillard, Simulacra and Simulation, 162.

1305 Truls Lie, "Jean Baudrillard: The Art of Disappearing," first published in Le Monde Diplomatique (Oslo), April 2007, Norwegian version, reprinted by International Academic Journal: Baudrillard Now, June 28, 2020, *https://www.baudrillard-scijournal.com/the-art-of-disappearing/*.

1306 See, for instance: Nick Bostrom, "Are We Living in a Computer Simulation?" Philosophic Quarterly 53, no. 211 (April 2003): 243–255, *https://academic.oup.com/pq/article-abstract/53/211/243/1610975*.

1307 Randy Laist (Goodwin College), "Bullet-Time in Simulation City: Revisiting Baudrillard and The Matrix by Way of the 'Real 1999,'" Alphaville Journal of Film and Screen Media 2 (Winter 2011), *https://cora.ucc.ie/handle/10468/692*.

1308 Dustin Broadbery, "Reality vs. Illusion: People Have Been Robbed of Their Ability to 'Decipher between Fact and Fiction,'" Center for Research on Globalization, GlobalResearch.ca, November 26, 2022, *https://www.globalresearch.ca/revelation-method/5779242*.

1309 Gary Genosko and Adam Bryx, trans., "The Matrix Decoded: Le Nouvel Observateur Interview with Jean Baudrillard," International Journal of Baudrillard Studies 1, no. 2 (July 2004), *https://baudrillardstudies.ubishops.ca/the-matrix-decoded-le-nouvel-observateur-interview-with-jean-baudrillard/*. Le Nouvel Observateur interviewed Jean Baudrillard on June 19–25, 2003. The reference to the New York–based Simulationist artist most likely included painter Peter Halley.

1310 Ibid.

1311 Jean Baudrillard, The Gulf War Did Not Happen, trans. Power Institute and Paul Patton (Bloomington: Indiana University Press, 1995). Originally published as: Jean Baudrillard, La Guerre du Golfe n'a pas eu lieu (Paris: Éditions Galilée, 1991).

1312 Paul Patton, "Introduction," Jean Baudrillard, The Gulf War Did Not Happen, 1.

1313 Ibid., 2.

1314 Ibid., 17.

1315 Baudrillard, The Gulf War Did Not Happen, 81.

1316 Ibid., 81–81.

1317 Ibid., 85.

1318 Ibid., 85–86.

1319 James Borman and William Rehg, "Jürgen Habermas," Stanford Encyclopedia of Philosophy (Fall 2017), ed. Edward N. Zalta, first published May 17, 2007, with a substantive revision August 4, 2014, *https://plato.stanford.edu/entries/habermas/*.

1320 Wiggershaus, The Frankfurt School, introduction, 2–3.

1321 Borman and Rehg, "Jürgen Habermas."

1322 Jürgen Habermas, The Theory of Communicative Action: Volume 1, Reason and the Rationalization of Society, trans. Thomas McCarthy (Boston: Beacon Books, 1984), 13. Italics in the original. Originally published in German as: Jürgen Habermas, Theory des Kommunikativen Handelns, Band I, Handlungsrationalität und gesellschaftliche Rationalisierung (Frankfurt am Main, Germany: Suhrkamp Verlag, 1981).

1323 Jürgen Habermas, "Discourse Ethics: Notes on a Program of Philosophical Justification," in Moral Consciousness and Communicative Action, trans. Christen Lenhardt and Shierry Weber Nicholsen (Cambridge, MA: MIT Press, 1990), 71. Originally published in German as: Jürgen Habermas, Moralbewusstsein und kommunikatives Handeln (Frankfurt am Main, Republic of Germany: Suhrkamp Verlag, 1983).

1324 Ibid., 197.

1325 Steve Hoenisch, "Habermas' Theory of Discourse Ethics," criticism.com, n.d., *https://www.criticism.com/philosophy/habermas-ethics.html.*

1326 Jürgen Habermas, "Morality and Ethical Life: Does Hegel's Critique of Kant Apply to Discourse Ethics?" in Moral Consciousness and Communicative Action, 197.

1327 Intergovernmental Panel on Climate Change [IPCC], Special Report: Global Warming of 1.5°C, October 6, 2018, *https://www.ipcc.ch/sr15/.*

1328 John Rawls, A Theory of Justice (Cambridge, MA: Harvard University Press, 1971).

1329 Thomas Hobbes, Leviathan (Oxford: Oxford University Press: reprint of the 1651 edition, 1929), chap. 19, part 2, 150.

1330 Ibid., chap. 13, part 1, 99.

1331 John Rawls, A Theory of Justice (Cambridge, MA: Belknap Press of Harvard University Press, 1971), 12.

1332 Ibid., 13.

1333 Ibid., 252.

1334 Ibid., 253.

1335 Thomas Piketty, A Brief History of Equality, trans. Steven Rendall (Cambridge, MA: Belknap Press of Harvard University, 2022), introduction, 1. Originally published as: Thomas Piketty, Une bréve histoire d l'égalité (Paris: Editions du Seuil, 2021).

1336 Ibid., chap. 10, "Toward a Democratic, Ecological, and Multicultural Socialism," 226–244, quotation at 226.

1337 Ibid.

1338 Frances Fox Piven and Richard A. Cloward, "The Weight of the Poor: A Strategy to End Poverty," The Nation, May 2, 1966, 510–517, *https://www.thenation.com/article/archive/weight-poor-strategy-end-poverty/.*

1339 David Horowitz Freedom Center, "Cloward-Piven Strategy (CPS)," DiscoverTheNetworks.org, n.d., *https://www.discoverthenetworks.org/organizations/clowardpiven-strategy-cps.*

1340 Friedrich A. Hayek, The Road to Serfdom (Chicago: University of Chicago Press, 1944), 25. Hayek quotes Alexis de Tocqueville from this source: Alexis de Tocqueville, "Discours prononcé á l'assemblée constituante le 12 septembre 1848 sur la question du droit au travail," found in Oeuvres completes d'Alexis de Tocqueville (1866), volume IX, 546.

1341 Hayek, The Road to Serfdom, 32.

1342 Ibid., 25.

1343 Ibid. The Alexis de Tocqueville quotation is again drawn from this source: "Discours prononcé á l'assemblée constituante le 12 septembre 1848 sur la question du droit au travail," found in Oeuvres completes d'Alexis de Tocqueville (1866), IX, 546.

1344 Hayek, The Road to Serfdom, 79.

1345 Ibid.

1346 Ibid., 80.

1347 Ibid., 118.

1348 Kimberlé Crenshaw, Neil Gotanda, Gary Peller, and Kendall Thomas, eds., Critical Race Theory: Key Writings that Formed the Movement (New York: The New Press, 1995).

1349 Derrick A. Bell Jr., "Serving Two Masters: Integration Ideals and Client Interests in School Desegregation Litigation," Yale Law Journal 85, no. 4 (March 1976): 470–515, *https://openyls.law.yale.edu/bitstream/handle/20.500.13051/15715/37_85YaleLJ470_March1976_.pdf?sequence=2&isAllowed=y*.

1350 Derrick A. Bell Jr., "Brown v. Board of Education and the Interest Convergence Dilemma," Harvard Law Review 93, no. 3 (January 1980): 518–533, *https://harvardlawreview.org/1980/01/brown-v-board-of-education-and-the-interest-convergence-dilemma/*.

1351 James Lindsay, Race Marxism: The Truth about Critical Race Theory and Praxis (Orlando, FL: New Discourses, 2022), 1.

1352 Crenshaw et al., Critical Race Theory, introduction, xiii–xxxii, quotation at xiv.

1353 Ibid., xxxii.

1354 Lindsay, Race Marxism, 25. Italics and parentheses in original.

1355 Kimberlé Williams Crenshaw, "Mapping the Margins: Intersectionality, Identity Politics, and Violence against Women of Color," Stanford Law Review 43, no. 6 (July 1991): 1241–1299, *https://www.berkeleycitycollege.edu/slo/files/2021/05/Crenshaw-Mapping-the-Margins-Intersectionality-and-Vioence-against-WOC.pdf*.

1356 Ibid., 1243–1244. Italics in original.

1357 Ibid., 1242.

1358 Ibid., 1297.

1359 Lindsay, Race Marxism, 199.

1360 Ibid., 199–200.

1361 Ibid., 200. Parentheses in original.

1362 Ibid.

1363 Coughlin and Higgins, Re-Remembering the Mis-Remembered Left, 111.

1364 Mary Grabar, Debunking the 1619 Project: Exposing the Plan to Divide America (Washington, DC: Regnery History, an imprint of Regnery Publishing, 2021), 251.

1365 Jeff Barrus, "Nikole Hannah-Jones Wins Pulitzer Prize for 1619 Project," Pulitzer Center Update, PulitzerCenter.org, May 4, 2020, *https://pulitzercenter.org/blog/nikole-hannah-jones-wins-pulitzer-prize-1619-project.*

1366 Nikole Hannah-Jones, Caitlin Roper, Ilena Silverman, and Jake Silverstein, eds., The 1619 Project: A New Origin Story (New York: One World, 2021).

1367 Nikole Hannah-Jones and Renée Watson, The 1619 Project: Born on the Water (New York: Penguin Young Readers Group, 2021).

1368 "Two Iconic American Writers Join Howard University to Create the Center for Journalism and Democracy," MacArthur Fellows, press release, MacFund.org, July 6, 2021, *https://www.macfound.org/press/press-releases/two-iconic-american-writers-join-howard-university-to-create-a-center-to-educate-the-next-generation-of-black-journalists.*

1369 Hannah-Jones, Roper, Silverman, and Silverstein, The 1619 Project: A New Origin Story, preface, xvii–xxxiii, quotation at xxii.

1370 Ibid, xxv.

1371 Mathew Desmond, chap. 6, "Capitalism," in The 1619 Project: A New Origin Story, 165–185, quotation at 167. The source for Desmond's quotation is: Sven Beckert and Seth Rockman, eds., Slavery's Capitalism: A New History of American Economic Development (Philadelphia: University of Pennsylvania Press, 2016), 3.

1372 Nikole Hannah-Jones, chap. 18, "Justice," in The 1619 Project: A New Origin Story, 451–476, quotation at 468.

1373 Ibid.

1374 President's Advisory 1776 Commission, The 1776 Report, originally published on the White House website, January 2021, *https://trumpwhitehouse.archives.gov/wp-content/uploads/2021/01/The-Presidents-Advisory-1776-Commission-Final-Report.pdf.*

1375 Ibid., 1.

1376 Ibid., 1–2.

1377 Grabar, Debunking the 1619 Project.

1378 Mary Grabar, Debunking Howard Zinn: Exposing the Fake History That Turned a Generation against America (Washington, DC: Regnery History, an imprint of Regnery Publishing, 2019), 86.

1379 Peter W. Wood, 1620: A Critical Response to the 1619 Project (New York: Encounter Books, 2020), 6–7.

1380 Ibid., 3–4.

1381 Ibid., 6.

1382 Ibid.

1383 Ibid.

1384 Riki Wilchins, Queer Theory, Gender Theory: An Instant Primer (New York: Alyson Books, 2004), 44–45. Pagination here is from the 2014 Magnus Books edition. Italics in original.

1385 Judith Butler, Gender Trouble: Feminism and the Subversion of Identity (New York: Rutledge, 1990).

1386 Ibid., 137–138.

1387 Jules Gleeson, "Judith Butler: 'We Need to Rethink the Category of Woman,'" The Guardian, interview with Judith Butler, September 7, 2021, *https://www.theguardian.com/lifeandstyle/2021/sep/07/judith-butler-interview-gender*.

1388 "Gender and Sexual Terminology," University of California, Riverside, Depts. ttu.edu, n.d., *https://www.depts.ttu.edu/lgbtqia/Documents/terminology-2015.pdf*.

1389 Marieta Pehlivanova et al., "Childhood Gender Nonconformity and Children's Past-Life Memories," International Journal of Sexual Health 30, no. 4 (2018): 380–389, *https://www.tandfonline.com/doi/abs/10.1080/19317611.2018.1523266*.

1390 Kathleen C. Gerbasi et al., "Furries from A to Z (Anthropomorphism to Zoomorphism)," Society and Animals 16, no. 3 (2008): 197–222, *https://www.animalsandsociety.org/wp-content/uploads/2016/04/gerbasi.pdf*.

1391 Pê Fiejó, "Doctors Herding Cats: The Misadventures of Modern Medicine and Psychology with NonHuman Entities," Academic.edu, 2016, *https://www.academia.edu/24718674/Doctors_Herding_Cats_The_Misadventures_of_Modern_Medicine_and_Psychology_with_NonHuman_Identities?auto=download*.

1392 Quoted in: "Why Be Human When You Can Be Otherkin?" University of Cambridge, Research, cam.ac.uk, July 16, 2016, *https://www.cam.ac.uk/research/features/why-be-human-when-you-can-be-otherkin*.

1393 "Michelle Forcier, MD, MPH," National LGBTQIA + Health Center, A Program of the Fenway Institute, lgbtqiahealtheducation.org, n.d., *https://www.lgbtqiahealtheducation.org/us/faculty-advisory-board/michelle-forcier/*.

1394 Jennifer Smith, "New Documentary Shows Pediatrician Saying Prepubescent Kids Are Ready for Trans Hormone Therapy 'Whenever They Ask for It' and Claiming You Can 'Pause' Hormones 'Like Music' with the Same Drugs Used to Chemically Castrate Pedophiles," Daily Mail, June 1, 2022, *https://www.dailymail.co.uk/news/article-10875017/Pediatrician-says-prepubescent-kids-ready-HRT-ask-new-documentary.html*.

1395 Wilchins, Queer Theory, Gender Theory, 26.

1396 Ibid., 35.

1397 Ibid., 36. Italics in original.

1398 Ibid., 139.

1399 Ibid., 143.

1400 Ibid., 139.

1401 Ibid.

1402 Ibid., 45. Italics in original.

1403 Thomas Harris, Red Dragon (New York: G. P. Putnam's Sons, 1981).

1404 Thomas Harris, The Silence of the Lambs (New York: St. Martin's Press, 1988).

1405 See: Lt. Ray Biondi and Walter Hecox, The Dracula Killer (New York: Pocket Books, 1992).

1406 See: Jem Tosh, Perverse Psychology: The Pathologization of Sexual Violence and Transgenderism (London: Routledge, 2014).

1407 Azeen Ghorayshi, "More Teens Are Choosing 'Top Surgery,'" New York Times, September 26, 2022, updated October 3, 2022, *https://www.nytimes.com/2022/09/26/health/top-surgery-transgender-teenagers.html*. The name of the physician is removed in order to protect privacy, despite the New York Times publication of the physician's name.

1408 Ibid.

1409 Calvin Freiburger, "BREAKING: Arkansas Legislature Overrides Gov.'s Veto; Ban on 'Transitioning' Minors Will Become Law," LifeSiteNews.com, April 6, 2021, *https://www.lifesitenews.com/news/breaking-arkansas-legislature-overrides-veto-ban-on-transitioning-minors-will-become-law/*.

1410 "ACLU Sues Arkansas over Ban on Health Care for Transgender Youth," American Civil Liberties Union, press release, ACLU.org, May 25, 2021, *https://www.aclu.org/press-releases/aclu-sues-arkansas-over-ban-health-care-transgender-youth*.

1411 Raymond Wolfe, "17 States Defend Arkansas Law Banning Child 'Sex Changes' and Puberty Blockers," LifeSiteNews.com, July 20, 2021, *https://www.lifesitenews.com/news/17-states-defend-arkansas-law-banning-child-sex-changes-and-puberty-blockers/*. See also: Amicus Brief of Alabama, Alaska, Arizona, Georgia, Idaho, Indiana, Kansas, Kentucky, Louisiana, Mississippi, Missouri, Montana, Nebraska, South Carolina, South Dakota, Tennessee, and Texas as Amici Curiae in Support of Defendants' Opposition to Plaintiffs' Motion for a Preliminary Injunction, Brandt v. Rutledge, United States District Court, Eastern District of Arkansas, Central Division, No. 4:21-CV-00450-JM, filed July 13, 2021, *https://www.alabamaag.gov/Documents/news/Arkansas%20Transgender%20Brief%20Amicus.pdf*.

1412 Amicus Brief, Brandt v. Rutledge, 1.

1413 Ibid.

1414 Ibid., 1–2.

1415 Spencer Lindquist, "Joe Biden: 'It's Wrong' for States to Ban Sex Change Operations," Breitbart.com, October 24, 2022, *https://www.breitbart.com/social-justice/2022/10/24/joe-biden-its-wrong-states-ban-sex-change-operations/*. The relevant segment of the NowThisNews.com interview with President Biden can be found here: "Joe Biden Answers Burning Questions of Our Young People in the NowThis Exclusive," NowThis News, YouTube, posted October 24, 2022, *https://www.youtube.com/watch?v=m8tT6gNej8A&t=1156s*.

1416 Hannah Nightingale, "Indiana Parents Lose Custody After Court Rules Not 'Affirming' Child's Gender Identity Is 'Abuse,'" ThePostMillennial.com, October 24, 2022, *https://thepostmillennial.com/indiana-parents-lose-custody-after-court-rules-not-affirming-childs-gender-identity-is-abuse#google_vignette*.

1417 Houston Keene, "Republicans Baffled That Ketanji Brown Jackson Can't Say What a Woman Is: 'It's a Simple Question,'" Fox News, March 23, 2022, *https://www.foxnews.com/politics/republicans-baffled-ketanji-brown-jackson-define-woman.*

1418 Ibid.

1419 "Liberation Theology: Roman Catholicism," Britannica, Britannica.com, last updated August 25, 2022, *https://www.britannica.com/topic/liberation-theology.*

1420 Gustavo Gutiérrez, A Theology of Liberation: History, Politics, and Salvation, trans. Sister Caridad Inda and John Eagleson (Maryknoll, NY: Orbis Books, 1973), 25. Originally published as: Gustavo Gutiérrez, Theología de la liberacíon, Perspectivas (Lima, Peru: CEP, 1971).

1421 Ibid., 41.

1422 Ibid., 170–171. Italics in original.

1423 Joseph D'Hippolito, "The Catholic Church Abandons Its Fundamentals in Favor of the New World Order," Human Events, September 12, 2022, *https://humanevents.com/2022/09/12/the-catholic-church-abandons-its-fundamentals-in-favor-of-the-new-world-order/.*

1424 Christopher Skeet, "The Next Pope Should at Least Be Catholic," American Thinker, September 6, 2022, *https://www.americanthinker.com/articles/2022/09/the_next_pope_should_at_least_be_catholic.html.*

1425 Ibid.

1426 The following is the source of this bullet point: Paul Vallely, "The Pope vs. America," Politico Magazine, September–October 2015, *https://www.politico.com/magazine/story/2015/09/pope-francis-america-washington-213092/.*

1427 The following is the source of this bullet point: Nicole Winfield, "Pope: Market Capitalism Has Failed in Pandemic, Needs Reform," Associated Press, APNews.com, October 4, 2020, *https://apnews.com/article/virus-outbreak-pope-francis-archive-capitalism-bcde0053314e65612add0709fada5519.*

1428 The following is the source of this bullet point: Nika Knight, "Pope Francis: Capitalism Is 'Terrorism against All of Humanity,' Canadian Dimension, CanadianDimension.com, August 5, 2016, *https://canadiandimension.com/articles/view/pope-francis-capitalism-is-terrorism-against-all-of-humanity.*

1429 Skeet, "The Next Pope Should at Least Be Catholic." All three bullet points come from this source.

1430 Ibid.

1431 Mark Devine, "Evangelists Fight Wokedom Without and Within," American Spectator, October 25, 2020, *https://spectator.org/evangelicals-social-justice-woke/*. The resolution can be found here: "On Critical Theory and Intersectionality," Southern Baptist Convention (SBC), 2019 Annual Meeting, SBC.net, June 1, 2019, *https://www.sbc.net/resource-library/resolutions/on-critical-race-theory-and-intersectionality/.*

1432 Wes Walker, "Those Woke American Churches Are Now All-In on Reparations and 'Racial Justice,'" ClashDaily.com, December 15, 2020, *https://clashdaily.com/2020/12/these-woke-american-churches-are-now-all-in-on-reparations-and-racial-justice/*.

1433 Noel Ignatiev, "My Debt and Obligation to Ted Allen," published on Noel Ignatiev's Blog, September 2, 2019, *https://blog.pmpress.org/2019/09/02/my-debt-and-obligation-to-ted-allen/*. Note: Noel Ignatiev is identified as Noel Ignatin (the name he used to join the CPUSA) in several works, including the following: Kirkpatrick Sale, SDS (New York: Random House, 1973). See also: Theodore W. Allen, Invention of the White Race: Racial Oppression and Societal Control (New York: Verso, 1994), vol. 1. Also see: Theodore W. Allen, Invention of the White Race: The Origin of Racial Oppression in Anglo-America (New York: Verso, 1997), vol. 2.

CONCLUSION

1434 Chambers, "Foreword in the Form of a Letter to My Children," 10.

1435 Carl Vogl, Weich Satan! (Altötting: Geiselberger, 1931), 31–32. Translation is drawn from: Kevin Symonds, Pope Leo XIII and the Prayer to St. Michael: An Historical and Theological Examination (Boonville, NY: Preserving Christian Publications, 2nd enlarged ed., 2018), 8.

1436 Symonds, Pope Leo XIII and the Prayer to St. Michael, 149–150.

1437 Taylor R. Marshall, Infiltration: The Plot to Destroy the Church from Within (Manchester, NH: Crisis Publications, 2019), 142.

1438 Ibid., 43–44. Latin and Italian phrases are in the original.

1439 Ibid., 46.

1440 Amy Mek, "Archbishop Carlo Maria Viganò: 'The New World Order Agenda Requires That Italy Should Perish' (Video)," Rair Foundation USA, RairFoundation.com, April 24, 2022, *https://rairfoundation.com/archbishop-carlo-maria-vigano-the-new-world-order-agenda-requires-that-italy-should-perish-video/*.

1441 Ibid.

ABOUT THE AUTHOR

Jerome R. Corsi has published over thirty books on economics, history, and politics, including six *New York Times* bestsellers, two at number one. From 2004 to 2016, Dr. Corsi was a senior editor at WorldNetDaily.com, where he authored hundreds of articles.

The Truth about Neo-Marxism, Cultural Maoism, and Anarchy is Volume II of Dr. Corsi's Great Awakening Trilogy. Volume I, *The Truth about Energy, Global Warming, and Climate Change: Exposing Climate Lies in an Age of Disinformation*, explained how neo-Marxists co-opted the post-war depopulation and environmental movements to demonize our use of hydrocarbon fuels.

Thus, Volume I explained that climate-change alarmists advance the pseudo-scientific hoax theories and climate lies in their ideological determination to destroy capitalism. This Volume II explains the ideology the neo-Marxists have constructed to self-justify their lying. Volume III will expose the ultimate utopian goal of these "New World Order" neo-Marxist, cultural Maoist atheistic anarchists by exploring transhumanism, artificial intelligence, and their "New World Order" dream of perpetual life extension and unlimited abundance for the select few and their machines.

Dr. Corsi has decided to reengage in the political discussion by establishing a new website and podcast, TheTruthCentral.com. As founder and CEO of Corstet LLC, Dr. Corsi has ventured into telemedicine, developing HablaConUnMD.com, offering Spanish-speaking patients an affordable electronic consultation with a Spanish-speaking physician licensed in their state, and GetLongevityMeds.com for those interested in medical consultations aimed at living longer and better.